ETHICAL ISSUES
IN
SIX RELIGIOUS
TRADITIONS

———

ETHICAL ISSUES
IN
SIX RELIGIOUS
TRADITIONS

Edited by
Peggy Morgan and Clive Lawton

EDINBURGH UNIVERSITY PRESS

© Individual contributors, 1996
Hinduism Werner Menski; *Buddhism* Peggy
Morgan; *Sikhism* Eleanor Nesbitt; *Judaism* Clive
Lawton; *Christianity* Trevor Shannon; *Islam*
Mashuq ibn Ally

Edinburgh University Press Ltd
22 George Square, Edinburgh

Typeset in Monotype Ehrhardt
by Nene Phototypesetters Ltd, Northampton, and
printed and bound in Great Britain

A CIP record for this book is available from the
British Library

ISBN 0 7486 0709 9

CONTENTS

CONTENTS

CONTENTS

SECTION E: CHRISTIANITY
Trevor Shannon

SECTION F: ISLAM
Mashuq ibn Ally

CONTENTS

A Note on Transliteration and Pronunciation

Most technical terms in original languages are italicised and linked with glossary entries. A few, such as guru, Brahmin and rabbi are used as accepted English terms without italicisation in the text.

For Indian languages, both classical and modern, there exists an internationally accented scientific system of transliteration. This involves many diacritical marks and it is therefore not always used, with the result that readers are confused. You could find *āshrama* written as āśrama, ashrama, ashram, aashrama or in other forms. In this text, all diacritical marks except the sign for vowel length on a, i and u have been avoided. All other vowels are long.

You should note that all vowels are best spoken as in German. So the vowel in *bhakti* sounds like that in 'bus', but the consonant is aspirated as in 'why'; *ātman* has the sound of 'father'. Note that i/ī sound like 'it' and 'eager', and u/ū like 'put' and 'mood'.

Accents in Punjabi differ from those in Hindi and Sanskrit; so gurū in the Sikhism glossary has an accent which it does not have in the Hinduism glossary. The Buddhism section contains both Sanskrit and Pali forms of words.

The Arabic transliterations are given with both aspirants where appropriate and vowel accents.

INTRODUCTION

This book has grown out of the conviction that crossing the frontiers of faiths, languages and races can enable people to deepen their understanding of issues that are important to us all. We live in an age when many different groups, particularly in Europe and North America, are expressing serious concern about human values – about how we should live, how we should treat each other and how we should treat our world. This concern is being articulated by politicians, members of the caring professions, in education and in discussions between members of different faiths. Often the most rigorous and challenging answers come from religious traditions. They challenge us with their different language worlds and starting points, but also startle us with answers that express values which are often shared. The central aim of this book is to make available the basic tenets of six world religions – their beliefs, experiences and convictions – in which these shared values are grounded. We acknowledge that many other religious traditions and world views have important contributions to make to this debate and their omission is not one of principle but of space.

Any context has its strengths and weaknesses. It is sometimes suggested that the treatment of values and ethical issues in the Western world, even when faiths come together, is dominated by a Christian or post-Christian agenda, and that this is a weakness. From this standpoint any list of common topics such as those to be addressed in this book may be seen to reflect the concerns of the majority culture rather than minority faiths; the concerns of the West and not of other parts of the world, for example in any distinctions made between public and private lives and the inclusion of issues such as homosexuality or euthanasia. It might well be suggested that each faith should set out its own themes and group them in its own way. This is a viewpoint with which the contributors are sympathetic. It would not, however, have produced a text which would be as useful when considering the question of shared values in the European and North American as well as other contexts. The text therefore does arise in a Western context, and the members of the minority faith communities who have contributed to it are happy that this is the case. It is also a major strength of the book that this has been done. For it is precisely the tensions between context and the world views of the various faiths which force reflection on assumptions and convictions which within that context are generally taken for granted – for instance, the private–public classification.

The topics were chosen for a variety of reasons. They provide an opportunity to focus on issues that are important within religions, even though in different ways or to a different degree. They are also being raised in professional groups and have been placed in some way or other on syllabuses in educational institutions. However, the editors have always kept an eye on any artificial moulding of material or traditions. Writers were asked to point out where any terminology or emphasis is not that used within a particular faith, or where there is as yet little material or debate on a particular topic. For example, the section on Buddhism has used the heading 'Human Nature' instead of 'Sin and Sins', which would not be appropriate terminology for Buddhists. At the same point the Jewish author writes that 'the overarching concept of Sin is not really present in Judaism'. In the Sikh section on euthanasia, it states that 'this is not a subject on which Sikhs have made any religious pronouncement'. What is apparent, though, is that questions on the agenda in a western context are drawing more and more response from the traditions whose roots have been until quite recently in quite different societies. Addressing these questions is part of the transplantation process of religious communities and not an artificial task. Each section has an introduction in which the concerns of each faith are explained in their own terms and in their own way. These passages 'set the scene', and hence prevent the common structure from moulding the material in an artificial way. There are also differences in the length as well as the contents of sections and this gives each faith an additional opportunity to show the balance and emphasis of concern for members of the traditions within it. The editors are very aware that there have been attempts, such as that linked with the centenary celebrations of the 1893 Chicago Parliament of Religions (see Küng and Kuschel 1993), to try to identify a 'global ethic' to which all religions might agree. This is an interesting enterprise but of another kind from the task undertaken in this book, where the contributors are attentive to differences even though working within agreed areas of concern.

INTRODUCTION

All of the writers have academic expertise in their given faiths and are sensitive to the kind of debate outlined above. They are also either members of the faith communities or have worked closely with those communities and are respected by them. They have tried at all times to reflect the viewpoints of believers. In doing this they have used ancient scriptural and other more contemporary written sources, and tried at all times to reflect the variety of views that exist on the many controversial issues within the different traditions. These varieties are to do with different historical contexts and the new geographical and cultural arenas in which members of faiths increasingly find themselves. Many of the issues are on the frontiers of debate in the faiths and there may be no such thing as a fixed or final view. It is often as important to understand how decisions are made and how guidelines are being laid down as to know what is being decided. Readers are encouraged to seek further views through meeting members of faith communities and through further reading, including journal and newspaper articles. The lists of addresses and bibliographies at the end of each section and the book as a whole facilitate this further exploration.

There are other important religions and communities that are not discussed here for reasons of space, rather than from any suggestion that they are not important. The viewpoints of these communities add further diversity and emphases to debates on ethical issues. As a result of the stimulus that this book gives, readers are encouraged to find out, for example, about Jain attitudes to animals and the environment, Bahai attitudes to peace and women, Zoroastrian views on other religions and marriage or Rastafarian attitudes to drugs and poverty, to name but a few. Priorities and populations vary, even in the so-called 'western' world. In the USA responses to the issues by the Afro-American populations are crucial and would add yet further perspectives to the material.

The section on each religion is presented separately as a free-standing and integral piece of writing. This is another way of trying to see each tradition in the round and in its own terms. If the themes had been dealt with across each religion and one at a time that would have given the reader much less sense of how aspects of a religion's viewpoint are part of a whole. As the text stands, cross-reference where needed is facilitated by the common structure used for each faith. Each religion begins with an introduction to what it means to be a member of that religion, with its own authorities, norms and ideals. There is no particular significance in the order of the religions being presented, but it seemed sensible to group the so-called 'Indian' traditions, the Hindu, Buddhist and Sikh traditions, together, followed by the Jewish, Christian and Islamic faiths.

INTRODUCTION

1. Religious Identity and Authority

Being a member of one religion rather than another is often a matter of people's country of birth, their general cultural background or the particular family from which they come. In this case the attitudes of that religion are absorbed gradually, becoming both as much a part of people's lives as the language they speak – something with which they feel 'at home' and towards which they have considerable loyalty and affection. Nevertheless, there are people who find that at some stage in life they want to change from the religion they grew up in to another religion or worldview which they feel is a better expression of what they really think or how they want to live. In addition, there are more and more people who grow up with no religious background at all, in what are usually called 'secular' societies. These people may never want to commit themselves to a religious view of the world or may become attracted to a religion and embrace it, often through meeting people whose ideas or way of life impress them in some way.

Many members of religions emphasise that it is not enough simply to believe certain ideas: a religion is a whole way of life. This is obviously a very important perspective for a book on ethics and so inevitably it is one which the authors have taken into account. Of course, not all members of a religion can or do follow the ideal path of life that the religion teaches, and hence many sections in this book contain examples of the gaps between theory and practice, or ideal practice and reality. The authors also set out to give expression to the diversity that exists within all religions, a diversity which often has something to do with where the religion is being lived. For example, Hindus or Muslims in Britain may make different decisions on marriage or family life from those in India or Saudi Arabia, and their religion provides for that possibility; Buddhists in Tibet may make different decisions about eating meat from those in Switzerland; Sikhs in the Punjab may find their struggle for justice of a different kind from Sikhs in Canada; some Jews in the USA may have a very different attitude to international politics from Jews in Israel. On top of this, all religions are made up of different groups, schools, denominations and sects and these often disagree strongly with one another, creating tension between members of different groups. There is also the feeling that belonging to a religion is like being part of a worldwide family which transcends other barriers.

One of the distinctive features of religions is the belief that this life and the world as we know it are not all there is. This does not detract from the importance of acting for the good of other people in the world, but it does mean that there is a further dimension to people's actions and the fruit those actions bear, a dimension unseen by other human beings. This makes teachings about *karma* and rebirth, heaven and hell, afterlife and the kingdom of God an important part of ethical discourse.

The religions in this book all have substantial collections of written texts or scriptures on which they draw for help in making ethical decisions. All these texts have a certain authority, even though believers describe it in different ways. Some texts, for example, have the status of revelation or 'givenness', while others derive their authority from being collections of traditions or the reflections of distinguished teachers on important issues.

Nearly every community, both secular and religious, has leaders. It is often instructive to discover how these leaders are chosen and by what kinds of qualities they are judged. Throughout history too, communities have tried to establish whether leaders are above the law or within it. Particularly important for communities who live under leaders of a different religious or secular tradition is the question of the appropriate attitudes towards such leaders: what duties do subjects or citizens owe, and what are the qualities to be looked for if these leaders are elected.

In the context of religious communities, it is important to discover the relationship between religious leaders, the tradition and the community's original inspiration which is often in the form of texts. In addition to texts, there are many people whom members of religions consider to be great ethical examples. These might be great figures at the origins of the religions, such as Moses, Sarah, Muhammad and Khadijah. They might be later historical figures such as Ashoka or Guru Gobind Singh. They might be well-known figures from the twentieth century, such as the Dalai Lama, or they might be people who live without any fame or publicity but whose lives of quiet love, self-sacrifice, bravery, honesty and loyalty to their faith greatly influence their families and friends.

2. Personal and Private?

The title of this section needs a question mark because the distinction that is often made in the western world between people's public and private lives is not one sustained in many cultures and religious traditions. This is pointed out very clearly in the sections on Hinduism, Sikhism and Islam particularly. People are seen in these cultures as essentially parts of a family, probably an extended family unit and a wider community. What they are and do is a part of the community's life, honour or blame. They do not make their decisions on such an individualistic basis as do many people in the secular West.

Nevertheless, religions offer guidance on the kind of qualities that should be admired or cultivated by individuals, even though they go about it in two broadly different ways. Some traditions lay down fairly clear guidelines and advice. They offer models, particularly early figures or founders, as prime examples of the kinds of qualities to be encouraged. Other traditions provide a looser kind of guidance, with inspirational ideas, parables and messages from which individuals can draw their own conclusions as to how the ideal life should be led.

Most of the religious traditions seem to agree that humility is a necessary quality, as are honesty, kindness and wisdom. Wisdom here is not the same as cleverness or even education; honesty is not the same as bluntness; kindness is not the same as sentimentality. One of the reasons for cultivating the personal qualities described in this section is so that the relationships one establishes with others are not only enriching but also inspiring. The way an individual relates to friends is perhaps the easiest test of the kind of moral life that she or he conducts.

For some religions, though, friendship is only a halfway house to the love of humanity as a whole, which is implied in the concept of the human race as one family. In others it is the highest form of human relationship, the one which sets goals and challenges and also provides a model of the kind of relationship that could be achieved either with God or with all humankind.

Best friends and early friends are often very important in people's lives. Every community has proverbs and sayings about the need to choose or have good friends and about the danger of having bad ones. In some, though by no means all, people's assessment of ethics and moral principles, relationships with friends need even more discussion than those with family members since people have the right to choose their friends. Therefore it is not only important how people behave towards a friend, but also how they go about gaining one in the first place, not to mention maintaining the friendship once it has been achieved. In most cases religions talk about friendships between people of the same sex. Nevertheless, this provides an intimation of the ideals that should lie within marriage (see section 3). This is especially important since for some, the most fulfilling friendship they will ever have is with their partner in life. Throughout history people have tried to anticipate or experiment with the preliminaries of this relationship through sex before or outside marriage. Since many religions place great stress on marriage, this is an area in which religious traditions may want to present strong views.

What is also stressed is the importance of the family. While the pattern of the family and one's responsibilities to it may differ from religious community to religious community, and sometimes even within the religions, it would still seem to be true that the responsibility of bringing forth new life is regarded as a serious one. Before the advent of what is seen as 'safe' sex for people in some parts of the world, there seems to have been particular concern about the consequences to the woman, either in terms of her reputation, her economic security or her emotional stability if bearing a child without a man to support her in its upbringing. It is technically possible now in most parts of the world for a woman to ensure that she does not have a child through sexual intercourse. Nevertheless, it would still appear that most religious communities consider that to have sexual intercourse if you are fertile without at least the general possibility of conceiving a child is almost a contradiction in terms since part of the function of having sexual intercourse is to do with having children.

Many religions seem to agree that the physical act of sexual intercourse in the appropriate loving context is a 'high' act rather than a 'low' one. It is usually linked with the procreation of children or the expression of a pure lifetime's love between two individuals. It would also appear that there is an attitude emerging on the part of the liberal wing of several communities that, while sex before marriage is still technically unacceptable, if it is performed by two individuals who intend to marry, it is less unacceptable than if performed by two individuals who have no intention of any particular mutual commitment.

For some religions, marriage is the norm and celibacy discouraged. But some communities teach that it is better not to be involved in the sexual act in any context and that sexual desire needs to be sublimated or ennobled. Celibacy is then an important ideal and may be seen as the highest way. These different views co-exist side by side within some religious traditions as well as between traditions.

Still more problematic for most religious traditions has been sexual activity with a member of the same sex. Deep relationships with people of the same sex are often set up as the highest form of friendship but many traditions seem to have deep taboos against homosexuality. Recently it has been stressed that even those traditions that feel most strongly about the subject do not condemn the homosexual, but the actual sexual activity. While that may seem to some like a very subtle line to draw in real life, it does at least make clear that the kind of abuse, ridicule and even physical attack that many homosexual men, for example, may experience in some societies cannot be justified by appeal to any of the religious traditions represented in this book.

3. Marriage and the Family

Marriage is one of the four rites of passage marked by religions, albeit in different ways and with different emphases. The other three rites are at birth, puberty and death. Some religions think of marriage as a path to follow for those who cannot be celibate and cannot devote all their lives to religious matters in an ascetic way. In these religions, married life is usually acknowledged as a lower path than that of a monk, nun or world-renouncer. Other religions view marriage as the norm, and getting married as a fulfilment of the religious life.

Whether it is seen as the recommended way or a lower path, all religions take marriage very seriously because it forms the most basic unit in society

into which children are born and nurtured in the faith. Most faiths emphasise that it has much wider implications than the attraction, personal happiness and fulfilment of one man and one woman. This is expressed in various
ways: for example, in accepting or approving a system of arranged or assisted
marriages where the extended family is involved in the process of choice and
commitment and the support of a couple. Marriage can be seen as one of the
sacraments of a religion, accompanied by special religious ceremonies in a
place of worship and in the presence of a priest. Alternatively there may be
emphasis on a publicly celebrated social contract with witnesses.

Marriage ceremonies have similar features wherever a religion is trans-
planted, but some are entirely dependent on the social customs, as well as the
legal requirements, of a particular country. Not all religions insist on monogamy, although they say that believers must observe the law of the country
in which they live. They all have a strong sense of an appropriate and ideal
relationship between a wife and husband, of the importance of having children and of mutual help in their different roles.

A marriage begins or extends a family unit, and family bonds are some of
the most important in people's lives. The relationships between parents and
children are emphasised particularly in religions because the child's early
spiritual as well as physical and emotional life is nurtured within the context
of a family. But many religions embrace an obligation to respect and care for
not only the closest family members but the extended family of grandparents,
aunts and cousins as well. This may have something to do with the traditional
societies in which most of the religions begin, but it may also express a deep
understanding of the network that is needed to sustain the life of an individual.

The principles of respect, obligation and love are also frequently extended
to the wider family of the religion. All these relationships are seen as an enrichment as well as a responsibility. They give security and help at crucial
stages in people's lives, as well as mutual obligations. The personal qualities
that are needed for family relationships are also those which the religions encourage in the wider world. It is important also to ask whether there are ever
situations when the demands of a religion might challenge and override the
commitments people have to their families and how these are resolved, as for
example if someone becomes a Buddhist or Christian monk or nun. Religions
may give different answers to this question in different circumstances.

All religions have a strong sense of the importance of marriages that last
a lifetime and ensure a stable home life for the whole family unit. This is the
ideal set before those about to be married, and to which members of the religion give their support. If a couple are encountering difficulties the extended
family and the wider religious community will usually do all they can to help
them, and to encourage them to stay together. There may be a stronger sense

of the rightness of staying within a marriage than in western societies at large which may accept more easily divorce as the lesser of two evils if a marriage is unhappy. People now often debate what is meant by a family and whether the unit in which one lives, whatever the mixture of human beings, counts as a family group. Members of religions may be sympathetic to this idea of what is meant by a family, emphasising that loving and supportive relationships are the touchstones of family communities, or they may be very critical of new ways of living together. There may also be considerable tensions between religious ideals and the custom of the land in which a member of a religious community lives, between the traditional sense of being a part of a community and modern individualism.

When traditional marriage relationships break down, there is often both compassion and realism in what is allowed by many religious groups, and in the last resort, practical arrangements can almost always be made for a divorce to take place. The reasons why a divorce may be permitted, if at all, will vary from religion to religion, and the nature of divorce will depend on whether the original marriage was a purely legal contract or a sacramental act. Like the original marriage, it should be acceptable to the laws of the country in which the couple are resident.

4. Influences on and Use of Time and Money

Education in the broadest sense is without doubt the main medium by which any culture or tradition transmits its values to others, particularly the next generation. There is a clear difference of opinion as to whether education in a faith should be given intensively to the leaders so that they can lead others effectively, or whether it should be given on a more widespread basis so that everybody has a fair knowledge of what the values might be and what is expected of them.

Whatever the preferred solution, it seems generally agreed that education is not primarily about developing skills to fulfil jobs or to become an economically productive member of society but more about developing the correct attitudes and personal qualities to be a fine human being. This is an attitude shared by people with religious as well as secular ideals. In trying to work out what should be taught as well as whom should be taught, every culture finds itself defining its major values and teachings. In many cases these are based on central and important texts and the understanding of them. What is particularly instructive is the wide variety of methods of teaching and learning that the different cultures have arrived at over the centuries.

As well as the influence that families and education have on people's values there is also the influence of the media and the power of advertising in people's lives. The media can be used for good purposes or to manipulate the minds and attitudes of people. Propaganda has always been used in societies, including by religious groups, but mass printing and publishing and the electronic media mean that more people can be influenced more quickly and therefore more potential harm done. Advertising presents another aspect of the potential misuse of these resources. Obviously a manufacturer or seller has the right to inform people of the goods or services available. However, with the increased power of the media and a growing understanding of how the human mind works, modern advertising can manipulate so that it is not offering the buyer an opportunity, but rather implanting an instruction to purchase the item in question. This clearly presents major moral and ethical challenges, and many societies have attempted to work out codes of practice. While the traditional teachings of the religions discussed in this book were established long before advertising was a major issue, there seem to be some guidelines that can be drawn from the ethical teachings embedded within them.

Although it has been said that education is primarily about wisdom rather than skills, each tradition nevertheless lays great stress on the importance of individuals playing a constructive part in society. This does not necessarily mean that the work done by each person must be of economic value but it does mean that everybody must contribute in some way or other to the success and improvement of the world in which they live. Besides the production of goods and services, people might be expected to work as teachers, religious professionals or even thinkers for the betterment of society. All the religions discussed in this book have at some time or another felt it important to enable certain individuals to devote almost their undivided attention to thinking and to extending their own learning for the enrichment of the society in which they live. This is also considered to be work.

The performing of a useful task is seen not only as important to society, but also to the individual in so far as it increases self-respect and dignity in the eyes of others. Any tendency to judge a job's worth by the money it earns is more alien to these religions than to society at large, where it is an important indicator of value. Many of the most valued jobs and workers in and for the community do not earn anything at all. Buddhist monks and nuns, for example, live entirely on the offerings of members of the lay community.

In Judaism the concept of leisure is enshrined as an absolute value through the concept of *Shabbat*. Any idea of leisure as self-indulgence seems alien to the religions and there is a greater sense that the time when an individual is not involved in his or her job might be spent not only on self-enrichment but also on social interaction and the enrichment of others.

The balance between these two sides of the coin – work and leisure – is seen differently by the different religious traditions. It is an important issue for modern technologically developed societies which are struggling with the apparent lack of jobs in relation to the number of people who wish to have them. It seems to be the message of all the traditions that every individual should have the opportunity to work, while the leisure that they have is that time which is in contrast to the work that they do. The balance seems to be important. At the moment employment and unemployment trends in western countries seem to have produced a situation where some people are overworked all the time and some people have enforced inactivity and the indignity of unemployment.

There may be some people who have excess leisure as a product of their wealth. The religions disagree as to whether or not individuals are to be allowed to accumulate wealth. The debate has a remarkably contemporary ring to it. Some suggest that since wealth can corrupt and provoke the evils of greed and selfishness, everyone should be allowed to have approximately the same amount and that the collective wealth should be shared for the good of society. Others argue that if individuals with the right kind of initiative are allowed to accumulate wealth, their affluence, if properly controlled and guided, can serve to benefit those less well-off than themselves.

One thing seems clear as far as these religions are concerned. Wealth is always given in trust to the individual and must be used responsibly and morally. The wealthy individual automatically has a responsibility to those who are poor, making the (compulsory) paying of taxes or the (voluntary) contribution to charity an absolute responsibility rather than an act of goodwill. Even those religions which agree that individuals have every right to accumulate wealth are nevertheless quite clear that there are correct and incorrect ways of accumulating it. Some money, however good the cause to which it is given, will be 'dirty' because of the way in which it has been earned.

One way in which some of the richest people in the world have achieved their wealth is through drug trafficking. This is widely seen as a way of life that exploits other people since it encourages and then trades on people's addiction. While there seems to be a case to be made by some of the traditions for the use of certain drugs or alcohol to heighten spiritual or mystical awareness and certainly to ease pain in the case of illness, when it involves the abuse of an otherwise healthy body it is roundly condemned. Certainly when people slip into addiction which can lead eventually to sickness, death, loss of personal autonomy and their destruction as individuals with integrity, each of the religions speaks out strongly to condemn.

It is a seeming paradox that drug abuse is a problem of the very rich and very poor. It would appear that people turn to them either out of boredom or despair. In either case perhaps some of the approaches to work and leisure could help to resolve the drugs problem that the world appears to face.

5. The Quality and Value of Life

The major religious traditions of the world all teach that human life is of great value and should be respected whether the individual is elderly, handicapped, sick, poor, dying or not yet born. In some ways they go even further than this and say that the life experience of some of these people may bring them especially close to the heart of their religion, in a way that the experience of youth, physical fitness, intellectual ability and wealth do not. The religions also teach personal qualities (see 2.a) which give priority to the practical care of the poor and sick. These include a sense of justice, unselfishness, generosity, love and compassion.

The attitudes of single religions, such as Christianity in the UK or Islam in Saudi Arabia, have sometimes permeated whole societies and influenced their laws on financial assistance and health care for those in need, and their attitudes to abortion and euthanasia. In other societies the existence of a plurality of religions has underpinned what might be called a 'caring' attitude and a respect for life, even when there is disagreement about the exact moment the human person comes into being. But religious people are now in the minority in many dominantly secular societies where people may value material success and a busy, efficient life in paid employment rather than anything else. These attitudes make the elderly, handicapped and poor feel useless and social failures. There is also a high level of scientific experiment and technical achievement which enables people to have safe abortions for social reasons, and which present death as a medical failure instead of the natural and acceptable end to life. Religious people are affected by and interact with these attitudes in many different ways and often share with humanists the attempt to improve values in their communities.

6. Questions of Right and Wrong

The law of the land in most countries is a secular legal system enforced by police, judges and a penal system. Because religions are ways of life as well as belief-systems, they too have ideas about how people should behave and what should be done when they behave badly. They also have their own teachings about justice and a way for people to show that they are sorry for what they have done. But one of the main characteristics of religion is its sense that order, truth and justice are ultimate cosmic values and realities, not just human ideas. They are part of the way God wants things to be, to put it in theistic terms, not just the creations of human societies.

There is obviously a great deal of overlap between what religions and the law of the land discourage – for example, theft and murder. The ideas of a religion about what are good and bad, right and wrong ways of behaving have often affected a society in which that religion has been a majority presence for a long time – for example, Christianity and the law of monogamy in Western Europe. Religious people are in any case almost always encouraged to obey the law of the land in which they live, except where they believe that the law is unjust or inhumane. Then they may feel that they have to make a protest, preferably, though not always, in a non-violent way, against injustice.

In these ways religions tend to think of two levels of law. There is the ultimate law, which some see as *Karma* and others as the Will of God, and which, for example, may condemn all killing. Then there is the lower law of a nation or state which asks soldiers to go to war to protect their country (see 8.b), or which inflicts capital punishment for serious crimes such as murder. Whilst all killing is wrong, there may sometimes have to be actions which are justified as a lesser evil because of the circumstances. Another example is that religions see punishment as a matter for God, who is both just and merciful; or as part of the law of *Karma*, which is based on the attitude and heart of a person, not just on their external actions. Repentance and forgiveness are then always a possibility between people and God, or between human beings. In human society, however, the state inflicts punishments for crimes, based mainly on external actions and with some reference to motive and intention, but independently of the issues of forgiveness and reconciliation. Crimes about which the state legislates are termed illegal. The religions have their own technical terms for what is considered wrong in their traditions. The Christian term is 'sin' but one should beware of using that term to translate the related concepts of other religions. Teaching about what is right and wrong is also related to beliefs about life after death and how a people's present life affects their future state.

7. Equality and Difference

People often point out that religions cause conflict and divide people (see section 8). In any consideration of the ethics of religious communities this challenge must be met. If religions create hatred and evil then their claim to present moral or ethical standards is almost totally undermined. It is necessary to examine what they have to say about differences between people. It would be facile to pretend that there are no differences, and quite clearly the different religions are in themselves responding to different kinds of cultural perceptions, experiences and attitudes.

While some find it relatively easy to accommodate the fact that people are infinitely varied, it is sometimes harder to find a way of coping with other religions as such, which often claim not only to know a different truth but sometimes exclusively to know the truth. It is interesting to note that there can be more problems in attitudes towards those religions closely related, than towards those religions at a distance. It is perhaps more common to conflict with members of one's family than with people who are strangers.

Related to this, but on a more political or social level, is the attitude of one community towards people of other races or nations. Some religions see themselves as very definitely relevant to all races or nations, while others are rather more restricted to a particular community or group. This has not prevented the large communities from breaking down into sub-groups related to race or nation, nor has it prevented the rather more restricted groups from opening up to embrace others not of their original community. Unless religions can provide an adequate and dignified response to these groupings, which sometimes conflict, they will be criticised as not able to teach much in the way of ethics.

Perhaps an even more fundamental split in humanity is that between the sexes; religions, like all cultural groups, have been challenged by the modern movement of feminism. The questions involve the nature of the relationship between the sexes. Are the sexes of differing status, of differing purpose, or merely different? Many religions have been influenced by the cultural environment in which they have operated, but equally many cultural environments have been influenced by the religions which operate within them. It is very hard to trace whether the contemporary experience of women is a product of local religious ideas, or whether the religious community can offer something in the context of modern feminism.

Overarching all these issues is the question of whether or not all people are equal and if so, what is the purpose of different religions and how does one deal with the various ways in which humanity tends to divide itself? Once again, and by easy reference to common knowledge, one can see that religious teachings have often been used to aggravate the sense of the inequalities between people, and to support the claims of one group against another. Is the religion being correctly interpreted in such a case, or is it being misused?

This section, with its various topics, points most specifically at the heart of the potential humaneness of religions, and their claim to moral and ethical insights worthy of being considered even by people of other religions or no religion at all.

8. National Divisions, War and Peace

This topic implies that the existence of different, separate nations is in some way a problem. Our experience of nations is as competitors and enemies rather than as collaborators and friends (7.c). The competition may be for trade, land, olympic medals or ideological superiority.

People tend to mean by a nation a humanly created nation-state rather than an ethnic grouping with an inherited common culture (7.a). Such a nation often has quite artificial, arbitrary geographical boundaries and separates related groups of people. The answer to the question of why different nations exist is most commonly given in historical, social, geographical and nationalistic, rather than religious terms.

The majority of the nation-states of today contain a diversity of cultures and religious groupings within them. It is possible for a nation to affirm this variety as a microcosm of the varied world in which we live. Members of religions might then feel secure living side by side. However, there is sometimes a tension between religious beliefs and commitment to separate nation-states. The state may be oppressive of religion or some religious groups. There may be a desire to create and live in a nation in which one can follow one's religious life and its ethical ideals with the minimum of compromise. This desire may lead to a radical reform of a nation from within (as in the case of the Iranian Revolution) or the setting-up of a new nation-state (as in the case of Pakistan in 1947 and the Sikh desire for a homeland). Religious beliefs may emphasise that fellowship with co-religionists in other nation-states transcends national divisions and loyalties. There may be a deep awareness of the final unity of all humankind whatever their religion or race (7.b and c), and a desire for the global village to see itself and act as one world. All of these views are reflected in this section.

Some of the above points are highlighted when nations go to war against each other. Many religions teach some form of non-violence as an ideal, and members of religions have often refused to fight. They maintain that their refusal to be involved in the killing of others is more important than blind loyalty to a nation-state or even more than its defence, if it is threatened by others. This has never been an easy option since people who take this stand might be imprisoned or expected to undertake dangerous tasks in war zones, such as working with ambulance crews. Some religions teach that war might be acceptable and even obligatory in certain circumstances such as self-defence or to end tyranny or oppression. If war becomes necessary, then careful conditions are traditionally laid down about how it should be waged, with as much respect given to civilian life and property and the humane treatment of prisoners, for example, as possible. Nuclear war is of quite a different kind from traditional warfare. It is not just a matter of degree and the number of people that would be involved in the present and the future, but also of its indiscriminate nature.

Many of the issues involved in discussion of war and peace overlap those involved in violence and non-violence amongst individuals. The ethics of some religions stress that families, societies and nations are no more than a collection of individuals, and that the best way to secure peaceful co-existence is to tackle aggression, hatred, greed, jealousy and so forth, on an individual level.

9. Global Issues

The modern awareness of the world as a 'global village' has brought to everyone's attention the problems of people around the world. Only a century ago it was possible to be fairly ignorant as to what was happening just a few hundred miles away, but nowadays it is almost impossible to ignore what is happening on the other side of the world, particularly when the happening is a crisis of some sort.

INTRODUCTION

There is much evidence to suggest that what is called the 'north–south divide' in the world demonstrates an injustice of monstrous proportions. Most of the countries in the northern hemisphere are relatively affluent and frequently waste a large amount of the food and resources that they have available, simply because they cannot consume them all. Meanwhile many of the countries in the southern hemisphere are starved and impoverished. Thousands of people die of famine, disease and natural disasters against which they cannot afford to establish proper defences. The problem of world poverty seems to be one which is to do with justice rather than resources, and challenges to solve it belong equally to all people.

Some people have blamed the poverty in the less technologically developed countries on the tendency of their populations to grow faster than those in the more affluent countries of the northern hemisphere. This is by no means a total explanation and in some ways a complete red herring. Nevertheless, each community is challenged by the situation to develop an attitude towards the growth of the world's population and the fact that humanity possesses the capacity to control or reduce its numbers, if it so wishes. Should people as it were, 'trust in God' and carry on producing children? Should people engineer a certain population size, in line with economic realities? A third possibility is, of course, to try to adjust economic realities to suit the size of population.

Nevertheless, the size of population in some impoverished countries has been seen as a major problem, and it is worth considering that the other side of the problem is the diminishing size of the populations of affluent countries. In time there is a fear that either there will be an insufficient workforce, or there will not be enough people to support the elderly, who through medical advances are living longer.

All this awareness and concern about global problems encourages a view of the world as a completely interrelated whole. Perhaps it was space travel that most dramatically established for all people that the world was a single unit spinning in space, and that everything that happened in one place would eventually have an impact on everywhere else. The development of concern for the environment, for ecological systems, for the conservation of fish stocks, for fossil fuels, and the attempt to prevent the atmosphere from deteriorating still further are all demonstrations of a growing awareness that regardless of differences, every community finally bears a relationship with and responsibility to every other community.

Even though this may not have been a major preoccupation in the days of the establishment of the main religious traditions, if they are to be relevant to the modern day they must say something about how human beings should respond to the concept of the world as a whole and its natural needs, in the light of the growing human capacity to affect the way the world progresses.

A. HINDUISM

Werner Menski

A.1. RELIGIOUS IDENTITY AND AUTHORITY

A.1.a. On Being a Hindu

The simple questions 'Are you a Hindu?' and 'What makes you a Hindu?' lead both the curious enquirer and the Hindu individual straight into a maze of interrelated concepts which one could not hope to describe adequately in a few words. The answer, even if the individual has thought about this point before, is bound to be something like 'Of course I am a Hindu, because I was born one', or 'My parents and my family are Hindu, we are all Hindus'. Quite often one will hear 'I am born in India, so I am a Hindu'.

But nowadays, not all Indians are Hindus, and a growing number of Hindus are born outside India, notably in the UK and North America. Clearly, it cannot be the birthplace alone that determines a person's religion. Being born into a particular family, however, does remain important. And this seems to be the same in all religions: the young ones grow up absorbing, more or less completely in traditional societies, the value system of their families, and thus become almost automatically an adherent of the religion of their ancestors, elders and peers. For Hindus, there is no formal point of entry into the group of 'the believers'. A young Hindu need never formally pledge his or her allegiance to Hinduism. That one is born a Hindu is, therefore, quite sufficient to the average member of this faith as an answer to the question 'What makes you a Hindu?' Some 'entry ceremonies' have been devised for converts to Hinduism, but it is still sufficient to simply adjust to a Hindu way of life (whatever that may be) and gain recognition that way.

Similarly, one could not simply stop being a Hindu by declaring oneself unreligious or 'of no religion'. Wearing western clothes, abandoning traditional dietary rules, neglecting or giving up worship of Hindu deities, all this may be seen by some as signs of 'Hinduism in danger'. But none of this means that those concerned have stopped being Hindu. In India, one would not cease to be counted as a Hindu unless one formally declared one's allegiance to another religion, for example, converted to Islam, Christianity, or another faith. The same is true elsewhere.

Because it does not constantly require confirmation of allegiance, Hinduism seems to make it comparatively easy for its followers to remain Hindu. Conversely, for a non-Hindu, the adoption of a Hindu way of life could well lead to recognition as a Hindu, particularly if the individual concerned has become a recognised and accepted member of a particular social group, for example through marriage.

Hinduism is, thus, clearly as much a way of life as a religion and Hindu individuals have a great deal of freedom in which to find their own path. Even though they remain at all times subject to overriding concerns when considering what is appropriate in particular circumstances, the religion offers considerable flexibility. This has, over time and among the various Hindu communities all over the world, created what can sometimes seem a confusing diversity of practice and belief. Yet all of this is part of one religion, Hinduism.

Unlike other world religions Hinduism cannot be defined by a central authority or dogma deriving from one spiritual entity or one scripture. Hindus know the theistic concept of the supreme deity and will often talk about God, while referring to a particular Hindu deity. Thus, Hinduism is also polytheistic and sectarian. In effect, Hindus have agreed to disagree over the very fundamentals of religious belief out of a tacit acknowledgement of the limits of human knowledge. As a result Hinduism puts more emphasis on action than belief, its ethical foundations being marked by an almost limitless plurality.

To the individual Hindu in India, this was rarely a problem. Hindus in other countries, however, are beginning to find it difficult to ascertain their identity as Hindus. It is often so cumbersome to maintain what is conceived of as a Hindu way of life, because there seems to be no formula to guide you.

Like all religions, Hinduism is concerned with the relationship between the individual and the spiritual – a relationship which is seen in various ways. This makes Hinduism as a religion complex and somewhat confusing to study. Having no single belief-system and no holy book as a focus, it is not concerned to divide the world into believers and non-believers. Essentially, Hinduism is concerned with the world, indeed, the universe as a whole, and in that context with the role and place of the individual. Hindus are thus firmly placed as tiny particles of the universe, whether they are aware of this or not. Being part of a larger whole all the time, not being able to declare oneself an independent individual goes much more to make the 'Hinduness' of a person than some particular way of life. Hindus perceive humanity as visibly

2

and invisibly linked with all aspects of the created world, whether gods, animals, plants and other creatures. The whole universe in fact, including the unknowable creative force behind everything. The Hindu's interlinkedness, strengthened by the concept that any activity has consequences (the *karma* theory), inevitably leads to a sense of the self as part of this world, inescapably tied in. For the Hindu, both these cosmological concepts and the realities of life are inseparable and they influence each other continuously and almost imperceptibly.

It follows that anyone studying Hinduism has to look both at the religious literature and the popular manifestations of Hindu existence. It may turn out that many Hindus know little about the former; this does not, however, mean that they are ignorant of their religion.

Hindu religious literature begins with the Vedas (*c.* 1200 BCE), vast collections of sacrificial hymns which are treated as *shruti*, 'revealed truth' or 'heard knowledge', a form of divine revelation. However, this sacred knowledge was not received by one Prophet but by an undefined group of ancient wise men or sages, who transmitted it to their pupils. This makes the origins of Hindu traditions difficult to identify and has had very important consequences. For example, belief in the divine nature of the Vedas is not a prerequisite for being a Hindu. In fact, the average Hindu has little idea of what the Vedas are, not least because they are written in difficult Sanskrit, the classical language of India.

This vast literature elaborates a central concept of early Hinduism, the idea of 'harmony' or 'order', called *rta* or *rita*. Observations of natural phenomena, such as the regularity of sun and moon, day and night, and the seasons, generated in the ancient Hindus a perception of their environment and themselves as governed by an invisible force with creative, preserving and destructive aspects. But disorder, like premature deaths, was also part of this created order. Hence, maintenance of balance and harmony came to be seen as an important aim of human life. A pantheon of Vedic gods, similar to that of ancient Greece, was perceived to be involved in the maintenance of this cosmic whole. Man's task became to worship these deities, to support them through rituals and sacrifices. An elaborate system of solemn sacrificial rituals developed at this time.

The Vedas were followed by layer upon layer of sacrificial and ritual literature handed down orally. Much later (*c.* 500 BCE) we find texts which aim to provide not only ritual detail, but also guidelines for human behaviour. In particular, two groups of works became important, the dharmasutras and dharmashastras, both handbooks of *dharma* or 'righteousness'. This developed into the central Hindu concept that still rules today. The dharma texts were classified as *smriti*, 'remembered truth', but in reality they were entirely the fruit of human efforts.

Dharma can be found translated as 'religion', 'law', 'duty', 'righteousness' and many other things. In fact, it is all this together. Its conceptual roots lie in the Vedic *rta*, but it goes further: *dharma* as 'duty' emphasises the systemic duty of every individual to act, in every life situation, in such a way that righteousness is achieved; in other words, to act appropriately.

It is during this classical period of Hinduism (*c.* 500 BCE to CE *c.* 200) that the concept of *dharma* is linked together with many other concepts to form a consistent body of Hindu socio-religious theories. What is provided in the end is a theory of the obligations of an individual according to his or her caste (*varna*) and stage of life (*āshrama*).

Childhood is not counted as a stage of life. The male Hindu should enter the stage of pupil or student (*brahmacarya*), depending on his *varna* (see A.7.a), at between 8 and 12 years old. In this classical theory, the lowest caste group, the *Shūdras*, as well as females, are not allowed to enter this stage. Impurity is given as a major reason, and they are thus denied access to the scriptures and to formal education in them. However, to understand Hinduism, it is necessary to learn to read such apparently inflexible rules as flexible guidelines. Clearly, what Hindus actually do is often not in line with orthodox preference.

After completing a period of study in this ideal system, the male Hindu would be about 24–32 years old. He should now marry and become a householder (*grihastha*) and partake fully in the maintenance and development of society, including as an important aspect the production of offspring. Although women are obviously crucial, at this stage this theoretical system does not seem to give them any importance. When the married man sees his grandchildren grow up (there is no definite time for this point) he should gradually withdraw from the worldly affairs that dominated the second stage of life and become what is called a 'forest-dweller' (*vānaprastha*). Again, this should not be taken too literally: here is a mental re-direction, not a sudden transit but a transition process, in which the older person should gradually focus attention increasingly on *moksha* or 'salvation', i.e. the spiritual sphere. Finally, when the old man finds that his end draws near, he should become a renouncer (*samnyāsī*), abandoning all concern for this life, fully concentrating on its termination.

For the female Hindu, an extended period of childhood is followed by marriage, which means a transfer of the bride to the husband's position. Thereafter a Hindu wife follows her husband's path. For *Shūdras* there are, in this theory, only childhood and married life.

It is important to emphasise that this neatly classified and predestined pattern is not a system of strict rules to be followed in every case. Rather it offers ideal guidelines which individual Hindus should strive to observe. The system also helps people to understand that no two Hindus are seen as alike, nor can they be treated in the same way. Even those in the same caste or stage of life are still different, and it is their individual circumstances which ultimately determine how they should live and what would be conducive to *dharma* for them. Hinduism explicitly recognises the importance of particular facts and circumstances in any given situation. Therefore there are no definite rules to be followed without exception by everyone in every situation. This realistic attitude to life's complexity is revealed by the fact that Hinduism has no central commandment that forbids killing. In fact, Hindu teaching is to the effect that sometimes killing may be inevitable and indeed necessary in order to follow *dharma*. A famous episode in the Bhagavadgita shows this with great drama.

How then is it possible to decide in Hinduism, and as a Hindu, what is appropriate, and who has the final say in such matters? It is very important to look at this question in some detail. The Manusmriti, the most important dharmashāstra, indicates the sources of *dharma*: 'The entire Veda is the source/root of dharma, next the smriti literature and the practice of those who know it, then the customs of good people, and finally one's own conscience' (Bühler 1975: 2.6; similarly 2.12).

Here is a clear-cut admission that the written sources of *dharma*, the ancient revealed truth itself, may provide some guidelines for human behaviour, but that in reality the final arbiter is the individual's conscience. The above verse seems to give us a hierarchy of the sources of *dharma* in order of importance. But in real-life situations, if there is some doubt as to what is appropriate behaviour, Hindus would intuitively turn first to their own consciences to find a proper solution. If this is not possible, if doubts persist, then they ought to look to the model of good people, leaders of society, elders perhaps; only if this also fails would they consult books on *dharma*, through experts who are presumed to live in accordance with its ideals. As a very last resort, i.e. when the complex *smriti* literature does not provide a solution, would they turn to divine revelation. In fact, it is certain that most decisions will be reached without reference to the scriptural sources and that an examination of conscience is generally quite sufficient.

The reality of Hinduism is, thus, that the *shruti* literature was very early on placed on a pedestal – and ignored for practical purposes. This method of ascertaining *dharma* achieves several things at the same time: it allows flexibility in view of tremendous local diversities, as well as adjustability to different circumstances and situations over time and space. Further, it gives the individual freedom, but not total discretion, while ensuring that any individual action, at any given moment, remains subject to wider considerations. This follows from the concept as a whole working in the context of a cosmic religion and worldview. *Dharma*, by placing the individual continuously under an obligation to act as a social being, as a small part of a larger whole, ensures that the repercussions of individual action, reinforced by the *karma* concept, remain constantly in the forefront of considerations. This need not be at the conscious level. The average Hindu is rarely familiar with the intricacies of the concept of *varnāshramadharma*, but such concepts have so permeated Hindu social practice that it is possible to speak of a 'Hindu way of life', which manifests itself in very many different ways, including forms of religious belief and practice.

A.1.b. Authority

Hindus have agreed to disagree about the central authority of the cosmic universe. Supreme authority rests in an invisible creative force, sometimes referred to as God or Brahma, but also seen as *brahman*, the 'all-pervading, self-existent power' (Stutley and Stutley 1977: 49). Brahma was apparently never prominent in Hindu worship; *brahman* has its equivalent on earth in *ātman*, the essence or principle of life (ibid.: 31). The divine manifests itself in a great number of incarnations (see A.1.c).

The same power also manifests itself in every human being, in fact in every creature, but it appears too weak now to bring about social control and to guarantee an ordered existence in the context of *dharma*. It seems that only in an early Golden Age was humankind so self-controlled that social life regulated itself. The matter is raised in the context of the need for law, more precisely litigation (*vyavahāra*), on which Nāradasmriti 1.1–2 say:

> When mortals were bent on doing nothing but their duty and were habitually veracious, there existed neither lawsuits, nor hatred, nor selfishness.
>
> Now that the practice of duty has died out among mankind, vyavahāra has been introduced; and the king has been appointed to decide suits, because he has the authority to punish. (Dutta 1978)

This gives the king or ruler (*rāja*) some kind of divine authority as supreme arbiter. Many other texts emphasise that the institution of the ruler has been created for the protection of humanity. In reality a *rāja* is 'a great deity in human form' (Manusmriti 7.8). As Hindu literature shows, the system is supposed to work through fear of the ruler's cruel and deterrent punishment. But the ruler must constantly be aware of his *rājadharma*, which implies first of all the protection of his subjects and the promotion of their *dharma* through self-controlled action.

At a lower social level, the heads of villages, clans and families have control functions similar to that of a major ruler. Here again it is possible to see how the Hindu concept of macrocosmic universal Order is composed of myriad microcosmic orders.

ETHICAL ISSUES IN SIX RELIGIOUS TRADITIONS

A.1.c. Authority Figures in the Faith

If Hinduism has no central doctrine that forms the essence of the faith, no one supreme God, no Holy Prophet and no one holy book, it is no surprise that central authority in this faith system is diffused. There is no Hindu Pope; no law giver, divine or human, dominates it. Divinely inspired scripture exists in the four Vedas and some later *shruti* literature, seen as divine truth or knowledge (*veda*) which was 'heard' by a large number of ancient sages. Centuries later this divinely inspired knowledge, passed on orally from teacher to student, was collected in new works based on the recollections of their authors, therefore classed as *smriti*, what was 'remembered'. These works constitute the main body of Sanskrit writing from the dharmasūtras of *c.* 800 BCE to *smriti* works composed in our day.

Since it is impossible to identify any one central authority figure in Hinduism, it has been called, with some justification, a group or family of religions rather than one religion. But there is a unifying bond despite the confusing mass of Hindu sects, schools of philosophy, incarnations and regional manifestations of the faith. This is the flexible concept of *dharma*. The Sanskrit literature provides ample moral and spiritual guidance, so do the various incarnations of deities, like Rama, Krishna or now Sai Baba and other leaders of the faith. No such Hindu bearer of authority, however, can claim to present the only truth, exclusively valid rules or universally applicable models, unless they are put in very general terms which can be interpreted flexibly. In the context of *dharma*, in order to maintain the necessary flexibility and adjustability to new circumstances, no two situations are seen as alike, and no rules that are fixed once and for all exist to be applied in the varied daily life situations of the Hindu.

Having said that, the power of guidelines and of model figures and their example can be strong. The heroic Arjuna in the Bhagavadgita, clearly unnerved by the prospect of having to kill his relatives in battle, is unequivocally told by Krishna that it is his *dharma* to go and fight them, regardless of the result, because he acts for the protection of *dharma*. For Hindus, this implies a general duty to act appropriately and less for one's own benefit. However, this does not answer the question, in any given circumstance, of what is the right thing to do. Thus, individual Hindus constantly have to balance their own personal interests and wider concerns.

A.1.d. Duties of Leaders

The guru's example (see A.4.a) shows that any leader figure has a particularly large responsibility for those under his or her supervision and guidance. Life at the top is thus more difficult than for the ordinary Hindu, since it involves additional, potentially very strenuous duties. High standards of model

7

behaviour and self-control would be expected of leaders of the faith as well as parents, teachers, and generally anyone in a position of responsibility for others, like the manager of a joint Hindu family.

The dharmashāstra literature sees monarchy as the normal form of government. Whoever had the 'power of command' (*kshatra*) became the ruler; clearly, he need not be a *Kshatriya* by birth because the function of ruling would make him into one. The texts are not concerned with how anyone becomes king, but concentrate on the duties of the ruler (esp. Manusmriti 7.1–226 and the Arthashāstra).

The ruler or king (*rāja*) is seen as necessary to maintain social order (see A.1.b) and his first duty is the protection of his people. The happiness of the king lies in the happiness of the subjects (Arthashāstra 1.19.34–5), and the king should behave like a father towards all people. Due to his royal functions he is sometimes viewed as a deity. Although he is seen as independent from his subjects (Nāradasmriti 1.32–3), the Hindu king is not an absolute ruler, because he operates within the contexts of *rājadharma*, a complex set of duties rather than rights.

Significantly, several verses emphasise the ruler's duty to uphold the laws of castes, guilds, certain localities and stages of life, i.e. to recognise local customary laws, which form the basis for much of Hindu law into our own time. The royal legislative power is therefore severely restricted, almost non-existent. Because Order is pre-ordained in the form of *dharma*, the ruler's duty is to make the legal processes work, not to make law. His judicial functions are discussed in great detail because in cases of danger to *dharma* he has to punish the offender (Manusmriti 7.19–22), and he must try to determine punishments that fit the crime and are just. It is very important that the ruler be accessible to anyone with a grievance. This was perhaps meant as a guarantee of fundamental human rights, although there is much evidence that Hindu rulers abused their powers. Naturally, the ruler was responsible for the efficient administration of his realm. The texts also place him under the constant obligation to support and honour learned Brahmins.

Modern India is officially a secular republic, while Nepal is the only Hindu kingdom in the world today. However, in practice, under a Western-type constitution, India today is a 'democracy with Hindu characteristics' and many Hindu concepts of government continue to be applied, although they often operate at a subconscious level. The fact that modern India combines a somewhat dynastic pattern of leadership with democratic elections shows how important leader figures continue to be. The functioning of modern India's democracy, much to the surprise of Western specialists, owes much of its success to the concept that those in positions of power are accountable to those whom they rule. The ancient Hindu notion of the ruler as a servant of *dharma* is clearly a strong force also in modern India.

A.1.e. Duties of Subjects

The *svadharma* of Hindus in positions of inferiority would inevitably include an element of obedience to elders and other superiors, particularly the king. Good examples set by leaders were to be followed and are an important element in ascertaining *dharma* (see A.1.a). The merits and demerits of the subjects were said to pass on to the king (Manusmriti 8.304–5), giving him an added incentive to control his subjects. The ruler was to be supported with taxes (up to one-sixth of income, according to some sources). Interestingly, Brahmins who were Veda experts could claim exemption from taxation.

The duty of obedience is prominent, but not often expressed in the texts, probably because it is taken for granted. Sensibly, Manusmriti 7.12 warns that whoever hates the king will soon be destroyed. The ruler's coercive force of punishment, embodied in the punishing rod or *danda*, has already been mentioned (A.1.b). Some texts (see Manusmriti 7.15–25) contain elaborate comments on this subject.

Should a ruler, however, be unjust and oppressive, since reality was often far away from the ideal of the shāstras, the requirements of an individual subject's *dharma* and the duty to obey the king or elder would inevitably clash. Oppressed subjects tormented by a ruler's injustice were not required to suffer in passive obedience. The moral right to oppose a wicked and tyrannical ruler appears to be accepted, although the texts do not discuss this topic in detail from the viewpoint of the subject. They do, however (esp. Arthashāstra 1.20–1), go into much detail as to how a ruler was to protect himself against being killed by enemies; it is not always clear whether these are rivals or dissatisfied subjects.

While there are few, if any, constitutional checks on the royal power (ancient assemblies may have played some such role), the most powerful sanctions against bad rulers were of religious and spiritual nature. Manusmriti 7.34 states the obvious when it insists that the fame of a bad king will diminish. Verses 7.27–8 say that an unjust ruler will be destroyed through his bad actions; destruction is the fate of an oppressive king in vv. 7.111–12. Injustice also destroys the judge (v. 8.14), whether he be the king himself or not. Such statements show that, apart from revolutions or public uprising, cosmic forces were believed to take care of grave violations of *rājadharma*. Similar concepts existed in ancient China, where the Emperor's 'Mandate of Heaven' could be forfeited if there were grave disharmonies and disorders. Similarly, Hindu subjects would blame any disasters on the king and a rival would be quick to step in. Ancient Indian history is not without reason so very confusing on the topic of who ruled what part of the country at what time.

The ancient concepts, often in disguise, operate in modern India, too.

The collapse of British rule in India appears in no small measure due to the fact that Mahatma Gandhi showed it to be morally wrong. Modern Indian governments, under democratic arrangements promise equality before the law for every Indian citizen. But when subjects see the government as both distant and not acting dharmically (righteously), they begin to ignore their obligations as subjects and base their actions on their individual concerns.

A.2. PERSONAL AND PRIVATE?

A.2.a. Personal Qualities

It could be argued that lack of central Hindu authority and the great variety of written Hindu sources would support almost any statement that might be made here and in the following sections. However, certain general ideas are quite clear and apparent. *Dharma* as well as *artha*, the acquisition of wealth or power, do not exist independently but are interlinked. Flexibility of rules is maintained, as we have seen, by the constant consideration of individual facts and circumstances. If some general rules are specifically given here, we must be aware that they are not necessarily binding for all times and in all cases.

Obviously the personal qualities of a Hindu depend a lot on a person's background and environment. The Hindu focus on the duties of a person, rather than on individual rights, means that any Hindu would constantly appear to be under an obligation to consider the needs of others. The Brihadāranyka-Upanishad, in part 5.2, brings this into a short formula: 'da da da', translated as 'be subdued, give, be merciful' (Limaye and Vadekar 1958). Manusmriti 3.72 puts it in different terms: 'But one who does not feed these five, the gods, his guests, the people he is bound to maintain, the ancestors, and himself, lives not, though he breathes' (Bühler 1975). Some texts appear to contain a catalogue of Hindu ethical values. Manusmriti 10.63 puts this in wider terms: 'Non-violence, truthfulness, abstention from unlawfully taking what belongs to others, purity, and control of one's organs, Manu has declared these to be the sum total of the dharma of the four castes' (ibid.).

There have been many attempts to define such a list of universal duties applicable to all life situations. Reciprocity is an important element in the Hindu system of obligations, despite the stress on duties. Quite realistically, many texts emphasise that the motivating force in human life, and in this world in general, has been, and continues to be, desire. Manusmriti 2.2, for example, reads: 'It is not laudable that one should act solely out of desire for rewards, but one hardly finds an exemption from such desire in this world: [already] the study of the Veda is based on desire, as is the performance of actions as prescribed in the Veda' (ibid.).

Innumerable texts promise rewards for certain actions, for example Manusmriti 2.5: 'He who continuously discharges these prescribed duties in

10

correct manner, reaches the deathless state and obtains, even in this life, the fulfilment of all the desires that he may have conceived' (ibid.). There is, thus, a strong moral force moulding behaviour with a view to future rewards. In family relationships, too, this underlying concept is at work. Young Hindu children have no duties yet, but many expectations may rest on them. This is especially true of little boys. At an early age, Hindu children may have the almost unlimited privilege of being cared for, to the point of being spoilt. The older child, however, is soon trained to take responsibilities, above all in the family context.

Adult Hindus, women in particular, often work in selfless devotion for both young and old members of the family. Many old Hindus tend to look confidently into the future, because it will in turn become the duty of those they once cared for to look after them. The joint family system, when operating smoothly, gives a tremendous sense of security to the individual. However, this can lead to dependency. Many individuals may not develop enough self-confidence to act independently, and many such Hindus find it difficult to live on their own, should this be required.

Local and caste ideals about individual behaviour and qualities seem to vary a lot among the many Hindu communities. Differences between the sexes and stages of life are particularly noticeable.

A.2.b. Friendship

Since many Hindus accept that we all come from one creator, there is much justification for the idea of 'brotherhood of all men'. Because of the theory of the individual's re-birth and re-incarnation, not necessarily in human form, Hindus include parts of the animal and plant world into this framework, and this has important implications for the approach to dietary rules, especially vegetarianism.

The philosophies of eminent Hindu leader figures like Mahatma Gandhi and Sai Baba do take account of such basic and universal theories. In practice, however, most Hindus are preoccupied with a much narrower realm. Regional and linguistic barriers continue to make communication within India difficult. The major concern of most Hindus would be with their more immediate social environment, i.e. their caste-fellows, clan, family and neighbours.

At the same time (see A.1.a) there is explicit recognition of diversity and the uniqueness of every individual creature. Social relations among Hindus involve, in normal circumstances, people belonging to one's wider or more immediate family and neighbours, especially those belonging to the same social group (formerly caste, now increasingly social class). It has been observed that in such situations it is often not an important consideration whether one 'likes' a particular person. One is related, and thus belongs together, and is expected to get on. In the joint family, where community of property is the accepted norm, 'Your shirt will be borrowed without your permission by anyone who is approximately the right size, and irrespective of whether you like him: in fact the very question ... is fatuous' (Derrett 1968: 61).

A good measure of self-control is involved in these relationships, and considerable restraint is exercised especially with regard to relations between individuals who are not of the same status. Such relationships may appear very formalised and hierarchical. However, such formalities do not preclude the growth of affection nor the development of personal friendships. Further, in a system of relationships that is duty-based, junior partners can expect protection and any help which may be needed.

The segregation of the sexes, in particular, is obvious in Hindu societies and has been much discussed. While small children are allowed to play together, from the age of about eight years there would often be minimal contact between boys and girls. This is not only because boys are trained to be men, and girls are prepared for women's roles. Coeducational facilities exist, but single-sex education is preferred because Hindu parents are much concerned about the chastity of their daughters, in particular. Such attitudes are well absorbed by youngsters. Many Hindu girls have an inbuilt reluctance towards friendships with the opposite sex and prefer to be in a circle of friends of the same sex.

A.2.c. Sex before Marriage

Pre-marital chastity ranks very high on the value scale of most Hindus. But there is also a place in the tradition as a whole for sexual pleasure.

Kāma or sensual pleasure is one of the four Hindu *purushārthas* or aims of life (*dharma*, *artha*, *kāma* and *moksha*). *Kāma* refers to the instinctive and emotional life of people. It involves an erotic element, but includes emotional and aesthetic experiences. The ideal for any human being is to maintain a proper balance between the four aims of life (see Manusmriti 2.224). Love and sex are, therefore, not denied their place, especially in married life, where they become an aspect of marital duties. But there is strong religious and social pressure to control the senses, and this is especially true for the time before marriage, where *kāma* seems to play a subordinate role only.

Clearly, in Hindu writings concerned with the *brahmacārī* (A.1.a) there is a marked emphasis on self-control and the sublimation of sexual urges before a person reaches the stage of the householder. Such notions have influenced the general social life of Hindus. For the higher classes especially, pre-marital chastity is an important value and it is achieved in a number of ways. Preaching sublimation alone is not considered sufficient, rather punishments are given for certain transgressions, and penances have to be performed. In general the topic of sex appears to have been suppressed. Indeed, several texts (for example Manusmriti 5.132) go as far as to declare that the lower parts of the body, those below the navel, are impure. Not surprisingly, sexual matters are more or less taboo in most Indian homes, with the result that Hindu youngsters are often quite ignorant about sex and so are not well prepared for the sudden transition to married life.

The major concern of Hindu society as regards sexuality is, without doubt, the preservation of female chastity. From about the beginning of the Christian era, society began to insist on the virginity of brides. One way to ensure the pre-marital chastity of women appears to have been to encourage pre-puberty marriages ('child marriages'), a practice later extended to males. It still occurs in India despite legislative intervention. What it reveals is that sex as such is not considered negative. To the contrary the enjoyment of marital sex, even at an early age (see Gandhi's autobiography) is fully acceptable to Hindus. Should a girl be subjected to intercourse before marriage, the man would be expected to marry her, but in reality this did, and does, not always happen.

The sexual purity of girls is expected so as to ensure that they belong to one man only. The requirement of pre-marital chastity for men or boys has different sorts of reason.

Within the system of *varnāshramadharma* (see A.1.a), the pupil or student is required to observe total chastity till the end of his studies. This could be, as we saw, up to a fairly late age, even above 30 years old, and must have been difficult to achieve and enforce. The overriding purpose was to ensure the student's total concentration on his studies, and the practice of self-control, both of which are believed to bring unseen merits. The student is required to avoid anything stimulating, like spicy diets and certain kinds of food, all forms of entertainment and, most important, contact with women. Masturbation and even the involuntary emission of semen are put under penance (Manusmrti 2.180), mainly because the potential for creating life should not be wasted. There are many stories of men under the vow of chastity who became overwhelmed by the mere sight of a woman. Females thus came to be seen as a temptation to be avoided and, typical of a male-dominated perspective, women are often blamed for male lapses of chastity.

Nowadays few Hindu boys go formally through the stage of *brahmacarya*, but a Hindu pupil or student would still be expected to remain chaste. Even 'modern' Hindu social reformers like Dayanand Saraswati, the founder of the Arya Samaj, have advised that the sexes should be kept at a safe distance from each other. Many young Hindus, thus, hardly encounter the opposite sex during adolescence.

There is much evidence of an evolving attitude among young Hindus that pre-marital sex is acceptable as long as marriage will follow. But there is just as much evidence that this attitude is creating new problems for girls, as there is also a continuing social expectation of chastity. If there is no absolute guarantee that marriage will follow, the 'lover' may subsequently despise the girl for agreeing to sex before marriage. While religious leaders tend to advise total abstinence and emphasise the ascetic elements of Hindu philosophy, in social reality many real problems are difficult to solve. At the end of the day, families and individuals try to find the right approach and then to live with the consequences against the background of Hindu teaching.

A.2.d. Homosexuality

The Hindu literary sources are remarkably silent on homosexuality. From traditional attitudes to chastity and sex it follows that homosexuality at any stage of life appears out of line with the standard norms and values of the *varnāshramadharma* system. In particular, not to marry and produce children could be seen as a violation of one's *dharma* (see A.1.a), although asceticism became acceptable in Hinduism for a small number of men concentrating on religious matters.

Actually, few Hindus remain unmarried, probably due to a wide range of social pressures. Homosexuality is not unknown, but is a taboo topic. Recent reactions in India to the rapidly growing AIDS threat are remarkable: the press created the impression, reflected also in letters from readers, that any form of sex outside marriage, including masturbation, would lead to certain destruction. The result is almost certainly even stronger pressure on individuals to remain chaste. Compensation or sublimation, not just for the few homosexuals that there may be, seems to take the form of quite remarkable narcissism, among young Hindus in particular.

In India and in other Oriental countries, but now also in Britain, one may observe groups of boys (less frequently girls) moving around together, holding hands and showing affection towards each other in different ways. This is not a sign of homosexuality, but socially acceptable behaviour between members of the same sex. It may be linked with the fact that physical affection, at this stage, is not permitted if it involves members of the opposite sex. In Britain now, neither form may be acceptable in public. If sex itself is sometimes a difficult topic for Hindus, homosexuality is virtually swept under the carpet.

A.3. MARRIAGE AND THE FAMILY

A.3.a. The Meaning of Marriage

A Hindu marriage is at the same time an intimate connection of two individuals and a relationship of great importance and interest for the social environment of the couple, with implications for society and, indeed, the whole cosmos (see A.1.a). It is perhaps mainly for this reason that Hindu marriages were traditionally arranged: the spouses were not left to choose for themselves, because marriage is clearly not an affair of the two individuals only. Although it was not unknown in ancient India for people to choose for themselves, the dominant view became that young people could not be trusted to select the best possible partner. In cases where the spouses were still children, the selection process was entirely in the hands of the families.

It is no doubt true that selfish parents have at times jeopardised their children's future by selecting an unsuitable life partner, due to some motive, usually connected with money or other possessions. But that does not mean that the system of arranged marriages is altogether bad. In most cases 'arranged marriage' does not mean that the spouses are absolute strangers to each other whose consent has not even been sought. In current practice, many parents take care of the selection of potential spouses, but the young person has the final say, a power of veto, as it were. Nowadays, in Britain as well as in India, young people often arrange their own selection and then have it approved and blessed by the parents, often after consulting horoscopes.

A Hindu marriage is considered a sacrament (*samskāra*), a divinely blessed indissoluble union. This irrevocable bond between the spouses is created by the performance of the marriage rituals. It is believed that the correct performance of the marriage rituals creates in the minds of the spouses an awareness of the state of being married, a realisation of the transition from unmarried youngster to married man or woman. This is important: if the marital tie is supposed to be irrevocable the spouses will have to adjust to each other in all respects. Consciousness about the essential oneness of husband and wife may help in this.

The Hindu marriage rituals not only dramatise the transfer of the bride from her paternal home (few Hindus are matrilineal) to that of the husband, they also express a number of important expectations connected with marriage. These are, above all, progeny, faithfulness and mutual support, and the expectation of a long life for both spouses. Marriage solemnisation is a public affair. Society accords its recognition to the union through the people that are present. There is, thus, no need for a formal registration of the marriage. Even the modern state law of India does not make marriage registration compulsory for Hindus. While Hindus in Britain and North America have quickly learnt about the importance of the registered ceremony, even there, for most Hindus, a complete and valid Hindu marriage is still only brought about by the Hindu form of marriage solemnisation. Recent research shows that the official registration ceremony may even be ritually incorporated into the Hindu wedding.

Hindu marriage rituals vary tremendously according to region and caste; priestly traditions and skills play an important role, too. The most ancient model of Hindu marriage is the union of the daughter of the sun god with the moon, described in Rigveda 10.85 (*c.* 1000 BCE) side by side with an ancient form of human marriage solemnisation. Some of those ancient rituals are still performed today, with the same verses or mantras, but there has been a lot of ritual change, too.

There is no one legally valid form of getting married as a Hindu. Even the modern Hindu law of India has left this matter to family custom, so it is possible to find marriage ceremonies with a minimum of ritual, almost mere cohabitation (this is customary if a widow remarries, for example), but elaborate ritualisation is more common.

An elaborate Hindu marriage should take place at an auspicious time and place, and it would contain all or most of the following elements, though not always in the same order.

• The ritual preparation of the place of marriage, not a temple, but the girl's home or a specially chosen place; this includes the creation of an auspicious atmosphere by invoking various Hindu gods.
• The groom and his party are welcomed by the bride's family.
• The bride is led in and is placed opposite or next to the groom.
• The girl's parents give her away (the ritual of *kanyādān*).
• In the ritual of *hastagrahana*, the spouses hold hands, often for the first time. The mantra used here may be Rigveda 10.85.36, which the priest recites for the groom: 'I take your hand for marital happiness, so that with me as your husband you may attain old age. Bhaga, Aryaman, Savitar and Puramdhi, the gods have given you to me for householdership'.
• The sacred fire is lit in a vessel and sacrifices are made to Agni, the god of fire, the heavenly witness of marriage. The spouses then walk round the fire (*agniparinayana* or *mangalphera*). This is done in many different ways, according to family custom. The ancient texts mainly use four circuits clockwise, now we find three, four, five or even seven rounds (odd numbers are seen as auspicious). Linked with this ritual are a number of others such as stepping on a stone, for firmness and strength, and various folk rituals, for example to predict who will dominate in the marriage. Often marital vows are recited by the priest prior to each round.
• The ritual of *saptapadī*, or seven steps, again with many variations. Often the bride steps on seven heaps of rice and with every step one vow is recited by the priest. This ritual, in which the spouses pledge total support to each other, culminates in the promise to be friends, which is sometimes beautifully ritualised. This ritual has now often became part of the *mangalphera* rite, which is why some Hindu couples walk round the fire seven times.
• A feast for the guests.
• In an often tearful ceremony, the bride is taken to her new environment.

Cohabitation should, according to the scriptures, take place on the fourth night after the marriage, following many more rituals. Nowadays, probably as a result of extreme concern over bridal purity, the marriage is often consummated as soon as possible so as to have proof of the bride's virginity. In North India, in particular, this is seen as very important (see A.2.c).

It is unrealistic to expect that Hindus can explain details of these rituals and the expectations expressed in them; many rituals are indeed performed just for good luck. Further, the ritual verses are mostly in Sanskrit, so that people cannot follow details unless the priest cares to explain. This has now become quite common in Hindu communities abroad. Still, detailed knowledge of the scriptures is an exception rather than the rule among Hindus.

The expectations of marital life have been amply expressed during an elaborate Hindu wedding. They are essentially that the couple will support each other faithfully, that children will be born, and that the spouses will grow old together. The purpose of some rituals is also to bring a step-by-step familiarisation of the spouses, for example the holding of the hands. Even in so-called 'love marriages', where the spouses themselves have selected each other, they may still be virtual strangers. Marriage rituals, thus, introduce a long process of adjustment of the spouses to each other. It would seem that often the wife has to make all the adjustments, while nothing much changes for the husband. In reality, this is a mutual process; ideally, both spouses will more or less consciously make efforts to become united. Love is supposed to grow and develop in marriage through this gradual adjustment process, which should lead to total mutual dependency and trust.

The period of married life is considered the central part of human existence (see A.1.a). Manusmriti 3.78 declares that the stage of the householder is the most excellent one, because it supports the members of all the other stages of life.

The bringing-up of children is easily identified as the most important aspect of marriage, because it vitally affects the future of society. Many texts contain elaborate rules for marital intercourse, making it a duty for the husband to cohabit during the fertile period of the wife, so that a child may be produced. In such circumstances, birth control really means considering how to increase fertility, and consequently abortion, the killing of an embryo, is taken as a severe crime (see A.5.c).

Sons are considered more important than daughters, because the latter have to leave the family and will produce children for their husband's family. Sons not only continue the family line, but also partake in the joint family property with all rights and obligations, especially care of elders and performance of rituals for ancestors. Should a marriage remain childless or only daughters be born, a Hindu husband was allowed to take another wife. Thus, in Manusmriti 9.81 it is said (Kautilya's Arthashāstra has the same rule in 3.2.38): 'One may supercede a barren wife in the eighth year, one whose children all die in the tenth, one who bears only daughters in the eleventh' (Bühler 1975).

In fact, a sonless Hindu wife, aware of her own *dharma* and that of her husband, should request him to take another wife and step back. By agreeing to this arrangement she would save her right to remain a wife and to be maintained by her husband. Traditionally, there was no limit on the number of wives that a Hindu could have, but there is a rule that the wife should not be of a higher caste than the husband. A wife, on the other hand, may not have more than one husband, and there are powerful taboos against the remarriage of Hindu widows, although the modern secular laws know no such restrictions.

More than anything else, a discussion of Hindu marriage demonstrates how, in the Hindu world view, the individual is seen as a vehicle for the purposes of a larger whole. Again it should perhaps be emphasised that this does not mean that the individual does not exist and that individual concerns do not matter, but it is the awareness of this interrelatedness which constitutes the core of the Hindu value system.

A.3.b. Family Relationships

The relationships between individuals in a Hindu family must be seen in the context of the Hindu joint family, an ancient institution which is far from dying out in India, and which also survives in Hindu communities overseas. Based on descent through the male line (for most Hindus), the traditional model of the joint Hindu family involves community of ownership of the ancestral family property by all male members in four living generations and three generations of ancestors, who are linked to the living through blood ties and sacrificial rituals. Women, in this model, are entitled to maintenance from family funds.

The fact that the joint or extended family live together reflects this common ownership of assets; it is also an economic way of using resources. However, it can also bring many problems: stronger members may exploit weaker ones, while constant supervision and crowded living conditions may not allow individual family members to develop their own way of life. If the system functions properly, it gives life-long help and security to all individuals, but there are also many families in which relations are disrupted and where members even litigate against each other. The joint family is led by the manager, a senior male member, who has the power to represent the family as a legal entity to the outside world.

Relationships in the family are hierarchically structured, based above all on the criteria of age and sex. Indian languages have subtle means of expressing these relationships. For example, the English 'you' can be expressed in various forms depending on whether the other person is superior, inferior, equal or very close to the speaker. Family relations are, thus, identified in minute detail. There are many different terms, for example, for different kinds of uncle. Family friends and even outsiders may be incorporated into this system, thereby at once showing everyone their place: if a young man is meant to refer to a young woman as 'sister' he has already been put under the obligation to avoid incest!

Concern for the segregation of sexes is all-pervading. Women are, in many families, under much pressure to behave with modesty towards males of the family as well as outsiders. Fear of incest can be traced back to the ancient works on *dharma* (see A.2.c). Thus the Manusmriti, having warned in 2.213 that women are out to seduce men, advises at 2.215: 'One should not sit in a lonely place with one's mother, sister or daughter, since the senses are powerful and master even a learned man' (Bühler 1975).

Various forms of *parda* or purdah (veiling the face and female body features) are practised by Hindu as well as Muslim women. As we have seen (A.2.c) talking about sexual matters is not acceptable in most households, a reticence which can lead to communication problems between the generations. Also relations between married couples within the family are governed by such restrictions: for example, public displays of affection between husband and wife are frowned upon.

Little needs to be added here about the husband and wife relationship (see A.3.a). If the wife, in the joint family, spends most of her time in the company of other women, and the husband consorts with his male relations and friends, a very close emotional relationship between the spouses may not develop. The extended family could cushion emotional crises if a marriage is under strain, while in a nuclear family husband and wife are much more directly dependent upon each other and have to work much harder to make their relationship successful.

Children, depending on age, are generally treated with much indulgence. A well-known proverb says that you should treat your son like a king for the first five years, like a slave for the next ten, and then like a friend. In practice this means that very small children are treated leniently, but the child also learns to become actively involved in the concerns of the family especially if there are many other children. Recognition as an adult would seem to come at different times in India and the West. Much value is placed by most Hindus on education (see A.4.a). In traditional circumstances, boys tended to learn the father's trade, but there is much more mobility now. A great deal of evidence suggests that Hindu mothers spoil their sons and prefer them to daughters. This is often so because a Hindu wife's position largely depends on whether she is able to produce the necessary male heir or heirs. This

19

focus on sons can have unfortunate effects in later life, when the mother-in-law resents the daughter-in-law's claims on the attention of the darling son.

In general, a Hindu individual's rights and duties are largely determined by the context of the family set-up and the socio-economic position of the family. It is impossible to give general rules: in emergencies, very young men and women may have to act as head of the family, while others will not even reach this position as grandparents.

A.3.c. Marriage Breakdown

Hindu spouses are irrevocably tied together once they have completed their marriage rituals. But this solemn concept of the sacramental nature of marriage is a typical high-caste Hindu ideal. In reality, a number of remedies have always been allowed in cases where a marriage did not work. As a general rule, Hindus of lower caste (the borders are not clearly defined in this context) have always allowed fairly easy divorce and the remarriage of both spouses.

Further, in the context of people strictly observing the rules of *dharma*, the sonless husband would, even had to, take another wife, maintaining the first if she followed her *dharma*. Fraudulent marriage contracts were null and void (Manusmriti 9.72–3). The father of a girl who had some blemish would have to declare this (Manusmriti 8.205) and could be punished by the ruler otherwise (8.224). Dissolution of the marriage was allowed in a number of situations: Manusmriti 9.77, for example, says that a husband should bear with a wife who hates him only for one year, while verse 9.81 advises no delay in getting rid of a quarrelsome woman. Verse 9.80 sums up the position as follows: 'A wife who drinks, is of bad conduct, is rebellious, diseased, mischievous or wasteful, may at any time be superseded' (Bühler 1975).

Certainly, supercession is not the same as divorce, but in practice such arrangements would terminate the marital bond. Should the husband not be able to fulfil his marital duties or treat the wife with cruelty, Manusmriti 9.79, for example, would not blame the wife for disliking him. But a rule system emphasising that women should have one husband only would not allow her to leave even such a bad husband. In the extreme, she is expected to put up with him, but in practice women also claimed the right, in these circumstances, to separate.

The Sanskrit texts take widely differing positions on adultery. Some see it as a minor offence: after menstruation and a number of penances, the woman is purified again. An adulterous husband may merely have to undergo some mild penances. But other texts advocate even the death penalty for either the man or the woman, depending on caste status.

The Hindu approach to the question of marital breakdown shows that, in a male-dominated society with clearly defined expectations, some female spouses can be made replaceable. As a result, it seems, Hindu women have been more concerned to preserve the marriage and their position and status as 'wife'. Modern case law shows that Hindu wives put up with their husband's adultery, cruelty and many other hardships, because it is still better to be part of a bad marriage than to live alone as a divorced woman (Mehta 1975). Sociological studies (see, for example, Balse 1976) have shown that arranged marriages do not break down as easily as 'love marriages', and that much seems to depend on the attitude of women in this context.

There is a great deal of evidence that the modern Hindu law of India works against the interests of women, despite the fact that it was introduced to give them better protection. Divorce was made permissible on the basis of certain faults, but in many cases weak husbands and mischievous relatives fabricate such grounds to drive out a wife who would not consider her marriage as broken down.

The modern law also does not lead to a satisfactory solution if the marriage has failed to produce the desired male progeny. The husband would now have to divorce his wife in order to be able to remarry, since bigamy was made a crime in 1955. But childlessness or failure to produce a son are not grounds for divorce under the modern law. So the spouses have to make an arrangement for the man to have another partner in addition to the wife, or some grounds for divorce will have to be manufactured. Either way, compared to the traditional system, the wife loses out. It has been suggested that bigamy should be allowed in certain cases, and indeed this is what some couples arrange. Adoption of a child has long been practised among Hindus and is allowed in the interest of spiritual benefits and continuation of the family, but this is not acceptable to all Hindus.

At present there is much discussion in India whether the irretrievable breakdown of a marriage should be allowed, as in Britain, as grounds for divorce. Many Hindus feel that the sacramental concept of marriage would then become totally meaningless, with disastrous consequences for society, and women and children in particular. Significantly, legislation seeking to introduce the breakdown principle in 1982 was withdrawn. Many Hindus think that India does better to rely on liberal interpretations of Hindu cultural traditions when reforming Hindu law than blindly following Western models. The latter may turn out to be inadequate and inappropriate because of their prominent focus on the individual and lack of consideration for wider concerns in the context of *dharma*. But some Hindus in the West are not unhappy to live within Western law rather than a traditional Hindu system.

A.4. Influences on and Use of Time and Money

A.4.a. Education

The traditional Hindu concept of education is best understood by looking at the *brahmacārin*, the Hindu student or pupil (A.1.a). In this formative stage, the aim is to build a person's character by training body, mind and soul. It provides education for life, not simply preparation for earning one's livelihood. During this stage the young are taught discipline and learn to subordinate their own ambitions and desires to the good of society. The training instils fundamental qualities through the teacher's example: gentleness, truthfulness, a kind attitude towards all beings. The guru, by his own example, demonstrates how to deal with others in the complex social network of inferior–superior relationships. While intellectual achievements are not neglected, on their own they are considered inferior to the development of an integrated personality (see, for example, Manusmriti 2.118).

This kind of education, fundamental though it may be, has an element of luxuriousness. The practice of spending many years of studentship under a guru's guidance was already becoming less and less common in Vedic times. The ideals, though, remain alive even today, and it appears that the Hindu family has taken over the task of building the young person's character. The father and other elders in the family now carry the burden of being a role model and guide for sons; the mother for daughters. Within the formal school system, expectations of the teacher remain very high.

A significant change in our times is that education has become a major means of achieving a better financial position and higher social status, especially in the middle classes where competition is fiercest. The abolition of occupational and caste barriers has increased expectations of the advantages of education. The dream of a white-collar job is very widespread. Many Hindus have high, often unrealistic ambitions with regard to formal education. Sociological studies (for example Ross 1973) have emphasised the pressures put on students who are well aware that their achievements as individuals are crucial for the future of whole families.

Since education is now more job orientated, and because there are still many reservations against working women since this would involve contact with strangers, there is less pressure on girls to become formally educated; their preparation for the roles of married life often takes place exclusively in the home. Today, however, very many Hindu women, from sheer economic necessity, have to work outside the home, so the attitudes to female education are gradually changing.

A.4.b. Work

The Hindu caste system is also a hierarchical model of division of labour in society. According to classical theory, the Brahmins were to be priests and teachers, carrying on the learning and providing links with the realm of the divine; the *Kshatriyas* were to be kings and local rulers, and also soldiers, i.e. leaders and protectors of society; *Vaishyas*, 'the people', were primarily agriculturists, traders and artisans, looking after the socio-economic aspects of society; the *Shūdras* were to be low-status artisans, agricultural and other manual labourers and, generally speaking, were to be in servile positions.

However, all parts of this system are closely interlinked. Society would be in turmoil if the king did not do his duty, but just as much if those who cleaned away rubbish refused to carry out their work. So there was an awareness, on all sides, that any form of work is socially useful and valuable. At the same time, however, society valued such works differently in terms of status. Being a priest, ruler, landowner or affluent trader brought with it influence in society, power and wealth. On the other hand, jobs involving some form of pollution brought lower status: the removal of carcasses and dead bodies, anything to do with leather, cleaning latrines and sweeping streets. Certain jobs are not even carried out by Hindus but, for example, their Muslim neighbours (see A.7.b). It is likely that there is no Hindu butcher anywhere in Britain or North America.

Significantly, the Sanskrit literature is often concerned with the status of Brahmins. For example, what occupations should still be allowed in times of distress? Brahmins were permitted to become farmers or traders in such circumstances (Manusmriti 10.81–2), and many Brahmins became cooks, since any Hindu could eat food prepared by them. But upward mobility was not allowed for the lower castes: by requiring a Hindu to follow his particular *dharma*, and promising a better next life, the system cleverly justified the status quo and precluded revolutions of the downtrodden. Although the traditional system may appear rigid and somewhat unfair to us, it did give security to the lower sections of society, too: those in positions of superiority had the duty to care for their subordinates. The hereditary nature of most occupations meant that even the lowest bonded labourer could expect to be fed and to survive. Recent court cases in India have shown that it does not help bonded labourers to release them unless it is also ensured that they are fed. The collapse of traditional hereditary exchange systems in rural areas is now creating severe problems for the rural poor.

In modern India, capitalist philosophies have found many followers in the upper classes but socialist and communist ideologies are also strongly represented. It appears that labour relations in India continue to be less aggravated than in Europe because they are worked out in the wider context of Hindu values. Thus, the 'boss' will not have exclusive concern for profits, and the workers are more ready to sacrifice for the benefit of the whole operation.

The concept of 'good work' is an integral part of the Hindu attitude to work. All and any work, unless it is manifestly against the interests of *dharma*, constitutes good work if *dharma* demands it. This includes, as in the famous scene in the Bhagavadgita where Arjuna hesitates to go into battle, the killing of one's own relatives, if necessary. Individuals may make special efforts to gain merit (again the force of desire creeps in here, see A.2.a), by making donations for good purposes or doing some form of social work. All Hindu religious leaders seem to emphasise this aspect: Gandhi devoted time to his spinning-wheel and a variety of aspects of social work. Sai Baba and other religious leaders teach that one ought to give several hours a week to the care of others. The danger here is, however, that split attitudes and hypocrisy develop (see A.4.f), that one only does such work because one expects certain benefits, not as an integral part of one's behavioural pattern.

A.4.c. Leisure and its Use

The Hindu approach to leisure is closely related to the concept of education (A.4.a). The traditional approach would be that there should be a balance of one's activities. Thus, in the Arthashāstra's rules for the king (1.19.14), certain parts of the day are given over to recreation and relaxation and the need for *kāma* is stressed (compare A.2.c). Verse 1.7.5 says that any one of the three aims in life, *dharma*, *artha* or *kāma*, if excessively indulged in, does harm to itself as well as to the other two. This approach may explain why some things move so much slower in India, and why life there can be so much more relaxing. '*Shanti rakho*', 'Keep calm', is an often-heard phrase, and this approach continues to influence Hindu attitudes.

Hindus tend to spend much time in worship, which also brings relaxation and mental peace. There are no special times or appointed days of Hindu worship but a great variety of festivals provide special occasions. Worship and social gatherings often go together. The communal singing of *bhajans* (devotional songs) is perhaps a typical example. Various folk dances (the Gujarati stick and clap dances of *dandiya ras* and *garba*, for example) incorporate elements of worship. The Panjabi *bhangra* is a vigorous folk dance re-enacting the times of hard work on the land and celebrating the joys of a plentiful harvest.

Generally speaking, though, there is a tremendous lack of recreational facilities and initiatives for many of the unemployed in India. There is a great deal of underemployment because of the seasonal nature of many jobs and people often do little more than sit around and pass the time dozing. Many seem to have given up the hope of finding work, or extra work (often the joint family cushions such lack of initiative), and drinking and various forms of drug abuse are not uncommon. Vandalism is as good as unknown, but inter-communal riots do sometimes happen. Card games, gambling and some sports activities such as cricket are enjoyed.

Much time is spent meeting friends and relatives, and playing with children. Women, in general, seem to have much less time for leisure, but they are, of course, less visible in public, so it is difficult to generalise. It must be stressed, however, that many people in India are so busy ensuring their survival and that of their family that they have very little time for anything else.

A.4.d. Wealth

The pursuit of wealth and power (*artha*) has a firm place as one of the legitimate aims of Hindu life (see A.2.c). Many studies have emphasised the other-worldliness of Hinduism and the prevailing spirit of renunciation. They are right to a point. Depending on his or her *dharma*, any Hindu may at times be required to be primarily concerned with *artha*. In all cases, however, the ideal of the balanced approach is prevalent and excessive concern for wealth itself is considered negative. This goes both for the acquisition of wealth and for methods of putting it to use.

In the classical model, the Hindu student is taught humility by being required to work for his *guru*, to beg food for him and for himself, and by the generally spartan living conditions imposed on him. The stage of *brahma-carya* is not concerned with worldly gains but with creating awareness of the priorities of Hindu existence.

The householder, however, should be actively engaged in gaining wealth because the other parts of society depend on him. Manusmriti 3.78 (see A.3.a) comments: 'Because people in the other three stages of life are every day supported by the householder through (the teaching of) sacred knowledge and with food, therefore the order of the householder is the most excellent one'.

Still, this does not amount to an unlimited licence to amass wealth. In the philosophical literature of the Upanishads (*c*. 1000 BCE) it is said in many passages that man is not to be satisfied with wealth alone (for example, Katha-Upanishad 1.1.27 and Brihadāranyaka-Upanishad 4.3.33 ff.). The example of eminent Hindus shows how this is being put into practice. Apparently, Sai Baba of Shirdi often demanded gifts from people who came to him, which is unorthodox for a holy man, but then he instantly distributed this to needy people. Satya Sai Baba regularly distributes food and clothes to poor people and Gandhi's teachings, reinforced by the Jaina concept of *nirgrantha*, 'non-attachment', also emphasise the sharing of resources and the benefits of putting them to good use.

25

The only restriction on the acquisition of wealth seems to be that it should be done in a righteous way. Thus, already in Rigveda 1.1.3, Agni, the god of fire, is invoked with a view to obtaining 'wealth, yes, plenty, increasing day by day'. In the Vedic hymns there are innumerable such invocations asking for strength, health, sons, power and other desirables. This tradition is continued into our times when Hindu businessmen, during the festival of Divali, pray to Lakshmi, goddess of wealth, for her blessings and generous support.

Individual detachment is also apparent in the operation of the Hindu concept of joint family property. The ancestral property of a Hindu joint family does not actually belong to the head of the family, although he is the powerful representative of the family as a legal entity (see A.3.b). Ownership rests in the family itself, a complex unit of up to four living generations and three generations of ancestors (see A.1.d and e). The living members act as trustees, so to say. Nobody has a clearly defined share (unless there is some form of partition), but a fluctuating interest, depending on births and deaths in the family. At the same time the concept of individual property is also known, with different rules for women's property.

An individual acting within the Hindu tradition would, in his later life at least, be expected gradually to abandon his concern for wealth and possessions. More or less rigid fasting and other renunciatory practices may constantly reinforce the fundamental message that wealth is not all that man should aim for.

Whenever a Hindu owns more than is needed for immediate survival the question would arise how to put such wealth, however little, to proper use. The mere giving-away of any surplus is considered meritorious, which explains why various forms of begging have such a firm root in Indian cultural traditions and also, to an extent, why hospitality is such a marked characteristic of Hindus.

Both giver and recipient, however, are warned of the potentially harmful effects of such transactions. The utterly selfless act of giving produces unseen merit, though acting with a view to acquiring that merit clearly defeats the purpose. A rich Hindu who installs, say, an image in a temple merely to enhance his or her status in the community may be envied by those who are easily impressed; but in Hindu terms, no unseen merit would accrue in such a case. Instead the allegation of hypocrisy could quickly arise. Thus, the mental state of the giver is very important and merit is not guaranteed. This is so even if it can be assumed that what is being given was acquired in a righteous manner.

Like many other texts Manusmriti 4.186–97 is concerned with the qualities of a deserving recipient of gifts. The mere caste status of a Brahmin does not suffice (4.190). Accepting gifts should not become a habit (4.186), otherwise there would be no unseen merit. Such attitudes explain why the wandering ascetic, who has visibly renounced all forms of attachment, is revered and is entitled to be supported by society. Indeed, in the right frame of mind, he provides an opportunity for the common Hindu to acquire merit, an idea which has developed more fully in Buddhist practice. There are, however, also 'bad ascetics' who merely take advantage of the Hindu tendency to give, and many Hindus appear to have become suspicious of holy men and make donations to a good cause rather than a person.

Several Hindu communities overseas expect their members to make regular and substantial donations for the purpose of establishing community centres and temples, often up to 10 per cent of their income. It is indeed the case that during the last decade or so, such centres have been established by many overseas Hindu communities, often through considerable personal sacrifice and self-denial.

A.4.e. Drugs

More or less vulgar displays of wealth are not entirely uncommon amongst status-seeking Hindus, especially to impress poorer relations and potential marriage partners. Here, the process of modernisation has occasionally meant the cheap copying of some bad aspects of Western society. The costly habit of drinking imported hard liquor and smoking particular brands of cigarettes has developed in certain classes of society, and is also observable among Hindus overseas. As more people count themselves as middle class and follow certain patterns of consumerism, Hindus seem to be involved in actual abuses more than before, but as indicated above (A.4.c) drinking, smoking, gambling and drug abuse were not uncommon in traditional India either. Men, in particular, seem to see it as a traditional privilege to indulge in one or several of those potentially very costly and destructive pastimes. Among the poorer sections of society, there is much disruption of family life due to such abuses. Several Indian states have introduced prohibition laws to control excessive consumption of alcohol, but this seems to be a growing problem in India which is difficult to control.

If we look at drugs more narrowly, we find that the rich plant life of India produces many intoxicating substances which have traditionally been used in the context of a fully developed science of homeopathy called *āyurveda*. Also, from the earliest literature onwards we find indications that even great sages were using some forms of drugs and that they were used in worship, too. Locally, many forms of indigenous drugs continue to be used in India today, and it is very difficult to draw a line between medical treatment involving drugs and actual drug abuse. It is recognised that this is a growing problem in India today, both in the trendy upper classes as well as among the very poor, who may seek to escape from an otherwise hard and unpleasant reality into a world of dreams. Any particular individual would be under an obligation, in the context of *dharma*, to ensure that he or she could continue to pursue what seems appropriate. Quite apparently, the use of drugs as such is not considered inappropriate, but the question of limits comes in, and this is, as always in Hinduism, a matter of individual discretion.

A.4.f. The Media

The Hindu concept of truth has on the one hand absolute, cosmic qualities as in *rita* or macrocosmic 'order' (see A.1.a), and is on the other hand a relative phenomenon to be worked out in accordance with *dharma*. The Sanskrit term for truth, *satya*, would always consider the two sides of a coin.

We have already looked at the question who controls knowledge of Hinduism as a religion (see A.1.a). We saw that initially it is a small elite group of learned sages. These few individuals, as is apparent from the concept of *smriti* (see A.1.c), had considerable power through their knowledge. There is ample evidence that their social attitudes have given a certain bias to the written works, which is a further reason why it is not possible to study Hinduism from books alone.

Since absolute truth, which was pre-ordained, was beyond human reach and control, knowledge of scriptures alone, however it was cultivated, was not sufficient. In the explicit relativity of the concept of *dharma* (A.1.a) it can be seen that Hinduism as a way of life became rather more prominent than the literary concepts, although both must be seen as intimately linked and mutually dependent.

This complex situation causes difficulties for contemporary Hinduism. There may be a lack of orientation, particularly in new socio-economic situations. There is no binding compendium of the rules of the faith. The current picture of Hinduism is that of a conglomeration of sects, following certain prominent leader figures, divine or human, who fulfil an important need in terms of guidance for their followers but who can also easily abuse that position.

Modern media, especially films, have played an important role in spreading knowledge about Hindu concepts. Prominent examples are a film about *Santoshimā*, a Hindu goddess whose cult was virtually 'created' by this film. The role of Hindu saints as political figures received a significant impulse due to the TV screening of the Mahabharata and Ramayana. Apart from the Hindi-based film industry, India also has very lively and important regional film traditions and a notable if small internationally oriented and English-focused section (Barnouw and Krishnaswamy 1980; Jackson and Nesbitt 1993).

The effect of the modern mass media and of international travel has been that the ideas of prominent Hindu leaders, who act as self-appointed spokesmen for the faith, are made much more widely available. Often such leaders have learnt about other faiths, and they seek to prove, in one way or another, that Hinduism is a world religion and is not inferior. Thus there is a tendency to give particular scriptures the status of a 'holy book', a Bible equivalent, and many rules which are quite clearly relative are stated as absolute truths of a universally binding nature. The modern mass media, mainly controlled by people not knowledgeable in Hindu matters, are thus often misrepresenting Hindu values, since they are unable to distinguish personal opinion from religious and ethical truth. A newspaper article in which a prominent Hindu leader is referred to as 'the Pope of the Hindus' illustrates the nonsense that may result, giving particular aspects of the faith an importance they never had.

A.4.g. Advertising

After the almost total collapse of the ancient system of education (A.4.a), lectures by wandering ascetics and learned individuals, as well as performances of dance and drama have contributed much to the spreading of Hindu religious and cultural traditions. All over the world today prominent public speakers on Hinduism attract large crowds. The success of such teaching in terms of individual education remains doubtful, but such events help to maintain a latent awareness of the higher aims of existence for many Hindus.

Traditionally Hindus have not sought to advertise their faith to others (see A.1.a and 7.c). The traditional Hindu caste system provides an elaborate hierarchical structure in which every individual has a place. Even though modern India has abolished the caste system by law, caste continues to act as an important factor in determining a person's status, although caste gradually gives way to class. The official abolition of many traditional restrictions relating to occupation has meant that the pressures of competition have increased (A.4.a) and that many Hindus find themselves with exaggerated ambitions that remain unrealistic.

Contemporary advertising all over the world projects the image of the joyfulness and success of a modern consumer society. At the same time, recent developments in consumer protection illustrate the Hindu culture of restraint, commonly referred to as Gandhian business ethics, with an important focus on avoiding misleading advertisements. Still, in contemporary India, as among Hindus abroad (A.4.f and e), there is a marked increase in materialism and greed, with cruel consequences. One example of this is seen in excessive demands in dowries and cruelty to brides as a result of dissatisfaction with the amount of the dowry. These are not only remnants of ancient traditions, but direct proof of modern Hindu society's excessive concern with *artha*, the acquisition of material goods. Modern advertising with its tempting displays of status symbols seems to have created an atmosphere where traditional values of restraint and self-control are not highly regarded any more. If it becomes more important to individuals to amass wealth than to value human lives, something must be wrong.

HINDUISM

A.5. THE QUALITY AND VALUE OF LIFE

A.5.a. The Elderly

For elderly Hindus there is no sudden shock of retirement after an active life. The stage of *vānaprastha* (see A.1.a) does not begin at a clearly defined point and does not have a special ritual to mark it. Few Hindu couples (the *vāna-prastha* does not normally abandon his wife) move physically 'into the wilderness', they rather move 'to the fringe'. Thus, retirement is more of a mental process and the elderly person remains an integral part of the joint family. In fact, many Hindu grandfathers continue to act as managers of the joint family as long as they are able to carry on such activities. Many older women do not give up major responsibilities in the household, even though a number of junior women may be there. In both cases this is not merely because the old folk are reluctant to give up control; if there is a genuine feeling and agreement on all sides that the expertise of such elders should be used to the benefit of the family, the younger family members will accept their junior status even though they may become old meanwhile. Many elderly Hindus, thus, remain active integral parts of their family all their life. Since they continue to be useful members, it helps both themselves and the family. An extra pair of hands is often very welcome and the relationship between grandparents and grandchildren tends to be a particularly close one.

There is much evidence found in sociological studies now that young women in India are becoming aware of the usefulness of having a granny at home if they have to go out to work to make ends meet. In cases where young women have resented joint family living and the presence of the husband's parents, the Indian courts have often lectured such women about their duties towards elderly parents-in-law. Public opinion in India was reflected by one judge who stated that the time had not yet come in India for old people to be pushed off into special homes.

Apart from situations where physical disabilities and the need for care arise, there is only one case in which an old Hindu should definitely live under the authority of his son, like a child, and that is when he has ritually entered the stage of *samnyāsin*, anticipating early death, but survives longer than he thought he would.

It is taken for granted that elderly single family members are taken care of. Hindu society looks with disapproval upon families who evict elderly members and leave them to fend for themselves. Caring for needy relatives is, of course, another way of acquiring unseen merit.

There is some evidence that the provision of old-age pensions makes elderly Hindus nowadays feel less dependent on their families. A growing number of elderly Hindus are living on their own, especially in overseas com-

30

munities, but it is unlikely that this will become a normal pattern among Hindus; the joint family system continues to exist also outside India.

A.5.b. Those in Need

Like elderly people, those who are mentally and physically handicapped or sick are ideally not excluded from the family, but are sheltered by it. Growing old was recognised as a natural process, and there was also an awareness that the elderly had, generally speaking, maintained the family at an earlier stage. Those born handicapped or subsequently afflicted with grave diseases may be treated differently, more so if they have not contributed anything to the family. It would be easy to see them as a burden, their maintenance as pure charity, and they pose, at times, ritual problems if they are considered inauspicious. But as in the case of elderly single relatives, social disapproval would be directed at families who abandon those in need. Still this does not give absolute security to the handicapped and sick: in times of distress, for instance famine, differing treatment of family members could mean that they, coming last in line, are not properly fed. The same has happened to many young girls, who were neglected by their families in times of famine. As there is evidence of the killing of baby girls, one wonders to what extent some handicapped babies suffer a similar fate in India. This is an example of where social practice does not match the ideal of the faith, that family members are cared for.

Generally speaking, the handicapped would have a low-status position in the family. In legal terms, they often remained perpetual minors, but as we have seen (A.5.a), this applied to many members of the Hindu joint family.

The dharmashāstra literature clearly supports different treatment of the handicapped and sick in a number of important social and legal contexts. They are exempt from taxation (Manusmriti 8.394) and, to an extent, enjoy legal immunity. But they are listed among the corrupt and bad when it comes to assessing their qualities as witnesses in court (for example, Manusmriti 8.64; Yajnavalkyasmriti 2.72–3). They are not even allowed to enter the court and their evidence is generally not admissible. They are not supposed to perform expiatory rituals (*shrāddha*), as in Manusmriti 3.150 ff. or to enter contracts and accept gifts (absolutely not in the case of lunatics and idiots), and they are debarred from inheriting within the joint family (for example Manusmriti 9.201).

Such discriminatory treatment is clearly based on the understanding that there are links between physical appearance or condition and the inherent past or present qualities of a person. Thus, incurable illness and physical deformity are often seen as the marks of a sinful individual, in other words, as a result of bad *karma* in a previous existence. Manusmriti 11.48 seems to contain the general rule: 'Some bad people suffer a change of their appearance in consequence of crimes committed in this life, and some in consequence of those committed in a former existence' (Bühler 1975).

This attitude seems to have justified the segregation of people with virulent diseases, lepers in particular, in special colonies. Social work institutions seem to have developed only during the nineteenth century. Some Indian rulers like the Gaekwads of Baroda have been very active in setting up such institutions, partly realising the ruler's *dharma*, partly as a result of Western influences.

In India today there are many homes for the disabled and sick, where they receive treatment and are sometimes taught skills to be able to help themselves. Other groups of people in need are also covered by such institutions now, especially orphans, destitute people, homeless children, and unmarried mothers, particularly if they are destitute or have been the victims of rape. The huge number of those in need in contemporary India poses great difficulties, but many organisations, as well as the government, are becoming increasingly involved in a wide variety of social work projects to ensure better implementation of the constitutionally guaranteed basic human rights.

A.5.c. Abortion

In the context of Hindu marriage (A.3.a) neither abortion nor birth control may be acceptable to many Hindus: one of the major life aims of a Hindu is to procreate so preserving life is a central aspect of *dharma* (see also A.1.a). The classical texts, therefore, see causing an abortion or miscarriage as a serious crime and sin. Some texts distinguish different forms of abortion and indicate different punishment for such actions. There are also distinctions in punishment according to whether the child was conceived in wedlock or not: aborting the child of a female servant may be seen as a less serious crime in the traditional hierarchies. Women causing abortions are treated as criminals and considered impure and inauspicious; some texts seek to banish them.

A Hindu woman with an unwanted pregnancy is, thus, not considered as being in need. Abortion would only be allowed if the mother's life is in danger due to the pregnancy. 'Social reasons' as understood in the West do not seem to count for Hindus here (see A.9.b).

But in real life, the situation is quite different, as the texts already imply when they discuss the subject. In today's hierarchy of values, the expectation that a married couple will have children continues to be strong. But people are content to have fewer children and various methods of birth control are fully acceptable (see A.9.b). The preference for sons, which has a number of reasons, mainly connected with the continuation of the family line, has been causing new problems here: since medical technology now makes it possible to determine the sex of an unborn child early in pregnancy, female foetuses are being aborted in large numbers. Both in India and overseas, doctors have become alerted to this practice. Several Indian states have now passed laws prohibiting sex testing, and this is certainly a matter of concern to many Hindus who would condemn such practices.

It is also not unknown that newborn girls are killed at once. Such practices, although not widespread, are cruel excesses of a male-dominated society and cause '*dharma* dilemmas'. Poor parents often justify this practice by arguing that a little suffering at this early stage is better than a life of misery later. The link with growing pressures to provide dowries for girls is also a factor here.

The killing of newborn babies seems hard to understand, but imagine life situations where the parents know they cannot hope to raise another child, perhaps because they have already seen so many young children die for want of bare necessities. There may be situations, thus, in which the individual conscience, that final arbiter of Hindu existence (see A.1.a) is swayed in favour of a rather cruel method of limiting the size of a family.

Abortion was legalised in India in 1971, but is not very popular, as far as we know. Research on family planning in Bombay (Lele and Kanitkar 1980: 142) reported that more than 80 per cent of women disapproved of abortion, and 56 per cent thought it was a sin; the Hindu concept of murder of an embryo is clearly present. Given the pressures of population explosion, this means that India's preferred way to control population growth must be the prevention of unwanted pregnancies in the first place.

A.5.d. Euthanasia

Generally speaking, Hindu respect for all forms of life, and negative attitudes against unnecessary killing, give little scope for the justification of euthanasia. A prominent Hindu attitude here is to say that the terminally ill individual has to wait till the right time (*kāla*) has come for him or her to die. Those that care for the terminally ill may well seek to lessen pain and suffering, but in principle they have no right to end the other person's life.

Yet again, the individual conscience of the terminally ill individual (see A.1.a) allows for radical solutions. The Hindu concepts of a 'good death' and a 'willed death' are relevant here. In the former, a person prepares for death, having finished all earthly business. In a 'willed death' people who are old and weak, but not terminally ill, may virtually wait till death arrives, refusing to take any food or drink. The model of the *samnyāsī* (see A.1.a) is certainly relevant here; renouncing life may be seen as a form of suicide.

The remarks above already indicate that in remarkable contrast to various prohibitions against taking a life, and also somewhat in contradiction to the ideal of non-violence, suicide may be morally and ethically acceptable to Hindus in a number of situations.

A clear situation, often found in the classical literature (see A.1.a) is the case of the old man who becomes a *samnyāsī*, performs his own funeral rites and then leaves this world (see Manusmriti 6.31). Similarly well known is the model of the ideal wife, *satī* (better known in English as suttee), who burns herself with her husband's body on the funeral pyre. Such cases may occur even today, despite the fact that the modern law strictly prohibits this practice because the *satī* ideal has been abused for murdering women.

Heroic medieval poetry promised great glory to the faithful wife of a king or warrior who seeks death rather than becoming the captive of another man. One may, thus, see *satī* as an ideal which takes the Hindu concept of marriage as an indissoluble union to its logical, if cruel, conclusion. By following this ideal, undergoing a form of self-sacrifice which demands great courage, a *satī* is believed to become instantly a goddess (*devī*) and is worshipped as a symbol of the ideal female.

A close analogy to *satī* can be found in texts showing a number of situations in which an individual, totally overcome by grief over the loss of a dear one, or in a situation of utter despair, commits suicide, often by burning. This practice is also followed by men, and there are no indications that this individual decision is not respected. Literature also gives examples of suicide as a penance, i.e. as an honourable way out of a life spoilt by a serious crime or sin. In some instances, there appears to be a moral duty to commit suicide, thus sparing the ruler the need to enforce the death penalty for a very grave violation of *dharma*. To have a more complete picture, it would be necessary to look at the Hindu evidence on suicide in the context of theories of rebirth and individual salvation, too.

A.6. QUESTIONS OF RIGHT AND WRONG

A.6.a. The Purpose of Law

In Sanskrit there is no precise equivalent for 'law' (which also in English can mean a number of things), but there are several relevant terms, among which *dharma* (A.1.a) and *vyavahāra* (A.1.b) are prominent.

The Vedic Hindus, looking at the way natural phenomena appeared with an invisibly guided regularity (for example, the sun rising in the east every day and setting in the west), saw a pre-ordained natural order behind this world (*rita*). This macrocosmic order was probably at first seen as self-supporting. But when the concept of *rita* merged with and developed into *dharma*, first the Vedic gods were seen as upholders of order, then the human action of performing rituals and sacrifices to these gods, and ultimately all human action itself was thought to have direct impact on the cosmic universe.

As a result it became not only necessary to formulate rules of *dharma* (as found in the *smriti* works), but also to support these rules through the concept of *vyavahāra* (legal processes) which is, thus, really a tool for the purpose of strengthening *dharma*. This is necessary, as several texts clearly tell us, because of the successive deterioration of moral standards. At the stage of worst deterioration, the *kali* era or *kaliyuga*, which we are living in now, *vyavahāra* is seen as essential to uphold order.

'Law' in the sense of *vyavahāra* has a purpose similar to that of modern laws only in one respect, namely that it provides sanctions. It is not the purpose of *dharma* to provide uniformly valid rules of law comparable to modern state law for all Hindus. Thus, it cannot be emphasised enough that works like the Manusmriti are not law books. They do not contain legislated law. All they do is give guidelines on *dharma* which may or may not be relevant in particular situations, depending on the circumstances. Hindu law provides basic guiding principles to be worked out in new situations but the actual 'rule of law' remains flexible. Hence, Hindu law is permanently concerned with achieving relative justice in the sense of appropriateness, rather than enforcing rigid compliance with any rule of positive law. This is seen to lead to injustice.

Viewed in this perspective it will be obvious that the modern Hindu law of India, which has largely adopted the positive law approach, based on Western models, cannot achieve justice in many circumstances (see A.3.c for an example).

A.6.b. Sin and Sins

Hindu literature has been much concerned with the topics of crime and punishment, sin and penance. While it is clear that sins require penance, and crimes some form of punishment (often penance, too), there are no theoretical discussions of the links between crime and sin, presumably because the underlying concepts were familiar to the writers.

In the Hindu world view, it is often impossible to differentiate between sin and crime. The Sanskrit term *pāpa* denotes both. The distinction of sin as an action which goes against God and his law, and crime, which violates a rule of state law, is a Western one and does not apply here. First of all, despite monotheistic tendencies in Hinduism, a Hindu does not generally think in terms of a direct relationship with God but acts in the cosmic context of *rita/dharma*, which does not separate the religious from the secular/social, the divine from the human. Sins, being a violation of the ideals of the cosmic order, affect the social sphere; and crime has cosmic dimensions and is not merely a violation of human laws.

The need for penances is amply discussed in the *smriti* literature. For example, Manusmriti 11.44 directs: 'Someone who omits a prescribed act, or performs a blamable act, or who is unduly attached to sensual matters, must perform a penance' (Bühler 1975).

This general rule is strengthened with sanctions in the case of non-compliance: Manusmriti 11.48–53 contains a list of illnesses and disabilities which are the result of bad *karma* caused by sin for which penance has not been made (see A.5.b). Various acts of stealing are included here. It is, thus, apparent that no clear distinction has been drawn between sins and crimes. Additionally, it appears that the idea of sin is attached to many offences of a secular nature; these, too, require purificatory rituals or, indeed, penances, as summed up in Manusmriti 11.54 which concludes the present discussion: 'Therefore, penances must always be performed for the sake of purification, because those whose sins have not been expiated are born again with terrible marks' (ibid.).

A.6.c. Punishments

The right to punish is seen by the *smriti* texts as the ruler's prerogative: only the ruler has this right, which is divinely ordained (see A.1.b). Punishment is personified and illustrated as *danda*, a stick or punishing rod in Manusmriti 7.14. Through fear of punishment, all beings should follow their *dharma*. Verses 7.18–19 are explicit on this:

> Punishment alone rules all created beings, punishment alone protects them, punishment watches over them while they sleep; the wise declare that punishment is identical with the law.
> If punishment is properly inflicted after due consideration, it makes all people happy, but inflicted without due consideration it destroys everything. (Bühler 1975)

Because the texts appear to concentrate on the king and his functions, there is little known about the role of local bodies in maintaining social order. It is unlikely that every incident was brought to a superior ruler. Several verses indicate that clan elders, village headmen, caste tribunals and professional bodies used to play a central role in maintaining social order (for example Manusmriti 8.41; Nāradasmriti 1.7). It is not known exactly to what extent they could punish offenders; it is quite likely that only grave matters went before the king.

The king, at the top of society, had to maintain a subtle balance between constantly competing claims. Should he not act properly, destruction would follow. The texts portray this as a decline to almost Darwinian conditions; in the 'rule of the fish', the big fish devour the small without any control, and this is ultimately fatal to all. Nāradasmriti 18.14–16 elaborates on this vision of social turmoil, and Manusmriti 7.20 ff. is even more imaginative.

Appropriate punishment by the king has several important consequences. If justice is seen to be done, this will deter potential offenders, and it also strengthens the ruler's position, increasing the security for his subjects. Offenders are either liquidated or re-instated in their position through punishments, often combined with penances.

Some authors (see for example Banerjee 1980: 7) are of the opinion that punishments were originally very severe and that a more lenient system of fines was introduced later, perhaps around 300 CE. Thus Vishnusmriti 5.1 states rather abruptly that 'great criminals should all be put to death', and lists forgers of royal edicts and other documents, robbers, thieves, adulterous wives (5.18). Equally worthy of such severity are men who have intercourse with a woman of the lowest caste (5.43). Similar rules are found elsewhere. Manusmriti 8.352–86 treats the subject of adultery in detail and advocates cruel death sentences, depending on the circumstances of the case.

There are various methods of ranking crimes and punishments according to severity, but even individual texts are often not consistent on this. Murder is identifiable as the most serious offence. Not all cases, though, attract the death penalty: intention seems to be an important consideration. Manusmriti 8.349–51 give instances in which killing is lawful, certainly 'by killing an assassin the slayer incurs no guilt' (v. 351). Arthashāstra 4.11 gives a survey of rules on capital punishment.

All texts are, not surprisingly, united in the opinion that the murder of a Brahmin is the most serious of all offences. *Brahmahatya* (killing a Brahmin) was clearly looked upon as the greatest sin and heads the list of the *mahāpā-takas* or mortal sins (for example Manusmriti 9.235). This list includes the drinking of a particular spirit by Brahmins, the theft of gold belonging to a Brahmin, and intercourse with the *guru*'s wife. The killing of a pregnant woman (Vishnusmriti 36.1) is listed among other serious cases of murder.

Generally speaking, the *varna* status of the criminal and the victim play an important part in assessing the severity of any particular crime and determining the punishment for it. It is remarkable that a Brahmin murderer, even if his victim was another Brahmin, should not be subject to the death penalty. The Vishnusmriti, which appeared so strict on death sentences, hastens to add that 'in the case of a Brahmin no corporal punishment must be inflicted' (5.2) and advises that a Brahmin murderer must be banished from the country, with a mark of his offence branded on his body (5.3). If guilty of other serious crimes, he should be banished, but not hurt, and he could take all his property with him (5.8). Such caste differentiations, as well as an element of retaliation, are apparent in rules like Manusmriti 8.280 and Vishnusmriti 5.19, which read: 'With whatever limb an inferior insults or hurts his superior in caste, of that limb the king shall cause him to be deprived' (Dutta 1978).

Public disgrace must have been a major deterrent in the case of minor offences. Loss of caste, i.e. relegation to a lower caste, was a powerful punishment. Manusmriti 11.181 ff., for example, gives ritual details of this punishment. Apparently, offenders can eventually be re-admitted to their original caste through the performance of penances.

Though not all Hindus believe in rebirth, the threat of punishment in the next existence has, of course, a potentially powerful deterrent effect, too.

In the context of the duties of the ruler (Manusmriti 8.1) the commentator Medhatithi (*c.* 900 CE) emphasises that he should not only guard his subjects against visible torment like robbers, but also against the consequences of their unexpiated sins. So the ruler is also put under an obligation to see that his subjects perform appropriate penances. The extent of such penances was decided by the Brahmin experts on *dharma*, not by the ruler himself. In this context, several texts emphasise that any act could be simultaneously sinful, immoral and criminal, and could thus require penal sanctions, penances and moral retribution. A dutiful ruler would have to consider all these aspects of punishment together.

It appears that at the local level the elaborate *smriti* rules on punishments and penances could easily be used as a means to terrorise and suppress less powerful and especially low-caste groups of Hindus. There is much evidence of such abuse in medieval India, when the institution of Hindu kingship was severely limited in operation, and there appeared to be no supreme ruler acting in the context of *rājadharma*. Such problems continue up to today when instances of cruel abuse of positions of power and influence come to light. The modern legal system with its constitutional guarantees seems badly to fail when it comes to delivering the great promises of human rights. It is interesting to see that the modern leadership of India currently punishes those who abuse positions of power and privilege with the aim of building up a 'clean' image and of putting 'public interest' before private concerns. This is precisely what the ancient Hindu ruler had to do to fulfil his *dharma*.

A.6.d. The Wrongdoer and the Wronged

Texts like Nāradasmriti 1.46 create the false impression that a wronged person had to rely totally on the king: 'One who tries to right himself in a dispute, without having given notice to the king, shall be severely punished and his case must not be heard' (Dutta 1978). The plaintiff himself has an important role to play in bringing a reluctant defendant to court. Verse 1.47 allows him to arrest a man who tries to abscond, while verse 1.51 has built-in safeguards saying that anyone who arrests a person improperly shall be liable to punishment. Self-help in the execution of judgements is allowed in some texts, for instance Manusmriti 8.50: 'A creditor who himself recovers his property from the debtor must not be blamed by the king for seizing what really is his own' (Bühler 1975).

Only the ruler, however, can use punishments to secure the execution of his orders. There is one significant exception showing again the privileged position of Brahmins: Manusmriti 11.31–3 tells us that a Brahmin who knows *dharma* need not bring an offence to the notice of the ruler and can punish the offender on his own because his power is even greater than that of the king, due to his knowledge of texts.

Since local forms of dispute settlement are explicitly allowed in many texts (for example Nāradasmriti 1.7), the relationship of wrongdoer and wronged at the local level would appear to be much more direct. Compensation rather than punishment or retribution, reconciliation and restoration of social harmony, also by penances, along with other conciliatory actions, must have been prominent. It is interesting to note that some modern reforms of criminal law return to the idea that not only is the wrongdoer liable to punishment from the state, but that the wronged needs to be compensated for any loss or injury.

A.7. EQUALITY AND DIFFERENCE

A.7.a. Differences between People

One important aspect of the Hindu 'unity in diversity' is the basic contradiction between the unity of all created beings and acute awareness among Hindus of differences between individuals. Thus, many Hindu religious leaders emphasise the 'brotherhood of all men', going beyond the group of Hindus, even while the hierarchical structure of Hindu society has by no means been abolished by the modern laws of India, which have made discrimination against people on the basis of caste illegal.

The realisation of individuality and an individual approach to the divine is especially cultivated by the various forms of devotion (*bhakti*) in Hinduism. The Bhagavadgita (9.29) indicates the non-partiality of the divine towards all creatures: 'I am the same towards all beings; to me none is hateful or dear'. Thus, it is up to Hindu individuals to realise the nature of the divine and to approach their chosen god – who in the process may become the equivalent of God in other religions – in a spirit of loving devotion. The Bhagavadgita indicates that Lord Krishna promises eternal peace (9.31) and salvation to all devotees. This includes women and *shūdras* (9.32), who appeared to be excluded from *moksha*, at least according to the orthodox view. Equality of all people is emphasised by many reform movements in Hinduism, for example the *Arya Samaj*.

In the classical literature, however, and in social life, differences between people play a large role. Already in Rigveda 10.90 we find a hymn on *purusha*, that is to say, the primeval man, which is later often used to legitimise the *varna* system: from the mouth of this being emerges the Brahmin, from his arms the *Kshatriya*, from his thighs the *Vaishya*, and from his feet the *Shūdra*. By the time of the Manusmriti (see 1.87) this symbolic description is presented as a manifestation of divine law.

The obvious differentiation, within the *varna* system, into regional and occupational sub-groups, also called caste (the Indian term here is *jāti*, not *varna*), reflects the very complex system of division of labour in society. This system also seemed to give every individual a clearly defined place and, in orthodox terms, little or no prospects of mobility. However, in practice there has always been intense competition between castes and there is by no means any agreement over the question of relative statuses; the system is much more complex and fluid than much of the literature suggests.

It is apparent that the caste system still operates wherever Hindus live today. At the same time, flexibility is emphasised more now, and mobility, urbanisation and education have all played their part in this. But particular areas of concern remain the selection of marriage partners and certain prohibitions in the context of occupations (A.4.a).

A.7.b. Attitudes to Other Religions

Hindus have no difficulties accepting that members of other religions have the right to believe and worship in their own way. This follows logically from the cosmic Hindu world view and the absence of any central Hindu dogma of belief and worship. Historically, this had the result that even among Hindus themselves there are widely diverging, but recognised ideas and practices so that it remains difficult to distinguish so-called reform movements that grew out of Hinduism.

Hindus often respond to this by pointing out that God is really one. You may find pictures of Christ, Sikh gurus and other symbols in a Hindu temple, thus reinforcing a principle of incarnation (*avatāra*), which transcends all boundaries. Hinduism sees no need to proselytise (see A.4.e), but does not refuse to acknowledge that non-Hindus may want to adopt Hindu practices. Many Hindus are irritated about the efforts of Muslims to win converts and about the activities of Christian missionaries.

The term *mleccha* (barbarian) was used for different people in different situations and could also mean 'foreigner' or 'outsider'. As such it is an ethnic term. Manusmriti 2.23 uses it with reference to the non-Aryans of Vedic India, 10.45 distinguishes between those emanated from *purusha* (see A.7.a) and the rest of the world's population who are referred to as *dasyus* ('enemies of the gods', 'barbarians'). They would mainly be forest and hill tribes living on the fringe of Hindu society. Many have, up to our days, not been Hinduised. The *smriti* literature is clearly not concerned with them.

Adherents of other religions, Muslims and Christians in particular, may do a number of things abhorrent to Hindus, like eating beef, and thus do not live in accordance with the high-caste ideals of Hindu *dharma*. They are therefore sometimes relegated to a position of inferiority (as with the Muslim butcher in A.4.b). On the other hand, adherents of Jainism, for example, are almost indistinguishable from their Hindu *Vaishya* neighbours, especially in

Gujarat. The feeling of superiority among Hindus, certainly those of the higher castes, led to the expectation that Hindus of lower-caste status as well as non-Hindus ought to conform to high-caste Hindu values and practices and would then gain a better social and religious status. This expectation occasionally creates difficulties in modern India in the context of freedom of religion, especially for Muslims. They feel under threat by the fact that the modern and nominally secular Indian legal system operates on the basis of a Hindu value system.

A.7.c. Attitudes to Other Races

There are two ways of looking at this. First, the Hindu world view necessitates a positive and supportive attitude to other nations and races because the world is, ultimately, seen as one interlinked whole. But second, in socio-political terms, other races and nations are also seen as competitors, rivals, even enemies; much of the Arthashāstra deals with various measures of foreign policy designed to conquer neighbouring states or to evade being conquered. Suppression of internal enemies and general statecraft are other major topics treated with much sophistication. However, if one looked only at the Arthashāstra alone one would get an unbalanced view. As a handbook on *artha*, it obviously concentrates on only one of the four aims of life but it is vital to view the attitudes to other races and nations from the perspective of the overriding principles of *dharma*, too.

In this, awareness of the complex, multi-racial nature of India is important. Not only modern Indian culture but also much of ancient Hindu tradition arose under the influence of quite different racial groups, among whom the Aryans were only dominant in certain areas. The term 'Hindu' originally meant 'the people inhabiting the land South of the river Sindhu or Indus'. The fact that South Indians are essentially Dravidians, and that South Indian Hinduism is in many ways different from that in the North is often overlooked, yet most Hindus are aware of this, as well as of their common roots. Thus the coexistence, for many centuries, of people of different castes and races has made it a fact of life for Hindus that there are different people with their own characteristics. Jokes and prejudices abound, as everywhere else in the world, but awareness of a higher unity is certainly there to be found in so many contexts.

Marriage between people from different groups was once apparently not uncommon, and there are many references to mixed castes, in particular. The *dharma* texts, however, developed a very restrictive attitude towards intercaste marriages and any other form of contact between different castes. In India one will often see a marked residential segregation of people belonging to different communities as a result of such attitudes. The pattern repeats itself in the West, particularly in Britain, where it is now quite clear that certain groups of Indians have tended to settle in particular cities, and even in certain localities within such cities.

A.7.d. Women and Men

Hinduism has not had a static view on this important topic (see A.2.c), about which there is much material and a lot of confusion. The major difficulty for understanding Hindu attitudes in this area arises from the fact that there have been dramatic changes in the Hindu approach to sexual ethics over time. Basically, the early Hindus were most concerned about procreation and were very conscious that only women could bear children. Women, thus, were more important for the continuation of society than men.

In practice this meant that an infertile husband who wanted children would require his wife to cohabit with another man, in the mythological literature even with a god. Modern Hindus do not identify with these practices and neither women nor men found this an ideal solution, as the literature clearly shows. There is a dramatic episode in the Mahabharata (1.122) in which a sage orders that from now on women are to be brought under control (*maryādā*). This reflects a shift in Hindu sexual ethics towards concern about chastity rather than progeny, with very important implications for gender relationships.

The *smriti* literature amply elaborates on this. An ambivalent attitude to women, which is still prevalent now, develops. On the one hand, women are to be honoured like goddesses, on the other hand they are not trusted. Seen as a moral danger to themselves and others, they are to be kept under strict control. On the positive attitude, Manusmriti 3.55–6 and 59 are frequently cited as an authority:

> Women must be honoured and adorned by their fathers, brothers, husbands and brothers-in-law, if they desire their own welfare. Where women are honoured, there the gods are pleased. But where they are not honoured, sacred rites yield no rewards.
>
> Hence men who seek their own welfare should always honour women with kind speech, with gifts of ornaments, clothes and good food. (Bühler 1975)

On the other hand, many texts elaborate on the need to keep women under control at all times. This position, too, is supported by the Manusmriti, which is certainly not consistent. Thus, 9.2–3, 9.5 and 9.7 provide:

> Day and night women must be kept under control by the males in their family, and if they attach themselves to sensual enjoyments they must be restrained.
>
> Her father protects a woman in childhood, her husband protects her

in her youth, and her sons protect her in old age; a woman is never fit for independence.

Women in particular must be guarded against evil inclinations, however trifling; for if they are not guarded, they will bring trouble on two families.

A man who carefully guards his wife preserves the purity of his offspring, virtuous conduct, his family, himself, and his marriage. (ibid.)

Of course, some of these texts have been highlighted by Western commentators and Indian feminists critical of Hindu society. The Manusmriti also gives some indication that it is difficult to guard women by force (v. 9.10) and considers it best if women of their own accord keep guard over themselves (v. 9.12), thus referring to the familiar theme of self-control. Verses 9.10–11 also advise the husband to keep his wife busy with a variety of household works; an attitude of suspicion and distrust of women is obvious from many texts. It may be explained by the fact that the verses we read tend to originate from ascetics.

In social reality, for many traditional Hindus the need to protect female chastity is indeed a major concern. This has important implications for life today, both in India and in the West. Many Hindu females are only very reluctantly allowed to go out to work. Older girls are under especially strict supervision, and a clear preference for single-sex education is a logical consequence of such attitudes.

It is too superficial to dismiss the Hindu approach to women merely as sexist. We have seen that Hindus are for a number of reasons concerned with the purity of the individual's mind and body; also men are governed by such concerns. The male chauvinist attitudes of many contemporary male Hindus are just as far away from Hindu ideals as the behaviour of the young Hindu girl who elopes with a lover.

A.7.e. Are All People Equal?

The answer to this question has already been given in different ways in a number of previous chapters and in A.7.a above. For Hindus, the answer to the question is clearly 'No', despite philosophical awareness of cosmic unity and the existence of the same *ātman* in all created beings.

The caste system would need to be looked at in some detail to study how religiously legalised inequality works in practice. There would also be much scope for discussing the conflicts arising for Hindus out of life in an environment that presupposes the equality of all individuals, especially in legal terms.

The Hindu awareness of inequality and of division of labour in society also means that no individual can be totally self-sufficient; other people are needed and they, too, have needs. In other words, a realisation of people as social beings and an integrated small part of a much larger whole lies at the core of Hinduness (see A.1.a). This is reflected in the affirmation of the extended family (A.3.b). However subconscious, this awareness of interdependency is characteristically Hindu and is fundamentally different from an individual-istic, self-centred approach to life, which does not really seem possible for a Hindu.

A.8. NATIONAL DIVISIONS, WAR AND PEACE

A.8.a. Why do Different Nations Exist?

This question was of little concern to traditional Hinduism. Throughout its long history, India has rarely been a politically united and unified country. Already the Vedic tribes formed a number of separate nations. Hinduism and its continuation did not depend on whether there was a Hindu ruler or not, as is clearly shown by the fact that centuries of Mughal rule in India have not wiped out Hinduism.

It is apparent that the idea of nation states based on adherence to a certain religion is a new phenomenon in the subcontinent. It is only in more recent history that the subcontinent has witnessed the creation in 1947 of Pakistan, a separate state for Muslims. This was accompanied by widespread com-munal violence and mass expulsions, as the physical separation of people who had for many centuries lived together caused severe problems and a great deal of suffering in border areas. The separation of Bangladesh from Pakistan in 1971 involved considerable bloodshed, too.

In terms of ethnicity, India certainly constitutes many different nations. However, there is also a wider awareness of belonging to the overarching Indian political unit, which is a modern federal state. In a sense, India's complicated federal arrangements are an attempt to keep very different groups of people under one political umbrella. This strategy has been tested in several crises. In particular, some sections of the Sikh population have been demanding a separate state for Sikhs, Khalistan. This is, however, directly against the letter and spirit of the Indian Constitution, which would not allow secession from the federal Union. The state is secular and treats the Sikhs as equal to Hindus. However, this is precisely the root of the problem, as many Sikhs have been objecting to being classed and treated as Hindus. Modern Indian politics, therefore, have to struggle with this par-ticular question and there is no easy answer when it comes to the subcontinent itself.

A.8.b. Conflict between Nations

The Hindu concept of *ahimsā* ('non-violence', 'avoiding harm to others') would seem to imply as an ethical ideal that conflicts between nations, as well as among individuals, are reprehensible, that violence must be avoided, and that the desire for harmony should prevail in all life situations.

However, the Hindu concern for balance and harmony remains at all times tempered by the reflection that maintaining a balance may involve handling imbalances to restore order. Thus, already the Vedic hymns contain many invocations to various gods for victory in battle (for example Rigveda 1.101). Armed conflict was certainly not uncommon in ancient India and all sides seem to have invoked their respective gods to help towards victory.

The notion of *ahimsā* is certainly an ancient concept. Mahabharata 12.254.29 appears to say that *ahimsā* has been considered the highest *dharma* from time immemorial. This seems exaggerated and is contradicted by the central passage in the Bhagavadgita in which Arjuna is admonished to go into battle to uphold *dharma*, even if it involves killing his own relatives. The notion appears more prominent in the philosophical literature of the Upanishads. We then find it applied by the Emperor Ashoka (*c.* 274–232 BCE, see B.1.d), who turned to Buddhism and renounced all warfare after a cruel war which he himself fought. In his 13th Rock Edict, containing not so much legislation as statements of moral principles, he advises that violence and war should be replaced by conquest through *dharma*: 'that conquest, again, is everywhere productive of a feeling of love. Love is won in conquest by dharma. That love may seem almost insignificant, but his Sacred Majesty considers it productive of great fruit also in the world beyond'.

The essence of this philosophy was adopted by Mahatma Gandhi, whose practice and teaching of non-violence did not mean absolute obedience in the face of injustice nor silent, passive suffering, but rather renunciation of aggression, despite a path of action against oppression.

Violence as such is not contrary to *dharma*, however, and we must see the ethical ideal of *ahimsā* in the context of relativity. If killing in self-defence and for the purpose of upholding *dharma* was not considered a crime, this means that killing as such does not necessarily damage *dharma*. As we saw, the Bhagavadgita teaches the necessity and moral justifiability of armed conflict, provided it is in the interest and for the preservation of *dharma*. Thus, Krishna tells Arjuna (2.37) that he will not incur any sin in battle: 'If you are killed in the battle you will go to Heaven; if you win, you will enjoy life on earth. Therefore arise, oh son of Kunti, ready to fight' (Radhakrishnan 1960).

In much stronger words, the heroic Arjuna is reminded of his duties as a *kshatriya* in upholding a righteous cause. Since he is acting in defence against the aggressive clan of the Kauravas, he is morally justified to use violence. Bhagavadgita 2.31 and 2.33 says: 'Consider also your own dharma, you should not hesitate; for a kshatriya nothing is better than a righteous war. But if you refuse to fight this righteous war, then, renouncing your own dharma and honour, you will certainly incur sin' (ibid.).

The concept of the just and righteous war (*dharmayuddha*) appears also in the Arthashāstra, which is above all concerned with the principle of expediency in the context of governing and administering a country. It is a sophisticated work on statecraft in which the considerations of self-preservation and political survival are prominent. Dangers arise from internal enemies of the ruler as well as from neighbouring states or rulers.

The principles of relations between states in ancient India are discussed in some detail by Bhatia (1977). His main aim is to prove that ancient India had a developed form of public international law which is much more civilised than later European concepts. He shows that relations between states were based on a number of considerations in the context of *dharma* and *artha*. Important among these are the concern for humanity and chivalry and the maintenance of agreements, i.e. the sanctity of treaties and alliances. Satisfaction of state interest is the main guiding principle, as shown especially in the discussion of foreign policy, which relies on book 7 in the Arthashāstra.

Bhatia (1977: 81) also refers to the Mahabharata to the effect that a policy of conciliation and compromise should be tried first to avoid armed conflict. A weak king should surrender to his enemies rather than go into a futile battle (Arthashāstra 7.15.13 ff.). War should only be a last resort, a necessary evil to determine the strength of equal partners. Similarly, Manusmriti 7.107–9 advises the ruler:

> When he is thus involved in conflict, let him subdue all his opponents as far as he can by the (four) expedients, conciliation and the rest.
>
> If they cannot be stopped by the first three expedients, then let him by the application of pressure gradually bring them to subjection.
>
> Among the four expedients, conciliation and the rest, the learned always recommend conciliation, and (only as the last resort) force for the prosperity of the kingdom. (Bühler 1975)

Manusmriti 7.193 and 7.200 reiterate the idea that conquest should not be made by fighting if it can be avoided. Should it come to war, however, Bhatia (1977: 93) argues that Hindus had a very high ideal of warfare. Arthashāstra 10.3.1–25 outline a number of methods for overcoming enemies, but in verse 26 it is stated that open warfare, in which the place and time for the fight are indicated by the combatants, is most righteous.

If in such a test of strength one party succumbed, peace should be sought to avoid unnecessary bloodshed (10.3.54–6). A broken enemy should not be embarrassed and harassed (10.3.57). It is apparent that an element of self-interest comes in here, too: the victor will become the new sovereign of the conquered nation and should be concerned to create an atmosphere of good-will. The warring kings of ancient India could not retreat to an isolated island after the combat, they had to live with the new situations which they had just created.

Similar reasons of expediency and concern for *ahimsā* seem to underlie the rule that atrocities against the civilian population should be restricted. The distinction between combatants and non-combatants is firmly recognised (Bhatia 1977: 94 and 99). Arthashāstra 13.4 is adamant that a wise ruler would not like to take over a country which has been destroyed and whose people have been killed. While taking booty was apparently not uncommon (Bhatia 1977: 107; Manusmriti 7.96–7), the treatment of prisoners of war, according to Bhatia (1977: 106) was subject to humane rules.

If humanity triumphed in ancient India over the desire for revenge, as claimed by Bhatia (1977: 108), this would probably not only be due to the ideals of *dharma*, but a few other factors. Wars in ancient India were secular in nature, a consequence of political contest and power struggles between neighbours. Wars were not fought to bring civilisation, or a better religion, to another country. The participants on both sides were probably mainly Hindus until the advent of the Muslims in India.

One could look at the role of modern India in the context of world peace and would certainly discover that awareness of the ancient concepts has had many effects, such as India's leadership of the non-alignment movement. Bhatia is not wrong to argue that the world could, perhaps, learn something from the Hindu approach to armed conflict.

A.9. GLOBAL ISSUES

A.9.a. Responses to World Poverty

Ancient Hindu ethics were discussed in contexts quite different from modern theories of economics and politics. The problem of poverty as such is not a prominent topic discussed in Hindu literature.

This could be explained, albeit not very convincingly, by saying that environmental and economic conditions were presumably such that people survived virtually from what nature offered. Hindu epics depict at times paradise-like conditions, and there seems to be little concern with survival as such. Only in a few places are hungry people mentioned (Arthashāstra 2.136 advises the ruler not to tax subjects suffering from famine). Reference to poverty is made in the context of appropriate methods of survival for Brahmins in distress (for example Manusmriti 10.104). Hunger is not a topic of the scriptures, and it does not appear as a punishment for bad *karma*.

In the context of *artha* (A.4.f) wealth and its effects play a role. Poverty is abhorred and material wealth is considered important (for example Manusmriti 12.8). Gopalan (1977: 75) has explained this by saying that the absence of material wealth and well-being is likely to hinder moral growth. A person who has to worry about survival is unlikely to have the peace of mind to develop the balanced approach to the aims of life which Hinduism considers ideal.

In connection with the forbidden occupations (A.4.b) we saw that in times of distress Brahmins were allowed to subsist by occupations other than those of their *varna*, while it is forbidden for non-Brahmins to live by the occupation of a higher caste (Manusmriti 10.96). The texts do not answer our question how society as a whole responded to poverty. Gopalan (1977: 84) indicates the presence of a social consciousness, as a result of which the affluent would part with a share of their wealth to support the destitute. Prominent Hindu leaders follow this model, for example, when they distribute food and clothes to poor people and admonish their followers to do the same. Also in other situations of direct relationship, for example master and servant, this solidarity comes through, supported by considerations of *artha* as well as *dharma*. A Hindu would most probably not turn away a destitute person who came begging. But what about concern for all those who do not come to the door but who are starving?

It may not be wrong to assume that in this case Hindus take a rather different attitude. The individual's range of effective action is seen as limited; total abolition of poverty is unrealistic and not achievable by an individual. Therefore, it seems easy simply to ignore the plight of others, or to explain it in terms of *karma* as a consequence of past actions.

The response of modern India to the present question is very interesting. India is a socialist, secular democratic republic, and the Indian Constitution of 1950 guarantees and promises not only social, but also economic justice. The underlying spirit and the execution of these policies appear decidedly Hindu in nature: it is a non-violent approach, not based on the dispossession of the rich and powerful by force, but aiming to create greater social consciousness among all citizens, leading to a gradual process of redistribution of individual and national wealth. A large variety of socio-economic measures (for example, land reforms and work-creation programmes) have had the effect that more recently, at least, starvation on a large scale has not been occurring in India.

A.9.b. Responses to Population Control

Population control in the sense of limiting the number of people born is totally alien to traditional Hindu thought, as we already saw (A.5.c). The unlimited desire to have children, sons in particular, is easily explained by the need for the family to secure its future. Lack of medical facilities and hostile climatic conditions once meant that many children died. The Hindu scriptures are therefore concerned with increasing fertility rather than birth control. The marriage rituals abound in verses praying for abundant and strong offspring, and there are early Vedic rules on raising extra-marital offspring. Even now prolonged infertility of the wife often means the end of her marriage (see A.3.c).

The *dharma* literature is concerned to put the husband, in particular, under a duty to cohabit at the right time so that a child is conceived (see especially Manusmriti 3.45–9 and 9.4). Wasting potential pregnancy time is in some texts even considered a crime equal to the killing of an embryo. Obviously the perspective at that time was fundamentally different from present concerns.

Modern India has a population of more than 900 million people, with a net increase of 17 million a year, equivalent to the whole population of Australia. This can be called a population explosion, but India is not really over-populated: that is a relative term, and a country the size of India can ideally feed many more people. The facts of rural poverty and urban slums, however, show the undoubted need for population control, and it is officially well recognised, with many Hindus practising birth control.

The number of births per thousand women from the age of 15 to 45 has come down significantly, but there are so many young people of child-bearing age now that the increase in real numbers will become a real problem even if every family had only two children. India has not, like China, used law to punish families with more than one child. Politicians were probably realistic enough to see that this would not work, not the least because India has a sub-stantial Muslim minority.

Hindus may not now be obsessed with fertility, but they continue to place much emphasis on having at least one son. Social and medical con-ditions have changed and it is sufficient to have only a few births to secure continuation of the family. Especially in the middle classes, having two or three children has become the norm. While there are some ethical problems connected with the prevention of unwanted pregnancies (see A.5.c), it is sometimes difficult to convince men of the advantages of birth control because of fears that women will abuse their new 'freedom from fear'. A major problem now is clearly education of the lower classes who, often out of pure ignorance, continue to produce more children than they want. The government is reasonably active in promoting birth control and has, on the whole, been quite successful in getting the message across to the people. Sterilisation for either spouse appears to be growing in popularity, but as we saw in A.5.c, new forms of termination of pregnancy have also de-veloped.

A.9.c. Planet Earth and Ecology

The realisation that the earth (*prithivī*, 'the wide or extended one', sometimes *bhūmi*, the actual world that we live in) is a limited resource is not documented in the Hindu scriptures. Stutley and Stutley (1977: 234) refer to one instance in the epics when the earth declares that she cannot bear so many people. However, this is not evidence of ecological problems, as the episode is clearly used to explain why there is death on earth.

The primeval importance of heaven and earth is not denied in Hinduism, but neither is it elaborated in worship. In a *smriti* version of the Vedic creation myths (Manusmriti 1.13) the male *purusha* (see A.7.a) is divided by the creator into two halves, heaven and earth, also representing male and female. But there are other creation myths in which *prithivī* plays no role. Some of the Vedic gods, sometimes seen as children of Mother Earth and the sky, became more important in worship than their parents. There is only one short, insignificant hymn to Prithivī in Rigveda 5.84. In the context of Vishnu worship, Prithivī appears more often. Some Purana texts see her originate from Vishnū and liken her to a lotus leaf.

Mother Earth is connected with fertility, but the connection with a more prominent Hindu symbol of abundance and fertility, the cow, is spurious. Sita, Rama's wife in the epic Ramayana, appeared from a furrow and is linked to the earth. She also appeals to the earth when Rama doubts her chastity (Ramayana 6.118). The ruler, Manusmriti 9.303 says, should emulate the actions of the earth, and verse 9.311 explains that because the earth supports all equally, the ruler should support all his subjects. The earth may be revered in certain situations, i.e. when a dancer does *namaskāram* to her and asks her for forgiveness in the beginning of the dance for trampling on her. One may see this as evidence of latent ecological consciousness among Hindus. The Arthashāstra is not only concerned with efficient agriculture and advises on the exploitation of forest produce for the benefit of the city, but also shows evidence of concern for the environment and the need for environmental protection.

Modern India does have severe environmental problems, both as a result of industrial exploitation and disasters such as the Bhopal gas leak, but also because of increased pressure on the environment of a growing population. Development of environmental consciousness seems to be more advanced among certain groups of Western people than among Hindus. A study on alternative development and 'the welfare of all' (*sarvodaya*) points out that voluntary simplicity in the face of hunger and need is much more difficult to achieve in India than in an affluent society (Kantowsky 1980: 162). *Sarvodaya* in the East must try to satisfy basic needs, while simplicity in the West simply has to resist the temptations of affluence.

Whether elements of Hindu philosophy can provide the basis for environmental ethics has been discussed in detail in a number of recent works. Crawford (1982: 149 f.) finds that a reverence for nature needs to be developed, that people must see themselves not as separate from nature, but as an integral part of it. This biocentric view, leading to a more fully developed ecological consciousness, is present in the basic Hindu concepts. However, it will not save India from grave environmental disorders unless more effective official steps are taken to protect the environment. More recently, the Indian higher judiciary has taken a lead in developing a uniquely Indian environmental jurisprudence which is fed by Hindu notions of an overriding order to which all life forms are subject. Thus, basic Hindu concepts continue to influence not only the way in which India develops, but also contribute to the discussion of many important issues in the world.

GLOSSARY

Ahimsā	Non-violence
Artha	Attainment of riches and power. One of the four goals of life
Āshrama	Stage of life
Ātman	Essence of life; individual self
Avatāra	Incarnation, or down-coming of God, for example Rama and Krishna
Bhakti	Loving devotion to a deity
Brahmacārin or Brahmacārī	Student or pupil in the first stage of life
Brahmacarya	The first stage of life; celibacy
Brahman	The all-pervading, self-existent power, trans-personal ultimate reality
Brahmin	Priest; member of the first caste
Danda	Stick, punishment
Dharma	Righteousness, duty, truth or teaching
Divālī	The Hindu festival of light
Grihastha	Householder, man in the second stage of life
Guru	Teacher; spiritual guide
Jāti	Caste (really sub-caste)
Kaliyuga	The world era of greatest moral deterioration
Kāma	Sensual gratification or pleasure. One of the four goals of life
Karma	Action, activity. The law of karma teaches that what you sow, you will reap
Kshatriya	Member of the second varna or caste, warrior
Mantra	Ritual verse or word
Manusmriti	Laws or Dharmashāstra of Manu
Mleccha	Non-Hindu; foreigner
Moksha	Liberation, being free from the round of rebirth, *samsara*

Namaskāram or Namaste	The Hindu greeting, spoken with folded palms
Pāpa	Sin; crime
Prāyashcitta	Penance
Purushārtha	The four aims of life
Rāja	King
Rājadharma	The ruler's set of rights and duties
Rita or rta	Eternal law, cosmic order
Samnyāsī or Samnyāsin	Man in the fourth stage of life; ascetic
Samsāra	Cycle of rebirth
Samskāra	Sacrament, ritual marking a rite of passage
Satya	Truth
Shrāddha	Expiatory rituals, especially for ancestors
Shruti	'What was heard', revealed truth or knowledge
Shūdra	Member of the fourth *varna* or caste
Smriti	'Remembered' knowledge
Svadharma	The individual's *dharma*
Vaishya	Member of the third caste or varna
Vānaprastha	Man in the third stage of the four stages of life
Varna	'Colour', caste
Varnāshramadharma	The system of individual duties according to one's caste and stage of life
Veda	Knowledge
Vyavahāra	Litigation, legal business

REFERENCES

Texts

Bühler, G., *The Laws of Manu* (Manusmriti), Motilal Banarsidass, 1975.

Doniger, W., *The Laws of Manu* (Manusmriti), Penguin, 1991.

Dutta, M. N., *The Dharam Shastra: Hindu Religious Codes*, vols I–VI, Cosmo Reprint, 1978. This includes the *smriti* literature other than the Manusmriti mentioned in the text.

Ganguli, K. M., *The Mahabharata*, vols 1–12, Munshiram Manoharlal, 1989.

Griffith, R. T. H., *The Hymns of the Rig Veda*, vols I–II, Chowkhamba Sanskrit Series, 1971.

Kangle, R. P., *The Kautilīya Arthashastra: Part III – A Study*, University of Bombay, 1965.

Limaye, V. P. and R. D. Vadekar (eds), *Eighteen Principal Upanishads*, Vaidika Samsodhana Mandala, 1958.

Radhakrishnan, S., *The Bhagavad Gita*, Allen & Unwin, 1960.

Shastri, H. P., *The Ramayana of Valmiki*, vols I–III, Shantisadan, 1962.

General

Altekar, A. S., *The Position of Women in Hindu Civilisation*, Motilal Banarsidass, 1962.

Balse, M., *The Indian Female*, Chetana, 1976.

Banerjee, S. C., *Crime and Sex in Ancient India*, Naya Prakash, 1980.

Barnouw, E. and S. Krishnaswamy, *Indian Film* (2nd edn), Oxford University Press, 1980.

Bhatia, H. S., *International Law and Practice in Ancient India*, Deep & Deep, 1977.

Coward, H. G., J. J. Lipner and K. K. Young, *Hindu Ethics*, SUNY, 1989.

Crawford, S. C., *The Evolution of Hindu Ethical Ideals*, University Press of Hawaii, 1982.

Day, T. P., *The Conception of Punishment in Early Indian Literature*, Wilfrid Laurier University Press, 1982.

Derrett, J. M. D., *Religion, Law and the State in India*, Faber & Faber, 1968.

Dumont, L., *Homo Hierarchicus*, Paladin, 1972.

Dwivedi, O. and B. N. Tiwari, *Environmental Crisis and Hindu Religion*, Gitanjali Publishing House, 1987.

Gandhi, M. K., *The Story of My Experiments with Truth*, Navajivan, 1927.

Gopalan, S., *Hindu Social Philosophy*, Wiley Eastern Ltd, 1977.

Jackson, R. and D. Killingley, *Moral Issues in the Hindu Tradition*, Trentham, 1991.

Jackson, R. and E. Nesbitt, *Hindu Children in Britain*, Trentham, 1993.

Jhingran, S., *Aspects of Hindu Morality*, Motilal Banarsidass, 1989.

Kantowsky, D., *Sarvodaya: The Other Development*, Vikas, 1980.

Lele, J. R. and T. Kanitkar, *Fertility and Family Planning in Greater Bombay*, Popular Prakashan, 1980.

Leslie, J. (ed.), *Roles and Rituals for Hindu Women*, Pinter, 1991.

Mehta, R., *Divorced Hindu Women*, Vikas, 1975.

Menski, W. F., 'Marital Expectations as Dramatised in Hindu Marriage Rituals', in Leslie, 1991, pp. 47–67.

Prime, R., *Hinduism and Ecology*, Cassell, 1992.

Ross, A. D., *The Hindu Family in an Urban Setting*, Oxford University Press, 1973.

Stutley, M. and J. Stutley, *A Dictionary of Hinduism*, Routledge & Kegan Paul, 1977.

USEFUL ADDRESSES

UK

Bharatiya Vidya Bhavan, 4a Castletown Road, West Kensington, London W14 9HQ.

HINDUISM

International Society for Krishna Consciousness (ISKCON), Educational Services UK, Bhaktivedanta Manor, Letchmore Heath, Watford WD2 8DP.

Maharashtra Mandal London, 30 Penney Close, Dartford, Kent DA1 2NE.

National Council of Hindu Temples (UK), Sri Sanatan Mandir, Weymouth Street, Leicester LE4 6FP.

North America

Canadian Council of Hindus, 5 Winterset Crescent, Etobicoke, Ontario, Canada M9R 4AU.

International Society for Krishna Consciousness (ISKCON) USA, 1030 Grand Avenue, San Diego, California 92109, USA.

Vishwa Hindu Parishad of America, 43 Valley Road, Needham, Massachusetts 02192, USA.

B. BUDDHISM

Peggy Morgan

B.1. RELIGIOUS IDENTITY AND AUTHORITY

B.1.a. On Being a Buddhist

Every Buddhist takes full responsibility for his or her deeds, words and thoughts, or to use a Buddhist phrase 'body, speech and mind'. What is important is the intention that motivates any of these, and it is this intention which bears spiritual fruit (Dhammapada vv. 1–2).

> If a man speaks or acts with an evil thought, sorrow follows him even as a wheel follows the foot of the drawer ...
> If a man speaks or acts with a pure thought, happiness follows him, like a shadow that never leaves him. (Radhakrishnan 1950)

Buddhists believe that no intention is ever wasted, whether it is good or bad, seen or unseen by others. People are all at different stages of development with different potentials (see B.7.a). This is an important part of the doctrine of *karma*, which teaches that 'what you sow you shall reap', if not in this life then in future rebirths when the fruit of *karma* ripens. Gautama Buddha points out in the Anguttara Nikaya that it is mental volition that he calls *karma*. This does not mean that Buddhists are not keenly aware of the need for combined practical social action as well as good individual intention, especially in Western societies which expect religious groups to be socially involved. But the Buddhist feels it is of prime importance that statements on social issues and involvement in social causes arise from the right individual intention, and that people are not at the mercy of undue social pressure or under manipulation to behave in a certain way. Good mental attitudes, with the appropriate *karmic* effects, can be developed when people are prepared to undertake certain rules for training themselves. Gautama Buddha never issued commandments to people; for example he did not say 'do not steal', but he did say 'it is wise not to steal'. He encouraged his followers to adopt certain precepts which commit them to the training of body, speech and mind in various key areas. The basic programme of training consists of ten precepts which are listed below.

The Buddhist community consists of two main groups. There are householders who lead ordinary lay lives, get married, have children and work in all kinds of occupations. Then there are those who join the *sangha*, the order of monks and nuns (*bhikkhus* and *bhikkhunīs*), who do not marry and who depend on the householders for the places they live, their food and their clothing; giving in return the gift of teaching, *dharma*. The householders usually take five precepts (*panca-sīla*) which are:

1. I undertake the rule of training to refrain from harming any living things (see *ahimsā*).
2. I undertake the rule of training to refrain from taking what is not given.
3. I undertake the rule of training to refrain from a misuse of the senses.
4. I undertake the rule of training to refrain from wrong speech.
5. I undertake the rule of training to refrain from taking drugs or drinks which tend to cloud the mind.

On special days householders may take another three precepts or even the complete list of ten for a short, set time; for example a day, a weekend or a month. Precepts six to eight are:

6. I undertake the rule of training to refrain from taking food at an unseasonable time, i.e. after the midday meal.
7. I undertake the rule of training to refrain from dancing, singing, music and unseemly shows; from the use of garlands, perfumes, and unguents; and from things that tend to beautify and adorn (the person).
8. I undertake the rule of training to refrain from (using) high and luxurious seats (and beds).

When the list of precepts is extended to ten, number seven is divided in two, in which case six to ten read:

6. I undertake the rule of training to refrain from taking food at an unseasonable time, i.e. after the midday meal.
7. I undertake the rule of training to refrain from dancing, music, singing and unseemly shows.
8. I undertake the rule of training to refrain from the use of garlands, perfumes, unguents, and from things that tend to beautify and adorn (the person).
9. I undertake the rule of training to refrain from (using) high and luxurious seats (and beds).
10. I undertake the rule of training to refrain from accepting gold and silver.

Novice monks and nuns live by the rules of training in the ten precepts (*dasa-sila*) and full members of the *sangha* take on many other disciplines which include limiting their possessions to a few items such as robes, a razor and an almsbowl. All these vows and precepts can be 'taken' or 'given back' if the burden becomes too onerous for an individual. People do what they can for as long as they can.

When Buddhists commit themselves to very broad precepts such as refraining from wrong speech, they will obviously want to discuss with others and then decide individually what counts as wrong speech. In the Buddhist scriptures this is further defined as telling lies, slandering people, talking frivolously and saying harsh things. Any discussions about harming living things will take into account whether the harm is done intentionally, and also what counts as a living thing and whether some lives are more important than others. These are very important questions in the debates about euthanasia and contraception, and will recur in topics five and nine.

Buddhists will always listen to the ideas and advice of others, especially anyone who is considered wiser than they are, and including members of other religions (see B.7.b). The Buddhist way includes not only morality (*sila*) but also the practice of meditation (*samādhi*) and the development of wisdom (*prajnā*). Wisdom involves having the right view of the world, a view outlined in the four noble truths (see B.6.b). The last of these truths is the noble eightfold path, which expands the areas of morality, meditation and wisdom even further, starting with wisdom.

wisdom

Right understanding is the perception of the world as it really is, without delusions. This involves particularly understanding suffering, the law of cause and effect, and impermanence.

Right thought involves the purification of the mind and heart and the growth of thoughts of unselfishness and compassion, which will then be the roots of action.

morality

Right speech means the discipline of not lying, and not gossiping or talking in any way that will encourage malice and hatred.

Right action is usually expanded into the five precepts: avoid taking life, stealing, committing sexual misconduct, lying and taking stimulants and intoxicants.

Right livelihood is a worthwhile job or way of life, which avoids causing harm or injustice to other beings.

meditation

Right effort is the mental discipline which prevents evil arising, tries to stop evil that has arisen, and encourages what is good.

Right mindfulness involves total attention to the activities of the body, speech and mind.

Right concentration is the training of the mind in the stages of meditation.

It is thought that truly moral action is not possible without wisdom. Meditation is also interdependent with wisdom: 'From meditation springs wisdom; from the lack of meditation there is loss of wisdom' (Radhakrishnan 1950, v. 282).

The ideal way of proceeding and putting belief into action is a measured balance between looking at the scriptures which contain the traditions of the various forms of Buddhism, listening to the advice of wise people, being aware of one's own inner motives and testing theoretical teaching in one's own experience. Buddhists then act with full responsibility for the consequences of their decisions on their own and other people's lives. Gautama Buddha did not claim to have found something new and unique, he said he had found 'an ancient noble path'. Buddhists are tolerant of the paths in other world views, and the way in which they can be an expression of true values.

B.1.b. Authority

Buddhist communities have always had within them a democratic ideal. From the beginning it was said that the *sangha* would flourish only if it met together regularly and made its decisions 'in unity and concord'. It is essentially a decentralised institution based on local communities. Seniority of respect is given according to the number of years a person has been a monk or nun; social status outside the *sangha* is left behind on entry. The World Fellowship of Buddhists does not pronounce in general terms on moral issues, although there are some Buddhists who would like it to do so.

On the other hand, traditional attitudes found in the scriptures and figures of authority (see B.1.c) are always listened to and respected, and most Buddhists seek out the opinion of someone who is wiser than they on important matters. In the end, however, individuals are responsible for their actions and have no obligation to test tradition by their own experience. The Buddha is quoted as saying:

> Yes, it is proper that you have doubt, that you have perplexity ... Do not be led by reports, or tradition or hearsay. Be not led by the authority of religious texts, nor by mere logic and inference, nor by appearance, nor by delight in speculative opinion ... nor by the idea 'this is our teacher'. But, when you know for yourselves that certain things are unwholesome and wrong, and bad, then give them up ... and when you know for yourselves that certain things are wholesome and good, then accept them and follow them. (Rahula 1959: 2–3)

B.1.c. Authority Figures in the Faith

Each Buddhist community, whether it is a village in Sri Lanka, Burma or Thailand or a *dharma* centre in the West, has a special relationship with a *dharma* teacher who in the majority of cases is a member of the *sangha* and may be the abbot of a monastery. All members of the *sangha* are honoured for the way of life symbolised by their saffron robes. However, not all members of the *sangha* are teachers and some teachers, especially in the Tibetan tradition, are not monks or nuns.

These figures have authority only in so far as those who go to them find their teachings helpful and true to experience (see B.1.b), and in so far as their own way of life has moral and spiritual integrity. Once there is a bond of confidence between a teacher and a spiritual pupil (see B.2.b) the pupil will be guided by the teacher's advice.

There is certainly no equivalent to the Pope in Buddhism, and statements made by figures such as the Dalai Lama have no automatic authority for other than their own school of Tibetan Buddhists, and even then only as subjected to the test of authority outlined in B.1.b. Ordinary Buddhists, however, would be considered foolish if they were not prepared to listen to people who are thought to be wise, and the authority of wisdom is likely to be found in those who have donned the saffron robe and devoted themselves to long years of study and practice. This still has to be tested out in one's own experience, however.

B.1.d. Duties of Leaders

The most developed model of leadership in Buddhism is that of the *dharma-rāja* or righteous king. The ideas involved in this model, however, can be adjusted to other forms of leadership and linked with the pattern of democracy, freedom and egalitarianism that is at work in the organisation of the *sangha*. 'Of course the term "king" should be replaced today by the term "government". "The Ten Duties of the King", therefore, apply today to the head of state, ministers, political leaders, legislative and administration officers, etc' (Rahula 1959: 84–5).

In the end, Buddhists believe it is good men and women who make good social systems, and the effect works from the top downwards.

> When kings are righteous, the ministers of kings are righteous. When ministers are righteous, householders also are righteous, the townsfolk and villagers are righteous ... The crops ripen in due season and men who live on these crops are long-lived, well-favoured, strong and free from sickness. (quoted in Anon., *Working Paper on a Buddhist Perception of a Desirable Society* 1985)

The ten duties of a king or government, as they are given in the Pali Canon, are as follows:

1. Generosity for the benefit of the people (see B.4.d).
2. A high moral character which observes the five precepts (see B.1.a).
3. Being prepared to give up all personal comfort and glory and even one's own life in the interests of the people.
4. General honesty, which means not being open to threats or bribes or deceiving people.
5. Having a kind and gentle attitude.
6. Ability to lead a simple life free from self-indulgence, and exercising great self-control.
7. Must be free from hatred towards anyone and not bear grudges.
8. Should try to promote peace by avoiding and preventing war and generally try to avoid violence and the destruction of life.
9. Ability to be patient, tolerant and understanding.
10. Should not oppose the will of the people but should rule in harmony with them.

Buddhists believe that these ideals were lived out by Ashoka, the great Indian Emperor who lived in the third century BCE. Here is an extract from one of his edicts: 'All men are my children. Just as I seek the welfare and happiness of my own children in this world and the next birth, I seek the same things for all men' (Morgan 1986: 24). In this century, the Burmese politician U Nu strongly linked Buddhism with the obligations of the ruling powers:

> Politics … has no other purpose than to protect the people from danger, to guard democratic rights, to give economic security to all, to wipe out malnutrition and disease, to banish ignorance, to develop human character, and to prevent wars. Religion should therefore be the guide. (King 1964: 264)

So Buddhists have the confidence that it is possible to rule without hurting anyone or causing grief, but through righteousness.

B.1.e. Duties of Subjects

There is far more material in Buddhism on the duties of rulers to their subjects than on the duties of subjects to their rulers. All the precepts and attitudes of Buddhists (see B.1.a and B.2.a) make them good citizens who respect the functions of rulers, as they respect all other roles and the human beings who fulfil them. If the individual relationships of children and parents, husbands and wives (B.3.b), teachers and pupils, friends (B.2.b) and employers with employed (see B.4.b) are functioning properly, then householders are playing their part correctly. The good of society depends on the individual worth of its citizens, and the goodness of society is but the sum of the goodness of its component individuals. No abstraction called 'country' or 'society' claims more loyalty than any individual being (see B.8.a): 'It is most worthy of notice that obedience does not occur in Buddhist ethics ... it does not occur in any of the clauses of the ethics of the Buddhist layman and it does not enter into any one of the divisions of the Eightfold Path' (Rhys Davids 1965: 181–2).

B.2. PERSONAL AND PRIVATE?

B.2.a. Personal Qualities

One of the most important qualities for Buddhists to develop is an alertness to, or awareness of, what is going on in their own minds and hearts, in their relationships with others and in the world in general. This means that Buddhists try to be mindful, not heedless. It is important for them to think and act as selfless people, those for whom the barriers between themselves and others, themselves and the world have disappeared. The disappearance of egoism and selfishness means that they are as concerned about others as about themselves (see also B.7.a).

Ideal personal qualities are summed up in the lists of six or ten perfections (*pāramitās*). The longer list of ten contains the following qualities:

1. *generosity (dāna)* – giving freely
2. *morality (sīla)* – acting virtuously
3. *renunciation* – letting go of anything that is unnecessary or harmful to the spiritual life
4. *wisdom (panna/prajnā)* – acting wisely
5. *energy* – acting vigorously in important things
6. *patience* – accepting life and people
7. *truthfulness* – being honest
8. *resolution* – applying oneself with determination to the important things in life
9. *loving kindness (metta)* – being kind and compassionate to all beings
10. *equanimity* – being stable, well-balanced and even-tempered, whatever happens.

Overlapping this list of perfections are four ideal states of mind that a Buddhist tries to develop. These are called the *brahma-viharas* and are loving kindness, compassion, sympathetic joy and equanimity. Together they form a basis for all good relationships. These qualities all overlap with the attitudes and path already described in B.1.a.

The following passage presents a general picture of the personal qualities of which Buddhists approve:

> The person who is kindly, who makes friends, makes welcome, is free from avarice, is understanding, is a conciliator, such a one obtains good

repute. Generosity, kindly speech, doing good to people, fairness in all things, everywhere, as is fit and proper, these are indeed the means on which the world turns, just as a chariot moves on quickly depending on the pin of a wheel axle. (Carpenter 1960: v. 192)

B.2.b. Friendship

Making friends and friendliness are natural results of the breaking-down of barriers between oneself and others, mentioned in the previous section (see also B.7.a). The interlinking of good states of mind can be seen from the fact that *metta*, translated in B.2.a as loving kindness, is sometimes translated as friendliness. Any relationship which exploits another person and involves taking what is not given (see precepts in B.1.a) is not true friendship. Friendliness extends towards all living things and not just people, for example towards a tree that has sheltered one from the rain or sun (see B.9.c).

Choice of friends is very important, because people tend to grow like those with whom they mix. Buddhists say that a wise enemy might do you less harm than a foolish friend. It can take time to know people and first impressions are sometimes misleading, so real friendship cannot be rushed. Friendship brings certain responsibilities, such as keeping promises, not listening to gossip about friends, staying with them through success and failure, happiness and unhappiness, and being sympathetic but never flattering them in a hollow way. It is possible to walk through life without meeting anyone who is an appropriate friend. In this case, Buddhists advise in verses 328–30 of the Dhammapada:

> And if, in walking, you do not meet a companion who might be suitable for you, continue resolutely your solitary walk. A fool is not company. The solitary walk is more worthwhile, a fool is no companion. Walk alone and do not do evil, having few desires, like an elephant in the forest. (Saddhatissa 1970: 140–1)

As well as ordinary friendships between equals, Buddhists talk about a special kind of friend called a *kalyana-mitta* or spiritual friend. These are often, but not always, monks or meditation teachers. The qualities of such friends are their own confidence and stability in the religious path they have chosen, their fundamentally moral character, their learning, their capacity to give and their wisdom in working for another person's well-being. They will then be able to help others question, practise and grow in religion under their guidance. Buddhists count themselves very lucky if they have such a friend.

B.2.c. Sex before Marriage

The kinds of friendships mentioned in B.2.b might be formed between members of the same or the opposite sex, but they do not involve sexual relationships. Falling in love can, of course, include all the qualities of good friendship mentioned in the first part of B.2.b, but also extends to sexual attraction and may lead to marriage.

In sexual as in all other relationships, Buddhists emphasise the intention behind words or deeds. Lying to another person about whether you love them, whether you want to marry them or whether you have had or are having sexual relationships with anyone else is expressly seen as wrong for anyone who has taken the precept to abstain from wrong speech (see B.1.a). Other precepts also have a bearing on sexual relationships, both before and after marriage. For example, the first precept raises the question of harm that may be caused, either to the other partner or to a child that might be conceived (see B.9.b). The harm done may be either physical or psychological. Precept two alerts everyone to the problems involved in taking what is not given. This does not indict only extreme behaviour such as rape, but also persuasion to sexual activity when the other person is unsure or unwilling. The third precept covers misuse of the senses to stimulate sexual desire, thus leading to un-mindful sexual activity. People can lose control of their emotions as a result of certain kinds of music, exotic perfumes, stimulating clothing or the general atmosphere at certain kinds of parties. Unwise sexual activity can also follow the taking of drink and drugs (see B.4.e) which are mentioned in the fifth precept.

For a Buddhist it is always unwise not to be totally aware of what you are doing and of its full implications. Birth control and the availability of abor-tions (see B.5.c) might help to avoid responsibility for the consequences of sexual activity, but they bring with them a larger responsibility for the harm-ing of life (see also B.9.b).

B.2.d. Homosexuality

Homosexual and lesbian relationships may be seen as unwise or unnatural for traditional Buddhism which identified only two types of sexuality; that of celibate monks and nuns and that of married householders engaged in hetero-sexual family life. Homosexual activity would seem to most Buddhists to break the third precept (see B.1.a) for either of these groups. Buddhists certainly see any uncontrolled desire as potentially destructive and un-wholesome (see B.6.b) and Buddhism has always taught that self-control and chastity, whatever one's sexual inclinations, are a high and wholesome path. In the monastic communities sexual misconduct is a cause for expulsion from the order.

Buddhists do, however, acknowledge that people are affected by the social conventions and dominant ethos of their century and country of origin. They accept that on issues such as homosexuality and lesbianism, opinions of what is right and wrong, permissible and forbidden, may change. They believe that 'right action' has to be worked out in whatever time, place and situation people find themselves, and that there are no moral absolutes which say that any particular action or type of relationship is always wrong or always right. Much depends not only on traditional guidelines but on the intention of those involved. Account has to be taken of individual people and the way they have been moulded by their social contexts.

B.3. MARRIAGE AND THE FAMILY

B.3.a. The Meaning of Marriage

To marry is to enter into the life of a householder with its own ethical bases and status (see B.1.a). Householders are highly respected and without them the *sangha* could not exist, but Theravada Buddhism emphasises how difficult it is to concentrate on spiritual matters when you have to earn a living, pay the mortgage, attend to the needs of partners and children, mend the drains, etc. Mahayana Buddhists are far more optimistic about the possibility of a householder attaining *Nirvāna*, and there is a famous illustration of this in the sutra about Vimalakirti.

There is no specifically religious marriage ceremony in traditional Buddhist cultures, although members of the *sangha* are usually asked to chant special texts of blessing after the legal state ceremony. Buddhists are bound by the marriage laws of the country in which they live. In the West, Buddhists are experimenting with forms of marriage blessings which link their faith with this important step in life. At the time of writing one Buddhist centre in Britain, Samye Ling in Dumfries, has been fulfilling the civil as well as the religious side of marriage on its premises. Here are quotations from two possible religious ceremonies. The first from the centre itself emphasises that marriage is a joyful state:

> May there ever be goodness, reknown, great riches and all life's necessities in their finest of forms: great joy, bliss and happiness, strength, good influence and the very best material life which is enduring, free of sickness and wherein all one's wishes are fulfilled. (Samye Ling 1984)

The second example from the Buddhist Society conveys a sense of sharing life and common ideals:

> Therefore let your love for one another be as the love between two pilgrims on the self-same way, sharing alike your joys and sorrows and the thousand incidents that form the day, in all things sympathetic, helpful, courteous to one another, caring only for each other's welfare and the common good.

It is not a religious custom for Buddhists to arrange marriages for their children, but it did happen in India where Buddhism began (see B.3.b), and it has stayed the social custom in some Buddhist countries, where it is seen as a dimension of parental care. Polygamy has also been practised by Buddhists when this was the social custom in a particular society.

Almost all the personal qualities and precepts of Buddhism outlined in B.1.a and B.2.a have direct bearing on the very close relationship which marriage involves. Loving kindness and compassion and mindfulness of the relationship are important at all times. The third precept (see B.1.a) is translated by many Buddhists as an undertaking not to commit adultery. Exploitation of a partner and hurting them by unfaithfulness are in disharmony with the intentions of the marriage bond. As long as the intentions are good, Buddhists accept the married state as a wholesome one for those who do not wish to be celibate monks and nuns. People are at different stages of growth, and there is an appropriate role for everyone.

B.3.b. Family Relationships

Husbands and wives both live under the same five householders' precepts, and aspire to the same perfections (see B.1.a and B.2.a). There should always be mutual respect and consideration between them. In the Pali Canon, Gautama Buddha outlined five ways in which a husband should treat his wife in his advice to Sigala (Rhys Davids 1965: 181–2):

1. being courteous to her
2. not despising her
3. being faithful to her
4. handing over authority to her
5. providing her with not only necessary clothing, but extra adornments too.

The wife in return:

1. orders the household well
2. is hospitable
3. is faithful
4. takes care of the family wealth
5. works hard.

Buddhism gives a very important position to mothers and the love mothers give their children. The Metta Sutta says of the ideal of loving kindness: 'Just as a mother would protect her only child even at the risk of her own life, even so let one cultivate a boundless heart towards all beings' (Rahula 1959).

In the Tibetan Buddhist tradition, teachers encourage their pupils to think of all beings as if they were their mothers and to vow to help them towards *Nirvāna*, as the following words at the Manjushin Institute, Cumbria, show:

These sentient beings are all my mothers. I contemplate again and again how they have cherished me with kindness. I request ... that I may soon give birth to the spontaneous great compassion, like a mother's compassion for her dearest child.

The role of the father is also seen to be a very caring one and the Lotus Sutra has two moving parables about a father's love for his children. In one the father uses great skill to rescue his children from a burning house. In the other the father takes off his fine clothes and dresses as a servant in order to approach, talk to and help a son who has lost all his self-respect and is glad to be given the job of clearing out the dung.

As well as those ideals, Buddhists would claim a very practical attitude to family relationships: 'at the moment I think it is important to establish peace and harmony in the world and in the family: it's in the family and among your friends that it's important' (quoted in Bowker 1983: 184).

Families should support each other emotionally. A family that is close and sticks together is like a forest of trees which can withstand the force of the wind, when a solitary tree would bend and break: 'Supporting one's father and mother, cherishing wife and children, peaceful occupations – this is the highest blessing' (Mangala Sutta, in Rahula 1959: 98–9).

In the Pali Canon the practical obligations of parents towards children are to restrain them from vice, encourage them to be virtuous, give them training in a profession (see B.4.b), arrange a suitable marriage for them (see B.3.a) and in due course give them their inheritance. In return children should respect their parents, support them when necessary, take over some of their duties when they become too heavy, respect the laws of inheritance and follow the correct rites when they are dead.

Buddhists, of course, realise that this general picture has to be adapted to different cultural conditions while the general principles of respect, courtesy, care and support are maintained. They would also emphasise that family love and responsibilities must always leave room for spiritual growth. Here, freedom is an important quality. Each individual needs enough emotional space to grow. Love is freeing, not imprisoning. So children may need to leave home, and even married couples may need to separate or divorce, painful though that is.

B.3.c. Marriage Breakdown

For a Buddhist, making a vow is a serious matter, whether it is done within a civil or religious ceremony. Since marriage involves the exchange of promises between two people, any breakdown of the relationship and the harm that this brings is to be avoided wherever possible. Stability in society is important for the happiness of everyone, and the family unit is seen as the core of this stability.

On the other hand Buddhists are realistic about the fact that people, circumstances and relationships are constantly changing and that in some instances people ask to be released from their vows. This is accepted if it seems the best course of action for all concerned. It must be borne in mind that the morality of any action for a Buddhist is based on the intention with which it is performed (see B.1.a). Selfishness is always discouraged and loving kindness is always better than hatred; but there is nothing in itself wicked or unforgivable about the breakdown of a marriage. Painful situations are often good teachers and can take people on to a deeper spiritual growth and insight. The important thing is that mistakes are faced and lessons learned from them.

B.4. INFLUENCES ON AND USE OF TIME AND MONEY

B.4.a. Education

Ignorance (*avijjā/avidyā*) is a basic evil in Buddhism and is portrayed twice in the wheel of life, as a blind man with a stick and as a pig. Another word for ignorance is delusion, or even illusion. This involves not knowing the truth about the way things are. The opposite of being ignorant is not being clever or knowing a lot, but being wise. Wisdom (*panna/prajna*) is the climax of the eightfold path (see B.1.a) and the perfections (*pāramitās*) (see B.2.a). It is the goal of all truly Buddhist education.

Before the state established schools in Buddhist countries, the monasteries provided children with the basics of reading and writing, gave an understanding of traditional Buddhist languages and literature, and generally passed on the cultural heritage. Initiation into adulthood usually involved a period of education in a monastery. Monks and educated lay Buddhists continue to offer classes in Pali and Buddhism, generally side by side with state schooling, even in the West. There have always been Buddhist universities and many new ones have been established in the twentieth century. 'The goal is to prepare the students to relate Buddhist doctrine to the contemporary situation and to train them for effective service in society. For the most part the students have gone on to teach ... and to participate in various community projects' (Dumoulin and Maraldo 1976: 55).

There are three stages in education which Buddhists believe are important for the development of wisdom. First of all material has to be listened to and learned in a conventional, factual way. Then there needs to be some consideration, study and discussion of its meaning, relevance and implications. The last stage is making the material one's own, integrating it into one's life, realising it and acting upon it. So wisdom is practical. In the end it is crucially what you do and are, not just what you know. 'A man is not learned simply because he talks much. He who is tranquil, free of hatred, free from fear, he is said to be learned' (Radhakrishnan 1950: v. 258).

Two further points are important to Buddhists. The word *citta* can be translated as mind or heart, and Buddhists try to educate the feeling as well as the thinking side of a person. There is also in Buddhism a remarkable sense of 'testing things out in one's own experience', which is very compatible with Western educational methods and scientific enquiry.

Two modern Buddhist comments on education spell out what is demanded. 'Since critical reflection is an important part of human potential, and essential for spiritual growth, we endorse the broadest possible expression of literacy and educational opportunity' (World Fellowship of Buddhists 1984: section 3.6). The importance of this critical faculty cannot be overstated since it is only by developing it that the young may be protected from a dangerous kind of conditioning.

> The education that is needed for the present time is one that can wash away from the innocent minds of the young generation all the dogmatic knowledge that has been forced upon them with the purpose of turning them into mere tools of various ideologies and parties. Such a system of education will not only liberate us from the prison of dogma but will also teach us understanding, love and trust. These qualities – understanding, love and trust – are the prescriptions needed for the revival of our society that has been paralysed by suspicion, intrigue, hatred and frustration. (Thich Nhat Hanh 1967: 57)

B.4.b. Work

The fifth stage of the noble eightfold path (see B.1.a) is right, correct or proper livelihood or vocation. The way one earns one's living is important to Buddhists and any jobs which involve going against precepts such as not harming, not taking what is not given and not making false statements are thought to be inappropriate or wrong (see B.1.a).

The traditional Buddhists' list of bad occupations includes dealing in arms, buying and selling slaves or any other living beings, buying and selling meat, and anything that involves alcoholic drinks, drugs and poisons except medicinally (B.4.e). This list can be linked with the seventh and eighth stages of the path which encourage both right effort and being mindful or alert whatever you are doing: 'he who does not get up when it is time to get up, who, though young and strong, is full of sloth, who is weak in resolution and thought, that lazy and idle man will not find the way of wisdom' (Radhakrishnan 1950: v. 280). The Buddha is said to have recommended that a person be: 'skilled, efficient, earnest and energetic in whatever profession he is engaged and that he should know it well' (Rahula 1959: 82).

One modern British Buddhist group, the Friends of the Western Buddhist Order, organise 'Right Livelihood Co-operatives' which seek to put into practice Buddhist ideals in relation to work. You do not have to be a Buddhist to join one, though you do have to agree with its aims. They are very varied and include building, painting and decorating, whole-food shops, secondhand shops, restaurants, photosetting and printing and arts and crafts. They are democratically organised and aim to fulfil the following:

> Right livelihood should involve no alienation. Work should be an integral part of a complete lifetype which, taken as a whole, fulfils all the needs of the developing individual. Work should never become so dominant in a person's life or be so boring and unpleasant that it can only be done for the sake of rewards. No more should it be necessary to compensate for the frustration and dullness of work with periods of indulgence ... Work and play, effort and relaxation, should be so balanced that the individual is always bright and alert, alive and joyful. The co-operative team must, then, consider the human and spiritual needs of each of its members, allowing sufficient material support, time for other activities ... and whatever personal help and encouragement each may need. (Subhuti 1983: 160)

Ernst Schumacher, the famous twentieth-century economist, was profoundly affected by Buddhist attitudes and wrote:

> The Buddhist point of view takes the function of work to be at least threefold; to give a man a chance to utilise and develop his faculties; to enable him to overcome his ego-centredness by joining with other people in a common task; and to bring forth the goods and services needed for a becoming existence. (Schumacher 1974: 45)

Lack of work often brings both poverty and despair which can only be detrimental to society (see B.4.a and B.9.a).

In Theravada Buddhism, monks and nuns are freed from the need to provide their own food, clothing and shelter in order to concentrate on meditation, which many of them refer to as their 'work'. In Zen monasteries and amongst many ordinary lay Buddhists it is emphasised that any work situation can be used for the practice of mindfulness (sati-patthāna) which is the basis of all meditation.

B.4.c. Leisure and its Use

Leisure is important for a balanced human life. It is entirely up to the individual Buddhist what he or she does with leisure time, and the possibilities vary with different cultures and different circumstances. The important thing is that all the precepts and attitudes outlined in B.1.a are kept in mind.

This means it is unlikely that Buddhists will spend their time hunting, fishing or drinking to excess, for example. Many Buddhists spend leisure time at *dharma* centres and *vihāras* where they meet friends, offer food to monks and nuns, chat, drink tea, listen to talks, plan outings together, meditate, take classes, help with maintenance and organisation and generally involve themselves with the company and care of a group of people who share their attitudes towards life. There are certain arts such as *ikebana*, calligraphy, painting and *tai-chi* which have cultural links with Buddhism and people with a particular interest in them will find groups with whom they can share it. Nature, whether in landscapes or gardens, has important lessons to teach about change, rebirth and beauty, so it has always been of particular interest to Buddhists (see B.9.c).

Festival celebrations are usually planned for weekends so that Buddhists can be together for them, and it is not unusual to find Buddhists spending their annual holidays in country retreat centres or summer schools. Others may spend a Saturday or Sunday on a peace march, hospital visiting or helping the community generally. Although every Buddhist will give a slightly different answer if asked about leisure and its use, most will mention that the sheer peace of a *dharma* centre or a period of meditation is one of the best refreshments from the noisy, busy and fragmented world in which most of us live. Another contrast with this world that is often commented on is the sense of belonging to a caring community, of the warmth and friendship that is found in a Buddhist group. Many Buddhist families are moving house so that they can spend as much of their leisure time as possible with members of the *sangha*, and bring their children up in an environment with deep religious values.

B.4.d. Wealth

Buddhism is sometimes called a middle way between extremes. The Buddhist attitude to wealth is a good example of this. Every human being needs enough basic food, clothing and shelter to be free from anxiety. However, if people have too much wealth and too many possessions they can spend all their time preserving and guarding them, while being in a permanent state of anxiety in case they lose them. This attachment to wealth does not bring happiness. Equally, if people have no food, and inadequate clothing or homes, they will inevitably have different obsessions or may fall into despair. Either way, they cannot lead fully human lives (see B.5.b).

In the advice to a righteous ruler (see also B.1.d) it is said: 'Whoever in your kingdom is poor, to him let some help be given' (Cakkavatti Sihananda Sutta, quoted in Ling 1981: 117). The same text points out that extreme poverty breeds crimes such as theft, and that it is the state's responsibility to see that no one is forced to act desperately because they are poor (see B.5.b): 'Thus because provision was not made for the poor, poverty became widespread, and from this stealing increased, from the spread of stealing violence grew, and from the growth of violence the destruction of life became common' (ibid.: 121).

The way of life of both Buddhist householders and members of the *sangha* is ideally free of greed as well as obsessive self-denial, and in this way non-attachment can be said to be the aim of both. The right attitude to all material things is: 'Look upon the world as a bubble, look upon it as a mirage ... for the wise there is no attachment at all' (Radhakrishnan 1950: vv. 170–1).

Gautama Buddha was born as a prince in a wealthy environment which cushioned him against understanding suffering and death. He felt that he had to leave this way of life, to find out the truth about the way things are. After a period of fierce self-denial he found that a gentler way with a minimum of possessions, one main meal each day and a simple shelter were a better foun-dation for contentment and he embarked on a life of service teaching others the truths he had realised. He gave the householders who listened to him the gift of the *dhamma/dharma* (truth or teaching) and help with their practical and spiritual problems. He had no personal wealth, so in return the house-holders provided him with food, cloth for robes and somewhere to stay.

This pattern of interdependence still continues. Buddhist monks and nuns could not survive if householders did not have enough excess food and wealth to support them. The householders would not bother if they did not believe that the *dhamma/dharma* is the greatest treasure a person can receive. Monks and nuns are living examples of happiness attained by non-attachment to wealth: 'Let us live happily, then, we who possess nothing' (ibid.: v. 200).

Ordinary Buddhist householders hope that their hard-working and honest lives will bring health, wealth, long life and happiness to themselves and their families. For them, wealth is a perfectly proper goal in life. What is import-ant is that it is honestly earned with a right livelihood (see B.4.b) and that it is properly used. Hoarding money and miserliness are condemned, as is the irresponsible dissipation of wealth: 'And which are the six doors of dissipat-ing wealth? Drink; frequenting the streets at unseemly hours; haunting fairs; gambling; associating with evil friends; idleness' (Sigalovada Sutta, quoted in Rahula 1959: 120).

The proper use of wealth involves looking after family and friends, proper investment in business, and if there is any excess, giving it to charitable causes and to the support of the *sangha*. Generosity (*dāna*) is one of the most im-portant lay Buddhist virtues (see B.2.a). The capacity to give shows that one is not unhealthily attached to wealth and possessions, and there is no better focus of giving than *Buddha*, *Dharma* and *Sangha*, known in Buddhism as the three jewels (*triratna*). Such gifts bring great merit and the desire to give them

71

can be said to be an important factor in Buddhist society. 'A certain stimulus to economic effort is provided by the Buddhist's need to have a surplus of wealth to be used for religious purposes but Buddhist culture acts as a brake on the accumulation of wealth' (Ling 1980: 106).

A person needs to be wise to handle wealth properly. 'Riches destroy the foolish, not those who seek the beyond. By a craving for riches the foolish person destroys himself as he destroys others' (Radhakrishnan 1950: v. 355). On the other hand, with the right attitudes, the lives of householders are no different in quality from those of monks or nuns. 'He who though dressed in fine clothes fosters the serene mind, is calm, controlled; is established in the Buddhist way of life, is chaste, and has ceased to injure all other beings, he indeed is a bhikkhu' (ibid.: v. 142).

B.4.e. Drugs

The fifth precept, which is taken by Buddhists throughout their lives (see B.1.a) says: 'I undertake the rule of training to refrain from drugs or drinks which tend to cloud the mind'. Buddhists emphasise the need to be alert in body, speech and mind in order to live mindfully and meditate properly. A person with a clouded mind will not be able to make wise decisions and will not have a firm grasp of the truth about the way things are, and the consequences of his or her actions. The Sigalovada Sutta in the Pali Canon lists six dangers connected with being addicted to intoxicating liquors. They are actual loss of wealth, increase of quarrels, susceptibility to disease, loss of good character, indecent exposure and impaired intelligence.

This discouragement of drink and drugs does not include the use of medicines for anyone who is ill. These are permitted by Buddhists when properly administered by a doctor and used for the health and well-being of the patient (see B.5.b and B.5.d). What is not permitted is drug and alcohol abuse. These prevent people from engaging in the full realities of the world and impede their capacities for moral and intellectual decision-making. They therefore come under the heading of causing harm to oneself. Dealing in drugs, which are like poisons, is categorised as a wrong livelihood (see B.4.b) as it involves harming others. Spending money on drink and drugs is categorised as wrong use of or dissipating wealth (see quotation in B.4.d).

B.4.f. The Media

If newspapers, magazines, television and radio inform people truthfully about the world in which they live and help them to be alert and mindful both of other people and events, then Buddhists are enthusiastic about them. If, on the other hand, they are vehicles for propaganda, and arouse hatred and greed or generate illusions, then Buddhists are critical of them. Many romantic magazines and television series encourage people to admire materialistic and self-indulgent life-styles which involve sexual promiscuity, over-indulgence in food and drink, and exploiting others. This obviously goes against the whole ethos of right living for a Buddhist who would emphasise simplicity, self-control, generosity and kindliness (see B.1.a and B.2.a).

Since watching television, listening to the radio or reading newspapers and magazines are entirely voluntary and since there are a large number of programmes and publications to choose from, the important thing for a Buddhist is to educate people to be critical. People need to understand the effect the media can have on attitudes and behaviour, and then appraise the options and try to make the wisest choice for their own lives and those of the people around them. There is no reason why the life-style and values of any one culture should be seen as normative, and Buddhists completely support the freedom of the press. The question of the media is closely linked to that of advertising: 'Asian cultures today are swamped beneath the flood of Western entertainment, advertising and propaganda. Thus Buddhists particularly sympathise with efforts towards cultural self-determination and the democratisation of communications' (World Fellowship of Buddhists 1984: section 3.7).

B.4.g. Advertising

Buddhists greet the subject of advertising with various searching questions. Do advertisements tell the truth or do they mislead people and therefore come under the heading of wrong speech (see B.1.a)? Are they harming anyone? Is it wrong to persuade people to want more and buy more than they need, in a world in which so many people do not have even the necessities of life? Does this create the wrong kind of economy, based on egotism and consumerism? Is the advertiser's view of the world in which perfumes, clothes, cars, and so on bring success and happiness a true picture or misleading? Does advertising have the effect of making people heedless of other values?

Close examination and a mindful approach to what is happening when goods are advertised, along with the knowledge that the motivation of the advertiser is to make money, show that advertising goes against almost every precept and attitude Buddhists respect (see B.1.a and B.2.a). As in the case of the media, Buddhists encourage education and a critical independence of mind so that people are not exploited, or basic human dignity and choice are undermined (see B.6.e): 'The dignity of human beings should be more important than consumers' culture, which encourages people to have more, and eat more than they really need' (Anon., *Working Paper on a Buddhist Perception of a Desirable Society* 1985: 16).

73

B.5. The Quality and Value of Life

B.5.a. The Elderly

In traditional Buddhist societies, the elderly are respected for their wisdom and for the way they have worked and cared for the community and their families. The practical care of the elderly is usually the concern of the extended family in the Anguttara Nikaya, vol. 1, section 61–2: 'We may carry our mothers on one shoulder, and our fathers on the other, and attend to them even for a hundred years, doing them bodily services in every possible way … still the favour we have received from our parents will be far from requited' (Tachibana 1992: 222).

If age has brought with it not just grey hairs but wisdom, parents and grandparents are thought to have a considerable contribution to make, especially in time spent with young children, passing on society's traditions through oral history.

Buddhists from this kind of environment might well be shocked at the way the elderly are treated in the West. State care guarantees a minimum pension, but the lack of an extended family, the great sense of 'being busy', and social mobility in the working generation all mean that the elderly are often treated as useless and rather a nuisance. They may live alone or spend their final years in the rather impersonal care of institutions. This is obviously an area where great loving kindness and compassion (see B.2.a) are needed to find the right ways of helping people grow old with dignity and care. Buddhists are concerned to help in any way they can, as with all examples of people in need (see B.5.b).

There is a very distinctive way in which the elderly are important in Buddhist teaching. A lot can be learnt from their situation, for they demonstrate the impermanence (*anicca*) of life. It was when he saw old age, sickness and death that Gautama Buddha was motivated to search for the true meaning of life. The elderly are a living example of the fragility of life and the impermanence of so many of the things that seem to make it worth while and give us our identity: for example, work, physical fitness and the beauty of youth. When these are things of the past, as they are in old age, there is time to ask what is of enduring value.

B.5.b. Those in Need

The Buddhist greeting is 'may all beings be happy'. A central part of Buddhist teaching has always been the acknowledgement of suffering (*dukkha*) and the need for its alleviation (see B.7.b). Gautama Buddha sent monks and nuns out into the world out of compassion and for the blessing and happiness of people.

The four noble truths (see B.6.b) are presented as a doctor's diagnosis of the human condition as one of suffering, along with an analysis of its cause and a prescription for its cure. One common Buddhist image is that of the *Buddha* as the doctor, the *Dharma* as the medicine and the *Sangha* as the nurse who administers the medicine. All of humankind is in need, but the highest ideal of help goes further than simply trying to cure disease and poverty, however important that is (see B.4.a–d):

> It is true and important that disease and poverty will decrease with economic and political improvement. However, even if such anxieties cease altogether, this does not necessarily mean the eradication of all human suffering. For example, death is inescapable. Death is certain. It may come tomorrow. This fact makes us think fundamentally about human existence. (Tamura 1960: 20)

This is always held in mind, even while Buddhists are involved in national and international consultations on Buddhism and social action. There is need for good works and more. The *bodhisattvas*, who hear the suffering cries of the world, and have the skilful means to help wherever they can, hope in the end to take all beings with them, beyond suffering, to the deathless realm of *Nirvāna*. The monk doing his 'work' or meditation (see B.4.b) bears witness to this other dimension and offers his help. 'No harm or violence will issue from him. The peace and purity he radiates, will have conquering power and be a blessing to the world. He will be a positive factor in society, even if he lives in seclusion and silence' (Venerable Nyanaponika, quoted in King 1964: 154).

This ultimate perspective towards need, witnessed to by monks and nuns, does not negate practical social concern. Communities of monks and nuns act like family units. Gautama Buddha once reprimanded a group of monks for failing to take care of a sick brother, saying that now they had left their families who else would take care of them?

When it is necessary, the monasteries also open their doors to those in need and have traditionally provided the people with both medicine and schooling. This is a description of what happened in Burma during World War Two:

> Monks, disregarding their personal convenience and the minimum comforts they happened to enjoy, gave accommodation to the people who sought refuge with them, protected them from all kinds of outward dangers and difficulties even at the risk of their own lives and looked after them with care and concern. (U Aung Than, in King 1964: 200)

A central part of all Buddhist practice is the cultivation of a heart that is loving and compassionate towards all beings (see B.2.a). People who are loving and kind feel the sufferings of others as much as their own, and treat others with the kind of love a mother has towards her child (see B.3.b). Anyone on the way to enlightenment will nurture these hopes for their fellows:

> May the blind see forms,
> May the deaf hear sounds.

> May the naked find clothing,
> The hungry find food;
> May the thirsty find water
> And delicious drinks.

> May the poor find wealth,
> Those weak with sorrow find joy;
> May the forlorn find new hope,
> Constant happiness and prosperity.

> May the frightened cease to be afraid
> And those bound be freed;
> May the powerless find power,
> And may people think of benefitting one another.

(Shantideva in Batchelor tr. 1981: chapter XV, 18–22)

This love extends beyond the human realm to all beings. Buddhists believe that human life is interdependent with all other forms of life (see B.9.c). The ideal of loving kindness (*metta*), and compassion (*karunā*), when combined with generosity (*dāna*) (see B.2.a), puts a great deal of emphasis on helping others.

The most obvious needs that people have are for food, clothes and shelter (see B.4.d and B.9.a). There is also the need for love and education and finally that need mentioned earlier, for a higher goal in life and the fulfilment of one's spiritual nature. All over the world members of both the *sangha* and Buddhist householders are helping those whose need is greatest by founding and running schools, orphanages, refugee centres, hospitals and clinics for the victims of drug abuse. They are also to be found visiting those in prison and raising funds for the homeless. The Indian emperor Ashoka who lived in the third century BCE is a powerful Buddhist exemplar for lay people. He encouraged kindliness to the poor and distressed and made many practical contributions to the needs of the people: building dams, sinking wells, founding hospitals and schools and planting trees to shade travellers (see B.1.d). In the twentieth century, the Indian Buddhist leader Dr Ambedkar worked tirelessly to improve the situation for the untouchable castes, while the modern Japanese lay movement Rissho Kosei Kai runs daily group counselling sessions to help members with the practical problems of their lives. In these ways Buddhists make every effort to ensure that basic physical and emotional needs are fulfilled (see B.4.a–d).

Buddhists are happy that in the modern world there is a great deal of emphasis on improving the quality of life for groups such as the disabled, and the mentally and terminally ill. They believe that trends towards caring for people in the wider community rather than in institutions are healthy, as they help others to see the whole of life as involving sickness as well as health. Importantly, they also demonstrate that the mentally retarded are just as much a part of society as other people and, equally, have a contribution to make. The development of medicine has, however, brought in a whole new set of ethical problems concerned with organ transplants, the use of life-support machines, not to mention abortions (see B.5.c) and euthanasia (see B.5.d). Buddhists will always ask about the motives and intentions behind some of the new technological possibilities. What is claimed to help people in need, can, in fact, prolong suffering, and cultivate the attitude that death can and should be avoided wherever possible, and that disease is somehow a failure rather than being part of the very nature of the world.

B.5.c. Abortion

Buddhists believe that the being comes into existence at conception so abortion is certainly the taking of life which they are committed not to do. Taking life is thought to be morally harmful to those who make the decision. In Japan, people dedicate statues and make offerings to the *bodhisattva* Jizo-sana to alleviate their guilt in cases of abortion. 'Thus, while the practice of abortion is easily accepted in Japan on account of its practicality, that is, at least, its social practicality, there is a well organised mode of religious expression to cover the sense of responsibility which people naturally feel' (Goodacre 1983: 27).

There might, however, be some circumstances where the life of an embryo is taken in order to save the life of the mother (B.5.b). Buddhists would acknowledge that this kind of reasoning and action is full of difficulties, and that decisions can only be made reliably by very wise and compassionate people. Heedlessness to the implications of either contraception (see B.9.a) or abortion is very serious. Each individual case is taken on its merits and judged on the intention behind the actions of the people involved. If suicide or abortion is an expression of despair, hatred or selfishness then it will be seen to produce nothing but bad *karma*. If, however, the actions are rooted in selfless compassion for others, they cannot be seen as entirely wrong. There is still some karmic responsibility for the taking of life, but it is balanced by good intention. Buddhists take a very pragmatic view – based on each individual case and the general guidelines of what is wise behaviour – rather than thinking in terms of moral absolutes.

B.5.d. Euthanasia

One important issue connected with the care of the elderly (B.5.a), the terminally ill or the badly disabled is that of euthanasia. The Buddhist precepts (see B.1.a) include the vow not to harm any living thing. This means that involvement in euthanasia has to be thought about carefully in terms of both physical and spiritual harm done to oneself or to another. Harm involves not only the taking of physical life but putting people under psychological pressure, so that the elderly, for example, might become afraid of becoming a burden on their family or society in general. Another important factor for a Buddhist is the intention (see B.1.a) of anyone arguing for euthanasia. Is it an expression of compassion for a person who is suffering and wishes to die, or is it a way of avoiding responsibilities towards that person? These are important considerations in deciding whether euthanasia is morally acceptable or not, and each case may vary within the generally agreed ethical guidelines of doing no harm.

For a Buddhist, death, through euthanasia or suicide, can never be an escape from suffering because a person's karmic forces continue into another life. These forces are affected by the state of mind at death, amongst other things. Death for a Buddhist does not have the finality that it might have for many people wanting to 'end it all' by either suicide or euthanasia. The best way through life, suffering and death is seen to lie in an honest and truthful understanding of a situation and the capacity to live through it, with the help and support of others.

B.6. QUESTIONS OF RIGHT AND WRONG

B.6.a. The Purpose of Law

The Sanskrit word *dharma* (*dhamma* in Pali) is important for Hindus as well as Buddhists. It can be translated as law, truth, teaching or righteousness. At its highest the law represents the ideal, the ultimate truth about the way things are, and also the way this ideal should be put into practice. *Dharma* is also an individual's obligations, according to his or her position in society and stage of life. In this sense *dharma* is a way of life; another name for the teaching of the Buddha is the *Buddha dharma*. His first sermon is called 'the turning of the wheel of the law'.

This presents the idea of law as a positive, upholding force in society, not just a prohibitive, punitive power. Buddhists believe that a good ruler upholds law in the sense of the ultimate ideal of life. He or she, or even a government (see B.1.d), is called a *dharma-rāja*, king of righteousness. It was in this spirit that Ashoka drew up his edicts and appointed *dharma* ministers to read them to the people. As one extract puts it: 'Ashoka now teaches you to respect the value and sacredness of life, to abstain from killing animals and from cruelty to living things, kindliness in human relationships and respect for mother, fathers and elders, for the poor and the distressed and for slaves and servants' (Morgan 1986: 24).

Law can also try to maintain the value of non-harming by prohibiting murder, the value of not taking what is not given by punishing theft, and the value of not indulging in false speech by prosecuting perjurers. But there will always be some tension for Buddhists between such precepts and the laws of state, the former are undertaken voluntarily and their consequences are based on motive and operate karmically; the latter threaten punishment if rules are not obeyed (see B.6.c). For Buddhists the utilitarian statement of someone like Helvetius in *De l'Esprit* in 1758 will always represent a much lower view of the purpose of law than the ideals contained in the word *dharma*: 'The whole art of legislation consists in forcing men by the sentiment of self-love to be always just to others'. Not only is self-love an inappropriate motive for a Buddhist, but the idea that habituation can transform humanity is also alien. It is the mind and heart which need transformation: 'All things are the result of what we have thought, are chieftained by our thoughts, and are made up of our thoughts' (Radhakrishnan 1950: v. 1).

B.6.b. Human Nature

It has been explicitly stated that 'there is no "sin" in Buddhism, as sin is understood in some religions. The root of all evil is ignorance and false views' (Rahula 1959: 3).

Certainly if the concept of sin in other religions implies disobedience to or turning away from God, then sin does not exist in Buddhism because Buddhists' idea of Ultimate Reality is transpersonal and not one of a personal creator God, who asks obedience. For Buddhists the fundamental problem lies in ignorance (*avijjā*), false views and a lack of wisdom. These do not flaw human nature (as does original sin in Christianity) but only obscure the enlightened mind like clouds obscuring the moon.

Another basic idea in Buddhism is that of *tanhā*, which literally means 'thirst', but can be explained more clearly by the terms clinging, grasping, desire or even greed. Like ignorance (see B.4.a) this is one of the three root evils (*lobha*, greed; *dosa*, hatred; *avijjā/avidyā*, ignorance) which are pictured at the centre of the wheel of life as well as round its rim. *Tanhā* is also the second of the four noble truths and is said to be the cause of suffering (*dukkha*). We shall return later to the four noble truths and the centrality of *dukkha* in Buddhism.

Sinful or wrong acts in Buddhism are denoted by the word *pap*, which can be translated as what is evil, or a demerit. The opposite of a demerit is *punna*, that which is good or meritorious. Breaking the precepts one has undertaken, for example, is a demerit (see B.1.a). A demerit involves harm done to one's relationships with other people as well as the production of bad *karma* (see B.6.d). Another way of expressing this range of ideas is to talk about what is karmically unwholesome, or karmically wholesome. This is what brings either a bad or a good rebirth. The things which make unwholesome roots and which will produce bad shoots in the future are greed, hatred and delusion, the three root evils mentioned earlier. *Karma* is formed on the basis of deed, word and thought (see B.1.a) but thoughts and motives are particularly important: 'A man should hasten towards the good (*punna*), He should restrain his thoughts from evil (*pap*)' (Radhakrishnan 1950: v. 116). In the end, evil (*pap*) like desire (*tanhā*) produces suffering: 'If a man commits sin (*pap*) ... let him not set his heart on it. Sorrowful (*dukkha*) is the accumulation of evil conduct' (ibid.: v. 117).

The social anthropologist Melford Spiro focuses on suffering (*dukkha*) as the central idea in Buddhism: 'The primary concern of Buddhism is not with sin, but with suffering ... for Buddhism, in which suffering is the inevitable element of existence, salvation consists in salvation from suffering. The message of the Buddha is "suffering and release from suffering"' (Spiro 1982: 38–9).

The emphasis on suffering is present in the most basic Buddhist formula, the four noble truths. The Buddha is seen as a doctor who describes the human condition, sees its cause, reassures the patient that it can be cured, and gives the medicine (see B.5.b). The stages are:

1. All is *dukkha*, suffering.
2. The cause of suffering is *tanhā*, 'thirst', seen as craving, greed and desire.
3. This can be 'stopped', *nirodha*.
4. The way to stop it is to follow the *magga*, 'path', in eight stages (the noble eightfold path (see B.1.a).

B.6.c. Punishments

As with all religions, Buddhism teaches and is lived at many different levels. From an ultimate perspective, Buddhists believe that our lives are part of a whole flow and chain of existence that goes beyond a single birth and death, and that ordinary beings do not know their past births or the next stages they will go through. Buddhists believe that in the end all beings will attain enlightenment and *Nirvana*, and that their growth towards that end and their destiny on the way is determined by their *karma*. The idea of *karma* teaches that 'what you sow, you will reap' and that 'you reap what you sow'. Morally no deed, speech or thought is ever wasted. Every good motive bears good fruit at some stage in the long series of births and deaths, and contributes to enlightenment. Bad *karma* might mean rebirth in the hell states, but none of these is permanent.

This ultimate perspective and the law of *karma* leads Trevor Ling to say,

> It is worth noting that there is no support for 'punishment' or a penal attitude in Buddhist social ethics – no cutting off the hand that steals, no capital punishment, no stoning of a woman accused of adultery, no criminal asylums. This lack of support for punitive laws is understandable in view of the Buddhist analysis of the human condition, which entails the idea that the only effective punishment is that which we inflict upon ourselves – sooner or later. (Ling 1981: 130)

However, on the level of ordinary life and social organisation, Buddhists are involved in systems of rewards and punishments for good and bad action (see B.6.a). Buddhist countries do have laws which involve punishment for crimes. The sharpest issue is always that of capital punishment, the taking of human life for crimes such as murder. Buddhists argue about its appropriateness or helpfulness in terms of prevention of crime, in the following ways. First, there is the fear that there would be more violence and murder, without the preventative threat of the death penalty. Then it is acknowledged that the decision must depend upon the state of development of a particular society, and that education is necessary to help societies advance ethically. Some Buddhists suggest alternatives to death penalties, such as banishment to prison islands. Others suggest that it is left on the statute books as a threat, but as far as possible never implemented. A very strong point is made by Buddhists who say that the whole concept of retribution is counter to the Buddhist teaching of *metta*, loving kindness and *karunā*, compassion. Some Buddhists would say that capital punishment can never be approved, as nothing can excuse the taking of life. These arguments are all put forward in Tamura 1960, chapter IX.

B.6.d. The Wrongdoer and the Wronged

A person who is wronged, whether by an individual or a social system, can respond in various ways. For a Buddhist the ideal personal qualities (B.2.a) need to be followed even more mindfully in this situation. Many of the *jataka* stories are told to illustrate great patience in the face of injustice and innocent suffering. Patience is not a negative virtue but a positive, active acceptance of all the implications of a situation (see B.2.a). Buddhists try to recognise negative emotions and then let them go, allow them to disperse; hanging on to them has a harmful effect on everybody and breeds more strain, tension and struggle.

Hand in hand with patience goes the knowledge that hatred is never overcome by hatred, but only by love. Friendliness or loving kindness (*metta*), even towards an enemy, is part of one particular meditation method which involves constant practice and self-discipline.

> The Buddha teaches us to be strict or rather unsparing in controlling ourselves, but at the same time we must be tolerant in forgiving injuries. Strict self-control and tolerance towards others are two prominent virtues. Be strict in controlling yourself, but be benevolent, liberal and tolerant towards others, and patience will be invariable for maintaining equanimity. It is through the power of patience ... that we can forgive the provocation, insult or injury, which we meet within our daily lives. (Tachibana rep. 1992: 133–4)

Verse 399 of the Dhammapada says that a spiritual person is one who, 'though he had committed no offence, bears patiently reproach, ill treatment, imprisonment, who has endurance for his force and strength for his army' (Rhadakrishnan 1950).

All of these attitudes involve confidence in the power of moral force and in the law of *karma* which teaches that nothing is ever wasted (see 8.6.b), and that the right motive in a person's heart will always bear good fruit, and a wrong motive bad fruit. Faced with someone who has stolen from them or been unkind, Buddhists reflect on the fact that everyone has different chances and capacities in life, and exercise compassion and skilful means to help such people improve their *karma*. A person involved in wrongdoing can always reverse his or her actions and undergo a change of heart, by asking forgiveness and repairing any practical damage. Buddhists are confident that the true nature and destiny of beings is enlightenment. Tolerance for other people's limitations, and even one's own, is combined with a high moral standard (see B.1.a and B.2.a) plus an emphasis on the need for considerable personal effort to transform an unenlightened person or situation into an enlightened one.

B.7. Equality and Difference

B.7.a. Differences between People

Buddhists believe that everyone has different potentialities, but that everyone is somewhere on the path to enlightenment (see B.7.b and c). People have a great deal of control over their lives and can choose the direction in which they want it to grow. For Buddhists, wisdom (*panna/prajñā*) is more important than cleverness, giving (*dāna*) more important than obtaining possessions, and loving kindness (*metta*) more important than hatred and aggression. Some people are thought to be at a higher spiritual stage than others, and these people are honoured. In human society the different kinds of people are like different limbs of the body or different members of a family, all dependent on each other. Even the separateness of complementary parts is, however, in the end an illusion. There is no eternal self or self-contained ego, and everyone is finally united in what Mahayana Buddhists call their Buddha Nature.

B.7.b. Attitudes to Other Religions

Buddhists are interested in the truth about the way things are. This is what they call *dharma*. The truth is to be found in Buddhism but is not the sole possession of Buddhists. It can be found in other faiths too. Buddhists picture the limitations of human beings' understanding of Ultimate Reality in the famous story of the six blind men who found an elephant. One felt the side of the elephant and thought it was like a wall; another felt the tusk and thought it was like a spear; the third felt the trunk and thought it was like a snake; the fourth felt a leg and thought he had found a tree; the fifth felt an ear and described it as like a fan; and the sixth felt the tail and thought the elephant was like a rope. They all had a limited grasp of the whole, and were impeded by their blindness (see B.4.a and *avijjā*). In a way they were all right and all quite wrong.

In the Paramatthaka Sutta, Gautama Buddha taught that views must be understood as provisional and limited:

> A man has a faith. If he says 'This is my faith', so far he maintains truth. But because of that he cannot proceed to the absolute conclusion. 'This alone is Truth and everything else is false' ... To be attached to one view and to look down upon other views as inferior – this the wise man calls a fetter. (Sutta Nipata: v. 796, quoted in Rahula 1959: ch. 1)

Religious teaching, Buddhists believe, is like a raft, the purpose of which is to carry people safely over the raging waters of life to the further shore. A raft is good if it serves its purpose, but it need not be carried about once the shore is reached. Ultimate truth goes beyond Buddhism, and the value of any belief needs to be questioned and tested out in a person's own experience, not accepted blindly (see B.1.a and B.1.b).

One of the highest values in Buddhism is tolerance, and one of the best statements of this is in Ashoka's twelfth edict (see also B.6.c):

> I desire men of all faiths to know each others' beliefs and acquire sound doctrines themselves. By honouring others one exalts one's own faith and at the same time performs a service to others. In dishonouring them one injures one's own faith. Concord alone is commendable. (Rahula 1959: ch. 1)

Winston King quotes a modern Burmese statement: 'Buddhism is not a religion which strengthens itself by persecuting others. Because it has loving-kindness as its basis, it can establish in strength the principles of Justice, Liberty and Equality to ensure peace and prosperity to all beings' (King 1964: 262).

In this context Buddhists feel confident in their choice of a spiritual path, but also encourage dialogue and co-operation between religions. They are interested to explain their ideas about selfless people, a trans-personal absolute and the importance of meditation to those whose beliefs are different, but they also want to listen and are willing to say that 'in this day and age some Christians and Muslims could really be our good friends' (see *kalyana-mitta*, section B.2.b). A Buddhist will usually teach his or her faith when asked to do so but, with one or two militant exceptions, will not deliberately seek out occasions to convert people but rather try to encourage them in whatever good they are already doing.

B.7.c. Attitudes to Other Races

Buddhism is a world faith and as such transcends national identities and seeks to unite individual people (see B.2.b), nations (section B.8.a and b) and the human race with its environment (see B.9.c). This aim was made explicit in the Green Buddhist Declaration, prepared by members of the international Buddhist community for discussion at the World Fellowship of Buddhists in Colombo, 1984.

> Buddhism is not the possession of any race or nation but aspires to the unity of the human race on earth. Nationalism and racism are seen as forms of greed, hatred and delusion. (Section 2.4)

> We support the United Nations as a means towards the transcending of national barriers and the unification of the human family. (Section 3.8)

The work and words of the Dalai Lama further illustrate these attitudes:

> There are many different philosophies, but what is of basic importance is compassion, love for others, concern for others' suffering, and reduction of selfishness. I feel that compassionate thought is the most precious thing there is. It is something that only we human beings can develop. And if we have a good heart, a warm heart, warm feelings, we will be happy and satisfied ourselves, and our friends will experience a friendly and peaceful atmosphere as well. This can be experienced nation to nation, country to country, continent to continent. (Gyatso 1984: 11)

B.7.d. Women and Men

In all the world religions, attitudes to the position of and relationship between women and men reflect those at the time the religion began; there is often ambivalence and some tension with modern attitudes. In the case of Buddhism, one of the main problem areas is the way in which the female *sangha* or order of nuns was founded. The story in the scriptures says that Gautama Buddha's aunt, who had brought him up after the death of his mother, wanted to become a nun and that Ānanda, one of the Buddha's most respected followers, intervened on her behalf when he saw her determination. The Buddha at first refused but was eventually persuaded to agree, but only on the condition that the women obeyed more monastic rules than the men and that they were under the authority of the men. This naturally suggests that the women were seen as inferior.

The situation seems to have been perpetuated historically by the fact that fewer women became nuns than men became monks, and that in the Theravada countries full ordination for women has faded out. This means that Theravada women in the West, for example, are only able to be ordained on ten precepts (see B.1.a) as novices, with the title *dasa-sīla mata* (ten precept mothers); although the Theravada *sangha* has controversially thought of restoring full ordination for women through a Chinese Mahayana group in the United States of America. There is now an international consciousness of the importance of women's participation (see Gross 1993), and an International Buddhist Women's Association with its own newsletter. It organised its Fifth International Sakyadhita (daughters of the Buddha) Conference in 1995.

In the early Buddhist situation the goal for a woman was very often rebirth as a man. As is often the case in societies where women are under the authority of men, another aspiration was the position of the mother, which brought increased respect. Mothers were greatly honoured at the time of Buddha and the ideal of *metta*, loving kindness (see B.2.a and b) is said to be like that of a mother towards her child. Both the Buddha and Moggallana took great pains to preach the *dharma* to their mothers. Killing either father or mother was seen as one of the most terrible sins (see B.3.b).

However, it is in Mahayana Buddhism that attitudes towards women seem to broaden considerably. There is a famous sutra about the enlightenment of Queen Shrimala, and one of the great *bodhisattvas*, Kwan-yin or Kannon, is female in form. In the Vimalakirti Nirdesa Sutra there is an incident where Sariputra says to a female goddess 'if you know so much, why are you a woman?' She answers, 'Sariputra, what is a woman?' She then uses her magical powers to change places with Sariputra so he is in female form, and demonstrates to him that male and female manifestations are of no real consequence. All beings have the Buddha Nature and the rest is an insubstantial and temporary covering. This is very much closer to modern attitudes towards female and male which were expressed in 1984 in section 2.7 of the Green Buddhist Declaration in these strong words:

> We believe that the Buddha expressed a fundamental insight into the equality of all being's buddha-nature, trapped within different karmic conditionings, when he founded the Sisterhood, recognising women's spiritual capacity. A Buddhist analysis of patriarchy points to the interdependence of social power and spiritual oppression, in that the organised power of men over women is rooted both in threat of violence, the greed to maintain privilege, and a subtle form of ego-ignorance, male chauvinism. Towards removing the patriarchal conditioning on women's full human potential, we oppose the making of women into objects of males' sense gratification from its extreme in pornography, rape and prostitution, to the use of dehumanising images of women in the media, to the limiting of women to subordinate social roles and occupations ... It is important that strong role models be rediscovered from Buddhist history for women *dharma*-practitioners, and that women actively ensure that the male bias be removed from *dharma* teaching in this generation. While the anger and extremism of some groups may be foreign to Buddhism, we are nonetheless in fundamental solidarity with the goals of political and economic liberation of women. We welcome the Naropa Institute (Boulder, Colorado) conferences on 'Buddhism and Feminism' and the Zen-feminist journal KAHAWAI.

It has to be said that not all Buddhists would agree with these sentiments, but the Buddhist Women's Movement is now strong in both the East and West.

B.7.e. Are All People Equal?

It is mentioned elsewhere (see B.7.a) that Buddhists believe all beings, not only humans, have within them the same Buddha Nature or nature of enlightenment, and that this is obscured to a greater or lesser extent like the moon by clouds, or stained by defilements such as greed, hatred and delusion (see B.6.b).

The things which seem to make people separate and unequal, such as colour, nationality (see B.8.a), religion (see B.7.b), social position, intelligence or beauty are in the end impermanent (*anicca*) and illusory. All beings are moving in *samsara* between birth and death. They are all in the same predicament of suffering (*dukkha*) and impermanence (*anicca*) while they grow towards enlightenment and *Nirvāna*. Power, cleverness or wealth, far from being advantages, can be great obstructions and may need to be laid aside to follow the path. What matters is a person's commitment to good deeds, words and thoughts (see B.1.a and B.2.a). The more enlightened people are, the more they treat all beings as equals without separate egos, and with the same love and respect they naturally show to children, parents or themselves. So there are Buddhist stories of human beings laying down their lives for animals, and of Gautama Buddha showing compassion for a leprous prostitute.

Being close to enlightenment and the respect that this brings is seen to be the result of much effort over many aeons. This is a possibility for everyone; the mark of great beings is their capacity to identify with others and their wish to take everyone along the path to *Nirvāna* with them. They are selfless persons (*anatta*) with all awareness of ego and distinctions gone.

Although such spiritual people may be easy to recognise and are likely to be members of the *sangha*, Buddhists are aware that life contains many surprises and paradoxes and that hasty judgements are dangerous. There is a story of the plump figure called Pu-Tai or 'old carpet bag' who lived in China in the tenth century CE. He spent his time telling stories to and playing with the children or just sitting around, a kind of combination of tramp and clown. But it was rumoured that he was the Buddha Maitreya (see Morgan 1986). Then there is a Tibetan story of an ordinary villager whose rainbow-light body after his death showed that he was an enlightened being, though he had spent his life working as a poor peasant farmer, happy that at least his son was a monk (see Hyde-Chambers 1981).

B.8. NATIONAL DIVISIONS, WAR AND PEACE

B.8.a. Why do Different Nations Exist?

Buddhists have no theories about the origins of the nations of the world. The earth is so old and the universe so large and constantly changing that no one can see its beginning or exactly how it has evolved. What can be done is to observe some of the processes of change that are currently at work within the world, and note that, along with the great variety in the number and types of living things, there is a great deal of interdependence in nature, especially between human beings and their environments (see B.9.c).

Buddhists believe that all sentient beings have within them the seed of enlightenment. Human beings are high in the spiritual chain and human birth is called 'precious'. But amongst human beings there are no special national privileges, no qualitative differences between African and American, British and Burmese. They all have the same potential for understanding *dharma*, the truth about the way things are, and for enlightenment. The variety of nations with their own ways of government, language and culture are viewed as different but equally valid human ways of organisation and expression. They can be likened to the variety of people within a single nation or the wealth of personalities within any one family. In the twentieth century, with a greater emphasis on world community, the nations can be called the human family. If criticisms are made against any one nation they will be of specific instances of injustice or oppression, not of the nation as a whole. Tolerance is an important Buddhist virtue and was particularly well expressed by the Indian Emperor Ashoka (see B.1.d) in his twelfth rock edit (see also the whole of section B.7).

Love for one's country and a desire to care for it and preserve its culture does not, for a Buddhist, mean abandoning larger interests. This could be called patriotism, not nationalism: 'Nationalism is an exaggerated, passionate and fanatical devotion to one's national community at the expense of all other national communities and even at the expense of all other interests and loyalties' (Sangharakshita 1984: 9). For a nation there is the need to go out to the world, but also within, to the hearts of individuals. Another twentieth-century Buddhist remarks:

> People are hypnotised, psychologically puzzled, blinded and deceived by the political and propaganda usage of such terms as 'national', 'international', or 'state'. What is a nation but a vast conglomeration of individuals? A nation or state does not act, it is the individual who acts. What the individual thinks and does is what the nation or state thinks and does. What is applicable to the individual is applicable to the nation or state. (Rahula 1959: 87)

B.8.b. Conflict between Nations

Many of the conflicts between nations are based on the same problems as those between individual human beings. Buddhists identify the most basic of these as greed (*lobha*), hatred (*dosa*), and ignorance (*avijjā/avidyā*) (see B.7.b), disrespect for the precepts (see B.1.a) and intolerance. The ideal Buddhist position is that 'Hatred is never appeased by hatred in this world; it is appeased by love' (Radhakrishnan 1950).

Since the first precept is non-harming (*ahimsā*), Buddhists obviously disapprove of violence. To look at a specific example; imagine that a gunman breaks into a house and threatens the life of the owners' children. How should they respond? First of all the Buddhist would advocate trying to disarm the man without harming anyone, while protecting the whole family. If it is necessary to hurt or even kill the man in the process, there are two ways of looking at the action. Theravada Buddhists say that killing is always wrong and brings very serious karmic consequences in this or another life, even when intention is taken into account. Mahayana Buddhists say that if the motivation for killing is care for other sentient beings, and if it is done in complete unselfishness with a willingness to take on all the bad *karmic* consequences for their sake, then it is not a wrong action and may not bring bad *karma*.

> In the Mahayana tradition, it is argued that if a robber is to kill 500 good persons, it is better to kill him first. Yet the act of killing that robber is still a sin. Mahayanists however are willing to commit sinful acts against oneself in order to save other beings. Hence Vietnamese monks who burnt themselves thought that such acts would contribute to the ending of the Vietnam War.
>
> In the Theravada tradition, to be pure is essential, otherwise wisdom and compassion would not be possible. So serious Theravadins cannot condone killing at all. (Anon., *Working Paper on a Buddhist Perception of a Desirable Society* 1985: 15)

These general principles can, of course, be applied to the question of war, which might involve a similar situation on a national scale: 'Theravada Buddhism has no theory for the Just War, nor could monks be directly implicated in political affairs' (ibid.: 8).

This does not mean that individual Theravadins have not disagreed with this general stand and acted differently. In all religions there are gaps between theoretical positions and the behaviour of many adherents. Mahayana Buddhists would say that there could be a situation when action for the benefit of sentient beings might necessitate political involvement and war. However, this idea is taught with some caution as it is obviously applied only for exceptionally skilful and wise beings with pure motives, and if taught carelessly might mislead people.

The general tenor of Buddhism, then, is one of pacifism and non-violence (*ahimsā*). There is a strong Buddhist Peace Fellowship in the West and many Buddhists are prepared to say quite bluntly 'it is better to be killed than to kill' (ibid.: 15).

When looking at national and international issues (see B.9.a), the most important emphasis for a Buddhist is still the heart and mind of the individual; for national action is seen as a collection of individual actions.

> If hatred can be appeased by love and kindness on the individual scale, surely it can be realised on the national and international scale too. Even in the case of a single person, to meet hatred with kindness one must have tremendous courage, boldness, faith and confidence in moral force. May it not be even more so in international affairs? If by the expression 'not practical' is meant 'not easy', you are right. Definitely it is not easy. Yet it should be tried. You may say it is risky trying it. Surely it cannot be more risky than trying a nuclear war. (Rahula 1959: 87)

Buddhists tend to work from the particular to its general implications. This is true with the issue of nuclear war. It is the horror of any act of killing that is multiplied so enormously in nuclear war, combined with the fact that harm extends from those living even to those yet to be born and to the whole environment. The scale of harm is much greater than in conventional warfare and therefore needs a more concerted response. It is their own experience of this scale of warfare, with all its implications that has made Japanese Buddhists particularly active for peace.

> Some Japanese Buddhist monks have indeed been very active against armaments and nuclear war. They walked around the island of Sri Lanka for reconciliation between the Sinhalese Buddhists and Tamil Hindus. They stood firm with the native North Americans who refused to be driven out of their lands, despite the fact that American police threatened to shoot them all. In Japan itself the lay Buddhist organisation Rissho Kosei Kai has established the Niwano Peace Prize and the Niwano Foundation which have encouraged studies towards a peaceful world. This foundation together with other leading institutions help support the World Conference on Religion and Peace, which could be very positive indeed. These are but a few examples that show the positive and active aspects of Japanese Buddhism. (Anon., *Working Paper on a Buddhist Perception of a Desirable Society* 1985: 10)

In addition the Nipponzan Myohoji group of Japanese Buddhists have built peace pagodas in many countries of the world.

While they are prepared to make every effort to stop harm being done to living beings and to work for world peace, Buddhists do not find the idea of the destruction of the world or the annihilation of mankind totally new. Traditional Buddhist cosmology describes vast universes and worlds within them, all of which come and go in cycles of evolution and dissolution. All worlds are impermanent (*anicca*). They develop and change and eventually pass away. What is important within this great movement of evolution and dissolution is the growth of sentient beings towards the state beyond extinction; the unborn, changeless peace of *Nirvāna*.

B.9. GLOBAL ISSUES

B.9.a. Responses to World Poverty

As was mentioned in the sections on leaders (B.1.d), work (B.4.b) and wealth (B.4.d), Buddhists believe that poverty is basic to all kinds of other problems in society. The Burmese politician U Nu said in the 1960s, 'The world is rich enough to provide sufficient food, clothing and shelter for everyone. The maximum standard of living is now enjoyed only by a few; but the majority of mankind has to live in extreme poverty' (quoted in King 1964: 265–6).

He saw the solution in a form of Buddhist socialism. The end of the Green

Buddhist Declaration presented to the Fourteenth General Conference of the World Fellowship of Buddhists in Colombo in 1984 states,

> We believe that since world resources and the ecosystem cannot support all peoples at the level of consumption of the advantaged nations, efforts towards global equity must be coupled with efforts towards voluntary simplicity, in one's individual life-style and through democratically-determined policies. The economic structures which encourage consumeritic greed and alienation must be transformed.

The western economist E. F. Schumacher also talks of voluntary simplicity of lifestyle in response to over-consumerism, and the problems of world poverty, in his chapter on Buddhist economics in *Small is Beautiful*.

This voluntary, individual simplicity combined with global, international planning is needed not just for panic famine relief when a particular situation gets out of hand, but as a sustained approach. Although Buddhists would support famine relief and any agencies helping those in need (see B.5.b) they would want to go further: 'The mere practice of benevolence without improving the political and economic conditions in which people need relief is not enough' (Tamura 1960: 85).

Buddhists would also want to go further in another way, in acknowledging that, 'Some in the industrial countries have learned at first hand that material prosperity without spiritual development is ultimately unsatisfying'. (Anon., *Discussion Points for United Nations University Project on Perceptions of Desirable Societies in Different Religions and Ethical Systems* 1983: 18)

B.9.b. Responses to Population Control

The idea of celibacy, of not marrying and having children but becoming a monk or nun, is very strong in Buddhism. It is often pointed out that in a society where a fair proportion of young males and females are members of the *sangha*, the dangers of overpopulation are greatly decreased. This is voluntary self-control which helps with population control.

When people do marry, Buddhists believe that the responsibility for having children is entirely theirs, and there should be no coercion or interference by the state on the matter of contraception. Individual freedom is important, and with it the responsibility for one's decision whether contraception is in harmony with the precept against harming or taking life (see B.1.a). This decision involves the now familiar debate about when life begins and whether the sperm or the unfertilised egg, or the fertilised egg before it is embedded in the womb, is actual or only potential life. The Buddhist is also interested in the motive a person may have for using contraceptives. If it is for the sake of the mother's health, or for the well-being of existing children, or even out of concern over population figures, then the action can be seen as a responsible one. If, on the other hand, a couple does not want the responsibility of children and see physical desire as an end in itself, or would rather have a bigger car or house, or more holidays abroad, then these might be seen as wrong attitudes towards sexuality and life as a whole.

B.9.c. Planet Earth and Ecology

The interdependence of human and all other forms of life in a finely balanced chain of being has always been a fundamental Buddhist belief: 'True development will arrange for the rhythm of life and movement to be in accordance with the facts, while maintaining an awareness that man is but part of the universe, and that ways must be found to integrate mankind with the laws of nature' (Anon., *Working Paper on a Buddhist Perception of a Desirable Society* 1985: 14).

The economist E. F. Schumacher points out that Buddhism is not so anthropocentric as the so-called Middle Eastern religions, and that its attitudes do not therefore allow for the possibility that mankind has the right to take from nature, to see nature as simply for humanity; particular use, or to dominate and oppress it. As he puts it, 'Man is a child of nature and not the master of nature' (Schumacher 1974: 84). Writing about Buddhist economics, he describes the Buddhist's attitude with reference particularly to trees.

> The teaching of the Buddha ... enjoins a reverent and non-violent attitude not only to all sentient beings but also, with great emphasis, to trees. Every follower of the Buddha ought to plant a tree every few years and look after it until it is safely established. He does not seem to realise that he is part of an ecosystem of many different forms of life. As the world is ruled from towns where men are cut off from any form of life other than the human, the feeling of belonging to an ecosystem is not realised. This results in a harsh and improvident treatment of things upon which we ultimately depend, such as water and trees. (ibid.: 49)

Another illustration of Buddhist respect for living things is the custom of buying fish and caged birds at the festival of *Wesak* in countries like Thailand, and setting them free. Liberation, which is an important part of the theme of the festival, is practically illustrated in these compassionate acts. In every way nature produces an atmosphere that is conducive to wisdom (*panna/prajñā*). This is well illustrated in the use of Japanese gardens as places of meditation, and Chinese landscape paintings.

Buddhists have always argued about vegetarianism. At the time of the Buddha, eating meat was not forbidden, although members of the *sangha* were not allowed to kill animals for food, or even to farm, as this involves taking life. They were, however, allowed to eat meat given to them by householders if it had not been killed specially for them, but was part of the householders' own surplus. Certainly not all Buddhists were or are vegetarian; it must be remembered that there were fishing villages in Japan where the basic food was fish, and that it was difficult in Tibet to grow enough vegetables to feed the population. The Tibetans were mindful of the basic principle of not taking life, and tried to kill the smallest number of animals necessary to feed people. For example, one yak can feed more people than one chicken.

On the other hand, texts such as the Lankavatara Sutra say, 'The *bodhisattva* who regards all beings as if they were his only child cannot indulge in flesh eating' (Suzuki 1930: 369).

The proper food of a *bodhisattva* is said to be rice, barley, wheat, all kinds of beans, clarified butter, oil, honey, molasses and sugar. Many Buddhists in the West believe that as it is possible to eat a very adequate vegetarian diet, then all Buddhists should do this. On the whole, however, Buddhists prefer not to be dogmatic on this or any other issue; they see clinging to views as if they are absolutes a mistake. It is left to the individual conscience, with the guidance of the precepts (see B.1.a) , to help in making the decision.

The following list of topics for discussion shows how closely linked with other issues is the question of planet earth.

> The problem of killing [see B.1.a] which would include war, racial disharmony [B.8 and B.9] peace and disarmament. The style of living, including vegetarianism in the modern world, which should not only be traditional, but must be really compassionate and must understand the way animals are bred just to serve human markets. This includes insecticide or vegetables that are really harmful to humankind as well as harmful to the whole ecological environment. (Anon., *Working Paper on a Buddhist Perception of a Desirable Society* 1985: 16)

Tibetans say very wisely that not too much of anything that is precious should be taken from the earth, as then its quality fades and the earth is destroyed.

GLOSSARY

Ahimsā	Non-harming, non-violence
Anattā (p), anātman (s)	The idea that there is no permanent, eternal soul or self in beings
Anicca (p), anitya (s)	Impermanence
Avijjā (p), avidyā (s)	Ignorance
Bhikkhunīs (p), bhikshunīs (s)	Almswomen, nuns
Bhikkhus (p), bhikshus (s)	Almsmen, monks

Bodhisattva (s)	An enlightenment-being. Describes someone who is on the way to enlightenment. One quality of such a person is their interest in helping others along the path.
Brahma-viharas	The four highest states of mind: loving kindness, compassion, sympathetic joy and equanimity
Buddha	A being who has attained enlightenment
Buddha-nature	The potential for and nature of enlightenment which is in all sentient beings
Citta (p)	Heart or mind
Dalai Lamas	Literally 'great ocean teacher', this is the title of the senior monk of the Gelukpa School of Tibetan Buddhism who is respected by all Tibetan Buddhists
Dāna	Giving, generosity
Dasa-sīla	Ten precepts
Dasa-sīla mata	Ten precept mothers. A term for Theravada nuns who are not yet able to take full ordination
Dhamma (p), dharma (s)	Truth, teaching, law, righteousness
Dharma-rāja	Righteous king
Dosa (p)	Hatred
Dukkha (p), duhkha (s)	Suffering, unsatisfactoriness, disease
Four noble truths	The basis of the Buddha's first sermon which teaches that life is suffering, that thirst or desire is the root of suffering, that suffering can cease and that there is an eightfold path which leads us out of suffering
Gelukpa	Literally 'those who follow the path of perfect virtue'. One of the schools of Tibetan Buddhism whose members are sometimes called 'yellow hats' because they wear these for ceremonials. The Dalai Lama is head of this school which dates from the fourteenth century CE.
Guru (s)	Teacher
Ikebana	The art of flower arrangement, developed particularly in Japan
Jataka	A story of one of the previous births of Gautama Buddha
Kalyana-mitta (p)	A spiritual friend
Kamma (p), karma (s)	Deeds or action which affect one's future birth on the principal that morally one reaps what one sows

94

Karunā	Compassion, one of the four *Brahma-viharas*
Lama	Tibetan term for teacher
Lobha (p)	Greed
Magga (p), marga (s)	Path
Mahāyāna	The great vehicle or way. The name of one of the two main schools of Buddhism found in Tibet, China and Japan, for example
Metta (p)	Loving-kindness, one of the four *Brahma-viharas*
Nibbana (p), nirvāna (s)	The Buddhist term for ultimate reality
Noble Eightfold Path	The way that the fourth noble truth teaches leads us from suffering. There are three parts to it: morality, meditation and wisdom. The path consists of right understanding, thought, speech action, livelihood, effort, mindfulness and con-centration
Pali	The ancient Indian dialect in which the Buddhist teachings were brought to Sri Lanka and in which they were written down
Pali Canon	The collection of Buddhist teachings in the three groups or *Pitakas* (baskets). These three are the *Vinaya* (monastic rules), *Sutta* (sermon) and *Abhidharma* (higher teachings). They form the scriptures of Theravada Buddhism and are in the Pali language
Panca-sīla	Five precepts
Panna (p), prajnā (s)	Wisdom
Pap (p)	Not meritorious, evil, bad
Pāramitā	Perfection
Punna (p)	Merit
Rebirth	Continued chain of life set in motion by *karma*
Samādhi	Meditation
Samsāra	The cycle of birth, death and rebirth
Sangha	Assembly, originally of all Buddhists, now usually monks and nuns
Sati-patthāna	Mindfulness
Shin	Another name for the Pure Land schools of Mahayana Buddhism found in China and Japan
Sīla	Morality
Tanhā (p)	Thirst, a synonym for desire and greed
Theravāda	The way of the Elders. Name given to school of Buddhism found in Thailand, Sri Lanka and Burma

Triratna (s), tiratana (p)	Three jewels: *Buddha, Dharma, Sangha*
Vihāra	An abode, used for a Buddhist temple or monastery
Wesak	Theravada festival celebrating the Buddha's birth, enlightenment and death
Zen	A Japanese school of Mahayana Buddhism. Its name means meditation

REFERENCES

Texts

Batchelor, S. tr. Shantideva, *A Guide to the Bodhisattva's Way of Life*, Dharamsala, 1981.
Carpenter, J. E. (ed.), *Dighanikāya*, vol. III, Pali Text Society, 1960.
Ling, T., *The Buddha's Philosophy of Man*, Dent, 1981.
Radhakrishnan, S. (tr.), *The Dhammapada*, Oxford University Press, 1950.
Rhys Davids, T. W. and C. A. F. (eds), *Dialogues of the Buddha III*, Pali Text Society, 1965.
Suzuki, D. T., *Studies in the Lankavatara Sutra*, Routledge, 1930.

General

Aitken, R., *The Mind of Clover*, North Point Press, 1985.
Anon., *Working Paper on a Buddhist Perception of a Desirable Society*, unpublished, 1985. See Sivaraksa, S., *A Socially Engaged Buddhism*, Inter-Religious Commission for Development, 1988.
Batchelor, M. and K. Brown (eds), *Buddhism and Ecology*, Cassell, 1992.
Bowker, J., *Worlds of Faith*, BBC Publications, 1983.
Cousins, L., *Ethical Standards in World Religions: Buddhism*, vol. 185, Expository Times, 1973–4.
Dumoulin, H. and J. C. Maraldo (eds), *Buddhism in the Modern World*, Collier Macmillan, 1976.
Eppsteiner, P. (ed.), *The Path of Compassion*, 2nd edn, Parallax, 1988.
Goodacre, D. (ed.), *World Religions and Medicine*, Institute of Religion and Medicine, 1983.
Gross, R., *Buddhism after Patriarchy*, SUNY, 1993.
Gyatso, T., *Kindness, Clarity and Insight*, Snow Lion, 1984.
Hyde-Chambers, F. and A., *Tibetan Folk Tales*, Shambhala, 1981.
Jayatilleke, K. N., *Ethics in a Buddhist Perspective*, Wheel Publications, n.d.
Jones, K., *The Social Face of Buddhism*, Wisdom, 1989.
Jones, K., *Beyond Optimism: A Buddhist Political Ecology*, Jon Carpenter, 1994.
Kapleau, P., *To Cherish All Life*, Buddhist Publishing Group, 1986.

Keown, D., *The Nature of Buddhist Ethics*, Macmillan, 1992.

Keown, D., *Buddhism and Bioethics*, Macmillan, 1995.

King, W., *In the Hope of Nibbana*, Open Court, 1964.

Ling, T., *Buddhist Revival in India: Aspects of the Sociology of Buddhism*, Macmillan, 1980.

Misra, G. S. P., *Development of Buddhist Ethics*, Munshiram Manoharlal, 1984.

Morgan, P., *Buddhist Stories*, private publication, 1986.

Rahula, W., *What the Buddha Taught*, Gordon Fraser, 1959.

Ruegg, D. S., 'Ahimsa and Vegetarianism in the History of Buddhism', in Balasooriya, T. and R. Gombrich (eds), *Buddhist Studies in Honour of Walpola Rahula*, Gordon Fraser, 1980, pp. 234–41.

Saddhatissa, H., *Buddhist Ethics*, Allen & Unwin, 1970.

Sangharakshita, *Buddhism, World Peace and Nuclear War*, Windhorse, 1984.

Schumacher, E., *Small is Beautiful*, Abacus, 1974.

Sizemore, R. F. and D. K. Swearer, *Ethics, Wealth and Salvation*, South Carolina, 1990.

Spiro, M., *Buddhism and Society*, University of California Press, 1982.

Stott, D., *A Circle of Protection for the Unborn*, Ganesha Press, 1986.

Subhuti, D., *Buddhism for Today*, Element, 1983.

Tachibana, S., *The Ethics of Buddhism*, Curzon Press, 1992.

Tamura, Y. (ed.), *Living Buddhism in Japan*, International Institute for the Study of Religions, 1960.

Thich Nhat Hanh, *Vietnam: The Lotus in A Sea of Fire*, SCM Ltd, 1967.

Thich Nhat Hanh, *Love in Action*, Parallax, 1993.

World Fellowship of Buddhists, *Green Buddhist Declaration*, WFB, 1984.

Journals

Florida, R. E., 'Buddhist Approaches to Abortion', *Journal of Asian Philosophy* 1, 1991, pp. 39–50.

Lamotte, E., 'Religious Suicide in Early Buddhism', *Buddhist Studies Review* 4, 2, 1987, pp. 1105–18.

NIBWA (Newsletter of the International Buddhist Women's Association).

Raft (the Journal of the Buddhist Hospice Trust).

Tricycle (The Buddhist Review).

USEFUL ADDRESSES

UK

Buddhist Directory (UK), The Buddhist Society, 58 Ecclestone Square, London SW1V 1PH.

BUDDHISM

For the European Buddhist Union, see the UK Buddhist Society Directory.

Forest Sangha Newsletter (with international news and detail of children's activities), Amaravati Buddhist Centre, Great Gaddesdon, Hemel Hempstead, Hertfordshire HP1 3BQ.

The Karuna Trust Aid Agency, St. Mark's Studios, Chillingworth Road, London N7 8QJ.

Pali Text Society, 73 Lime Walk, Headington, Oxford OX3 7AD.

Throssel Hole Priory, Carrshield, Hexham, Northumberland NE47 8AL.

Tricycle (The Buddhist Review), The Sharpham Trust, Ashprington, Totnes, Devon TQ9 7QT.

Western Buddhist Order (including the journal, *Golden Drum*, with international coverage), Padmaloka, Lesingham House, Surlingham, Norwich NR14 7AL.

Addresses of local Buddhist peace fellowships, networks of socially engaged Buddhists, prison chaplaincies, hospices and therapy groups are in the Buddhist Society Directory.

Overseas

American Buddhist Directory (USA and Canada), American Buddhist Movement, 301 West 45th St, New York 10036, USA.

Buddhist Studies Department, The Naropa Institute, 2130 Arupahoe Avenue, Boulder, Colorado 80302, USA.

International Buddhist Directory, Wisdom Publications, 361 Newbury Street, Boston, MA 02115, USA.

Newsletter of International Buddhist Women's Association, c/o Dr Chatsumarn Kabilsingh, Faculty of Liberal Arts, Thammasat University, Bangkok 10200, Thailand.

Shasta Abbey, PO Box 478, Mt Shasta, CA 96067, USA.

Tricycle (The Buddhist Review, which includes many addresses), Dept TRI, PO Box 3000, Denville, NJ 07834–9897, USA.

World Fellowship of Buddhists, 33 Sukhumwt Road, Bangkok 10110, Thailand.

C. SIKHISM

Eleanor Nesbitt

C.1. RELIGIOUS IDENTITY AND AUTHORITY

C.1.a. On Being a Sikh

According to Rahit Maryādā: A Guide to the Sikh Way of Life:

> A Sikh is any person whose faith consists of belief in one God, the ten Gurus, the Guru Granth Sahib and other scriptures of the Sikh religion. Additionally he or she must believe in the necessity and importance of *amrit* (the Sikh baptism ceremony).

The word Sikh means a learner and, more specifically, a disciple of the spiritual teacher or Guru. For Sikhs the word Guru means God, as well as each of the ten human masters from Guru Nanak (1469–1539 CE) to Guru Gobind Singh (1666–1708), and the Guru Granth Sahib (the scriptures, a 1430-page volume of hymns).

Since Sikhs respect all religious paths (see C.7.b) theirs is not a proselytising faith. Although there are a few converts from Western countries, the vast majority of Sikhs, in whatever continent they now live, share a common cultural heritage. They originate from Punjab in North-East India, speak Punjabi, and every aspect of their lives is affected if not moulded by Punjabi cultural norms. Since 1947, when Punjab was divided between Pakistan and India, it has been the Indian state of Punjab with which Sikhs have identified. This cultural factor has to be borne in mind when looking at Sikhs' moral decisions, especially those conerning family life (see C.2.c, C.3.a, C.3.b and C.5.a).

Sikhs share many values (such as hospitality) with members of other faiths in the Indian subcontinent. For example, the maintenance and enhancement of one's family's *izzat* (honour) is a dominant concern (see C.2.c). Misconduct, especially a woman's real or imagined sexual misconduct, brings shame on the whole family.

During the twentieth century many Indians have emigrated. Although Sikhs constitute only 1.9 per cent of the population of India, they make up a much higher proportion of emigrants to the West. In Britain they probably outnumber Hindus and are a large community in Canada. Largely as a result of family dislocation, the younger generation of Sikhs are facing different issues from their parents at the same age. It is traditionally on the older family members that the responsibility for decision-making rests. They are acutely aware of social pressures to conform within the Sikh community and these are likely to determine their conduct and advice. Certain major decisions are regarded as less a matter for the individual than in many families of non-Asian origin. Choice of career and, in particular, selection of a spouse are concerns for older relatives (see C.3.a). Traditional behaviour, in terms of age, gender and status roles, is often at variance with contemporary non-Asian pre-suppositions and values. For young Sikhs in the West, faced with ethical choices in an environment far removed from Punjab, and for those in contact with them, it is helpful to be able to distinguish between time-honoured regional custom on the one hand, and Sikh religious principles on the other. For example, family custom may dictate that sons and daughters marry members of the same *zāt* (caste, see C.3.a). In rejecting this, as many Sikhs wish to, they are in fact not abandoning Sikh teaching, but acting in accordance with it (see C.7.a).

Those whose daily life is a constant remembrance (*simran*) of God will express God's will (*hukam*) in their actions. This is the shining message of the Gurus as set down in the Guru Granth Sahib, the sacred scripture otherwise referred to as Adi Granth. Sikhs must recall God constantly, work honestly and share what they earn. Self-centredness (*haumai*) must give way to the Godward orientation of a *gurmukh*. The *gurmukh* is a person who shuns lust, anger, greed, attachment to things temporal and pride (*kām*, *krodh*, *lobh*, *moh* and *ahankār*). Sikhs must resist the temptation to renounce secular responsibilities, and must seek to live like a lotus, which is rooted in the mire, but unsullied by it.

Because certain values were and are a basic part of Indian society, the Gurus did not emphasise them. Thus, a Sikh knows it is necessary to show hospitality to strangers and respect to the elderly (see C.5.a). But because caste discrimination and religiosity were common problems, Guru Nanak and his successors proclaimed tirelessly the irrelevance of caste distinction and of superficial ritualism to the soul's reunion with God. This emphasis on certain aspects of behaviour should not be taken to mean that other values are less important.

A Sikh's conduct may find inspiration in certain compositions and traditions not included in the Guru Granth Sahib. Among these are the Vars of Bhai Gurdas (a saintly contemporary of four of the Gurus) and the numerous stories of Guru Nanak's life known as the *janamsākhīs*. Equally inspirational are the compositions of Guru Gobind Singh, comprising the Dasam Granth, and also the accounts of later Sikhs' heroism and martyrdom. Ever since the time of Guru Gobind Singh (d. 1708 CE), codes of conduct (*rahitnāmās*), for example Rahitnāmā Bhai Chaupa Singh and Prem Sumarg, have been in circulation. These lay down the behaviour required of Sikhs. Sikhs can decide questions of individual and corporate, moral and ritual conduct in the light of the most recent of these codes of practice, the Rahit Maryādā, a guide to the Sikh way of life. This was approved for issue by the Shiromani Gurdwara Parbandhak Committee, the central advisory body of the Sikhs, in 1945. It is available in both Punjabi and English.

The few comprehensive studies of Sikh ethics so far undertaken do not tackle many major, highly complex and controversial contemporary issues such as nuclear war. These await serious scholarly attention and indeed recognition by most preachers.

In *gurdwārās* generally those who are regarded as religious authorities – the *giānīs* and *granthīs* – are traditionalist, ill at ease with English and unfamiliar with the dilemmas facing those growing up in the West. Many Sikhs, young and old alike, act on the guidance of revered spiritual masters known as *sants*. They may have complete faith in their pronouncements, regardless of how little first-hand experience a *sant* has of some of his followers' perplexities.

Some ethical issues, such as abortion (see C.5.c), euthanasia (see C.5.d) and homosexuality (see C.2.d), have not been publicly debated or discussed by scholars. Others, of central concern to Sikh identity, such as the cutting of one's hair or smoking, have received a great deal of attention. In the latter case, contemporary medical research is used to support the religious prohibition.

Currently most Sikh concern is focused on the uneasy situation of Sikhs in India. This means that other controversial ethical issues are unlikely to receive so much attention. However, Piara Singh Sambhi and Gobind Singh Mansukhani have provided a Sikh response to important contemporary questions (see, for example, Mansukhani's *Introduction to Sikhism*, first published in 1986).

C.1.b. Authority

Guru Nanak's vision of truth did not divide the world into spiritual and secular. Political and social order are for him inseparable from the universal order, a divine harmony in which every part has its role to play, its *dharma*. Humans who forget God, abuse earthly power. The fundamental issue is spiritual, not political:

> Lords of the ocean and kings with mountains of wealth
> Are not equal to an insect
> That never forgets God in its heart. (Ādi Granth: 5)

But the tyranny of unjust kings may itself be divinely ordained punishment on those who have forgotten Him. Guru Nanak witnessed Babur's invasion of India:

> How hard it is for the captives ...
> They never gave God a thought.
> Now they have no leisure in which to remember him (Ādi Granth: 417).

All authority is ultimately God's. From analogy with the Sikhs' conduct of their religious affairs (see C.1.c) it might be imagined that they disapprove of monarchy or favour democracy. In fact the Gurus never criticised the political system of kingship, only its abuse. After the death of Guru Gobind Singh in 1708 CE, many of his followers flocked to his nominated deputy, Banda Bahadur, and treated him as king. Throughout the eighteenth century Sikhs fought as members of *misals* (military groups), each with its chieftain who exercised more or less princely power. More successful than his contemporaries in his pursuit of power, Maharaja Ranjit Singh ruled a united Punjab from 1799 to 1839. Although regarded by some as the golden age of Sikh polity, by others Maharaja Ranjit Singh's period is perceived as one in which Sikhism lost its distinctive character and lapsed into Hinduism. The difference between his reign and that of the eighteenth-century Sikh rulers was one of degree and not of kind (see, for example, Grewal 1972: 160–7).

C.1.c. Authority Figures in the Faith

Authority is God's, and as the Guru uniquely mediates the divine to other human beings, the Guru is the ultimate human authority. During the lives of the ten Sikh Gurus, this spiritual authority was recognised by their followers and evident in a style of sovereignty increasingly parallel to the Mughal rulers' administration. The *chaurī* (an emblem of authority) was waved above the Guru as he gave audience. From at least the time of Guru Arjan Dev, representatives called *masands* had responsibility for devotees in designated areas (*manjīs*). This reflected Mughal imperial administration and continued until the system was abolished by Guru Gobind Singh. On assuming Guruship in 1606 CE, Hargobind also assumed military leadership – *mīrī* (temporal power) – as well as *pīrī* (spiritual authority), symbolised by two swords. The Guru was *sache pādshāh*, the true emperor.

In 1699 Guru Gobind Singh established a new model of authority. Guruship was henceforth vested not only in his person but also in his *khālsā*. This consisted of those Sikhs who had taken *amrit* (that is, made a distinctive act of commitment) and accepted the responsibilities and identifying marks now required of them. From Guru Gobind Singh's death in 1708, the scriptural compilation of hymns, the Ādi Granth, was to be Guru, the Guru Granth

Sahib. The Guru Granth Sahib continues to be treated with the external signs of respect due to the highest authority. For example, most Sikh families do not have a complete volume of the scriptures at home, because as Guru it requires an upstairs room to be devoted exclusively to it. A random reading is accepted daily as the Guru's *hukam* (order, guidance) for the day.

The Guruship of the Khālsā or the *Panth* – the term used for the religious community of Sikhs – has been emphasised less. However, a *gurmatā*, a decision taken by consensus of the congregation in the presence of the Guru Granth Sahib, is binding. This is particularly true of any *gurmatā* taken in the Akāl Takht, the building facing the Golden Temple in Amritsar, and issued as an edict (*hukamnāmā*) to all Sikhs. A recent instance was the *hukamnāmā* issued in 1978 CE which ordered all Sikhs to boycott the Sant Nirankārī sect (see C.7.b). At times of crisis during the eighteenth century, the *Dal Khālsā* (Sikh army) would gather at Amritsar and act on the basis of whatever *gurmatā* was reached. Akāl Takht is the principal seat of authority but there are four other Takhts recognised by Sikhs.

For religious purposes, such as administering *khande dī pāhul*, the initiation ceremony inaugurated by Guru Gobind Singh in 1699, authority is represented by the *panj pyāre* (five beloved ones), that is, five Sikhs of known orthodoxy and good character.

In the *gurdwārā* all are equal, although only those proficient in reading the *Gurmukhī* script can publicly read the scriptures and act as *granthī*. *Giānī* (learned) is the respectful title given to Sikhs proficient in interpreting the Guru Granth Sahib.

There is no priesthood in Sikhism. It is important to realise this, especially as the media and many Sikhs now use the words 'priest' and even 'high priest'. The latter usually refers to the senior *jathedār* (leader of the *panj pyāre*) at the Akāl Takht, Amritsar.

A *sant* is a religious teacher who attracts followers. Some *sants* wield enormous influence on Sikh religion and politics. Sant Jarnail Singh Bhindranwale in India and Sant Puran Singh (Kerichowale Baba) in Britain are recent, very different examples. Although the election of office holders on *gurdwārā* management committees is ideally by consensus of the gathered congregation (*sangat*), individual *gurdwārā* constitutions differ on the best procedure. In *gurdwārās* set up by the followers of a *sant*, his choice is final.

C.1.d. Duties of Leaders

In accordance with Guru Nanak's insights, both ruler and ruled must be disciplined. The pursuit of power and pleasure leads both astray, and a conflict of interests results (see C.1.b). The ruler has, above all others, the task of maintaining justice. He or she must be a person of integrity. Guru Gobind Singh re-emphasised this in his Zafarnāmā (Epistle of Victory) addressed to the emperor Aurangzeb, reproaching him for his faithlessness in breaking an oath.

When the tenth Guru died, Sikhs had political leaders, but the community (*Guru Panth*) were careful that they did not have religious powers since the Guru Granth Sahib was the spiritual leader. In the nineteenth century Maharaja Ranjit Singh ruled over an independent Punjab which was not a Sikh state but a place where people were free to practise any religion. He, like any ruler, Sikh or other, could be challenged if they abused their power. The ideal of the *Kshatriya* or ruler (see A.7.a) for the Sikh is expressed by Guru Amar Das when he said: 'He alone is a *kshatriya* who is brave in good deeds. He yokes himself to charity and alms giving. Within the field bounded by the protecting fence of justice he sows seed which benefits everyone' (Ādi Granth: 1411).

C.1.e. Duties of Subjects

Sikhs must always keep the law if it is in accordance with Sikh principles (see C.6.a). However, when those in power are unjust, Sikhs are exhorted to resist the oppression. In the last resort this will possibly involve armed resistance (see C.9.b). Unfortunately, acts which one Sikh regards as justified violence against an otherwise immovable oppressive regime can appear to others, Sikh and non-Sikh alike, as irresponsible terrorism. The killing of Mrs Indira Gandhi, the Prime Minister of India, on 31 October 1984 was one such act, during the Sikhs' struggle for greater autonomy for Punjab. A positive example for Sikhs is Guru Tegh Bahadur (1621–75) who pleaded the cause of the Kashmiri Brahmins to the Mughal rulers and his execution is seen as a death for religious liberty. See also C.8.b.

A favoured method of drawing attention to injustice is the *morcha* (campaign), a mass protest, as when Sikhs protested peacefully against the abuse and corrupt managements of their *gurdwārās*. This led to the passing of the Sikh Gurdwārās Act in 1925. Similarly Sikhs courted arrest in the early 1960s, demanding a state where Punjabi was the officially recognised language. In Britain, Sikhs have campaigned successfully against legal discrimination against those wearing the turban. But in 1982, for example, the Court of Appeal had ruled that a headmaster was not breaking the law by refusing to admit a pupil who wore a turban.

C.2. PERSONAL AND PRIVATE?

C.2.a. Personal Qualities

Certain virtues recur in the hymns of the Guru Granth Sahib, in the compositions of Guru Gobind Singh and in the stanzas of Bhai Gurdas. One of the best descriptions of the personal qualities encouraged in Sikh teaching is by Professor Avtar Singh (see Singh 1983).

Good qualities are not abstract or passive, but virtues to be cultivated diligently and practised unremittingly.

> Let your mind be the farmer and deeds the farming; and let your body be the farm: water it with effort. Let the spiritual word be the seed, and contentment the furrowing, and let the fence be of humility. If you do the deeds of love, the seed will sprout and fortunate will be your home. (Ādi Granth: 595)

Virtues flourish in social interaction with good people, and are to be exercised in the service of others. They cannot develop in isolation from one's fellows.

Above all the virtues, Sikhs are to exemplify truthfulness in thought, word and deed. 'Truth is above everything but higher still is truthful living' (Ādi Granth: 62). They must seek wisdom, not merely theoretical knowledge (see C.4.a). In eating, sleeping and speech they must show self-control, taking a path between the total abstention of some ascetics and the indulgence which is careless of consequences. They must behave justly, never exploiting others. 'Depriving others of their due is [like] eating pork for a Muslim or beef for a Hindu' (Ādi Granth: 141).

When other means fail, the righting of injustice may require bravely taking up arms (see C.8.b). The readiness to risk all in defence of another is epitomised in the Sikh's ideal of the courageous saint-soldier (sant-sipāhī). Courage may also demand endurance to the point of non-violent martyrdom, as demonstrated by Guru Arjan Dev and Guru Tegh Bahadur.

Realising the matchless greatness of God, a Sikh should be humble, like a mango tree which bends lowest when most richly laden with fruit. A Sikh should not retire from life's struggles fatalistically, but continue striving in a spirit of contentment (santokh) unperturbed by seeming failure.

C.2.b. Friendship

Since one's character is affected by one's choice of company, one should associate as far as possible with those of a godly disposition. Most social relationships in traditional Sikh society were likely to be within one's caste and kinship group and with members of one's own sex (see C.2.c and d).

The lives of the Gurus demonstrate friendship across human frontiers – for example, the devotion of the Muslim Mardana and the Hindu Bala to Guru Nanak – and prove their readiness to accept the risks inherent in friendship. Guru Tegh Bahadur died in order to protect the Kashmiri Hindus' religious freedom. God is without enmity (nirvair), as Sikhs daily recite in the opening credal statement of the Guru Granth Sahib, the Japjī (Ādi Granth: 1). A person who remembers God constantly will likewise feel hatred for no one. Sikhism emphasises sevā, that is, service to all humanity regardless of colour, caste, class and creed.

105

C.2.c. Sex before Marriage

Central to Sikh teaching and practice is the exercise of family responsibilities and self-restraint. Marriage is a spiritual union, not only the union of two bodies (see C.3.a).

Sikhism arose in the cultural context of North India where marriages were arranged at an early age, often before puberty, although the couple might not live together for several years. Older members of the family chose spouses for their children with care. Every marriage was an alliance between two extended families. In a society where people lived together as families and youngsters did not move away to lead individual, private lives, the question of living together unmarried was unthinkable. The honour (*izzat*) of the extended family depended upon the respectable conduct of every member. In particular, *izzat* was threatened if a girl behaved without *sharam* (decent modesty). Tongues would wag if she was even seen looking at a boy. There was no question of sex before marriage as a practicable, let alone defensible, proposition.

Sikh parents' attitudes today have been shaped by these connections. 'There is no courting. Our grown-up girls don't generally go to discos and parties' (Bowker 1983: 197). As might be expected in a traditional society, such restrictions apply less to boys. 'Boys have more freedom as they grow older but teenage girls are not allowed to go out unchaperoned' (Sambhi, in Cole, 1982: 228).

These statements were made by Sikh parents living in Britain's more permissive society. Clearly this 'no' to the unsupervised mixing of boys and girls means 'no' to sex before marriage.

In practice, relatives may punish severely a woman who transgresses this code (see C.6.c). The woman concerned needs to consider carefully the shame which she will cause her family, with its possible implications, and the suffering she may incur for herself. For her male counterpart, retribution is unlikely to be so harsh.

The restriction of sexual activity to its responsible use within marriage is consistent with the reference to *kām* (lust) in the scriptures (see C.2.d).

C.2.d. Homosexuality

Sikhs have not written on this subject. They expect every man and woman to marry and have children. A woman without children, particularly sons, is regarded as extremely unfortunate. There is no respected or desirable alternative to the role of wife and mother. In such a scheme there is no place for an unmarried – let alone a lesbian – lifestyle. Nor would such possibilities occur to most women. Sexual activity for both sexes must be confined to members of the opposite sex and within marriage.

It is regarded as right and natural that only those of the same sex hold hands or embrace in public (see A.2.d). Much of the individual's emotional support is provided, as in other South Asian communities, by companions of the same sex (see C.2.b). It would be totally incorrect for a westerner to assume that this physical contact between men or women indicated a tendency towards homosexuality.

In the Guru Granth Sahib, *kām* (lust) is cited as one of the five evil passions. Union with God is not possible while one is at the mercy of wayward impulse. Any surrender to instincts incompatible with conjugal fidelity or to the proper role of men and women as marriage partners would be condemned.

C.3. MARRIAGE AND THE FAMILY

C.3.a. The Meaning of Marriage

The Sikh Gurus had a very high regard for the state of marriage, and they themselves entered into matrimony. They insisted that marriage is not merely a civil or social contract, but that its highest and most ideal purpose is to fuse two souls into one so that they may become spiritually inseparable.

(McCormack n.d.)

In Guru Amar Das' words:

They are not husband and wife
Who only dwell together.
Only they who have one spirit in two bodies
Can be called husband and wife. (Ādi Granth: 788)

Verses such as the one above are used in the *Anand Karaj* (literally 'Ceremony of Bliss'), the Sikh marriage service, to impress upon the bridal couple the significance of marriage. The volume of the scriptures is the Guru in their midst, witnessing the marriage. Without the Guru Granth Sahib's presence no valid Sikh marriage can take place, and conversely, wherever it is appropriately installed is a fit place for the *Anand Karaj*, whether in a Western *gurdwārā* or in India under an awning near the bride's home. While the couple are in front of the Guru Granth Sahib, stanzas of Guru Ram Das' hymn, *Lāvān*, are read. These affirm the life of the *grihasth* (the married householder as opposed to the celibate) and suggest the progression of conjugal devotion, while on the spiritual plane evoking the soul's gradual advance towards union with God.

Anand Karaj has been recognised as legal marriage in India since the passing of the Anand Marriage Act in 1909. In Britain, some *gurdwārās* have registering officers who conduct a brief civil marriage on the day of the religious ceremony. Most Sikhs who marry in the West have a civil marriage in the Registry Office near the time of their engagement, but do not live together until after the *Anand Karaj* has been solemnised.

Indian tradition, rather than specific Sikh religious teaching, demands that the couple have children, in particular a son to carry on the family name and to care for his parents in their declining years (see A.3.a). In practice, women's sexual morality is more strictly enforced, but the Gurus condemned the adultery of men – even in thought.

> Do not cast your eyes on the beauty of another's wife. (Ādi Granth: 274)

> The Sikh's underwear (*kachh*), worn by both sexes should remind them of the need for their marital fidelity. (Mansukhani 1986b: 20)

Monogamy has always been the Sikh norm. However both Guru Hargobind and Guru Gobind Singh had three wives, probably resulting from the fact that some devout Sikhs dedicated their daughters at birth exclusively to the Guru and his relatives.

Marriage is lifelong but there is no religious reason why Sikh widows and widowers should not remarry. In practice, perhaps influenced by the attitudes of Hindus, a woman is less likely to remarry than a man, although marriage to a close relative of her late husband is socially sanctioned (Bedi 1971: 60).

Unlike Muslims, Sikhs of most castes may not marry cousins. In fact, they observe the general, unwritten Punjabi Hindu rules restricting marriage to members of the same subcaste (*Jat*, *Ramgarhia*, etc.) but of different *got* (clan). This precludes marrying anyone with the same family name as either of one's parents or any of one's grandparents. In villages men always marry women from a different village, in order to avoid moral laxity in village society where the men regard each other as brothers and the women as their sisters. This is a social convention and is not strictly observed among Sikhs living in the cities, whether in India or overseas.

Similarly, in the majority of Sikh marriages, parents and senior family members play a leading part in selecting the spouse (see C.2.c). This is simply the way things are done in South Asian society; it is not a religious require-ment. From a religious point of view what is required is that the future bride or groom be a Sikh. In practice, inter-marriage with Hindus has often occurred, but only according to the caste and *got* rules already outlined. For a Sikh girl to marry a non-Sikh would be considered more reprehensible than for a Sikh boy to marry out (see C.7.b), for it is assumed that wife and chil-dren follow the father's faith.

Also, since marriage is a union of two families, it is felt that care must be taken to avoid needless future friction. This means ensuring that one's son's or daughter's life partner is from a background similar in its religious orientation and general outlook, as well as in its levels of education and income.

C.3.b. Family Relationships

In practice, but not by any religious requirement, family relationships are based on the same expectations and presuppositions as in Punjabi Hindu society. Parents tend to indulge small children, especially boys, and to discipline older ones more strictly. A girl is brought up knowing she will one day be lost to another family whose love and respect she must earn, but looks to her brother for lifelong moral support. Boys know that they will be responsible for caring for their parents in their old age (see C.5.a). Folk songs, particularly those sung at the time of weddings, draw out the usual relationships of love (between mother and daughter, brother and sister) and potential friction (notably mother-in-law and daughter-in-law). In the West, many families conform outwardly – in terms of the number of relatives living under a single roof – to the norms of the nuclear family, but frequent reunions, especially at marriages, make children keenly aware of kinship ties, obligations and relative status.

For example, a man will feel bound to please his daughter's or his sister's in-laws. Since they have, as it were, taken a wife from his family, they enjoy higher prestige than those who gave the wife. Similarly, with her husband's younger brothers, a woman has an altogether more relaxed, joking relationship than with his elder brothers who have the greater status. This is very different from Western family life in which individual preference, rather than the nature of the relationship, determines relations (or the lack of them) with relatives and in-laws.

As in Hindu families (see C.3.c) cousins are regarded as brothers and sisters. Indeed in Punjabi villages there is a sense of blood relationship between all members of a *zāt* (sub caste).

In Punjab, as in Indian society generally, a child would not say 'thank you' to his or her parents. That would suggest that parental love is conditional and uncertain, rather than the perogative of every child. To thank a relative in so many words would be to impose a distance and formality. Love is reciprocated in non-verbal ways. Parents know that they can rely on their sons to care for them in old age (see C.5.a), and that their children will in turn lavish care on the next generation.

Among Sikhs resident in Western society, fewer relatives live together, both wives and husbands are at work and family ties are put to the test. More subtle influences are also at work. For example, the younger generation may think in terms of 'my friends' and 'my mother's friends'. In the past a parent's friend would automatically be a child's 'aunt' or 'uncle', and would be treated with the respect given to other older members of the family. Friendship was not seen in such an individualistic way as it often is nowadays in Western society.

C.3.c. Marriage Breakdown

Although marriage is regarded as the union of two souls and a lifelong bond, divorce increasingly occurs. Although it is permitted by Indian law, divorce is rarer among Sikhs in India than among Sikhs in the West. One reason is that in India women of all religions are less likely than those in the West to be financially independent of their spouses.

Wherever possible, Sikhs will endeavour to achieve a reconciliation between husband and wife. Consideration for the children may prevent divorce. 'If the wife and husband break off, their concern for their children reunites them' (Ādi Granth: 143). When it does occur, divorce is regarded as extremely unfortunate. By many it is seen as a punishment for past wrong. Whatever the reason for the breakup, for divorced women the stigma persists.

Parents will usually arrange a second marriage for their son or daughter if the first union has ended in divorce. A divorcee can be remarried in the *gurdwārā*.

Sikhs are, however, required to abide by the law of the country in which they live. In India it is now illegal for a man to remarry simply because his wife did not bear a child or bore only daughters. As Mansukhani writes: 'Generally grounds like cruelty, adultery, change of religion, suffering from an incurable disease and in some cases incompatibility of temperaments are accepted by courts for purposes of divorce' (Mansukhani 1986b: 182).

C.4. INFLUENCES ON AND USE OF TIME AND MONEY

C.4.a. Education

Sikhs generally encourage their children to study conscientiously at school and college, so preparing for the best career available to them. The professions of medicine and engineering are most attractive to parents and grandparents whose attitudes were moulded in rural Punjab. Teaching is also a respected occupation for both men and women.

As the word 'Sikh' means literally 'learner', and the concept of Guru or teacher is central to the faith, one might expect education to be a key concern. So it is, but in the sense of spiritual enlightenment rather than courses in the arts, sciences or practical skills. Before the provision of state education in Punjabi villages, children could learn in the *gurdwārā* to read and write in *Gurmukhī*. This is the script used for the Sikh scriptures, and it is also used by Sikhs to write Punjabi. In Britain, Punjabi classes are held in many *gurdwārās* in order to make children literate in their mother tongue and enable them to read the Guru Granth Sahib.

Guru Nanak's compositions reveal his understanding of Sanskrit, Persian and Arabic in addition to the local vernacular, and as a young adult he used his skills as an accountant. Guru Gobind Singh was a proficient poet in Hindi, Punjabi, Sanskrit and Persian and set great store by training in martial as well as literary skills. In the late nineteenth century the Singh Sabha, a Sikh reform movement, set out to eliminate the social evils of illiteracy and ignorance by establishing schools and colleges. Since 1905 the Educational Committee of the chief Khālsā Dīwān, Amritsar, has promoted education, providing scholarships and setting up educational institutions, for example for women and in backward areas. Despite this positive regard for secular education the Rahit Maryādā makes no reference to education except to advocate that 'Every Sikh should learn Gurmukhi and read the Guru Granth'. From a religious point of view this is the most vital source of knowledge.

> When the lamp is lit darkness is dispelled; similarly by reading religious books evil mindedness is destroyed. (Ādi Granth: 791)

> What matters ultimately is not book-learning but spiritual enlightenment and truth.

> An educated person ... is one who puts the garland of God-remembrance round his neck. (Ādi Granth: 938)

> The scholars study more and more to gain knowledge. But they use it for vain discussion. (Ādi Granth: 152)

> True learning springs from reflection and is manifest in goodness of character. (ibid.)

In the *janamsākhīs*, the young Nanak tells his teacher how useless all his book knowledge is, by comparison with perpetual mindfulness of God's name. Western-style education encourages the student to assume increasing independence. For Sikhs a central truth is our dependence upon God and upon each other, and particularly the priority of family interests over individual concerns. The clearest statement on education by a Sikh writer is probably Piara Singh Sambhi's in Sutcliffe's *Dictionary of Religious Education* (1984: 316–18).

C.4.b. Work

> He alone has found the right way who eats what he earns through toil and shares his earnings with the needy.
>
> (Ādi Granth: 1245)

Sikhs are proud of their reputation for hard work and initiative. Since they are expected to marry and live as householders, they are also expected to work hard to earn and to keep their families (see C.3.a). After Partition in 1947 the

111

hundreds of thousands of refugees from the Pakistan side of the new border built their lives anew without resorting to begging. In the rural, unmechanised economy of Punjab's still-recent past there was some work for everyone. All but the handicapped had to work, and if performed in the right way, every work was noble.

According to Sikh teaching caste considerations should not affect one's attitude to accepting the work available. In practice hereditary caste preference has played its part, so that, for instance, only Sikhs of the leatherworking caste would be shoemakers. From a religious standpoint, however, only occupations incompatible with the Sikh code of conduct should be avoided, such as running nightclubs, selling alcohol and, in particular, selling cigarettes and tobacco (see G.4.e).

C.4.c. Leisure and its Use

Leisure is a necessary element of life. Festivals, marriages and the agricultural cycle in Punjab ensure periods of recreation. *Bhangrā* dancing (for men) and *gidhā* (for women) are enjoyed to the full. Rhythmic drumming, vivid costume and often humorous verses add to the fun. Reading and singing the hymns of the Guru Granth Sahib brings peace of mind and spiritual refreshment. These are the traditional pastimes.

In urban and Western society, leisure pursuits are to be enjoyed provided they do not conflict with morality and health. The company one keeps is vital to one's well-being. Smoking was forbidden by the Gurus. Together with drinking and gambling, it is prohibited for all Sikhs (see Rahit Maryādā). In practice, the ban on smoking is almost universally observed, whereas many men see no inconsistency between their Sikh faith and the consumption of alcohol (see C.4.e).

Sikhs have not yet thought out the implications of a world in which a growing number of individuals are destined to be technically unemployed for long periods of their lives. In the West, the *gurdwārā* is a place where the elderly, with time on their hands, find fulfilment in acts of services such as preparing tea or cleaning. But what of school leavers? Families may start a business, thereby avoiding the compulsory leisure of unemployment particularly for the young. Whether paid or unpaid Sikhs believe that work is essential for everyone's character to develop (see C.4.b). Noblest is the work offered to God and the congregation as *sevā* (service). *Kār sevā* is voluntary manual work, sometimes on a vast scale, as when a *gurdwārā* is under construction. By extension, voluntary service to the wider community accords well with Sikh teaching and is to be undertaken by those who might otherwise be idle. So it would be appropriate for young Sikhs to be involved in local community projects of various kinds. Those in paid employment must be willing to share with those whose equally hard work is unpaid.

C.4.d. Wealth

Sikh teaching is realistic in its approach to wealth: 'Those who have money have the anxiety of greed: those without money have the anxiety of poverty' (Ādi Granth: 1019). Poverty is not essential for holiness. All Sikhs are to earn honestly and share generously. They should give at least a tenth (*dasvandh*) of their earnings to others. Often they give in kind rather than cash: food for the *langar* (corporate meal) or building materials for a *gurdwārā*. There is no place for dishonesty or avarice. Nor should money be spent on pursuits such as gambling or drinking (see C.4.c).

Riches must be honestly earned, not the result of exploiting the poor. This point is made most graphically in the *janamsākhī* story of Malak Bhago, the rich man who insisted that Guru Nanak should dine with him rather than with the carpenter, Lalo. Guru Nanak squeezed Bhago's fried 'puri', and blood dripped from it. When he squeezed Lalo's simple, hard-earned bread, milk flowed out (see McLeod 1980: 87). A popular *janamsākhī* story recounts how the youthful Guru Nanak struck a 'true bargain'. Instead of making financial profit with the money his father gave him for business, he spent it on feeding some religious mendicants (see C.5.b).

According to the Ādi Granth, wealth must not distract its owners from life's spiritual purpose:

> If the world were to be encrusted with diamonds and rubies, my bed studded with rubies;
> And if there were to be an alluring damsel, her face glistening with jewels, tempting me with seductive gesture,
> Forbid it, O Lord, that beholding such temptation I should forget Thee and fail to call to mind thy name. (McLeod 1980: 96)

Wealth must be seen in perspective. In comparison with *Nām* (God's name, or essential reality) wealth is nothing. Material wealth is impermanent: 'Wealth, youth and flowers are short-lived as guests for four brief days' (Ādi Granth: 23).

A *janamsākhī* story illustrates the point that money cannot accompany us beyond death. Duni Chand advertised his treasure by flying flags. Guru Nanak gave him a needle, bidding him keep it safe as he would need it again in heaven. Duni Chand then realised the futility of hoarding wealth which he could not possibly retain after his death (McLeod 1980: 125–6).

Wealth in one life may be the karmic reward for virtue in a previous existence. This is one way of understanding an episode narrated in the Puratan *janamsākhī*. When Mardana asked why one man rode in a palanquin while his six bearers walked naked, Guru Nanak replied: 'Joy and pain come in accordance with the deeds of one's previous existence' (ibid.: 85).

C.4.e. Drugs

Sikhs in Punjab and elsewhere are increasingly aware of addictive drugs and their harmful effects on the individual and on society. Preachers speak out against intoxicants. These include both alcohol and drugs, although alcohol consumption is socially acceptable among Sikh men in a way that smoking has never been (see C.4.c). On alcohol the message of the Guru Granth Sahib is clear. Lines such as the following also apply to drug taking: 'By drinking wine one loses sanity and becomes mad, loses the power of discrimination and incurs the displeasure of God' (Ādi Granth: 554).

Intoxicants and tobacco are forbidden for Sikhs (see Rahit Maryādā). By implication this includes drugs. If an *amritdhārī* (baptised) Sikh breaks these rules he or she is *patit* (lapsed) until readmitted to the *Khālsā* by taking *amrit* (see C.7.c). However, the *Nihangs* of Punjab, the defenders of historic Sikh shrines, take an infusion of cannabis to assist meditation. In general, though, the Sikhs' emphasis on physical fitness rules out drug taking.

C.4.f. The Media

Sikhism stresses truthfulness. The media must be used as honestly as possible. Sikhs have enthusiastically adopted all means of mass communication. Bhai Vir Singh was a pioneer of mass communication in the vernacular. One of the demands of Sikhs in 1981 was the installation of radio transmitters at the Golden Temple, to broadcast *kīrtan* (hymns).

Sikhs are a minority and acutely aware of the way in which the media may misrepresent them. Some Sikhs regard publications which are unsympathetic to their own political stance as propagandist.

C.4.g. Advertising

Contentment is one of the virtues taught by the Gurus. 'The Sikh who works hard limits his needs, and so he does not feel frustrated if he cannot keep up with the Jones' (Mansukhani 1986a: 21). If advertising leads to discontentment it is contrary to Sikh teaching. *Lobh* (greed) and *moh* (attachment to worldly things) must be resisted.

All statements must be true and commodities advertised must not be injurious to health or morality. Advertisements for tobacco and alcohol are contrary to the teachings of Sikhism (see C.4.c).

C.5. THE QUALITY AND VALUE OF LIFE

C.5.a. The Elderly

Respect for one's elders is a key principle of Asian society (see A.5.a). Only through prolonged contact with Western values does care for the elderly become an issue to be discussed. Sikhs, in common with Indians of all other faiths, have always accepted the duty of sons to care for their parents (so the need for mothers to give birth to male children) in a society with minimal state welfare provision. Given the prevailing Punjabi attitudes there was little need for the Gurus to urge what was common practice. However, on the subject of respecting one's parents, Guru Ram Das said: 'Son why do you quarrel with your father due to whom you have grown to this age? It is a sin to argue with him' (Ādi Granth: 1200).

An initial reaction of Asians settling in the West was horror at a society in which the younger generation consigned their parents to institutions for the elderly. Fearful of the shame their family would suffer if fellow members of their community suspected neglect, Asians were reluctant to utilise such services as the local authority provided. Sikhs need to realise the increasing isolation felt by aged parents as they grow old and frail in surroundings where their earlier expectations of support and respect can't be realised and where they are cut off from neighbours and officials by lack of English.

The *gurdwārā* plays an important role in the West as a welcoming, familiar centre for the exchange of gossip; it also promotes an enhanced sense of self-worth through acts of *sevā* such as hoovering or preparing tea for others. But the *gurdwārā*'s potential as a day centre for the elderly, both Sikh and non-Sikh, has yet to be developed. In Tarn Taran, Punjab, the Bhai Vir Singh Birdh Ghar, established in 1958, provides a free home for the elderly, funded by Sikhs' donations. This is a pointer to the future, when in India, as in the West, families may be more fragmented. Along with other Asians, Sikhs have much to teach Westerners about family support for those needing care (see C.5.b), and in turn their commitment to *sevā* must extend beyond immediate kin and community.

In the life of Guru Amar Das, whose twenty-two-year Guruship commenced at the age of 73, Sikhs have a reminder that age need not bring diminished responsibility or service.

C.5.b. Those in Need

Sikhs are to share their earnings with the needy. In the West, gifts to charities are one means of carrying out this obligation. In India, the Chief Khālsā Dīwān set up an orphanage in 1906 in Amritsar. The Pingalwara, also in Amritsar, is a centre supported by voluntary donations, caring for the sick who are desperately in need of shelter. There is a Guru Nanak hospital for the handicapped in Ranchi. In Thakur Nagar, West Bengal, Guru Nanak Niketan has grown from a home for refugee children and orphans into a large community welfare centre.

As medical skills become more expensive and specialised, Sikhs realise that the family and *gurdwārā* may not always be in the strongest position to care directly for the suffering.

Sikhs are always ready to provide temporary assistance. When the Pope visited the English city of Coventry, in 1982, the Ramgarhia Gurdwārā provided refreshments for passing pilgrims, and during the miners' strike of 1983–4 *gurdwārās* in West Yorkshire provided free weekend lunches for miners and their families.

C.5.c. Abortion

There are no injunctions in Sikhism against the use of contraceptives. Abortion is taboo as it is an interference in the creative work of God. If the conception has taken place it would be a sin to destroy life.

(Mansukhani 1986b: 183)

Despite the serious consequences of population growth in India, women have never been pressurised (as in China) to limit their family by abortion (see C.9.b). If an unmarried girl became pregnant and her relatives felt that family honour could be maintained by speedily ending the pregnancy, they might compel her to have an abortion, although this is not defensible on religious grounds. Quite recently it has been emphasised that 'While Sikh teachings do not have any direct advice on abortion, they do teach a respect for life which provides Sikhs with guidance on issues like abortion' (*The Sikh Messenger* Spring/Summer 1988: 32).

Despite Sikh teaching, sons are often more prized than daughters as they carry on the family name, look after their parents and do not require dowries (see C.3.b). As a result, it has happened that in the past many female babies were suffocated at birth. This is contrary to Sikh teaching. Indeed, Rahit Maryādā instructs that: 'The newly baptised Sikhs are told not to associate with those who practise infanticide'. Now that tests enable parents to know the sex of their unborn child some families, influenced by cultural pressure, may wish to abort a female foetus. This needs to be examined in the light of Sikhism's condemnation of infanticide.

C.5.d. Euthanasia

This is not a subject on which Sikhs have made any religious pronouncement. Certainly they would emphasise loving care of any sufferer. Clearly an attempt to end a life for financial motives is immoral. There is also no place in Sikh thought for deliberately ending the life of the incurably ill or irreversibly senile. All Sikhs are to accept what God gives as an expression of the divine will. They must also sympathise with those who crave death as an alternative to being a burden to dear ones. (See Mansukhani 1986b: 183–5 for an outline of 'the Sikh attitude to mercy killing'.)

C.6. QUESTIONS OF RIGHT AND WRONG

C.6.a. The Purpose of Law

Human society is an inseparable part of a universe which exists in accordance with *hukam* (divine order). Good law ensures the harmonious management of human affairs. Justice is the key principle of law. It must protect the weaker sections of society.

Sikhs have nearly always lived under laws imposed by non-Sikhs. They are therefore very alert to legalised discrimination against their community. They expect the law to recognise them as a distinct community (see C.9.a). The inclusion of Sikhs in the category of Hindu in Article 25 of the Indian Constitution has aroused anger.

Sikhs are to keep the laws of the state in which they reside unless these conflict with Sikh principles. In that case Sikh strategy is non-violent mass campaigning. So, in 1975, Sikhs in Britain campaigned for exemption from the law enforcing crash helmets for motor cyclists (see C.1.e).

Sometimes individuals break the law, not on religious grounds, but because they feel that *izzat* (honour) is at stake. In such cases relatives may prefer to punish the offender in their own way rather than by involving the public judiciary. To the outsider this can appear to be an attempt to hamper the course of justice.

C.6.b. Sin and Sins

In the Gurus' terms, humans are either *manmukh* or *gurmukh*, depending on their spiritual orientation. The *manmukh* is wayward and prone to do wrong on the impulse of *man* (mind or caprice in Punjabi). The *gurmukh*, on the other hand, looks to God, the divine Guru, for guidance. Everyone has the natural tendency to be *manmukh* and also, through sustained effort and God's grace, the capacity to lead the life of a *gurmukh*. Ego (*haumai*) and the propensities to lust, anger, covetousness, worldly attachments and pride must be checked, for they give rise to sinful thoughts, words and deeds. One's conduct accords with God's will (*hukam*) only if one's life is spent in unceasing remembrance of God. Otherwise, the five so-called evil passions listed above sway one's judgement.

Through *simran* (remembrance of God) and *sevā* (service to others), it is possible to make good the deficiencies carried over from previous births. According to the law of *karma*, one sows what one reaps, either in this human lifetime or the next. Sikhs do not, however, dwell upon remote concepts of heaven and hell, but upon the here and now. It is possible to achieve release from the cycle of rebirth, and experience oneness with God, through divine grace during one's present lifetime.

Such was the teaching of Guru Nanak and his successors. However, with the institutionalisation of Sikhism in later centuries, a process symbolised by Guru Gobind Singh's inauguration of the *Khālsā* on Baisakhi Day 1699, specific rules and regulations were formulated. These helped to unite Sikhs as fighters for religious freedom. The rules were circulated in the form of *rahitnāmās*, codes of practice, and served the function of the present Rahit Maryādā (which spells out what Sikhs may and may not do). Sikhs must keep the five Ks (the external signs of Sikh faith), learn Gurmukhī, recite prescribed daily prayers and give one-tenth of their income for religious and social work. The gravest offences (*kurāhit*) are cutting the hair on any part of one's body, eating meat slaughtered in the Muslim way, committing adultery and using tobacco. It is also an offence, but less grave, to associate with breakaway or lapsed Sikhs or with those who oppose Sikhism; with those who practise infanticide; with those who arrange a son's or daughter's marriage for profit; with those who dye or remove their grey hairs; with those who indulge in drugs or alcohol; or with those who perform any ceremony contrary to Sikh principles or break the *amrit* vows.

C.6.c. Punishments

Many Sikhs assume that, in accordance with cosmic law (*karma*), individuals are likely to suffer for their wrongdoing, either in this life or in a future birth.

Some offences are specifically religious. They contravene the Rahit Maryādā, but do not necessarily hurt others and are not in breach of the civil law code. Any *amritdhārī* Sikh who deliberately disobeys one of the injunctions laid down in the Rahit Maryādā (for example, by smoking or cutting his or her hair) is termed *patit* (lapsed). The offender must apologise publicly to the congregation and perform whatever *tankhah* (penance) the *panj pyāre* recommend. This is usually community service in the *gurdwārā*, such as looking after worshippers' shoes, or increased daily devotions such as repeating the hymn Japji a certain number of times. The apostate should take *amrit* (be ceremonially reinstated) and make the vows anew.

The death penalty for certain grave offences does not run counter to the Sikh world view. However, when Sikhs are put to death for fighting in what they believe to be a noble cause, such as achieving independence from British rule over India, they are revered as *shahīd* (martyrs), like, for example Shahid Bhagat Singh.

C.6.d. The Wrongdoer and the Wronged

Sadly, many Sikhs have suffered bereavement and injury during the violence of the 1980s and 1990s, particularly in Punjab and Delhi in 1984. Their grief is exacerbated by seeing innocent individuals victimised while murderers are not brought to justice. As noted (C.6.c) and (C.8.b), some have taken the law into their own hands. Many Sikhs turn to a political solution.

Sikhs have also shown a capacity for self-sacrificial non-violence in the face of violent injustice (C.9.b). The qualities of detachment and of compassion (*daya*) are extolled. Forgiveness is not singled out as a scriptural concept but is consistent with the emphasis on overcoming one's ego and being like God, who is without hatred (*nirvair*). This spirit of forgiveness is clearly expressed by Farid:

> Farid, if someone hits you
> Do not hit him back.
> Go home – after kissing his feet. (Ādi Granth: 1378)

Once Guru Angad's son angrily kicked Guru Amar Das off his throne. The Guru's gentle response was 'Great king, forgive me. You must have hurt your foot' (Macauliffe 1978: 64).

C.7. EQUALITY AND DIFFERENCE

C.7.a. Differences between People

The Sikh Gurus stressed the oneness of God and the oneness of the human race, although God was apprehended differently in different religious traditions, and society was divided by differences of culture and wealth. In his Akal Ustat, Guru Gobind Singh declared:

> Though they use different dresses according to the influence of regional
>   customs
> All men have the same eyes, ears, body and figure
> Made out of the compounds of earth, air, fire and water.

The division of Indian society into high and low castes had no place in the Gurus' teaching. Members of all castes must sit together in worship and eat together in the *langar* on the same level. The hymns of two men, Kabir and Ravidas, from low castes, are included in the Guru Granth Sahib. Ever since Guru Gobind Singh baptised the first Khālsā Sikhs in 1699 CE, Sikhs have used the names Singh (lion) and Kaur (princess). Unlike the family names which often indicate caste status, these two titles suggest the equality of all. (See also C.7.b, c, d and C.8.a.)

C.7.b. Attitudes to Other Religions

'Sikhs must in no way give offence to other faiths', states Rahit Maryādā. The lives of the Gurus unequivocally affirm deep and, if necessary, costly friendship with those of other faiths (see C.2.b). The honour paid by the Sikh Maharaja, Ranjit Singh, to Muslims and Hindus in the early nineteenth century is cited by Sikhs with approbation.

'Although the Guru Granth is the centre of Sikh belief, non-Sikh books can be studied for general enlightenment', states Rahit Maryādā. In compiling the Sikh scriptures, Guru Arjan Dev deliberately included not only the Gurus' hymns but those of Muslims such as Farid and Hindus such as Sain. Sikhs are brought up to respect the scriptures and religious insights of non-Sikhs.

However, Sikhs must discriminate in the practices they condone and the company they keep. 'A Sikh should have no dealings with caste, black magic, superstitious practices such as the seeking of auspicious moments, eclipses ... the wearing of sacred threads and similar rituals' (Rahit Maryādā II (d)). This refers to Hindu customs to which, in their homeland, Sikhs might easily revert. Guru Nanak did not teach that all religious rituals were inherently wrong, but that God's truth lay beyond outward limitations. He went to Mecca as a pilgrim, but pointed out that God did not lie only in the direction of the Ka'aba.

Guru Nanak opposed religious groups which ran counter to the social fabric. He chose as his successor a family man, Guru Angad, not his ascetic, celibate son, Sri Chand. One of Guru Nanak's compositions, *Sidh Gost*, reports his criticism of extreme yogic cults.

Sikhs are enjoined, in the Rahit Maryādā, to avoid association with sectarian Sikh splinter groups. In particular, a 1978 *hukamnāmā* commanded Sikhs to boycott the Sant Nirankārīs (see C.1.c). Marginal groups such as these, whose members maintain certain outward signs of Sikh identity, are felt to confuse others and to represent a threat to Sikh unity and integrity.

The prohibition of *halāl* meat enforced the historic division between Sikhs and Muslims. During Mughal times, Sikhs fought political oppressors to break their tyranny, not to destroy their Islamic faith.

The separatism of more institutionalised Sikhism is not to be found in Guru Nanak's hymns. His famous words, 'There is no Hindu, no Muslim. Whose path shall I follow? I shall follow God's path', convey his conviction that God's truth is beyond religious affiliation. In Akāl Ustat, Guru Gobind Singh proclaimed: 'Hindus and Muslims are one ... The temple and the mosque are the same ... All men are one, it is through error that they appear different.'

The Sikh is called to see God's light shining in others whatever their religious persuasion. Conversion from one faith to another is irrelevant.

Sikhs do not proselytise as they believe that the devout and sincere in all faiths attain salvation and truth. To quote Dr Gobind Singh Mansukhani:

> As all water eventually reaches the sea, so spiritually this is also possible by following the various religious paths conscientiously and with understanding. It is this thinking that the layout of 'Golden Temple' at Amritsar illustrates materially. Its four doors welcome visitors to enter from any direction. (Mansukhani 1986a: 20)

In practice, the Sikh acceptance of the validity of other faiths does not extend to ready acceptance of marriage into another faith, except for marriage with Hindus of the same caste (see C.3.a). In particular, few parents would permit marriage between their daughter and a Muslim. In telling her own story, Sharan-Jeet Shan highlights this seeming paradox (Shan 1985: 35). What seems at first inconsistent can be justified (see C.3.a.).

C.7.c. Attitudes to Other Races

During the Gurus' period, Northern India was split along lines of religion, caste and political status, that is, the Mughal rulers and their powerless subjects. Sikhs are aware of the continuing need to affirm the equality of different nations.

According to Indarjit Singh:

> In stressing the equality of all human beings, men and women, their emphasis on social and religious tolerance and their brave and forthright attack on all notions of caste, class or racial superiority [the *Gurus*] gave us, in a sense, the forerunner of the United Nations ideal, the key, not only to sanity and survival in the world today, but also to the positive realisation that different cultures, different ways of life, are not barriers between people, but gateways to a fuller understanding and enrichment of life itself. ('Thought for the Day', BBC, 23 October 1985)

C.7.d. Women and Men

It is a frequently heard Sikh claim that the Gurus revolutionised the status of women. According to prevailing Hindu belief, women were often ritually unclean through menstruation or childbirth. Girls were a liability whose marriages drained the family's financial resources. Widows were regarded as the bearers of bad luck. Such attitudes contributed to the practice of female infanticide, the ban on widow remarriage and the ideal of *sati* – the loyal wife immolating herself on her husband's funeral pyre. The Gurus' condemnation of these customs is reiterated in successive *rahitnāmās* (codes of practice). Sikh women were not even to veil their faces.

Unfortunately convention has not always tallied with the Gurus' teachings. Baby girls were often smothered at birth until this century (see C.5.c), and even in Britain Sikh women of the Bhatra subcaste frequently cover their faces in the presence of senior male in-laws. Dowries continue to be given and expected. Women themselves are perpetuating the custom (see Bhachu 1985). Dowries are sometimes seen as a gift to the girl rather than as a demand by the boy's parents which can improve the woman's situation.

The Gurus established *grihasth* (the life of the householder or married person) as the ideal and normal way of life. This meant that both men and women could achieve union with God through constant remembrance of the divine in the course of faithfully discharging family responsibilities. A woman need not await rebirth as a man in order to achieve *moksha* (release from the cycle of rebirth), and since celibacy was not the noblest state for a man, women need no longer be feared as seducers and temptresses. According to the Gurus, sexual continence and fidelity to one's spouse are as important for men as for women (for example, Ādi Granth: 403 and 8117), although in practice Sikh society more readily condones men's sexual promiscuity (see C.2.c and C.3.a). According to Guru Nanak:

> It is through woman, the despised one, that we are conceived and from her that we are born. It is to woman that we get engaged and then married. She is our lifelong friend and the survival of our race depends on her. On her death a man seeks another wife. Through women we establish our social ties. Why denounce her, the one from whom even kings are born? (Ādi Granth: 473)

In these much-quoted lines, esteem for women is linked to the dependency of men on them.

Although Sikh history and public life are still dominated by men, and the Guru Granth Sahib consists only of compositions by men, women of courage have played a conspicuous part in the Sikhs' struggles. Sikhs remember with respect Guru Nanak's first follower, his elder sister Nanake; the Gurus' wives for their contribution to Sikh corporate life; and women preachers and ladies such as Mai Bhago who fought in battle. Sikh women of the eighteenth and nineteenth centuries showed themselves skilled in diplomacy. In 1699 Guru Gobind Singh's wife added sugar sweets to the first *amrit*. Women are as eligible as men for initiation. In the *gurdwāra*, acts of *sevā* and ritual participation are open to men and women equally, although in practice men far outnumber women on management committees and women preponderate in the kitchens. Woman's noblest role is seen as that of loving wife and mother.

The five Ks (*kesh*, *kanghā*, *kirpān*, *karā* and *kachh*) are worn by both sexes. Among some groups, for example those influenced by Bhai Randhir Singh, women cover their hair with a turban (*keskī*). Here we have a visual demonstration of sexual equality in Sikhism.

Essential to Sikh spirituality is the image, as in the Lāvān marriage hymn of Guru Ram Das, of the human soul's relation to God as that of a devoted wife submitting in joy to her husband. Different readers will react in various ways to the implications of this image, with regard to women's status.

C.7.e. Are All People Equal?

Individuals differ in ability, personality and material circumstances. At different stages in life, each person has different roles to play. From sections

C.7.a–d it should be clear that Sikh teaching emphasises the equality of all people in relation to God: 'God is one and we are all his children. The poor and the rich are brothers' (Ādi Granth: 611). Reunion with God, through the grace of the Guru, is open to all.

C.8. NATIONAL DIVISIONS, WAR AND PEACE

C.8.a. Why do Different Nations Exist?

Sikhism regards the differences between nations as less important than the oneness of the human race (see Indarjit Singh 1987: Section 7). However, sensitive to their vulnerability as a minority community, Sikhs increasingly perceive and present themselves as a distinct nation. In 1983 the British House of Lords ruled that Sikhs: 'are more than a religious sect. They are almost a race and almost a nation. They qualify as a group defined by ethnic origins because they constitute a separate and distinct community.' This statement was the culmination of a case brought by S. S. Mandla, whose son had been refused admission to a private school unless he removed his turban. For Sikhs concerned to promote their nationhood, this was a notable vindication.

In contemporary Sikh controversy over Khalistan (a state separate from India for which some are campaigning), Sikh understanding of nationhood emerges. However, this draws more on nineteenth- and twentieth-century world history and political theory than on Sikh religious teaching. Its causes are economic as well as ideological. Those who share a common religion, language and homeland (Punjab) should, the separatists feel, be prepared to struggle for political sovereignty. A community's shared identity and sense of grievance must fuel a fight for independence. Only then is their nationhood acknowledged by the rest of the world, as happened with Pakistan in 1947 and Bangladesh in 1971. Inspiration is drawn from Sikh history – especially the reign of Maharaja Ranjit Singh. Some Sikhs would justify acts of violence in a nationalist cause on the religious grounds of fighting against oppression so that right may prevail (see C.8.b).

Sikh views differ. But in the *Ardās*, the daily prayer in which all participate, after commemorating their community's costly history, Sikhs pray for God's blessings not only on Sikhs, but on all people.

C.8.b. Conflict between Nations

Khālsā Sikhs are characterised by the five K's, religious symbols beginning with the Gurmukhī equivalent of the letter 'K'. Of these, probably the *karā* (steel wristlet) and certainly the *kirpān* (sword) have military significance. However, Sikhs are enjoined to take up arms against others only in defence, and only as a last resort: 'When all efforts to restore peace prove useless and no words avail, Lawful is the flash of steel, it is right to draw the sword' (Guru Gobind Singh, Zafarnāmā).

The violence of Sikh extremists is frequently reported, but Sikhs generally oppose wanton destruction, believe in the right of others to live, and have never engaged in warfare to compel conversion to their faith. There is no Sikh equivalent of the Crusades or of holy war, although the term *dharamyudh* (religious war) has been applied emotively to the Sikh campaign of the 1980s to wrest greater autonomy for Punjab from India's central government (see C.8.a).

To the non-Sikh, it can appear that the non-violent stance and teaching of the first five Gurus was considerably altered by the decision of Guru Hargobind (Guru 1606–44) to militarise his followers, and by Guru Gobind Singh's martial leadership. (Both Guru Hargobind's father, Guru Arjan Dev, and Guru Gobind Singh's father, Guru Tegh Bahadur, had died as unresisting martyrs.) However, in Sikh faith the ten human *Gurus* were one in their divine spirit. As political circumstances changed and Sikhs and Hindus felt increasingly threatened by the repressive measures of Mughal rulers, a different emphasis was needed, although this was totally consistent with the vision of Guru Nanak.

In Guru Gobind Singh's poetic compositions, a military metaphor is often used to convey God's greatness. God is addressed as the sword and All-steel. So, for example, Guru Gobind Singh wrote in Bachitar Nātak:

I bow with heart and mind to the holy sword …
The sword cuts sharply, destroys the host of the wicked, and has power
   to make the battlefield glorious …
The sword brings peace to the saints,
Fear to the evil minded, destruction to sin,
So it is my refuge.

In his Akal Ustat, Guru Gobind Singh requests:

May we have the protection of All-steel
May we have the protection of All-death.

In Jāp Sāhib he proclaims:

Salutations to God who wields the sword,
Salutations to God who can throw arrows.

Elsewhere God is addressed as 'musket', 'cannon' and 'lance'. Through such hymns, Guru Gobind Singh no doubt intended not only to portray one aspect of divine power, but also to awaken his followers to fearless acts of valour.

Sikhs keep alive, in paintings and narrative, historic examples of their forebears' heroism, such as Baba Dip Singh's return to Amritsar from battle, bearing his severed head. In many cases Sikhs showed their bravery as they underwent barbarous torture rather than surrender their faith. Bhai Taru Singh's scalp was removed because he refused to allow his hair to be cut.

Sikh history clearly shows that armed conflict springs from greed, from power over others and from the anger of those in power at the dissent of a minority. In practice, within the Sikh community violent actions result from outraged *izzat* (family honour).

Sikhs have shown themselves heroes of non-violent action against oppression. Their passive resistance to police brutality in 1921 at Guru Ka Bagh, a shrine near Amritsar, greatly impressed Gandhi's friend C. F. Andrews, as recalled by Khushwant Singh (Singh 1977: 204).

As yet few Sikhs have turned their thought seriously to the issues relating to nuclear arms. Resorting to traditional weapons could not genetically affect unborn generations or destroy life on the planet as nuclear war could, nor could it divert such vast sums of money from other purposes at a time when millions are on the verge of starvation. In a paper given at a plenary session of the World Conference of Religious Workers in Moscow, 1982, Dr Rajinder Kaur declared that all nations must stop the arms race:

> The very idea of nuclear weaponry is repugnant to Sikh religious thought because it can exterminate the whole of life [and bring about] total destruction of mankind, the highest expression of the Supreme Self, God Himself. (Kaur 1982: 20)

C.9. Global Issues

C.9.a. Responses to World Poverty

Action to redress the unjust distribution of the world's resources is in keeping with the message of the Gurus. Sikhs are Punjabi, except for a few Western converts (see C.1.a), so they have a different world view from people who are culturally rooted in materially affluent Western consumer societies. As industrious members of a developing society, Sikhs have brought relative prosperity to India's Punjab state. Here they have increased agricultural yields markedly in the last few decades, and they are keen to develop new industries. Sikhs' prime concern is bettering the lot of their immediate family, caste-community or village. However, greater material security should free resources for global use. In 1971 British *gurdwārās* collected funds to help rehabilitate refugees from Bangladesh. Such acts of organised giving make one hopeful that in future, Sikhs will be increasingly ready to provide relief for those in need, far beyond, as well as within, the borders of India (see C.5.b).

C.9.b. Responses to Population Control

Over-population was not an issue facing the human race until the twentieth century. Now it is more pressing in the Sikhs' homeland, India, than in countries to which they have emigrated. Since Independence (1947), India's government has publicised the need for a reduced birthrate and has offered inducements. During India's State of Emergency (1975–7) the campaign was intensified and many citizens underwent compulsory sterilisation or vasectomy.

In Sikhism marital fidelity, not celibacy, is the goal for all, so population growth has never been limited by encouraging men or women to be monks or nuns.

The Sikh religion does not forbid the use of contraceptives. In practice, the more educated Sikhs tend to have fewer children. In Punjab, prior to the Emergency, Balwant Singh, a prominent member of the Akali cabinet, promoted family planning. The Shiromani Gurdwara Parbandhak Committee is the most influential elected body in Sikh Affairs. In January 1973 its official journal, *Gurmat Parkash*, reported that the SGPC had discussed the forced sterilisations and vasectomies and decided that these contravened the Sikh injunction to maintain *kesh* (uncut hair), as pubic hair was shaved off before surgery.

Sikhs are currently more preoccupied with Punjabi affairs than with global considerations. Nothing in their scriptures or tradition contradicts the widely held view that, as the average life expectancy increases and resources run down, adults should be encouraged to limit their families. From a religious viewpoint, self-control is the preferred method (see Mansukhani 1986b). However, with the fear of losing their narrow majority in Punjab, Sikhs may prefer to have large families.

C.9.c. Planet Earth and Ecology

Punjab is an agricultural state. Of its many farmers, the majority are Sikh. Their concern for improved yields made them wholehearted supporters of the Green Revolution which began in the 1960s. They have welcomed modern technology and use of chemical fertilisers. The long-term effects of these innovations, both economically and environmentally, will affect their lives profoundly and not only for the good. However, despite the Bhopal disaster of 1984, environmental concern in India is less developed than in the West.

In Western countries television has alerted people to the unjust distribution of world food supplies. Many argue that vegetarianism would reduce the waste of protein-rich grain which could be used to feed humans but is currently diverted to feed cattle. Others argue against human exploitation of fellow species on planet earth. Sikh vegetarians would concur with these views – in particular the Nāmdharis, whose leader campaigns actively to promote vegetarianism. But such considerations have never been fundamental to the Sikhs, and diet remains a matter for individual choice.

Continuing the ruling of Guru Gobind Singh, the Rahit Maryādā forbids the consumption of *halāl* meat, that is, animals slaughtered in the Islamic manner. Some Sikhs interpret this as permission to eat animals killed by other methods. For others, it constitutes a total ban on meat.

The Guru Granth Sahib and traditional stories of the Gurus' lives are also ambiguous. Guru Nanak's verses (Ādi Granth: 1289–90) addressed the contemporary Brahminical Hindu view that anyone who ate meat was polluted. He pointed out that we are caught up in the chain of life and that it is difficult to be completely free of exploitation (ibid.). He suggested that plants are also living organisms.

There are stories of later Gurus eating meat and even hunting. In practice, most people's diet in Punjab includes meat more rarely than in the Western diet. In conformity with Hindu respect for the cow, the Sikh diet excludes beef. (In this way the cattle stock, vital for milk and haulage, was conserved.) *Langar* (the Sikh's shared meal) is vegetarian, so that anyone can eat there.

In Western societies the prevailing norms force Sikhs to make a conscious decision on the basis of Guru Nanak's teaching: 'The food which causes pain to the body and breeds evil in the mind is baneful' (Ādi Granth: 16). In reaching a personal decision the Sikh may also take into account Hindu teachings on non-violence and on the correlation between categories of food and types of character, as well as such twentieth-century issues as factory farming, starvation and the effects on health of excess cholesterol and food additives.

Glossary

Ādi Granth	The Sikh scriptures, Guru Granth Sahib
Ahankār	Pride
Akāl Takht	'Throne of the Timeless One', a building facing the Golden Temple in Amritsar. The most binding decisions on religious matters are taken here
Akāl Ustat	A composition in the Dasam Granth
Akālī	Member of a political party representing Sikh interests
Amrit	'Ambrosia', the sanctified sweetened water used in initiation (*amrit*) ceremonies. Although it is not altogether satisfactory, 'baptism' is sometimes used to translate this
Amritdhārī	A Sikh who has received *amrit*, one who professes commitment to Sikh principles

127

Anand Karaj	'Ceremony of bliss', wedding ceremony
Ardās	Formal prayer offered in most acts of worship
Bachitar Nātak	An autobiographical composition in the *Dasam Granth*. In this, Guru Gobind Singh declares his mission
Bhāī	'Brother', respectful title for male Sikh
Chaurī	Fan, usually made of yak-tail hair or nylon. This is waved over the scriptures as a traditional mark of respect
Chief Khālsā Dīwān	The political arm of the Singh Sabha movement. It was formed in 1902
Dal Khālsā	The undivided army of the Khalsa
Dasam Granth	Volume (*granth*) of compositions by the tenth (*dasam*) Guru
Dasvandh	Tythe, the tenth part of one's earnings which should be given to charity
Dayā	Compassion, sympathy
Dharamyudh	'Righteous War', a name used for the current Sikh campaign against injustices
Dharma	One's rightful function. Dharam in Punjabi
Giānī	'Knowledgeable', title for person who is well versed in the Sikh scriptures
Got	Exogamous group within the *zāt* (in Hindi this is *gotra*)
Granthī	A reader of the Guru Granth Sahib. Sometimes the *granthī* is a paid custodian employed in a *gurdwārā*
Grihasth	Householder, married person. This is the ideal and expected lifestyle for Sikhs
Gurdwārā	Sikh place of worship, a place in which the Guru Granth Sahib is installed
Gurmatā	A decision, affecting the Sikh community, taken in the presence of the Guru (nowadays the Guru Granth Sahib)
Gurmukh	A person whose life is directed towards God
Gurmukhī	The script in which Sikh scriptures and Punjabi (in the Indian State of Punjab) are written
Guru	Teacher. For Sikhs this term is used only for God, each of the ten human Gurus and the scriptures
Guru Granth Sahib	Scriptures. The 1430-page volume consists of hymns by six Gurus and other religious poets
Halāl	Permissible in Islamic Law. Meat of animals killed in the Muslim manner

Haumai	Egoism
Hukam	Order, God's will
Hukamnāmā	Binding pronouncement issued by the highest Sikh authority; a directive from the Guru Granth Sahib
Izzat	Honour, reputation. This is a powerful force in South Asian community life
Janamsākhī	Hagiographic account of Guru Nanak's life. There are several manuscript traditions. One of these is known as Purātan (ancient) and it includes a manuscript which can be seen in the India Office Library, London (MS Danj, B6)
Jāp (Sāhib)	Introductory invocation in the Dasam Granth
Japjī (Sāhib)	The opening stanzas of the Guru Granth Sahib. Devout Sikhs repeat these each morning. *Jap* means 'repeat'
Jat	The dominant caste community (*zāt*) in Punjab, traditionally land-owning farmers
Jathedār	Leader of a political or religious group
Jihād	Islamic obligation to wage war in the cause of the faith
Ka'aba	The building in Mecca that is most revered by Muslims and towards which they pray
Kachh	Trousers which do not come below the knee. One of the Five Ks, symbolising self-restraint
Kām	Lust
Kanghā	Comb. One of Five Ks used to keep the hair clean and tidy
Kār sevā	Voluntary work such as constructing or repairing a gurdwārā
Karā	Steel band worn on the right wrist, one of the Five Ks
Karma	Action, the law of cause and effect. Hence the adjective *karmic*. Karam in Punjabi
Kaur	Prince (usually translated princess), the title of all female Sikhs
Kesh	Uncut hair, one of the Five Ks
Keskī	A small turban
Khālsā	'Pure', 'owing direct allegiance', i.e. to the Guru. The family of initiated Sikhs formed by Guru Gobind Singh, maintaining his rules of conduct and dress
Khande dī pāhul	Initiation (*pāhul*) with the two-edged sword (*khandā*) which is used to stir the *amrit*

Kirpān	Sword, one of the Five Ks
Kīrtan	Congregational singing of the hymns from the Guru Granth Sahib
Krodh	Anger
Kurāhit	Any breach of Khālsā code of discipline
Langar	Free meal served to anyone visiting the *gurdwārā*; the area where it is prepared and served
Lāvān	Stanzas composed by Guru Ram Das. These are the core of the Anand Karaj
Lobh	Greed
Man	Mind, whim
Manjī	An area of jurisdiction during the Mughal period. Guru Amar Das adopted a similar system
Manmukh	Any self-centred person (as contrasted with the *gurmukh*)
Masand	A representative of the Guru, preaching and collecting donations on his behalf (Guru Gobind Singh discontinued this as the *masands* became corrupt)
Mīrī	Temporal power (see *pīrī*)
Misal	(Arabic 'equal'.) Name for the twelve bands of Sikh fighters that emerged in the mid-eighteenth century
Moh	Materialism, attachment to worldly affairs and relationships
Moksha	Liberation of the human spirit from the cycle of rebirth
Nām	The name of God, God's essential nature
Nāmdhārī	A group whose nineteenth-century founder and leader, Ram Singh, urged a strictly disciplined life, including vegetarianism
Nihang	'Without anxiety'. Nihang Singhs arose in the time of Guru Gobind Singh. They particularly revere the Dasam Granth. Nihangs often wear tall, dark blue or saffron coloured turbans and carry steel weapons
Nirvair	Devoid of enmity, a characteristic of the divine reality
Panj pyāre	Five (*panj*) beloved ones (*pyāre*). Those who administer *amrit* to candidates for initiation share this name with the first five Sikhs who publicly demonstrated their loyalty to Guru Gobind Singh in 1699
Panth	'Religious way', the Sikh community
Patit	'Lapsed', one who transgresses the Khālsā code of discipline
Pīrī	Spiritual authority

Purātan	See Janamsākhī
Rahit Maryādā	Code of discipline
Rahitnāmā	Written codes of discipline issued from the eighteenth century
Rāmgarhīā	Title adopted by Sikhs of certain artisan castes, for example woodworkers and masons
Sache Pādshāh	'True Emperor', a title accorded to the Guru and God
Sāhib	A title of respect which Sikhs confer on historic shrines, certain hymns in the scriptures and to the scriptures as a whole
Sangat	Congregation
Sant	An acclaimed leader exercising considerable influence on spiritual and sometimes political affairs
Sant Nirankārī	Name of a twentieth-century group related historically to Sikhism but differing from it on central principles of belief and conduct
Santokh	Contentment
Sant-Sipāhī	'Saint-Soldier', the Sikh ideal of spirituality combined with disciplined courage
Satī	A wife whose devotion is so great that she chooses to die on her husband's funeral pyre
Sevā	Service to others, especially in the *gurdwārā*
Shahīd	Martyr
Sharam	Modesty, a sense of shame
Shiromani Gurdwara Parbandhak Committee	Chief Gurdwara Management Committee, Amritsa. This is a powerful, elected body, referred to as SGPC
Sidh Gost	One of Guru Nanak's hymns
Sikh	A learner (from *sikhna* 'to learn'), a believer in God, the teachings of the ten Gurus and the Guru Granth Sahib
Simran	'Remembrance', meditation
Singh	'Lion', second name of Sikh males (see also *kaur*)
Singh Sabhā	Late nineteenth-century movement to reform and revive Sikhism
Tankhāh	Penance, i.e. for disobeying the basic rules of Sikh discipline
Vāhigurū	A title for God, the wonderful Guru
Vār	Heroic ballad, a poetic composition
Zafarnāmā	Guru Gobind Singh's *Epistle of Victory*, addressed to the Emperor Aurangzeb. It forms part of Dasam Granth

Zāt   Endogomous community, traditionally sharing a hereditary occupation. (*Jāti* in Hindi)

REFERENCES

Texts

Ādi Granth

Singh, G. (trans.), *Sri Guru Granth Sahib*, 4 vols, Delhi, 1962.

Singh, M. (trans.), *Sri Guru Granth Sahib*, 8 vols, Amritsar, 1962–9.

Singh, T. et al. (trans.), *Selections from the Sacred Writings of the Sikhs*, Allen & Unwin, 1960.

NB *The references within this chapter do not follow a particular translation, and the page numbers refer to the Gurmukhī text. The reader will be able to trace quotations in any of the above translations.*

Dasam Granth

Loehlin, C. H., *The Granth of Guru Gobind Singh and the Khalsa Brotherhood*, Lucknow, 1971.

NB *No complete English translation of Guru Gobind Singh's compositions has been published.*

Janamsākhīs

McLeod, W. Hew, *Early Sikh Tradition: A Study of the Janamsākhīs*, Oxford University Press, 1980.

McLeod, W. Hew, *The B40 Janamsākhī*, Guru Nanak Dev University, 1986.

NB *This is the only complete English translation of a janamsākhī.*

Rahitnāmās

Grewal, J. S., *From Guru Nanak to Maharaja Ranjit Singh: Essays in Sikh History*, Guru Nanak Dev University, 1972. (In this the Prem Sumarg is discussed.)

McLeod, W. Hew, *The Chaupa Singh Rahit-nāmā*, University of Otago Press, 1985.

McLeod, W. Hew, 'The Problem of the Panjabi rahit nāmās', in Mukherjee, S. N. (ed.), *India; History and Thought: Essays in Honour of A L Basham*, Subarnarekha, 1982, pp. 103–26.

Rahit Maryādā (Rehat Maryada)

Kaur, K. and I. Singh (trans.), *Rehat Maryādā: A Guide to the Sikh Way of Life*, 1971.

The Sikh Code of Conduct, Sikh Missionary Resource Centre, n.d.

McLeod, W. Hew (trans. and ed.), *Textual Sources for the Study of Sikhism*, Manchester University Press, 1984, pp. 79–86.

ETHICAL ISSUES IN SIX RELIGIOUS TRADITIONS

General

Bailey, J. R., *Religious Leaders and Places of Pilgrimage Today*, Religion in Life: a Religious Education Course for Secondary Schools, Schofield & Sims, 1987.

Bedi, S. S., *Folklore of the Punjab*, National Book Trust, 1971.

Bhachu, P., *Twice Migrants*, Tavistock, 1985.

Cole, W. O. and P. S. Sambhi, *The Sikhs: Their Religious Beliefs and Practices*, Sussex Academic Press, 1995.

Hawley, J. S. and G. S. Mann (eds), *Studying the Sikhs: Issues for North America*, State University of New York Press, 1993.

Hershman, P., *Punjabi Kinship and Marriage*, Hindustan Publishing Corporation, 1981.

Kaur, R., 'Paper Given at a Plenary Session of the World Conference of Religious Workers, Moscow', in *The Sikh Courier*, Autumn/Winter 1982, p. 20, and *Spokesman Weekly*, June 1983, p. 4.

Kohli, S. S., *Sikh Ethics*, Manoharlal, 1975. On pp. 66–7, original sources for Sikh ethics are listed.

Macauliffe, A. H., *The Sikh Religion*, 4 vols, S. Chand & Co. Ltd., 1978.

McCormack, M. K., *The Sikh Marriage Ceremony*, no. 7, Sikh Society of Great Britain, n.d.

McLeod, W. Hew, 'Ethical Standards in World Religions – The Sikhs', in *Expository Times*, vol. 85, no. 8, 1974, pp. 233–7, and *The Sikh Courier*, vol. 7, no. 5, Spring 1975, pp. 4–9.

Mansukhani, G. S., 'Sikhism and its Ethical Values', in *The Sikh Messenger*, Summer 1986a, pp. 17–21.

Mansukhani, G. S., *Introduction to Sikhism*, Hemkunt Press, 1986b.

Pettigrew, J., *Robber Noblemen – a Study of the Political System of the Sikh Jats*, Routledge, 1975.

Sambhi, P. S., 'Sikhism', in W. O. Cole (ed.), *Comparative Religions*, Blandford Press, 1982.

Sambhi, P. S., 'Sikhism', in J. M. Sutcliffe (ed.), *A Dictionary of Religious Education*, SCM, 1984.

Sambhi, P. S., 'Alcohol and Religion: a Comparative Study, *The Sikh Messenger*, summer 1985, pp. 28–30.

Sambhi, P. S., 'Sikhism: a family religion', *The Sikh Messenger*, summer 1986, pp. 7–11.

Sambhi, P. S., 'A Survey of Religious Attitudes to Meat Eating', *The Sikh Messenger*, winter 1986/spring 1987, pp. 27–31.

Shan, S.-J., *In My Own Name*, The Women's Press, 1985.

Singh, A., *Ethics of the Sikhs*, Punjabi University, 1983.

Singh, Bhai Vir, *Sundri*, trans. G. S. Mansukhani, Hemkunt Press, 1983.

Singh, H., 'The Place of Women in Sikhism', *Khera*, vol. 9, no. 3, 1990, pp. 64 ff.

Singh, I., 'Thought for the Day', BBC, 23 October 1985; 'Thought for the Day', BBC, 31 August 1987, published as 'Sikhs and Race' in *The Sikh Messenger*, summer 1987, p. 22.

Singh, K., *A History of the Sikhs, Vol. 2, 1839–1974*, Oxford University Press, 1977.

Singh, N., *The Sikh Moral Tradition: Ethical Perception of the Sikhs in the Late Nineteenth and Early Twentieth Centuries*, Manohar, 1990.

Singh, Teja, 'Women in Sikhism', in id. *Essays in Sikhism*, Sikh University Press, 1989, pp. 44–9.

Singh, Trilochan (trans.), *Autobiography of Bhai Sahib Randhir Singh*, Bhai Sahib Randhir Singh Publishing House, 1971.

Talib, G. S. and H. Singh (trans. with Yann Lovelock), *Bhai Vir Singh: Poet of the Sikhs*, Motilal bonarsidas, 1976.

Talib, G. S., 'The Basis and Development in Ethical Thought in Sikhism', in L. M. Joshi (ed.), *Sikhism*, Punjab University, 1980, pp. 86–130.

USEFUL ADDRESSES

Information and books on Sikhism not easily available elsewhere can be obtained from:
Sikh Education Society, Box 1103, Postal Station A, Vancouver, British Columbia, Canada V6C 2T1.
Sikh Missionary Society (UK), 10 Featherstone Road, Southall, Middlesex UB2 5AA.

Copies of *The Sikh Code of Conduct* (*Rahit Maryādā*) are also available from:
Sikh Missionary Resource Centre, 411 Dudley Road, Birmingham B18 4HD.

For books published in India contact:
Books from India (UK) Ltd, 69 Great Russell Street, London WC1B 3BQ

Articles on ethics can be found in:
The Sikh Messenger, 43 Dorset Road, Merton Park, London SW19 3EZ.

A list of Sikh organisations worldwide is published in:
Shergill, N. S., *Shergill's International Directory of Gurdwaras and Sikh Organisations*, available from Virdee Brothers (Booksellers), 102 The Green, Southall, Middlesex UB2 4BQ.

D. JUDAISM

Clive Lawton

D.1. Religious Identity and Authority

D.1.a. On Being Jewish

Being Jewish is primarily to belong to a people, an extended family, a tribe, a historical community. Most Jews will grow up knowing something of their recent and distant history and will feel themselves part of the destiny which is that of the Jewish People.

Since Jews have lived so long scattered outside their own homeland, they have become skilful at absorbing the cultures and traditions of the societies in which they live, while at the same time retaining their own distinctive identity. This scattering or dispersion is known as diaspora. As the world's population becomes more mobile, more and more religions which were established in one place, or associated with one culture, are learning to cope with the diaspora experience which has been the 'normal' experience of the Jew for centuries.

A Jew may frequently be wholly indistinguishable from his non-Jewish neighbours, but for many Jews the traditions of their religion give them distinctive practices and perceptions that enrich their lives.

Jewish religious tradition stems from the Torah, the first five books of the Bible, in which are to be found a large number of rules and commandments, for example, 'Love your neighbour as yourself' (Leviticus 19:18), and 'Honour your father and your mother' (Exodus 20:12). In addition, it sets out the early history of the Jewish People.

This collection of rules and laws merely acts as the headlines for an extensive system of rules which are known as the Oral Torah. These have been discussed over the centuries and are still discussed to this day. The largest encyclopaedia of this discussion is the sixteen-volume Talmud, which includes the thoughts and teachings of over a thousand rabbis over a thousand years up to about the sixth century CE.

The discussion centres around how one performs or fulfils the *mitzvot* in the Torah. (The word *mitzvah* is not easy to translate but it carries the compound meaning of a good deed which is required of the Jew and which adds to his or her dignity and status in the sight of God.) Each *mitzvah* is seen to be a directive from God and therefore its precise mode of fulfilment becomes crucially important. It is disagreement about the authority and interpretation of the Torah that is the basic division between the Orthodox and the groups known as Reform, Conservative and Liberal Jews. The latter groups are sometimes known as Progressive Jews.

In the first instance, a person who is learned in the Torah and qualified to teach – a rabbi – will be consulted on a specific problem or situation and he (and for Progressive Jews, she) will rule as best as possible within the context of personal understanding based on learning. For example, when the electric light was first invented, a debate arose as to whether or not turning on such a light on *Shabbat* would constitute lighting a fire, which is forbidden. Each rabbi asked to rule would make his own decision (the majority decided it was like lighting a fire), and now therefore the *halakha* (the accepted consensus as to the proper course of action or ruling) states that it is forbidden to turn an electric light on or off on *Shabbat* since it is like lighting or extinguishing a fire.

Each rabbi's decision is independent and carries weight only within his or her own community, until a body of rulings has built up which will then be collated and considered by a scholar who has specialised in such a subject. If the resulting assessment of the majority mood is inaccurate, then other rabbis will not accept the scholar's view and the *halakha* would simply not be according to his or her decision. (No rabbi will automatically agree with another rabbi and no rabbi has greater authority than any other unless the rabbis agree to submit to such authority.) Eventually, as consensus grows on the correct way to act in a given situation, this becomes the *halakha*.

There are, of course, always new areas where the *halakha* is being considered and the atmosphere of debate and argument is vigorously cultivated in the Jewish community. It is recognised that there is a need to thrash out the various arguments for and against a given course of action. Further the traditional perception of the Torah is that it is multifaceted and deserves the subtlety of human ingenuity in recognising the possibility of a vast number of legitimate interpretations. Nevertheless, when a community is deciding how to behave there can only be a single ruling in order that the community retains a coherent identity.

This has resulted in Jews valuing study, articulate discussion, and free thinking, but against a background of communally responsible action.

Dominant in the life of the practising Jew will be commitment to family (see Genesis 29:10 and the stress on 'his mother's brother') and to community in terms of respecting, honouring and offering charitable and welfare support. As the mystical book, the Zohar, says: 'It is the duty of the righteous to aid the wicked; of the wise to aid the unwise; of the rich to aid the poor. Each person should aid his fellow man according to his talent' (Zohar 1:208a). Other dominant concerns are commitment to dietary rules (for example Deuteronomy 14), observance of the festivals (of which there are many, for example Deuteronomy 16) and *Shabbat* which is, in a way, a weekly festival. The degree of commitment will, of course, vary from person to person.

Support for the Jewish People is another way in which Jews are affected by their Jewish identity on a regular basis; this means that many Jews are actively involved in support for the State of Israel, the plight of Soviet and Arab Jewry, concern for the rehabilitation of Ethiopian Jewry and charitable activities at home.

D.1.b. Authority

Strictly speaking, authority is only really possessed by certain texts. As soon as human beings are involved the matter is open to human error and interpretation, and we are at the mercy of individual opinion. Alongside this statement must go the consciousness that a text is read by people and perceived by them in different ways. It is extremely difficult to arrive at what a text 'really' means – only what most people *think* it means.

The orthodox Jewish belief that the text of Torah is God given makes the text the only infallible item. All human beings, however great, are fallible and therefore no one person has absolute authority. Even Moses made mistakes and could be advised by his heathen father-in-law, and Abraham's impulse to be excessively merciful to the inhabitants of Sodom and Gommorah was corrected by God.

The key text is the Torah and the second most important text is the Talmud. Because of the complexity of the Talmud and the brevity of the Torah, it is quite probable that on simple issues the easiest way to arrive at a fairly authoritative answer to a dilemma is to consult the Shulkhan Arukh (A Set Table) which, as its name implies, is codified in a much more straight-forward way.

However, in order to understand these texts and their authority, scholars and teachers must learn about and transmit their contents. A person's authority to interpret depends on their learning, and a rabbi's authority is based on his knowledge and understanding of these texts and the traditional commentaries and interpretations arising from them.

D.1.c. Authority Figures in the Faith

No single individual holds authority over the whole Jewish community. Even those who are nominated chief rabbi in a given locality merely hold that authority through the consensus of the other local rabbis, or by virtue of having been appointed by the lay leadership. Because of the democratic structure of synagogue life, the lay leaders of the community (who are normally elected on a regular basis, or achieve their position by virtue of seniority or the respect they hold in the eyes of the community) have considerable authority in terms of the running of day-to-day communal affairs, including charitable activities, social life and the conferring of honours.

As the basic authority of Judaism lies in the text, no single character in the past, in terms of his or her sayings or teachings, has absolute authority in preference to anyone else whose teachings and sayings lie within the traditional ambit of Judaism. The Talmud demonstrates this excellently. This encyclopaedic work was compiled over the space of eight hundred years or more, and quotes more than one thousand rabbis. Nowhere between its covers is it indicated that one rabbi has superior status to another, and while it becomes clear that the rulings and interpretations of some rabbis are usually preferred to those of others (usually the more lenient), all are recorded equally. Indeed there is a story in the Talmud which indicates it is possible for two conflicting interpretations both to be right!

It is worth mentioning, however, that in the Hasidic community it is slightly different. Each Hasidic sect has its *rebbe* (teacher) who is normally part of a dynasty tracing back to the disciples of the original Hasidic teacher, the Baal Shem Tov. Hasidim often attribute to their *rebbes* almost mystical and supernatural powers, so that most Hasidim submit many of their life choice decisions (marriage partners, career directions and so on) to the *rebbe* for his approval.

D.1.d and e. Duties of Leaders and Subjects

The duty of a rabbi is to teach Torah and rule in specific cases, according to the teachings of the Torah. When a case reaches beyond the normal domestic or simple problem a panel of rabbis is invoked – this is called a *Bet Din* (Court of Judgement). Where such a *Bet Din* is permanently established, the members of it are known by the title *'Dayan'* which means 'judge'. A *Dayan* is always a rabbi; he does not necessarily have superior status to another rabbi, except in so far as he is considered sufficiently learned to be able to judge, together with colleagues, on matters which an individual rabbi may not be able to decide.

A rabbi's teaching and leading must always be based on his (or her in Progressive communities) understanding of Torah and its related teachings, rather than on his or her own wisdom and accumulated experience.

Lay leaders are responsible for the financial and social running of the community. Any lay person is able to lead the services in the synagogue, read from the Torah or teach what he or she knows. Both men and women are free to teach, but the Orthodox community will only allow women to lead services amongst women, while the Progressive community will allow women to lead services for men and women together.

Sometimes 'ministers' are not rabbis at all but learned lay people. A person becomes a rabbi by being approved by other rabbis, who agree that he or she has reached a requisite level of learning. It is only in recent years that the Progressive Jewish community has introduced women rabbis in some communities, where they have the same function as their male counterparts.

Jews are required to pray for the welfare of the State in which they live. The traditional blessing on seeing a monarch or president is to express recognition that it is God who gives power to some mortals rather than others. However, Deuteronomy is explicit about the limitations of the power of any monarch that Jews may set over themselves. In chapter 17 it is made clear that he should not accumulate wealth or wives to his own selfish benefit, and that he should be learned and just. The failure of even the greatest kings such as David and Solomon to match up to these requirements was staunchly criticised by the representatives of religion at the time, and it is hinted in the Midrash that these excesses sowed the seeds for the downfall of their united kingdom.

The democratic nature of Jewish life blurs the distinction between leader and led, so that at one time the led can become the leaders and vice versa. Clearly there is a responsibility laid upon all Jews to ensure that the things which enable a person to become a leader, namely communal activity and knowledge of Torah, never become exclusively the property of any leader at any time. Hence every Jew is expected to have a fair knowledge of Torah and to play a fair part in communal affairs. By and large Judaism has prevented the growth of a learned clergy, holding the knowledge to be powerful, while the majority remain ignorant. If anything, the opposite has been the case. The tendency in Jewish communities is for the congregation or community to challenge and argue with its leaders, or for the congregation to establish a large number of committees to deal with various activities, to appoint or elect chairpersons and then to argue with them all the time!

D.2. PERSONAL AND PRIVATE?

D.2.a. Personal Qualities

The rabbis point to Abraham as the model of hospitality and urge all Jews to

139

imitate him. Abraham, they say, stood at the door of his tent to seek out guests and so Jews are encouraged to find people to invite to their table for all the various festive meals of the year. If a Jew cannot cater for guests personally, at the very least the community should provide for them.

For the principle of humility, the rabbis point to Moses who, even when directed by God to save the Jewish People from Egypt, protested his inadequacies.

Jews are encouraged to create peace between people. The rabbis point to the fact that God did not tell the whole truth when relaying to Abraham what Sarah had said, for fear that it might have created conflict in their household (Talmud, Yevamot 65). Jews are encouraged to honour teachers and parents as directed by the Ten Commandments and are required when doing good to be self-effacing (Maimonides, Mishne Torah, 10:1–14). The ideal form of charity is giving anonymously.

However, Jews are not required to be self-deprecating, nor are they discouraged from exercising all their ingenuity, skill and ability to achieve comfort and convenience for themselves and their fellows (Talmud, Nedarim 10a and Nazir 19a). They are not asked to deny human appetites and drives, but rather to harness them and control them for the benefit of humanity.

D.2.b. Friendship

There are many examples of friendship in the Tenakh – the Jewish Bible – the most famous of which is that between David and Jonathan (I Samuel 20). Jonathan sacrificed his own claim to the throne in recognising David's superior claim to kingship in Israel, and David honoured Jonathan in all that he could.

Jews are commanded in the Torah to love their neighbours as themselves (Leviticus 19:18). The great rabbi Hillel in the second century set a minimum standard by telling an enquirer that the whole of Judaism was summed up by the expression 'Do not unto others as you would not have done to yourself'.

The highest form of charity, identified by the rabbinic master Maimonides, was to take a poor man into partnership, in this way recognising and preserving his self-respect and dignity (Maimonides 1956, 10:14). The tendency of Jews to operate in an extended family makes the inclusion of friends in family events still easier. Since one is already inviting second cousins three times removed, it is not hard to include friends who are almost as closely related!

D.2.c. Sex before Marriage

One of the Ten Commandments, a section of the Torah which enshrines several of the basic concepts of Judaism, is that Jews should not commit adultery. Adultery is defined as indulging in a sexual union which is prohibited, that is with someone else's husband or wife.

Strictly speaking, sex before marriage in Judaism is impossible to achieve, since having sex is one of the three stages of marriage. Although the traditional order is betrothal, contract and consummation, this order is not categorically fixed – what matters is that, by having sex with one's partner, one has already embarked on the marriage process.

While this is the technical definition, in practice there can, of course, be sex before marriage. The general Jewish view is that, particularly when performed promiscuously, it can be destructive to the best qualities of human relationships, can cheapen sexuality and can undermine self-respect. A child born from such a union is not, however, illegitimate in Jewish law. To be illegitimate, the child would need to be the product of adultery only.

While the letter of the law in Judaism is fairly lax, the general interpretation of it has been reasonably strict through the ages. The incidence of children born outside marriage in the Jewish community, until fairly recently at least, has been low in comparison to the figures of the wider community within which Jews live. This is one of the reasons why adoption for Jewish parents has customarily been so difficult. There are simply not enough unwanted Jewish babies.

Another reason for this apparent conformity to law may well be that the subject of sex is not necessarily taboo, nor has it ever been in the Jewish world. Rules relating to sexuality, for example, are studied by quite young children, and menstruation, sexual intercourse and sexual organs are necessary aspects of life which are not avoided in conversation. When a subject is not taboo it is harder to be intrigued or tempted by it.

D.2.d. Homosexuality

There appears to be nothing in Jewish sources which recognises that people may be homosexual, merely that they indulge in homosexual practices. The most influential text is to be found in the Torah (Leviticus 19:12), 'You shall not lie with men as with women; it is an abomination', and a little later in Leviticus (20:13), 'If a man lies with a man as with a woman, both of them have committed an abomination; and they shall certainly be put to death.' It is worth noting, though, that there is no record of such a death sentence being applied.

The possibility of lesbian activity is recognised in a discussion in the Babylonian Talmud (Shabbat 65a). A ruling is offered there that a woman who indulges in lesbianism would not be eligible to marry the High Priest. Since this prohibition also applies to divorcees and prostitutes, it is not clear what moral statement the comment is making but it certainly appears as if male homosexuality is taken more seriously than female. Without doubt, it is the activity rather than the person that is condemned. This is in line with general Jewish thinking that people perform activities more or less out of their own free will, rather than because they 'cannot help it'.

Interestingly, the Talmud considers whether or not two men should be alone together but decides that it is acceptable because 'Jews do not behave in such a way'. By the sixteenth century and the writing of the Shulkhan Arukh, Rabbi Joseph Caro advises that owing to current standards of behaviour amongst some people, it would be wiser for two men not to be alone together.

D.3. MARRIAGE AND THE FAMILY

D.3.a. The Meaning of Marriage

Marriage in Judaism is a contract between two individuals on which the blessing of God is invoked. The written contract which changes hands from husband to wife is called the *Ketuba*. Marriage is intended to imitate the relationship between Adam and Eve, where each supported the other in the cultivation of a harmonious home and world. In the Babylonian Talmud (Yevamot 62b), we are told that a man should 'love his wife as himself and respect her more than himself', and the wedding blessings include a prayer that the new couple should rejoice in each other as God 'gladdened his creatures in the Garden of Eden'.

While it is considered desirable to have children (most authorities agree that one of each sex is the minimum) the absence of children does not obviate the need for marriage, since it is considered by the rabbis to be the ideal state for any man, though not, interestingly, for woman. They are not like men required to marry, as it is only upon men that the duty to have children lies (Babylonian Talmud, Yevamot 65b). The rabbis are also at pains to point out that Eve was taken from a rib of Adam, indicating that she stands by his side and near his heart, rather than below or above him.

The traditional performance of the marriage ceremony under a *huppa* visually stresses the implication that marriage is not merely about relationship but also about the establishment of a home. Traditionally, the marriage is seen not merely to be the business of the two individuals involved, but the developing of an alliance between two families. The marriage celebration, therefore, will invoke the involvement of the extended families of both sides. This could well be the reason why Jewish wedding celebrations often include so many people, and wedding feasts with three hundred and more guests are not rare.

Orthodox Jews have always been strongly against outmarriage – a Jew marrying a non-Jew. When one considers how much of Judaism is centred on the home, it is hardly surprising, but it is often misunderstood. The reason why Jews do not want their children to marry non-Jews is not because they feel a non-Jewish partner is not good enough, but because, however good, no non-Jewish partner can help a Jewish child fulfil its essential role and destiny, that of propagating the Jewish People and keeping alive the Jewish heritage.

The more unwilling a section of the community is to make converts, the more problematic the issue of outmarriage will be. Progressive Jews, who have a fairly open approach to would-be converts, find that many non-Jewish partners will convert to Judaism, thus solving the problem as far as the Progressive Jewish community is concerned. In the Orthodox community not only is conversion harder, but a would-be convert will not be accepted if there is the faintest suspicion that the reason for wanting to convert is to marry. The Orthodox rabbinate feel that converts should only be accepted if there is no ulterior motive for conversion at all.

In the past parents have even gone into mourning when their children have married out, and it was not rare for parents never to talk to their children again. This may seem very harsh, but probably parents who took such action would argue that it was the child who was cutting them off rather than the other way around: they were only making it explicit. All this is compounded by the memory of a long history in which Jews have suffered and sometimes died to keep their heritage alive for future generations. In this light it seems to many like a particular betrayal to give it all up now that society is at last being kinder to the Jews.

D.3.b. Family Relationships

The ideal wife is thoroughly expressed in Proverbs 31 in a famous passage starting 'Who can find a woman of worth for her value is far more than precious jewels?' A husband has a prime responsibility to ensure that his wife and children are housed, clothed and fed, but marriage is greatly to his advantage as well, since the rabbis say that the Holy Spirit can rest only upon a married man, for an unmarried man is but half a man, and the Holy Spirit does not rest on what is imperfect.

The responsibilities of parents to children and the respect required from children to parents are enshrined in Jewish biblical teaching. The Ten Commandments require of children that they 'honour' their parents. This does not mean that they must always obey them, rather that they must always give them due respect. Parents have a range of responsibilities towards their children. The Talmud, for example, requires them to teach the children a trade, teach them to swim, and teach girls and boys to understand sexual matters. Overarching all of these, parents are required to teach their children about Jewish practice and religion (Babylonian Talmud, Kiddushin 1:11).

These responsibilities are binding therefore, even if a child does not honour its parents, they must still perform their duties for the child, and vice versa. We are told in the Babylonian Talmud (Berakhot 10a) 'Let not the fear of bad offspring deter you from having children; you must do your duty and God will do what pleases him.' Elsewhere in the Talmud (Sotah 49a) the rabbis aver that 'A father loves his children; they love their children.'

It is assumed that families will look after all their members so that grandparents are allocated a place of respect as well as affection in the family framework. The extended family structure means that Jews will see a special bond even with those who are their brother's wife's aunt's third cousin! This may be a product of the feeling that all Jews are in some way related through their common ancestors; Abraham, Isaac and Jacob, Sarah, Rebekah, Leah and Rachel. Family relationships are cherished and all members of an extended family are invited to family celebrations.

It is worth noting that one of the Ten Commandments is against adultery and one of the three rules that a Jew should give his life for rather than break is the rule against adultery or incest. (The other two are against public idolatry and murder.) This seems to indicate that the sanctity of the family and the marriage tie is such that if people tried to save their lives at its cost, more will have been lost than saved.

D.3.c. Marriage Breakdown

Strictly speaking divorce is easy in Jewish law. All that it requires is mutual agreement between the two partners and the giving of the divorce document (a *get*) by the husband to the wife. The reason it is done in this way is a legal, technical one, since in the first instance the marriage contract is given by a husband to his wife (see D.3.a). She makes no contractual promises to him (except by implication in accepting the marriage contract from him). Since all the promises are made by him to her, breaking the contract requires that he who made it in the first place must do so.

However, this has led to many problems, when, for example, the man is reluctant to give such a divorce document or he cannot be found. In the past Jewish courts have even imprisoned a husband in an attempt to coerce him into divorcing his wife, when they agreed that the wife's request for a divorce document was reasonable.

Not surprisingly, much effort will be expended on trying to keep the marriage together. First, there will be an attempt to counsel the couple so that their marriage can survive. While divorce is easy, it is never considered desirable. Generally the Jewish community would like to avoid the situation where two people state they want a divorce and no one argues with them.

The Talmudic discussion on grounds for divorce remarkably ends by suggesting that a man can divorce his wife for even the most trivial reasons. (Rabbenu Gershom in the eleventh century finally established the *halakha* that a man could not divorce his wife against her will.) This is not to make divorce more popular but to make it easier when necessary, so that the entrapped couple do not have to go through an unpleasantness in order to justify their incompatibility.

It would be a mistake therefore to see the view in the Talmud as aiming to popularise divorce and indeed it also says (Yevamot 37b) 'A man should not marry a woman with the mental reservation that, after all, he can divorce her.' More strongly in Gittin 90a, the Talmud tells us that 'Tears fall on God's altar for whoever divorces his first wife'.

The crisis that faces the Jewish community in the matter of divorce is that in most countries the courts cannot or will not compel husbands to provide their wives with a religious release, even if they agree to a civil divorce. The Progressive Jewish community has decided that in such cases the Jewish rabbinic court can abrogate to itself the right to annul or divorce the marriage. The Orthodox community is looking into the possibility of civil courts making the provision of a religious divorce a condition of receiving a civil divorce. This already happens in New York State and the aim of such an attempt is to free the woman by preventing the man from gaining a civil divorce until he allows his wife a religious divorce. It is still theoretically possible in Jewish law for a man to have several wives but not for a woman to have several husbands. If the man does not provide the *get* then the woman cannot remarry in the Jewish community and the man can. Most rabbis would not countenance such behaviour on the part of the man, and would refuse to officiate at his wedding, but strictly speaking he does not need a rabbi to marry. Even if he did feel constrained by such disapproval he could still wait until it suited him, not his wife, to present the *get*.

The issue of divorce is one of the most vexing current concerns on the Jewish community agenda and is one of the best examples of how Jews suffer from not being in control of the application of their laws. In Israel, where the law courts apply Jewish law on this matter, there are far fewer trapped would-be divorcees.

D.4. INFLUENCES ON AND USE OF TIME AND MONEY

D.4.a. Education

From the earliest times and as a fundamental directive, the need to educate the children of the community has been seen as a central responsibility. The *Shema* refers twice to the command to parents to 'teach your children diligently' (Deuteronomy 6:7 and 11:19). In Deuteronomy 31:10–13 the responsibility is laid upon the leaders of the people to gather them together from time to time and read them the whole of Torah.

This tendency towards democratic education led to a situation where every synagogue was also known as the *Bet Hamidrash*, 'the Place of Study'. The Mishna states in a passage which is read every morning as part of the morning service:

> These are the things which a man benefits from in this world and is also rewarded for in the World to Come [afterlife]: honouring father and mother, acts of loving kindness, punctual attendance at the synagogue morning and evening, hospitality, visiting the sick, dowering the bride, attending the dead, devotion in prayer and making peace between people; but the study of the Torah leads to all of them. (Peah 1:1)

Nineteenth-century European Jewry established a vast network of rabbinical colleges called *Yeshivot*, in which learning of Talmudic and related subjects went on at a remarkably high level. Study at a *Yeshiva* was available to all, and one of the most desirable things for a person to do with his money was to maintain a student at *Yeshiva*. The mental training required to cope with the complex thought processes of Judaism, and the vast range of areas of study that Jewish learning could cover meant that Jews were not only skilled in Jewish learning but could also perform well in secular fields of study.

Following the Enlightenment in Europe and the breakdown of the ghetto walls, Jews found themselves able to take a leading part in the development of scientific, technological and social scientific study.

D.4.b. Work

The value of work is stressed repeatedly by the rabbis in the Talmud. In Nedarim 49b they say: 'No labour, however humble, is dishonouring'. Many of the Pharisees were themselves manual workers, being carpenters, shoemakers, charcoal burners and so on, and the rabbis of Talmudic times stressed that knowledge of the Torah should not be the means by which one earned one's living.

It has been pointed out that the commandment about *Shabbat* in the Ten Commandments also requires people to work for six days: 'Remember *Shabbat* in order to keep it holy. You shall work on six days and do everything; but the seventh day is *Shabbat* for the Lord your God' (Exodus 20:8–10).

Wage and employment ethics are also discussed both in the Torah and the Talmud, and it is legislated that a creditor is not allowed to take the tools of a person's trade in payment of a debt, nor is an employer allowed to withold payment from an employee for a job done.

The image of work, labour and service is used repeatedly in order to stress the relationship between God and humanity, where the human being is talked of as a willing and enthusiastic servant in the service of the Master. In the Mishna, Rabbi Elazar says: 'Know before whom you are toiling and who your employer is who will pay you the reward of your labour' (Pirke Avot 2:19–21).

Rabbi Tarphon says: 'The day is short, the work is great, the labourers are lazy, and the reward is much, and the Master is urgent.' He is further quoted as saying: 'It is not your duty to complete the work but nor are you free to desist from it; if you have studied much Torah, you will receive much reward, for your employer is faithful to pay you the reward of your labour.'

D.4.c. Leisure and its Use

One of the central features of Jewish practice is the day of rest each week – *Shabbat*. This is a day of leisure rather than inactivity; it is only through the proper balance of leisure and work that the world was created according to the Bible and that humanity can remain sane and survive.

The Bible says: 'God finished all the work that He had done on the seventh day and He rested' (Genesis 2:2), and the rabbis ask how He could have done both. The answer they offer is that by resting, He finished the creation. The invention of *Shabbat* is an essential part of the future of the world.

Leisure on *Shabbat* is to be used for meeting one's God, oneself and one's family and community. The day is devoted to social activities rather than private ones; praying in synagogue is a communal event and much of the rest of the day is devoted to family meals, learning, singing, playing and talking together.

While Jews over the years have played a significant part in sporting activity of various sorts, the traditional way of using leisure time in Judaism is not through the development of fitness of body or through competitive activities, but rather through communal activities which develop the mind and social communication. The role played by this leisure day of *Shabbat* cannot be overstated. In the words of the Jewish Zionist thinker, Ahad Ha'am: 'The Jews did not keep Shabbat; Shabbat kept the Jews.'

D.4.d. Wealth

There is nothing in Judaism that prohibits the accumulation of wealth, the only guidance is about how one should use this wealth. Too many Jews have been poor through the ages to be able to ennoble or idealise the value of poverty.

The collective Jewish memory of slavery in Egypt reminds them of the value of being their own masters so that they can more effectively serve God. A wealthy person, however, is expected to put her or his wealth at the service of the community while not necessarily denying self or family any comforts or even luxuries that they can afford.

The Shulkhan Arukh – 'the Code of Jewish Law' – asks how much one should give to charity and answers:

If a man can afford to do so, he should satisfy the needs of all the poor who require help. If he cannot afford so much, then, if he wishes to carry out his duties in the best way possible, he should give up to a fifth of his wealth. A tenth of his wealth is the average amount and one who gives less than this is ungenerous ... but a man should not give away more than a fifth of his wealth so as to avoid becoming himself a recipient of charity. (Yoreh De'ah 249:1)

The Hebrew word for charity is *Tzedaka* which is also the word for justice. This indicates that the idea of charitable giving is not about largesse or generosity but is more to do with the simple justice of the 'haves' giving to the 'have nots'.

Maimonides, a great rabbi of the twelfth century, identified eight levels of *Tzedaka*, the lowest being that which is given unwillingly while it is less than the donor can afford, the middle stages depending on the anonymity of the donor and/or the recipient, and the highest stage bringing a poor man into partnership with oneself, so that not only is he helped but his dignity is retained and his ability to establish his independence is created.

D.4.e. Drugs

In so far as the use of drugs is dangerous there is no doubt that in Jewish law it is forbidden. The current head of the *Yeshiva* (rabbinic academy) in Gateshead in Tyneside, one of the leading *yeshivot* in the world, has forbidden his students to smoke in the presence of others and urged them not to smoke on their own either. Maimonides makes it clear that no one has the right to endanger his or her own life and the Shulkhan Arukh rules that it is better to eat unkosher food than to put oneself in danger.

If drugs are merely producers of euphoria or even 'liberators of the spirit', it is less clear what the Jewish view might be. Certainly as far as alcohol is concerned, the Talmud comments that there is 'no celebration without wine' and Hasidim have been enthusiastic users of alcohol 'to loosen the spirit'. On the festival of *Purim*, the Talmud actually requires (Megillah 7b) that Jews get a little tipsy to the point that they are not sure 'whether you are blessing Mordechai or cursing Haman'. However, it is also recognised that alcohol clouds the judgement and the Talmud says in Ketubot 10b that a rabbi may not give a judgement if he has drunk a little wine.

Such practices that constitute self-abuse, as injecting drugs, are unacceptable in view of the responsibility to treat the body with respect.

Overall, it should be remembered that mainstream Judaism, at least, lays great stress on the use of the reasoning mind and conscious recognition. Anything that diminishes that capacity should be treated with some suspicion.

Hanging over all this, of course, is the broad rabbinic principle that the law of the land is Jewish law (so long as it does not constrain a Jew to act against Jewish law). Therefore, so long as certain drugs are illegal, their use in Jewish law is automatically wrong.

D.4.f. The Media

The need to be well informed on both current and general affairs dictates that, in general, Judaism would encourage adherents to follow the media. The sixteenth-century text, the Shulkhan Arukh (Orah Ha'im 307:1), allows people to pass on the latest news on *Shabbat*, since it adds to the joy of *Shabbat*: knowing about current affairs is an enlivening experience. (The comment is worth making in the Shulkhan Arukh otherwise someone might have argued that one could not talk about the news because it would not be suitable for a day that should be 'holy'.)

The entertainment that the media offers is also not to be ignored. In so far as certain kinds of entertainment also make some individuals more aware of social problems and therefore heightens their compassion, it would be viewed with positive approval rather than indifference.

However, one of the greatest vices, at least to the Jewish way of thinking, is the transmission of gossip or slander, and today's mass media can multiply this alarmingly. The Jerusalem Talmud in Peah 1 puts slander in the same category as murder, and the Midrash in Genesis Rabbah (56:4) wisely comments that 'even if all of a slander is not believed, half of it is'. The mystical work, the Zohar, states that 'God will accept repentance for all sins except one, giving another man a bad name', and the Book of Proverbs (10:18) comments 'Righteous lips cover up hatred but he who lets out slander is a fool.' The Koretser *Rebbe*, a Hasidic Rabbi of the nineteenth century, perhaps taught the lesson most clearly of all. 'For thirteen years I taught my tongue not to lie; for the next thirteen, I taught it to tell the truth.' Therefore, Judaism would require of the media that they place upon themselves the most stringent ethical standards to ensure that they are never responsible for the transmission of slander or misinformation. Even the kind of gossip which damages someone's reputation but has no practical value is disapproved of. The fact that it may actually be true is irrelevant.

The demand for such self-restriction, however, should not aim to inhibit the freedom of editorial comment. The tendency of Jews to challenge leaders and insist on the right of comment, with reference to the organisation of their community or country, requires that the media have the greatest editorial freedom and that the consumers exercise discrimination to decide what is good and what is not.

D.4.g. Advertising

The Talmud, in a discussion on how a man may sell his wares, decides that it is acceptable for him to paint designs on pots to make them more attractive to the buyer, but that it is wrong to paint old pots to make them look new. A text in Baba Metzia says: 'Rabbi Pappa ben Samuel allowed baskets to be painted. But did we not learn "Utensils may not be painted"? (Midrash) – there is no difficulty: one referred to new, the other to old' (60b). This provides the distinction between what is acceptable in selling and advertising, and what is not.

While the individual is free to encourage the buyer to find his goods more attractive or to extol their virtues, this should not spill over into fraudulently misrepresenting the goods, and suggesting they have properties or potential which they do not really possess. In short, the standards established by groups such as the Advertising Standards Authority are roughly those laid down by the Talmud two thousand years ago!

D.5. THE QUALITY AND VALUE OF LIFE

D.5.a. The Elderly

The definition in Isaiah of a society that has gone bad includes the expression, 'The child shall behave insolently against the aged' (3:5). In Leviticus 19:32 we are instructed, 'You shall rise up before the grey head, and honour the face of the elderly, and you shall fear your God; I am the Lord.' Traditional Jewish interpretation always sees significance in the expression 'I am the Lord': it is seen either to stress a certain requirement or to make it clear that even though there may be no one else to enforce a rule protecting the weak or underprivileged, God requires it. The Talmud in Kiddushin 33a informs us that Rabbi Yochanan would stand up for aged heathens because, he said, they had experienced so much.

While one hopes that the extended family unit will be able to look after its own elderly, it has not always been possible, and every Jewish community has set up, as almost a first priority, a secure and respectable home for the elderly.

In view of the fact that the elderly deserve their respect through their accumulated wisdom, it is quite clear that in Jewish terms the older someone is the better, and therefore any cult of youth is very much contrary to the trend of Jewish thinking. The suggestion that as people become older and more frail they become less useful is considered quite wrongheaded, and it is noteworthy that the term 'elder' is automatically one of respect, to be applied to the leaders of the community.

D.5.b. Those in Need

The Torah explicitly recognises various categories of people in need. Those it names are the fatherless, the widowed, the poor and strangers (for example, Deuteronomy 24:17–22).

The fatherless and the widowed are, in Jewish terms, clearly disabled. They lack the proper family structure which enables a secure family life. Judaism, so much based on the home, not surprisingly stresses the disadvantage of the fatherless and the widowed, and requires the community to look after them, as it were, in collective fatherhood.

Interestingly, the motherless are never referred to as a category. This may be a reflection of the social contexts in which such texts were recorded, where it was possible to employ a nursemaid or even have a second wife who could take over the children of the dead mother. This certainly seems to be the case in the story of Jacob's sons in Genesis, for example. The death of Rachel, the mother of Joseph and Benjamin, is perceived as a tragedy for Jacob who loved this wife above Leah (his other wife) and his two concubines, but we do not hear anything of the loss to her two sons. Loss of a father would have more significant financial and economic, rather than social reper-cussions, whilst the loss of a mother would be an emotional one for which the community could not easily provide a substitute. This indicates that the Torah's legislation is intended to be practical rather than merely to provoke sympathy.

The poor are again, not surprisingly, a category deserving of concern. Charitable funds are always established and it was quite normal (long before it became the norm for the government to do it) for the community to pro-vide free education for poor children. One of the first priorities of the Jewish community, on arrival in large numbers in London, was the establishment of the Jews Free School which by 1911 had grown to accommodate more than 4,000 pupils. In addition, many communities established funds to provide dowries for poor brides. This concern for the poor is once again not merely sentimental. In Exodus 23:6 Jews are advised not to pervert justice (*Tzedaka* see D.7.a) on the side of the poor out of misplaced compassion.

Care of the sick and visiting the sick are still recognised as a basic and necessary responsibility of every Jew. While the Jewish community delegates its rabbis and ministers to act as chaplains at hospitals, this does not dimin-ish the duty of each Jewish individual to visit people in hospital or on their sickbed.

It might be mentioned here that one of the most important acts of caring or charity is to the one section of society which cannot repay a good deed under any circumstances, that is, the dead. The highest act of goodwill that one can perform is care of the dead, and in the Jewish community there are no commercial undertakers. The job of preparing and burying the dead is done by community groups, often volunteers trained for the purpose.

The last category to be specifically mentioned as a group to be looked after are strangers. This perhaps surprising category is stressed again and again throughout the Torah; more than twenty times the Jews are admonished in one context or another to care for the stranger. 'A stranger you shall not oppress; for you know the heart of the stranger, seeing you were strangers in the land of Egypt' (Exodus 23:9), is an example of such a commandment, as is Deuteronomy 10:18–9, 'He executes justice for the fatherless, the widow and loves the stranger in giving him food and clothing. Love the stranger therefore; for you were strangers in the land of Egypt.' This concern for the immigrant, the foreigner or simply the non-Jew is a crucial one in defining the Jewish relationship with people outside the Jewish community.

When the word 'immigrant' became a dirty word in Britain in the 1960s, the relatively well-settled and integrated Jewish community immediately went on record, calling itself an immigrant community and insisting that any attack on newer such communities was also an attack on itself.

D.5.c. Abortion

This issue centres on when a foetus becomes a person, or in religious terms, when the soul enters the body. Clearly, in Judaism, the killing of non-humans is allowed – the slaughtering of meat for food, the swatting of flies, the cutting-down of trees and so on. Indeed, even the killing of humans under certain circumstances, for example self-defence and fighting in a war, is also allowed.

The rabbis consider that there seem to be only two logical moments for deciding that a foetus becomes a person; either at the moment of conception or at the moment of birth. All other moments in the intervening nine months are nothing but arbitrary decisions. (The current debates on abortion indicate that with the development of medical science one can change one's decision as to how fully a person a foetus is.)

Since the rabbis were well aware that it was impossible to fix the time of conception until some time after the event, it seemed foolish to refer to a person that one was not even aware of existing. They therefore decided that the foetus became a full person at the moment of birth, so that the problem of murder does not apply in the case of abortion.

Nevertheless, it is important to respect the foetus and abortion should not be performed merely for convenience. The main view is clearly laid down in the Mishna, 'If a woman is in difficult labour (to the point that her life may be in danger) her child must be cut up while it is still in her womb since the life of the mother is more important than the life of the foetus. But if the greater part of the child has already emerged it may not be damaged, since one life cannot be more important than another' (Oholot 7:6).

Quite clearly, it is the moment of emerging that makes the foetus a separate person and after that point the doctors must simply carry on their normal procedure of trying to save all people as they come to them rather than making a judgement of one over the other. Therefore, in Judaism abortion is not forbidden even up to the very moment of birth. Indeed, it is required if it is necessary in order to protect the life of the mother.

The current thinking in Judaism is divided as to possible justifiable causes for abortion, however. No one thinks that simple convenience is an adequate reason, but possible reasons put forward are that the pregnancy is the product of rape, the child might be seriously disabled mentally or physically, or that the mother's sanity or health might suffer severely.

D.5.e. Euthanasia

The Talmud makes it clear that he who shoots a man as he falls off a cliff to certain death is guilty of murder, even though he shortened his victim's life by only a few seconds. Nothing should be done to shorten a person's life but nor should anything be done to prolong agony. As a general principle, no one has the right to cut short anybody's life except in cases of self-defence or war or punishment (see D.6.c and D.8.b). But if something will ease someone's last hours even though it accelerates his or her death, that may not be unacceptable. One example would be the administering of pain-killing drugs which may also reduce the individual's will to fight for life.

The issue of euthanasia is also relevant in the matter of organ transplants, since that depends on the right to determine that someone is dead and then clinically to take from them something without which they definitely cannot live. Maimonides, who besides being a great rabbi was a great physician, commented that the only way of being absolutely sure that somebody was dead was if their head was missing. Certainly, the view seems to be that principles such as brain death are not clear and objective enough. A doctor needs irrefutable evidence that the individual is not conscious and is not likely to be so again – particularly when he or she is driven by the urgent possibility of saving another life through organ transplant. Nevertheless it is given to every doctor to exercise his best wisdom and conscience in keeping alive the maximum number of people as they fall into his or her care.

It is for the reasons stated above that Jewish authorities have greeted the possibility of organ transplants from animals with great enthusiasm. It is their feeling that these must be less problematic than transplants from human beings, since one need be less concerned about the life of the donor than if it were a human being – always accepting that animals deserve care and kindness from our hands as we use them for whatever needs we can legitimately justify. This view is taken from the account of creation in Genesis in which humankind is given control over, and responsibility for, the world in whichever way it likes to use it. Further, the rabbis note that during the Flood the animals that weren't saved in the ark all drowned, although they had committed no sins. From these texts, the rabbis concluded that the function and purpose of animals is to be of use to mankind and that they were only created and preserved for that purpose.

It is also worth noting at this point that the main discussion on the use of animal organs has centred around those from pigs. Despite the stringent prohibitions on *eating* pigs, no rabbinic authority has suggested that the use of their organs would be a problem for a Jew.

D.6. QUESTIONS OF RIGHT AND WRONG

D.6.a. Purpose of Law

While the term 'law' is an insufficient translation of the word 'Torah', a large proportion of Torah is law, and is taken up with the expression of 613 rules or commandments for living. These commandments are themselves merely the headings for larger and more complex codes of legislation and guidance. The purpose of such laws is to define for the Jew the right and ideal life in relationship with his or her fellow human being and with God. The laws prohibit certain actions and command others, but in all except three cases are designed to enrich the individual's life.

The rabbis, when interpreting the comment that the law is given so that Jews might live by it, added (as it were in the margin) 'and not die by it'. In the passage in Deuteronomy where the Israelites are presented with the choice of a blessing or a curse, depending on whether or not they choose the Torah, they are recommended and encouraged to 'choose life'.

> I call heaven and earth to witness before you today that I have set life and death in front of you, the blessing and the curse; therefore choose life, that you may live, you and your descendants; love the Lord your God, to listen to His voice and cleave to Him; for He is your life and the length of your days; that you may live in the land that the Lord swore to give to your ancestors, Abraham, Isaac and Jacob. (Deuteronomy 30:19)

As a result, virtually every one of the rules can be broken if the purpose is to save life, and in only three cases should life be sacrificed rather than the laws be broken. These three cases indicate quite clearly the overall purpose of the laws. They are murder, idolatry and incest (or adultery). These three laws which accentuate respect for life, for God, and for family, should be kept even if it is at the cost of one's own life. The implication is obvious; it would be absurd to endanger the concepts that preserve life in general, in order to save one's own. However, there is no great enthusiasm for martyrdom in Judaism and rabbis are at great pains, for example, to limit the definitions of idolatry so that people do not leap too willingly into the flames of religious martyrdom.

Jewish law exists to keep society stable and protect the individual from exploitation. It also serves to encourage a spiritual life and awareness. It is more interested in people's responsibilities than in people's rights and the personal fulfilment of the individual.

D.6.b. Sin and Sins

The overarching concept of sin is not really present in Judaism. There is a large range of sins which an individual can commit, but these do not change the state of the individual but rather his or her relationships.

The rabbis identified two kinds of *mitzvot*. One is between people and God and the other is between people themselves. If one breaks or fails to fulfil a *mitzvah* relating to God, then clearly one's relationship with God is damaged, but if one breaks or fails to fulfil a *mitzvah* relating to one's fellow human being, then one's relationship with both humanity and God is damaged.

It is interesting to note that out of the 613 *mitzvot* in the Torah, 365 are negative (that is, they are 'Thou shalt nots') and 248 are positive (that is, 'Thou shalts'). The rabbis suggest this indicates that one should perform the *mitzvot* every day of the year (365 days equal the 365 *mitzvot*) and with every bone and organ of your body (there are taken to be 248 of these). Like most law codes, secular and religious, there are more negatives than positives. What is perhaps surprising is that there are so many positives. If one looks at British law, for example, one will find very few positive precepts. Law, by and large, usually exists to prohibit wrongdoing, and the proof that the Torah is more than simply law is the large number of ethical positive directives included in it.

To tell people that they must not damage another's property is a reasonable rule to prevent society collapsing, but when the Torah commands them to help their fellow human beings it is clearly trying to improve the quality of social relationships beyond the merely tolerable. When it commands people to help their enemies (Exodus 23:4–5), it is clearly intending to stretch their moral capacity to create a society that is reaching for higher standards, taking it not only from tolerance to respect, but beyond. It requires of the believer that irrespective of how others behave, she or he must struggle against and overcome 'natural impulses', in order to help create a godly world.

The tendency of the rabbis to summarise the Torah in terms of people's relationships with each other indicates their sense that if these relationships are good, then probably relationships with God will fall neatly into place. A talmudic discussion between Rabbi Akiva and Ben Zoma makes this point quite clearly. They were discussing which was the most important line in Torah, and while Rabbi Akiva argued that it was 'Love thy neighbour as thyself', Ben Zoma argued for the line 'These are the generations of Adam'. This is a relatively obscure line from the book of Genesis which begins the genealogical list of the descendants of Adam. Not surprisingly, those listening to the debate demanded an explanation of this apparently idiosyncratic choice.

Ben Zoma explained that it was not sufficient to love other people as you loved yourself, because this was dependent on how much you loved yourself. Self-deprecating, self-hating, self-denying people could therefore give others quite a hard time. He suggested that the fact that all people are descended from Adam (thereby making them all of equal ancestry) and that Adam was created in the image of God (thereby making it clear that all human beings deserve respect as descended from someone created in the image of God) meant that whatever you think of yourself, you must always award dignity and respect to every human being.

D.6.c. Punishments

In biblical times and up to the year 70 CE, when the Temple was still standing, there was a wide-ranging and complex system of sacrificial offerings which the individual could give, should she or he act incorrectly. A large proportion of these sacrifices were to do with grain, oil and incense. Contrary to popular imagination, only a small proportion were related to animals and most of these pertained to small animals and birds which were easily affordable. Very rarely was some large sacrifice required of an individual or a family. With the destruction of the Temple, the entire sacrificial system ceased, and in its place the system of prayer and repentance, which had already been running side by side with the sacrificial framework for about three or four hundred years, grew in importance.

Nowadays, if a Jew performs some wrong act, there are three courses of action available which manifest repentance. The central statement in the repentance sequence in the Yom Kippur service is 'Repentance, Charity and Devotion can change a grim fate.'

The first, and apparently the simplest, is prayer itself. If the individual sincerely repents, Judaism believes that that prayer is accepted. But it must involve more than just an apology for the wrongdoing; a genuine resolution to avoid repeating such a misdemeanour must also be present. The second is to commit oneself to charity giving, and the third is fasting. In Judaism fasting involves neither eating nor drinking for a period of time, never more than twenty-five hours.

On the Day of Atonement which falls in September or October, the Jew makes a total reckoning of his or her year's behaviour along with resolutions for the coming year. All three facets of punishment play their part: the day is spent in prayer and repentance in synagogue; neither food nor drink are taken for a full twenty-five hours; and customarily a commitment is made to give charity, not in a generalised way, but of a specific amount.

On this day confession is made for sins. There is no individual who intercedes in this confession – it is made directly to God – but the whole confession follows a formula framework in which everyone confesses in the plural for every possible sin. By so doing, Jews manifest the principle of collective responsibility and perhaps more sensitively, the need not to expose each individual to some public statement of his or her misdeeds. The idea of giving testimony or publicly stating where one went wrong in the past is not normal in the Jewish community, and it is generally felt that the individual would do better to guard personal dignity and self-respect and privately resolve to improve.

D.6.d. The Wrongdoer and the Wronged

The rabbis are convinced that a person who sincerely repents will receive forgiveness. One rabbi in the Talmud recommends that everybody should repent the day before they die. In response to the perfectly justifiable question as to how one knows when one is going to die, he replies: 'Exactly. One should repent every day.' However, if the wrong committed is to another human being, it is not good enough simply to try and square one's account with God. First, one needs to make a genuine attempt to repent and gain the forgiveness of the individual one has wronged.

In the month preceding the Ten Days of Repentance in the Jewish calendar, many Jews will take it upon themselves to telephone people whom they feel they may have offended, speak to people they feel they have neglected, and generally try to correct their relationships with their fellows before embarking on a programme of becoming 'at one' – atoning to God.

Obviously one of the means of making clear one's repentance to one's fellow human being is accepting the punishment that human society metes out. Therefore, if a Jew has committed a criminal act, it is no good to repent to God and yet try to escape fine or imprisonment. The acceptance of the fine or imprisonment is one stage towards proper repentance.

The wronged have a more difficult role to play. Jews are advised in the Torah 'not to hate your brother in your heart' (Leviticus 19:17), and the rabbis are at pains to make it clear that the wish to take revenge, or even bearing a grudge, is not acceptable. In the Talmud, the following example is given:

> What is revenge and what is bearing a grudge? If one said to his fellow: Lend me your sickle, and the other replies: No, and tomorrow the other asks the first: Lend me your axe, and the first replies: I will not lend it to you just as you would not lend me your sickle – that is revenge. And

what is bearing a grudge? If one says to his fellow: Lend me your axe, and the other replies: No, and on the morrow the second asks: Lend me your garment, and he answers: Here it is. I am not like you who would not lend to me – that is bearing a grudge. (Yoma 23a)

This does not mean that no one is justified in attempting to bring a wrong-doer to justice. If that were the case, then there would be an open charter to anyone to act unscrupulously. However, the point is stressed that it is the responsibility of each individual to participate in a properly constituted legal system, rather than to carry out their own private or personal revenge. Neither is it the responsibility of any individual to continue to parade in front of the wrongdoer his or her misdeed, even before he has repented – that would be bearing a grudge.

It is interesting to note that the rabbis, when they identify 'Seven Laws to the Sons of Noah' – those basic laws required of all humanity to establish a moral society (see D.8.c) – exclude several of the Ten Commandments which are specifically Jewish (keeping *Shabbat* and so on). They do nevertheless include one which is not to be found amongst the Ten Commandments, namely the need to establish a proper legal system and to comply with the ruling of the law courts. In the rabbis' understanding, this is an essential prerequisite of a civilised society. Even Rabbi Akiva, who was himself eventually martyred by the Romans, advised that one should pray for the Roman administration, because without it 'men would eat each other'.

D.7. EQUALITY AND DIFFERENCE

D.7.a. Differences between People

The rabbis readily recognise that all people are different. Not only are they created differently – short, tall, fat, thin, black, yellow and so on – but also human experience establishes differences between them, for example rich and poor, learned and ignorant, even healthy and unhealthy. It is every individual's responsibility to attempt to diminish any man-made differences and the prejudices they evoke. (Note here that a difference in colour is God-made, a difference in education is not.) The term for charity is *Tzedaka*, which also means 'justice' in Hebrew. For example, it is the responsibility of every learned person to teach those who know less, in order to try and bring them to the same standard.

God-made differences are of a different order and clearly are part of God's good purpose for the world. If one can alleviate any disadvantage that arises out of such a difference then one should try to do so, and certainly one should not suggest that a person is any the less for their difference. Thus someone with a disability (mental or physical, see D.5.b), with a different skin colour, or born into a different religious community or social class should not be disdained or looked down upon.

The rabbis of the Midrash (a vast compilation of homiletic teachings almost paralleling the Talmud itself) teach that when God created Adam he selected the soil that he used from all four corners of the earth. Not only that, they say he used dark, light, red and yellow earth in order to make up the first human being. This determination to use variety in the creating of Adam is proof enough in the eyes of the rabbis that God's desire is for humanity to be varied, and that no single person can claim to be more the original, or pure style of human.

They also point out that when God created other creatures, he made many different kinds; when he made humankind he made only one species. The Talmud asks why God began with only one man Adam and answers, 'So that no one of his descendants should be able to say: my father is better than your father' (Sanhedrin 37a). It offers a further reason: in this way no race can say that it is better than others.

There is a great desire in rabbinic teaching, therefore, to recognise differences, to insist on the divine spark in every individual, and to argue that where differences are disadvantageous it is the responsibility of every human being to try and lessen the disadvantages. However, it is not always within people's power to correct the disparity between individuals; sometimes it appears that great injustice is purely a product of chance, fate or God. A whole book of Tenakh is devoted to this problem, namely the Book of Job. In this book, a perfectly righteous man is subjected to all sorts of suffering and when he demands an explanation, God replies 'You wouldn't understand if I told you'! While this may be unsatisfactory, it appears to be the only authoritative answer that Jews are prepared to give.

However, the broad belief in reward and punishment for good and evil, bestowed beyond this life after the Day of Judgement (whenever that may be), maintains the broad principle of belief in justice in the world, even though Jews readily admit that they do not understand how it works.

Different countries and different languages are explained simply in the Tenakh by the story of the Tower of Babel (Genesis 11:6–9) and the suggestion that the three sons of Noah were the fathers of three races: negroid, caucasian and semitic. While this does not in fact allow for all the people of the world, we need not become too obsessed by the scientific accuracy of the Tenakh – it is after all not intended to be a scientific text.

D.7.b. Attitudes to Other Religions

Other religions can be divided broadly into two categories in Jewish thinking: idolatrous and God-fearing. Judaism sets its face against idolatry, by which it means religions which purport to destroy the sense of the morality of God's world, or to demote it. Although a bald understanding of idolatry would suggest something to do with idols, in fact the rabbis were much more concerned about how others behaved rather than how they represented their understanding of God. Nowadays, few would argue that the primary issue is whether or not statues are used; in fact the Spanish rabbi and poet Ibn Gabirol, of the twelfth century, suggested that even those who worship the sun and the moon are striving to recognise God's greatness and therefore should not be judged too harshly.

The sharp end of this problem is that Jews should rather give up their lives than publicly approve idolatry, and yet they have often been faced with forcible conversion to either Christianity or Islam. The general consensus has been that both of these religions are essentially moral and recognise God, and therefore if it is a matter of saving life, the Jew can publicly accept conversion. This does not relieve Jews from privately maintaining their religious position, which is the reason for the phenomenon of the secret Jews, or Marranos, who arose in the fifteenth century in Spain during the Inquisition and have left their mixed practices amongst their descendants in Spain and Portugal. Sikhism is clearly in the same category as Christianity and Islam as a monotheistic religion, but Buddhism and Hinduism are less easily definable.

To most Jews Buddhism is a non-theistic religion, and Hinduism is pantheistic. While there are many different opinions and it is only recently that Jews have needed to engage in dialogue with either of these two communities, the consensus appears to be that since both propagate a moral perception of the world, and neither categorically deny the existence of an ultimate reality (God for Jews), it would be more desirable to make no particular judgement on them.

It must be stressed that all of the above relates to Jewish attitudes to the religions themselves. As far as the adherents of these religions are concerned, they are deserving of every respect that human dignity demands. For while a Jew may anathematise and condemn any particular philosophy, that does not mean to say that he or she should not respect the individuals who hold such a philosophy, provided they do not act in such a way as to harm other human beings. There are limits to tolerance in Judaism.

Jews are unequivocal about the belief that Judaism is the best possible way for the Jew to live. Jews who had clearly converted to another religion, although they could not ultimately deny or destroy their Jewish identity which is a product of their birth, would be considered to have done real damage to their chances of a coherent relationship between themselves and God. Indeed most Jews would see such a conversion as an act of betrayal in view of the hardships so many generations have undergone to preserve Judaism through the ages. Conversion is a sharp act of dissociation from the family and community as well, so the pressures against such a move are intense.

This requisite to practise Judaism, however, is only placed on Jews, and non-Jews would be encouraged to seek out their own moral/religious position rather than consider adopting Judaism. This view enables Jews to engage in dialogue with other religions perfectly comfortably, because at root Jews are not concerned to convert others. Jews do not want a world full of confused Jews, rather a world full of good Christians, Muslims, Sikhs and so on. As has been stressed, Judaism is an identity and a way of life and Jews tend to view all religions in this light. It is not a matter of changing belief, therefore, but of changing identity if an individual wishes to convert. That is a much more thoroughgoing venture and much less likely to succeed.

D.7.c. Attitudes to Other Races

In the Jewish perception, the world is broadly divided into Jews and Gentiles. It is quite clear that according to the Bible, Jews are allocated a specific and special role. In Exodus 19:6 God is quoted as saying to Israel 'You shall be for me a kingdom of priests and a holy nation.' Isaiah also describes the role of the Jews to be a 'light to the gentiles'. The Jews are called *a* – not *the* – chosen people. This does not diminish the responsibility or significance of any other people, but in Jewish terms, the Jew's preoccupation must inevitably be with the role and responsibility of Jews. Therefore, all other people are considered as equal, and it makes little difference if they are French, Greek, Catholic, Sikh, black, white or anything else.

The Talmudic principle that 'the righteous of all nations will inherit the World to Come' indicates the belief that provided people are good, they will receive their reward. There is no need to be Jewish and, in fact, there is a strong suggestion that the only effect of being Jewish is to lay more and tougher demands on the individual in order to gain salvation.

However, in a characteristically Jewish and thorough way, Jews do not simply demand of others that they be good but they attempt to define what that goodness requires. In so far as all humanity is descended from Noah according to the Torah, the rabbis identified Seven Laws to the Sons of Noah or the 'Seven Noahide Laws'.

Very approximately these are the Ten Commandments, with the exclusion of some of those which might be identified as specifically Jewish, for example the need to keep *Shabbat*. Two laws are significant for their inclusion. One is that people should not eat meat torn from a live animal, and the second is that all should set up or comply with the rulings of a properly constituted legal system. (The other five are the prohibition of blasphemy – in deed rather than word – of idolatry, of incest, of bloodshed except under certain circumstances such as self-defence or war, and of robbery.)

161

JUDAISM

Provided people comply with these basic rules of humanity, then no Jew could have any quarrel with them. The Jews appreciate the diversity with which God has created the world and therefore would not wish to do anything to diminish it. The unification of Mankind is anticipated in God's good time with the coming of the Messiah; prior to that it is the Jewish responsibility to ensure that Jews are good Jews and that other people might benefit from their example of leading a life influenced by the teachings of God.

D.7.d. Women and Men

While both Orthodox and Progressive Jews would agree on the equality of status of women and men, Progressive Jews have also established their equality of function. Men and women can perform exactly the same roles in the synagogue service and exactly the same parts in all legal and social functions.

Within the Orthodox community, women and men have traditionally had clearly defined and separate roles. Women are given total superiority in the home which is the primary focal point of the development of Jewish life – where children are taught and the table prepared for *Shabbat* and other festive occasions. Men are given total supremacy in the public aspects of religious life, in the synagogues and courts. This has many repercussions on the life of the Jewish community and in the twentieth century the religious appearance is often misleading in respect of how people actually live together. For example, women are not prevented from holding down jobs or developing careers, while men are actively encouraged to participate in the maintenance of the home and the nurture of children. The man is recommended, for example, to participate in the preparation for *Shabbat* and for the *Shabbat* meals, and the ideal type of woman as outlined in the Book of Proverbs (chapter 31) is described as not only the mainstay of her home and family but also as an active businesswoman.

Women are relieved from the responsibility of fulfilling those rules which are bound by time. The rabbis explain that their responsibility to nurture children is paramount and cannot be interrupted by the need, for example, to say the daily services. This does not prevent them from performing these deeds if they wish, and it is notable that many women do what they are not required to do while many men neglect even their basic responsibilities.

In addition, some rabbis explain that women do not need daily services as men do because they are necessarily, by virtue of their spirit and body, in closer relationship with God. The late British Chief Rabbi Hertz commented on the line in Genesis that a man should cleave to his wife 'and not the woman, physically the weaker, to cleave to her husband, because in the higher sphere of the soul's life, woman is the ethical and spiritual superior of man' (quoted in Hertz 1933:9).

Men need rules fixed by time because without them they would more rapidly forget God. The rabbis in the Midrash comment that it is because of the virtue of the women of Israel that the Israelites were saved from Egypt, Jewish status is transmitted through women and the maintenance of most of the key and distinctive aspects of Jewish practice are in the care and control of women. The Talmud is succinct: 'If your wife is short, bend down to listen to her advice.'

In Western secular society where the status of individuals is judged either by their economic capacity or the job they hold, it is tempting to see women in Judaism as second-class citizens, but it is noteworthy that in the Bible Miriam was a prophetess, Deborah was a judge, Esther was a queen and all three saved the Jewish People. Women are not able to lead services in the Orthodox Jewish community but the Liberal and Reform traditions now have women rabbis.

There has never been a time when the woman was the property of the man, nor was she ever unable to own her own property. What is more, if her husband went bankrupt, she had an automatic prior right as creditor to that which was left.

The Jewish ruling that the law of the land is the law of Judaism (so that Jews do not come into conflict with the law of the country in which they live except where the matter is of deep moral or ethical significance) means that many of the most enlightened aspects of Jewish legislation in relationship to women have become dead letters, and women have suffered from the same disadvantages that they have encountered in the wider, non-Jewish community.

D.7.e. Are All People Equal?

The Talmud is categorical on this issue. 'The righteous of all nations will inherit the World to Come', say the rabbis, and in Baba Batra 10b they comment: 'Deeds of mercy are the Gentiles' sin offerings, reconciling them with God.' In the Midrashic book, Bamidbar Rabbah (8:2), we are told that even an idolator can be a righteous man and in another rabbinic text (Eliyahu Zuta 20) we are told: 'The just among the Gentiles are the priests of God.'

All humankind is descended from a common ancestor, Adam, and all humankind is produced in the image of God. In the sight of God, therefore, all people are equal and every human being has the responsibility to respect the godliness in everyone. However, experience makes it clear that people do not proceed through life equally – some will be more or less intelligent, more or less good-looking, more or less physically fit, more or less wealthy – and the responsibility of the just society is to attempt to negate these inequalities.

Further, the Talmud states that if someone has destroyed one life, it is as if he has destroyed the whole world. The Jerusalem Talmud in Sanhedrin 4:5

gives this as a reason why God began from one person, Adam: 'In order to teach us that whoever destroys a single life is as guilty as if he had destroyed the entire world; and that whoever saves one life, earns as much merit as though he had saved the entire world.'

In the Torah the Jews are called 'a chosen people'; by such a phrase they indicate their awareness of having a special role to play. This does not suggest a sense of superiority, rather of distinctiveness which is to live according to Torah and manifest through their lives the goodness and authority of God. There is a sense, therefore, in which it is more difficult for Jews than non-Jews to achieve their reward in 'The World to Come', since the Jew might be judged by the more exacting standard of Torah observance.

While Judaism is vague about 'The World to Come' or any future reward, it is clear that it is available to all humanity and not just to Jews. This is one of the reasons why Jews do not feel the need to win converts to Judaism. It is only if one considers others to be remote from God through their own understanding or religion that one would feel it necessary to try and persuade them to adopt one's own path.

D.8. NATIONAL DIVISIONS, WAR AND PEACE

D.8.a. Why do Different Nations Exist?

The simplest and shortest answer to this question can be traced back to the story of the Tower of Babel (Genesis 11:6–9). Humankind attempted to reach God in an arrogant and short-sighted manner by building a tower to the heavens. God himself frustrated the project by introducing different languages to them so that they were unable to communicate and co-operate with each other. But this explanation begs many questions. Are Jews meant to believe that God prefers people to be unable to communicate with their neighbours, or that international communication is working against God's original intention of introducing different languages?

The ideal, as expressed in messianic aspirations, is that all humanity should come together once again in unity. Therefore, obviously, God does not require our disunity. The reasons for dividing people at the time of the Tower of Babel was because their co-operation was leading towards unconstructive ends. This clearly indicates the line that Jews would draw. When nations co-operate in order to challenge God, such co-operation should be undermined. An alliance between oppressive countries, for example, cannot be approved of. But when nations come together in order to encourage goodness and enrich the world, then this is working towards the messianic dream and should be supported.

It is interesting that the quotation on the side of the United Nations headquarters in New York, which refers to the dream of world peace, comes from the Jewish Bible – Isaiah. Certainly the basic purpose of the UN is one of co-operation towards an ideal world.

In Midrashic teaching it is clear that the rabbis were more than ready to accept the possibility of national characteristics. This might seem strange when Jews have often had to bear the brunt of unpleasant generalisations based on prejudice and ignorance. However, the existence of national characteristics is not only borne out by experience, but by reason as well. Different nations are influenced by different philosophies, different climates and different manners of upbringing, so that one nationality might tend to be more phlegmatic, passionate, or adventurous, and so on. This should not blind anyone to the possibility of individuals within that nation not conforming with the norm or stereotype, nor should the stereotype or norm be used to attack a given nationality or define it as a weakness. Each national characteristic gives a nation, after all, its character, and therefore its strength.

Once again, the Jewish ease with the pluralistic nature of human society emerges. Indeed, even in the midst of the critical tensions of Israel in the Middle East, the rights of Muslims, Christians and Bahais have been carefully respected and protected in Israel. The military and political conflict that exists between Israel and its neighbours should not be misunderstood as a doctrinal conflict. Isaiah is explicit about God's concern for Egyptians and Assyrians just as much as for Jews, even though they were traditional enemies, but neither he nor any other Jews would wish to argue that they are all identical. If that were so, it would remove the sublimity of the teaching of the equality of humankind.

So the differences between nations exist in order to prevent their arrogance and to control their combining for destructive purposes. While on the face of it, it may appear that divisions between nations bring about destruction or at least bring it nearer, it may also be argued that alliances between nations have been even more dangerous on some occasions. Humanity needs to be sure that in its pursuit of the messianic age, it does not end up instead striving after the Tower of Babel.

D.8.b. Conflict between Nations

Judaism does not have a pacifist philosophy but it does believe in peace as the highest good. While revenge and unprovoked aggression are immediately condemned, self-defence is considered to be a justifiable course of action, and refusal to act at the cost of one's life is generally to be criticised. So while people are not allowed to take an innocent life in order to save their own, they are certainly allowed, and indeed encouraged, to take the life of the aggressor if that is the only way to save themselves. Not only that, but responsibility to save one's own life is almost paramount. This is the reason why Israel was able to mobilise easily without any crisis of conscience when it was attacked on Yom Kippur, the Day of Atonement, the most holy day of the Jewish year on which customarily people would not even travel, let alone drive tanks.

Necessary violence in self-defence is quite acceptable according to Judaism. Unnecessary violence is not allowed, so even war is bound by strict rules. In Deuteronomy, Jews are required to warn their enemies first that if they continue with their course of action, they will be attacked (Deuteronomy 20:9–12). Jews are also exhorted to limit damage to the environment in a war as much as possible. The example given is that they should not destroy the fruit trees round a town when besieging it (Deuteronomy 20:19–20). Generally speaking, the concept of total war is alien to Jewish thinking. In today's warfare, where the pre-emptive strike becomes a necessary manœuvre owing to the speed and efficiency of modern weapons, these principles may seem inapplicable. None the less, as far as possible, Jews still believe that one should try to warn enemies of the consequences of their actions so that they cannot say they did not know that whatever they were doing would lead to retaliation of some sort.

Sometimes, of course, Jews have found themselves helpless. During the Holocaust, for example, Jews in the camps were often unable to fight back. Where they were able, they did, and there were many breakouts, revolts and sabotage attempts in even the worst deathcamps of eastern Europe. The Warsaw Ghetto resistance is a famous example of Jewish determination to fight, if not for self-defence, at least for self-respect. Where one is unable to fight, one should at least maintain one's dignity to the end. The Jews in the camps often manifested a strength of spirit and a determination not to drop to the level of their Nazi oppressors, which was in itself a kind of resistance.

The story is told of a Jew standing by a rabbi in one of the concentration camps, compulsorily watching a fellow inmate being flogged to death. He asked the rabbi why it always seemed to be the lot of the Jew to be the victim of such persecution. The rabbi replied: 'In this camp, where you can only be a victim or a perpetrator, we should be proud we are the victims.' This manifested the indomitability of the human spirit and as such was a slap in the face for any totalitarian regime.

Recently, Jewish thinkers have been pondering the issue of nuclear arms. It would appear that if nuclear arms serve as a deterrent or as a means of self-defence, then clearly, according to Jewish thinking, they must be acceptable. Any means of self-defence is a desirable thing. Other thinkers argue that nuclear arms encourage war, and it has often been pointed out that no weapon has ever been devised that has not eventually been used. If this is the case, then the holding of nuclear arms is a provocation to war, but no more severe a provocation than the holding of any other kind of arms.

Nuclear arms, however, are different in quality, not just power, from conventional arms, because they have a different effect both on the enemy and the environment. At this point, many Jewish thinkers would argue that the rules laid down in Deuteronomy come into play. The opposition to the concept of total war on the one hand, and the command not to damage the environment in a lasting way on the other, could be said to prevent the use of nuclear arms. The debate is by no means closed and, as has been seen, centres around the question whether nuclear arms are the ideal form of self-defence or the ultimate weapon of destruction.

Finally it might be mentioned that a former Chief Rabbi of Britain, Lord Immanuel Jacobovits, has with typical pragmatism argued that while one might be distressed by the idea of nuclear arms, they have not yet been used in any conflict since their effects were discovered in Hiroshima and Nagasaki at the end of the Second World War. On the other hand, conventional weapons are used every day around the world and are manufactured in vast numbers. He, therefore, would rather oppose the arms race in general and the use of conventional arms in particular, rather than join the bandwagon of nuclear arms opposition. This is as good an example as any of the way in which Jewish thinking, while contemplating from within its own tradition a reaction to a current issue, adopts a pragmatic as well as idealistic stance. The problem of arms is not discussed on the basis of a pacifist ethic but rather on the issue of their danger to the future of human life.

D.9. GLOBAL ISSUES

D.9.a. Responses to World Poverty

As has been shown elsewhere (see D.4.d), Jews have never wished to make a virtue out of poverty, so as soon as they were allowed to join in international activity and thought, the issue of the distribution of wealth concerned them greatly. Left to themselves, Jews had always brought prosperity to the country in which they lived.

It is no surprise to discover that Jews were in the forefront of the development of trade unionism and the socialist ideal and ethic. At the same time Jews are traditionalists, and therefore they have tended to be on the less radical side of left-wing politics. They are also individualists and were to be found leading the entrepreneurial revolution of the 1980s. In a word, it is impossible to generalise about Jewish political and economic positions except to say that Jews play a vigorous and constructive part in the development of new movements and ideas.

As previously stated, the Jewish religion does not (except in the most general terms) legislate for the behaviour of others. Therefore how people in different countries respond to the poverty they experience is very much a matter for the individual society concerned. However, now the world has shrunk to a global village, so that we are increasingly visibly responsible for people thousands of miles away, Jews, as well as others, are required to respond to the plight of people with whom they might previously have felt little association.

In this case the principle of *Tzedaka* applies, as it would in any other (see D.5.b and D.7.a). It becomes the responsibility of the rich to help the poor, since charity is only another word for justice. Quite clearly, world poverty is a product of the misdistribution of resources since there is already enough food, wealth and industry to provide for everyone.

It is significant that in 1956, while the State of Israel was still a new and financially weak country, it established a programme of aid to Third World Africa which is still going on. It even continued this aid when Black African countries cut off diplomatic relations with the State of Israel. This is fully in keeping with Jewish ethical principles as to how one behaves to the poor, as is the fact that the main aspect of that aid was training and technological support so that the recipients could become independent. This was recommended by Maimonides as the highest level of *Tzedaka*. The fact that the recipient may be neither grateful nor gracious does not relieve the donor from performing the act of *Tzedaka*. In addition, the State of Israel was the first to open its doors to the Vietnamese boat people.

While Jews only constitute a tiny proportion of the world's population, they have always been disproportionately active in the alleviation of poverty in whatever society they are living.

D.9.b. Responses to Population Control

Jews note that they are commanded in the Bible to be fruitful and multiply (Genesis 1:28) and therefore they view it as desirable for all people to have children. There is no concept of celibacy in the mainstream of Jewish thinking (see D.3.a), and the general view is that the more children, the better.

However, this is only true if the increase in the number of children is not damaging to the health and sanity of the parents. In the matter of abortion (see D.5.c), if the choice is between saving the life of the mother and saving the life of the embryo, then Judaism unequivocally says you must choose the mother, since she is a full independent person. Clearly then, in a situation where population increase threatens the future of society, Judaism would exercise population control. Preventing births is definitely better than allowing deaths.

At this point, we should be careful to establish two things. First, Jewish teachings and principles are primarily for Jews. Secondly, Judaism never advocates choosing the easy answer without carefully investigating its implications and alternatives. For example, if it is possible, it would be better to increase food supplies than limit population. It would be wrong to prevent individuals from choosing the size of their families. It is the responsibility of the parents to decide how many children they have; but the Jewish ideal is that parents should have the minimum of two children in order to fulfil their responsibility of 'replenishing the world' (see D.3.a).

Generally Jews accept and understand the view that large families are happy families, and that children grow up to provide for the elderly. While this may not seem to be true in the welfare state, one must not overlook emotional needs, and it is quite clear that a society which is not producing young people to be the wage earners of the future will not be able to maintain the welfare state that provides for the elderly.

Family planning is often about choosing *not* to have a family at present, and population control often seems to be a programme imposed upon others. When people choose it for themselves it is often true that the choice is a fairly selfish one. Therefore, while Judaism would not consider population control altogether wrong, it would be wary of it because it so easily exploits the most shortsighted and selfish tendencies of humanity.

At this point it should be mentioned that Judaism has considered the various systems of contraception that exist. The broad principles that guide the acceptability or otherwise of a form of contraception are that it must not spoil the pleasure of the sex act, and it should not act abortively, but rather preventatively. Therefore, the withdrawal method is completely unacceptable but many scholars would suggest that the pill is completely acceptable.

D.9.c. Planet Earth and Ecology

The issue of conservation is well recognised in the Torah, and further developed in the Talmud and later writings. The Torah deals primarily with the land of Israel and it legislates that the land should be allowed to lie fallow for one year in every seven (Exodus 23:10–11). No profits should be taken from the produce of the land at that time. Many religious kibbutzim today grow their produce in trays suspended above the ground during the Sabbatical year.

There are rules defining how early one could take fruit from a tree: one could not take the fruit from a tree less than two years old, one could not profit from the third year's produce, and one could only start to sell produce from a tree in the fourth year (Leviticus 19:23–5). Such agricultural legislation has been subsequently identified as most enlightened; there are still many countries which have not been able to start the kind of programme of tree planting which is implicit in Jews having a specific festival called 'The New Year for Trees' (*Tu B'Shevat*).

Over the last hundred years, one of the most commonplace gifts from Jews to each other on special occasions such as Barmitzvahs, weddings, anniversaries or birthdays is to plant trees in the land of Israel in the name of the person concerned. Through such programmes, a land which was originally mostly desert or marsh has been extensively re-afforested.

The rabbis note that the account of the creation consistently describes the world as good. It is clear, they say, that the world in itself is beneficial. The only component of the creation which God did not describe as good was Man, on whom he announced no judgement. The rabbis interpret it that when God said in Genesis 'Let us make Man in our own image', he was enlisting the help of Man in this process. By so doing he required Man to become a partner in the whole development of the world's creation.

What is more, Torah legislation requires that during a war, people should not gratuitously damage the environment (see D.8.b). In Deuteronomy, for example, Jews are required to avoid damaging the trees around the city that they are besieging. By such concerns, Jews have always been encouraged to conserve and respect their environment. Add to that the tendency of the Jewish time cycle to observe the processes of the sun, the moon, the seasons and agricultural events, and however urbanised the Jewish community may have become, it has an important system for ensuring that it does not forget its relationship with the land and its responsibility for it.

GLOSSARY

Bet Din	A Jewish court of authority consisting of at least three rabbis
Diaspora	The world outside the Land of Israel and the Jewish community that lives there
Gentile	A non-Jew
Get	A document of divorce
Ghetto	An area in which people are forced to live. The first ghetto was established for the Jews of Venice. At their worst they were surrounded by high walls and the Jews were only allowed out under certain restrictions
Halakha	The established consensus as to the correct interpretation of Jewish law
Hasidism	A charismatic, mystical movement which developed in eastern Europe in the eighteenth century. Its adherents are now characterised by their distinctive dress
Holocaust	The systematic destruction of seven-eighths of European Jewry by the Nazis. About six million Jews were killed between 1933 and 1945

Huppa	The canopy under which a marriage takes place
Ketuba	A marriage contract
Kosher	Acceptable or fit. Usually used of food that complies with the dietary laws but in fact applicable to anything defined by Jewish law
Marrano	A 'secret' Jew. During the time of the Spanish Inquisition a number of Jews took on the outward trappings of Christianity but maintained their Jewish commitment in private to avoid persecution
Messianic Age	The ideal Age to which Jews look forward and for which they work. It is so called because of the belief in the Messiah who will inaugurate the Age. Belief in the Age is much more important than belief in the person
Midrash	The major compilation of homiletical teachings or a homiletical teaching
Mishna	The first authoritative attempt to codify the Oral Torah completed by Judah the Prince in the second century CE
Mitzva (s.) Mitzvot (pl.)	A rule of Torah of which there are 613 in the written Torah. Also a good deed
Orthodox	Those Jews who give the traditional interpretations of Torah full authority
Pharisee	A democratic and innovatic teacher of Judaism of about two thousand years ago. Pharisees mainly operated through the synagogues and were largely responsible for the survival of Judaism after the destruction of the Temple in Jerusalem in 70 CE
Progressive	Those Jews who do not feel that traditional interpretations of Torah are binding. This term is used by Orthodox Jews to include the Reform, Conservative and Liberal Communities
Purim	Early spring festival celebrating the events recounted in the biblical book of Esther. Carnival time
Rabbi	A teacher and scholar. Now also often a minister to a congregation
The Seven Noahide Laws	Seven basic rules of human behaviour defined by the rabbis as the prerequisites for a civilised society
Shabbat	The weekly day of peace commemorating the creation and the exodus from Egypt
Shema	Paragraphs from the Torah forming a twice-daily prayer which includes a declaration of faith and several important Mitzvot

Shulkhan Arukh	A compilation of *halakha* made in the sixteenth century by Joseph Karo and considered to be the most comprehensive and authoritative
Talmud	An encyclopaedic work recording the discussions of over a thousand rabbis covering several hundred years concerning the *halakha* and general principles and traditions. Its core is the Mishna, and the two Talmuds – the Jerusalem and the Babylonian – are a product of two different discussions on the Mishna. The Babylonian Talmud is the more complete and the more authoritative
Tenakh	The acronym for the Jewish Bible standing for Torah, Nevi'im and Ketuvim – Torah, Prophets and Scriptures
The Ten Commandments	A group of fundamental laws of Judaism
Torah	The first five books of the Bible. The entire body of Jewish teaching and law
Tzedaka	Justice/charity
The World to Come	The context in which the system of reward and punishment after death will demonstrate itself
Yeshiva (s.) Yeshivot (pl.)	A centre of advanced Jewish study
Yom Kippur	The Day of Atonement. The most solemn day of the Jewish year
Zionism	The movement that supports the right of the Jewish People to a homeland of their own in Israel
Zohar	The fundamental work of Jewish mysticism (*kabbala*)

REFERENCES

Texts

Danby, H. H., *The Mishnah*, Oxford University Press, 1933.

Epstein, E., *The Babylonian Talmud*, Soncino, 1952.

Friedman, H. and M. Simon, *The Midrash Rabbah*, Soncino, 1977.

Ganzfried, S. (ed.), *Code of Jewish Law*, Kitzur Shulkan Arukh, Hebrew Publishing Co., 1961.

Hertz, J. H. (ed.), *Pentateuch and Haftorahs*, Soncino, 1933.

Maimonides, M., *The Guide for the Perplexed*, Dover, 1956.

Newman, L. I. (ed.), *The Talmudic Anthology*, Behrman, 1945.

Sperling, H. and M. Simon (trans.), *Zohar*, vols I–V, Soncino, 1933.

Steinsaltz, A., *The Essential Talmud*, Basic Books, 1976.

General

Biale, R., *Women and Jewish Law*, Schocken, 1984.

Borowitz, E. B., *Choosing a Sex Ethic*, Schocken, 1972.

Breslauer, S. D., *Contemporary Jewish Ethics: A Bibliographical Survey*, Greenwood, 1985.

Breslauer, S. D., *Modern Jewish Morality: A Bibliographical Survey*, Greenwood, 1985.

Carmell, A. and C. Domb (eds), *Challenge: Torah Views on Science and Its Problems*, Feldheim, 1978.

Cohn, H., *Human Rights in Jewish Law*, Ktav, 1984.

Dorff, E. N. and E. Newman (eds), *Contemporary Jewish Ethics and Morality: A Reader*, Oxford University Press, 1995.

Encyclopaedia Judaica, Macmillan, 1972.

Feldman, D. M., *Health and Medicine in the Jewish Tradition*, Crossroad, 1986.

Haut, I. H., *Divorce in Jewish Law and Life*, Sepher Hermon Press, 1983.

Herring, B. F., *Jewish Ethics and Halakhah for Our Time*, Ktav, 1984.

Jacobovits, I., *Jewish Medical Ethics*, rev. edn, Bloch, 1975.

Jacobs, L., *What Does Judaism Say About ...?*, Keter Publishing House, 1973.

Jacobs, L., *Jewish Personal and Social Ethics*, Behrman, 1990.

Kellner, M. M., *Contemporary Jewish Ethics*, Sanhedrin, 1978.

Plaskow, J., *Standing at Sinai: Judaism from a Feminist Perspective*, Harper, 1991.

Rose, A., *Judaism and Ecology*, Cassell, 1992.

Rosenbaum, I. J., *The Holocaust and Halakhah*, Ktav, 1976.

Rosner, F., *Modern Medicine and Jewish Ethics*, Ktav, 1986.

Silyer, A. H., *Where Judaism Differed*, Collier, 1973.

Solomon, N., *Judaism and World Religion*, Macmillan, 1991.

Strassfeld, S. and M. (eds), *The First Jewish Catalog*, Jewish Publication Society, 1973.

Strassfeld, S. and M. (eds), *The Second Jewish Catalog*, Jewish Publication Society, 1976.

Strassfeld, S. and M. (eds), *The Third Jewish Catalog*, Jewish Publication Society, 1978.

Wigoder, G. (ed.), *Jewish Values*, Keter Publishing House, 1974.

USEFUL ADDRESSES

UK

For general information and contacts on specialist subjects:
Central Jewish Lecture and Information Committee, Board of Deputies of British Jews, Woburn House, Tavistock Square, London WC1H 0EP.

JUDAISM

Jews College Library, 44a Albert Road, Hendon, London NW4.

For an extensive range of books on a wide variety of topics of Jewish relevance:
JMC Bookshop, Woburn House, Tavistock Square, London WC1H 0EP.
Leo Baeck College Library, Manor House, 80 East End Road, London N2.

For authoritative Orthodox Jewish positions on ethical issues:
Office of the Chief Rabbi, Adler House, Tavistock Square, London WC1H
    0EP.

For access to Reform and Progressive perspectives on ethical issues:
The Sternberg Centre for Judaism, Manor House, 80 East End Road,
    London N2.

North America

B'nai B'rith International and Co-ordinating Board of Jewish Organisations,
    1640 Rhode Island Avenue, NW Washington, DC 20036, USA.
Canadian Jewish Congress, 1590 Docteur Penfield Avenue, Montreal,
    Quebec, H3G 1C5, Canada.
Hebrew Union College, Jewish Institute of Religion, 3101 Clifton Avenue,
    Cincinnati, Ohio 45220, USA.
Jewish Education Service of North America, 730 Broadway, New York, USA.
Jewish Information Referral and Service, 130 E 59th Street, New York City,
    10028, USA.
National Jewish Community Relations Advisory Council, 443 Park Avenue
    S., 11th Floor, New York City, 10016, USA.

E. CHRISTIANITY

Trevor Shannon

E.1. RELIGIOUS IDENTITY AND AUTHORITY

E.1.a. On Being a Christian

It is important to understand that for Christians, living a good life or doing what is right is not a way of winning God's approval. The basic belief of Christianity is that God loves people as they are – 'warts and all'. Christians believe that this love of God was demonstrated in the life, death and resurrection of Jesus. This has overcome people's fallen nature and original sin (see E.6.b). Once people realise that God loves them however bad they may be, they can then respond with gratitude and joy. The Christian does not earn the love of God by being good. He or she realises and accepts that God loves him or her, and then responds by trying to live in accordance with God's commands – the process known as sanctification.

When faced with a particular moral dilemma, a Christian will often make the same decision as people of other faiths, or even as agnostics, or atheists. The difference for a Christian will be in the reasons for making the decision. We can use two questions which are both ways of asking whether a moral decision is distinctively Christian.

The first question is 'What would Jesus have done?' Of course, no one knows what Jesus would have thought, said or done about questions such as abortion, nuclear weapons, or the destruction of wildlife. But the urge to imitate Jesus has been a continuous one. Jesus said to his disciples, 'If I, your Lord and Master, have washed your feet, you also ought to wash one another's feet. I have set you an example: you are to do as I have done for you' (John 13:14–15). St Paul took up the theme. In one of his letters he urged his fellow Christians, 'Follow my example, as I follow Christ's (1 Cor. 11:1). St Francis of Assisi is revered as one of the greatest saints of Christianity because he set out deliberately to imitate Jesus, giving up his possessions and caring for the outcasts of society. One of the great Christian books outside the Bible is *The Imitation of Christ* by Thomas à Kempis. It was originally written for monks who had devoted themselves totally to following Christ, but many ordinary Christians have gained and still gain help and inspiration from it.

So Christians try to imitate Christ and can check their moral decisions by asking 'What would Jesus have done?'

Another way of asking whether a moral decision is a Christian one is to ask 'Is the decision in accordance with the law of love?' Amid all the rules and regulations that can be found in the Christian tradition, this one stands supreme. Again it begins with Jesus. In the same chapter from which we traced the theme of the imitation of Christ, we read that Jesus said to his disciples, 'I give you a new commandment: love one another; as I have loved you, so you are to love one another. If there is this love among you, then all will know that you are my disciples' (John 13:34). The Synoptic Gospels record that Jesus summarised the Ten Commandments in the words, 'Love the Lord your God with all your heart, with all your soul, with all your mind and with all your strength', and 'Love your neighbour as yourself' (Mark 12:29–31, Matt. 22:37–9, Luke 10:27–8).

Once again the theme is taken up by St Paul in his observation that 'All [commandments] are summed up in one rule, "Love your neighbour as yourself". Love cannot wrong a neighbour: therefore the whole law is summed up in love' (Rom. 13:9–10). Paul also wrote the great 'Hymn of Love' (1 Cor. 13) in which he defines the love that is central to Christian morality:

> Love is patient; love is kind and envies no one. Love is never boastful, nor conceited, nor rude; never selfish, not quick to take offence. Love keeps no score of wrongs; does not gloat over other men's sins, but delights in the truth. There is nothing love cannot face; there is no limit to its faith, its hope and its endurance. (1 Cor. 13:4–7)

Another New Testament writer, St John, stresses that the love that is demanded of Christians is not a human faculty to be striven after, but a gift from God to be received and shared. 'Dear friends, let us love one another because love is from God ... God is love; he who dwells in love is dwelling in God, and God in him ... We love because he loved us first' (1 John 4:7, 16, 19).

So, again, a Christian can check any moral decision by asking 'Is it in accordance with the law of love?' Imitating Jesus and fulfilling the law of love are, for the Christian, different ways of speaking of the quest for the ideal standard of Christian morality.

Against the background of the ideal standard, the individual makes decisions. Rarely does a person have the time, the clarity of thought, the advice and information that would ensure a properly considered decision.

But in an ideal situation, a Christian might take the following steps on the way to a decision.

A Christian will pray for guidance. In doing this she or he is demonstrating a belief that God can guide the individual through the work of the Holy Spirit, which Jesus promised the disciples would guide them into 'all the truth' (John 16:13). He or she also demonstrates the belief that God's Holy Spirit can speak to people through their consciences. No one, of course, can prove that they are right about being guided by the Holy Spirit, nor that their conscience is properly informed. This qualification is an important part of Christian humility.

Further, all Christians believe that the Bible is in some sense the Word of God, and that as such it is a proper source of guidance. Different Christians use and interpret the Bible in different ways. Some see it as an infallible guide. Others say that the moral teaching of the Bible must be studied in its context, and then applied to particular circumstances.

In making a decision the Christian may also look to traditional teaching on moral issues. Such teaching does not exist on all moral issues and often it is the traditional teaching of one part of the Church. For example, there is clear guidance for Roman Catholics on the question of contraception and abortion, whereas Christians of other traditions may have no precise teaching from their leaders. Once again Christians believe that God's Holy Spirit guides them, in this case by working through the tradition of their Church as a body rather than through individuals.

It is common and useful to speak of different approaches to the guidance given in the commands and rules found in the Bible and in the teaching of the Churches. Some people see in the words of Scripture and in the traditional statements of the Churches unchanging laws which are valid for all times and in all places. Thus, if the Bible says 'You shall not steal' (Exodus 20:15), then stealing is always wrong. Christians who believe that biblical and other authoritative statements are unchangeable are sometimes called Absolutists or Traditionalists, Conservatives, Legalists or Fundamentalists. None of these terms are derogatory: they are simply shorthand for a certain approach to moral decision-making.

Other Christians believe that all rules are guidelines which must be applied individually, and the particular circumstances of a case must be taken into account. Thus, while stealing is wrong, there may be cases in which it would be the lesser of two evils, for example if a person stole to feed a child who would otherwise die. Christians who think like this are called Situationists, Casuists or Radicals. Again none of the terms are derogatory. As we later consider specific moral issues we shall need to take into account these different approaches.

In addition to asking the two questions mentioned earlier and taking the three steps outlined above to try to arrive at a moral decision, the Christian inevitably brings all the conditioning of his or her situation. A twentieth-century Christian is a twentieth-century person, and the attitudes and pressures of modern life cannot be avoided. We live in a largely secular society, we have many material comforts, we prize individuality, we applaud success and though these modern attitudes may sometimes contradict the law of love or the imitation of Christ, modern Christians are still affected by them.

It can be seen from what has been said so far that there is not, never has been and never can be *one* Christian ethic. Basing one's response on love gives flexibility of action and variety to the possible answers to a problem.

E.1.b. Authority

Christianity was born in a more authoritarian age than ours. Not only was the authority of parents and religious leaders accepted and sustained by law, the first-century world was the world of the Roman Empire – a world in which the authority of the Emperor and his representative was inescapable and upheld by force.

There is little in the New Testament to suggest that Jesus was a rebel against the political authorities. Some scholars believe that any protests were edited out as Christianity tried to commend itself to the Roman world. Certainly several books of the New Testament try to stress that Christianity did not present a political challenge to Rome.

Paul seems to have accepted the authoritarian structures of his day. He recommends obedience to the powers of the state: 'Every person must submit to the supreme authorities. There is no authority but by act of God, and the existing authorities are instituted by Him' (Rom. 13:1). He tells husbands to love their wives (Eph. 5:25) but only after he has told wives to obey their husbands (5:22). Children must obey their parents (6:1) and slaves their masters (6:5). Paul does not seem to suggest that slavery is wrong: he suggests that masters should be gentle and considerate (6:9). Paul has been criticised for a lack of sensitivity about the rights of women and the underprivileged. The criticism may be justified, but perhaps Paul was simply a man of his time and accepted many of the social standards of his day not seeing them as contradicting the ethic of love. Also, like many early Christians, he thought the world would not last for long and therefore social reform was not an urgent issue.

On one level, therefore, the New Testament seems to suggest that Christians should accept the authorities that exist. But there is another side. The New Testament presents Jesus as a man who acts with a self-confidence born of a natural authority. When He spoke and acted, people said, 'What is this? A new kind of teaching! He speaks with authority. When He gives orders even the unclean spirits submit' (Mark 1:27). Christians believe that Jesus' authority came from God, that he was God's son and acted on God's behalf. He said 'I do nothing on my own authority, but in all that I say, I have been taught by my Father' (John 8:28). Christians also believe that Jesus passed on His authority to His followers – 'As the Father sent me, so I send you' (John 20:21) – when he spoke to Peter, who became the disciples' leader:

> You are Peter, the Rock; and on this rock I will build my church, and the powers of death shall never conquer it. I will give you the keys of the Kingdom of heaven; what you forbid on earth shall be forbidden in heaven, and what you allow on earth shall be allowed in heaven. (Matt. 16:18, 19)

This has been used as a central text for the authority of the Church.

E.1.c. Authority Figures in the Faith

Leaders in the Church today are seen as possessing the authority which Jesus passed on to his disciples. The Pope, as it were, stands in the shoes of St Peter. It is important to remember, however, that all the people who have this authority are known as 'ministers', which means 'servants'. Even the most influential Christian leaders should consider themselves to be servants of God and of God's people. When Christian leaders speak or write in their official capacity they do so with the authority they have as people chosen by God and the Church.

Many Christians emphasise the equality or priesthood of *all* believers and do not accept structures of authority within Christian communities. Other Christians derive their authority from their personal qualities or the gifts given them by God. Mother Teresa and many other Christians do not hold official positions in the Church, but exercise a powerful personal authority.

E.1.d. Duties of Leaders

Christian leaders, local, national and international, have the responsibility of maintaining the faith and making it relevant to their own day, while preventing it from being moulded by passing fashions of thought. They have the responsibility to speak on matters of faith and morals. Even people who are not Christians often expect Churchmen to give a lead on moral questions of the day. On some topics often considered, for example abortion and euthanasia, many people expect the Pope or the Archbishop of Canterbury to speak out. Some Church leaders find it more difficult than others to do so because, as we have seen, there is often no simple, single Christian view.

The Christianity of New Testament times was the religion of a persecuted minority and contains no teaching for a Christian head of state. Later, when Christianity became a state religion and a powerful force, it borrowed teaching about the place of rulers from the Hebrew Scriptures (see D.1.d and D.1.e). Kings and emperors were seen as God's anointed, with authority derived from Him and with divine rights. Historically, there has often been considerable collusion of power between the Church and State. Nowadays, where there are Christian rulers, presidents or prime ministers, the expectation is that they observe Christian moral teachings in their private lives and perhaps be more concerned than others for justice, mercy, the poor and the oppressed.

E.1.e. Duties of Subjects

In the modern Western world the idea of being a subject, having duties or owing obedience is not a popular one. People are likely to say, 'Why should we obey the Pope or the Archbishop?' So modern Christians find themselves in a dilemma. Life is easier if all you have to do is obey: most of the difficult decisions are taken away from you. But Christians believe that their reasoning ability is God-given and that they have a duty to think for themselves. All parts of the Christian Church hold that people must obey their consciences which they also have a duty to 'inform'. This will involve taking seriously the pattern of Jesus' life and listening to what Christian leaders say to tradition (see E.1.a). But in the end they must obey their own conscience. Christians accept that they have a duty to obey the proper authorities of their state. But if that authority is corrupt or unjust a situation might arise in which Christians should revolt against it. Dietrich Bonhoeffer made a decision of this kind in Hitler's Germany. In modern Central and South America many Christians have sided with rebels against oppressive regimes, and teach 'liberation theology'. They believe that the will of God and the teaching of Jesus are clearly against the sort of social and economic oppression found in some countries. In those countries, they claim, reasoned argument will have no effect on those in authority. The only avenue left is revolution, violent if necessary. This Christian liberation theology is symbolised by the poster showing Jesus (with halo) carrying a sub-machine gun: a portrait of Jesus the revolutionary. It may also be the case that some people claim that their conscience has led them to act in a way which seems wrong to other Christians. Although a state or even Churches may punish such people, trial and judgement – Christians believe – is in the hands of God, who knows people's intentions and the secrets of their hearts.

E.2. PERSONAL AND PRIVATE?

E.2.a. Personal Qualities

In his letter to the Galatians (5:22) St Paul wrote 'the harvest of the spirit is love, joy, peace, patience, kindness, goodness, fidelity, gentleness and self-control'. It is difficult to find a better list of the personal qualities which Christians find admirable. These qualities are all positive. Love is the supreme Christian virtue (see E.1.a) while joy comes next in the list – a reminder to those Christians who show a joyless, negative face to the world. Christianity has also identified the Seven Virtues all of which are very close to the harvest of the spirit. There are three Theological virtues – faith, hope and love – and four cardinal virtues – prudence, justice, temperance and fortitude. The cardinal virtues overlap the classical virtues in Greek and Roman culture.

Christians believe these qualities are gifts from God, not the result of human endeavour, and therefore possession of any of them is not a cause for boasting. Nevertheless, they are all to be encouraged and developed; the stories of many Christian saints give excellent examples of the Christian struggle to achieve supreme qualities such as love.

E.2.b. Friendship

Friendship is not a specifically Christian virtue, and Christians would say that loyalty and love for a friend, though admirable, is extended further by the Christian ideal of love for all, including enemies.

It is sometimes said that we choose our friends but are stuck with our family. This may be true at first, but a real friendship should bring with it the demands and support that is found in family life. Jesus spoke of the great demands of friendship when He said 'There is no greater love than this, that a man should lay down his life for his friends' (John 15:13). This sets out the standard of friendship required in Christians.

Friendship of the sort described by Jesus has been seen as so important by some Christians that they call themselves 'The Society of Friends'. They are more generally known as Quakers. Their fuller title stresses the joy, loyalty and mutual support they find in their friendship with Christ and with each other.

In Christianity the ties of friendship have often been spoken of in family terms. From the earliest days Christians often referred to each other as 'brother' and 'sister'. Senior members of the Christian community have been called 'Father' and 'Mother'. These terms are still used in communities of monks and nuns, and many Christians call priests 'Father'. The term 'sister' survives in secular life in hospitals, where originally the nursing was done by nuns.

E.2.c. Sex before Marriage

Fifty years ago no one mentioned sex in public; today you cannot avoid it. Sex sells everything from newspapers to cars. Books, magazines and films gain popularity (and profits) because of their sexual content. Perhaps the main reason for this new attitude to sex is the ready availability of contraceptives, making sexual activity comparatively safe and freeing people from the fear of conception and infection. Another factor is the stress on individuality; the idea that people should not be constrained by old attitudes or values, but free to – as it is said – 'do their own thing'.

The Christian view of sex is that it is God's gift and is to be used and enjoyed. Like other gifts of God it ceases to be a joy and blessing when it is abused. Traditional Christian belief has been that it is only within marriage that sexual activity can properly fulfil its role of being both unitive and procreative (see E.3.a). This means that sexual intercourse should express and deepen the love of the partners for each other. Christians also see the conception and upbringing of children as an extension of the love between the partners and as a desirable result of sexual activity. This teaching is more strongly emphasised in the Orthodox and Catholic Churches than by Protestants.

The term 'pre-marital sex' can be understood in two ways. It can mean either indiscriminate sexual activity before a person settles to one partner in marriage, or the sexual expression of the love existing between two people who intend to marry. The Christian view of humanity is that it is fully achieved by the coming together of male and female, both of whom are separately incomplete. Jesus taught that when man and woman come together they complete each other and become 'one flesh' (Mark 10:8). St Paul taught the same (1 Cor. 6:16). A casual multiplicity of partners is in this view damaging to the person and belittles the sexual act. Quite apart from Christian objections to promiscuity, the practical consequences such as venereal diseases – which have developed new strains not easily treated – and, of course, AIDS have given strength to the arguments against casual sex.

Still, many young people are wary of marriage. They may be worried by the high divorce rate, they may themselves be the children of unhappy marriages, or they may have had an unsuccessful marriage of their own. Some choose to live, without marriage, in a loving and stable relationship. Others have a 'trial marriage', living together before taking the formal and legal step of marriage.

Many Christians find it hard to condemn a sexual relationship which unites the partners, deepens and expresses their love and results in the procreation of children who can be brought up in a stable and loving home. The strains and pressures of marriage are not caused by the taking of vows but exist because living closely with another person is difficult. The difficulties are not removed by omitting marriage. Indeed the taking of legal vows, before family and friends, can give both incentive and support to the partners. In Christian marriage the support of the Christian community and the grace of God are also available.

E.2.d. Homosexuality

It is important to understand the distinction between homosexuality and homosexual acts. The condition of homosexuality means that a person, whether a man or woman, is sexually attracted by persons of the same sex. The exact causes of this are unknown: they may be social, genetic or hormonal but the recognition of its existence is quite recent. Consequently, biblical and secular laws concerning homosexuality deal with homosexual acts, usually called sodomy or buggery, because people were thought to *choose* to feel and act in this way.

The Old Testament condemns homosexual acts in Leviticus 18:22 'You shall not lie with a man as with a woman: that is an abomination', and 20:13 adds the penalty 'they shall be put to death'. In the New Testament Jesus makes no statements directly about homosexuality; he simply speaks of the married state, in which man and woman become 'one flesh', as being God's plan. St Paul, however, speaks forcibly of the wickedness he sees in society. He says, 'women have exchanged natural intercourse for unnatural, and their men in turn, giving up natural relations with women, burn with lust for one another; males behave indecently with males' (Rom. 2:6–7).

In 1 Corinthians 6:9–10, Paul is again outspoken, but notice that it is not only homosexuals who receive his condemnation here. 'Make no mistake: no fornicator or idolator, none who are guilty either of adultery or of homosexual perversion, no thieves or grabbers or drunkards or slanderers or swindlers, will possess the kingdom of God'. Such straightforward condemnation influenced not only people's opinions down the centuries, but also the formulation of laws in Western society. Consequently, until fairly recently most Christians (and others) would have simply and righteously condemned homosexuals. To most people the condition itself was unimaginable and homosexual acts seemed repulsive and unnatural. Public opinion of this kind made homosexuals feel guilty and dirty: they were driven to secrecy and subterfuge, becoming targets for blackmailers and swindlers.

Attitudes began to change in the 1950s and in the United Kingdom the *Wolfenden Report* (1957) led Parliament to do away with the severe sentences for any homosexual behaviour. It became lawful for homosexual acts to take place privately between consenting adults. Great care was taken to protect anyone at risk, particularly children. Since this report, homosexuals have been able to come out into the open. They have (to some people's distress) taken over the word 'gay' and campaign for a wider acceptance of their way of life. As with most campaigns, the activities of some people have brought reactions. For example, books were introduced in certain schools which suggested homosexual relationships, partnerships and the rearing of children within them were normal, and in December 1987 the UK Parliament ruled that such books were not permissible.

For Christians there are several important facts to bear in mind. First, it is pointless condemning someone for being homosexual: it is a condition that is not arrived at by choice. To be homosexual is no more morally culpable than to be blind. Secondly, if it is believed that God made male and female complementary, then sexual acts between persons of the same sex are not normal nor ideal. Some Churches certainly teach that homosexuals should not give physical expression to their desires, whilst others are more tolerant. But most important the homosexual, whether he or she indulges in homosexual acts or not, is a person loved by God and for whom Christ died. The Christian, therefore, should not condemn, but give love, compassion and help.

E.3. MARRIAGE AND THE FAMILY

E.3.a. The Meaning of Marriage

The Christian understanding of marriage is that it is given by God for the proper ordering of relationships between the sexes (see E.2.c), for ensuring the best conditions for the raising of children and for the stability of society. Christians have also emphasised celibacy as a high ideal, especially since Jesus himself did not marry. Monks, nuns and priests in the Roman Catholic Church take vows of celibacy.

Christian marriage is not unique: it shares the nature of marriage in most societies. It involves a legal contract between the partners. In those parts of the Church which regard marriage as a sacrament it is the partners, not the priest, who are the ministers of the sacrament. The priest is present to give God's blessing. Old forms of the marriage service gave three reasons for marriage:

1. having children
2. mutual society, help and comfort, and
3. the avoidance of sin.

In modern services, the reasons given are:

1. mutual help and comfort
2. delight in bodily union, strengthening the union of hearts and lives, and
3. having children.

Based on biblical teaching, Church tradition and social custom, Christians hold that marriage is permanent. In Mark 10:1–12 Jesus taught that ideally, husband and wife become 'one flesh' and this bond, once made, is indissoluble. Jesus did not ignore the fact that in His day divorce took place, but

He clearly regarded it as a departure from the ideal. It seems clear too that the stability and security of a permanent union is desirable for society and for the children of the marriage. But it is also supposed to benefit the married couple through its premiss of 'mutual society'. Sex is important of course, but more than this husband and wife should be each other's confidant, critic and best friend.

Modern forms of the marriage service make it possible for the marriage to be a contract between equals. In the past, the man was dominant both in law and in social practice. That is not the case now, and generally both partners take identical vows and make identical promises to 'have and to hold ... to love and to cherish'. Provision is, however, still made for the woman to promise to 'obey', if that is what the couple wish.

Christianity has often been criticised for its repressive attitude towards women in society and the many scriptural passages which seem to support this. Of course there is truth in the charge and Christians need to address these issues. But it is also true that Jesus' 'liberal' attitude to women in His day, and St Paul's general statement that 'in Christ Jesus there is neither male nor female', set examples and standards that fighters for women's rights have found useful.

E.3.b. Family Relationships

When we speak of 'the family' in the West today we usually mean the so-called nuclear family of a man and woman who freely chose each other as partners and who live in their home with their children. In many cases both parents will work. If, when the children are young, one parent needs to be at home, it will usually, though not always, be the mother.

This pattern of family life is comparatively recent. In the past, marriages have been the means of economic survival or of family or tribal alliances. It was most unusual for partners freely to choose each other. In the past fifty years, other changes have occurred as people have moved around the country and world, and married people from other areas, nations, religions, races and social groupings. Families can now be isolated from in-laws and other relations in a way that would have been unthinkable before the Second World War. In this new situation Christians still maintain that the family is the best environment for raising children and ensuring the stability of society.

Christian values regarding the family are rooted in Judaism (D.3.b) along with the teaching of Jesus, other teaching in the New Testament and present social conditions. The fifth of the Ten Commandments requires that parents should be honoured and Jesus used the relationship of father to child as an analogy for the relationship between God and humankind – 'This is how you should pray: "Our Father ..."'. But Jesus did not place the family above

185

all else. For him and for his followers, the Kingdom of God had to have priority, and might require a person to leave his family. When his mother and brothers went to take Him home He said: 'Who is my mother? Who are my brothers?' And looking round at those who were sitting in the circle about Him He answered Himself: 'Here are my mother and my brothers. Whoever does the will of God is my brother, my sister, my mother' (Mark 3:33–5).

In giving advice to young Christian communities, St Paul spoke of the relationships that should exist within families:

> Be subject to one another out of reverence for Christ. Wives, be subject to your husbands, as to the Lord; for the man is the head of the woman, just as Christ also is the head of the church.
>
> Husbands, love your wives, as Christ also loved the church and gave Himself up for it ...
>
> Children, obey your parents, for it is right that you should ...
>
> Father, provoke not your child ...
>
> (Eph. 5:21–3, 25; 6:1, 4)

In modern society the duties of love and obedience which St Paul requires from husbands and wives respectively are more often understood as being equally binding on both partners.

Christians have often referred to Jesus' upbringing in a family in Nazareth as confirmation that family life is what God intended. That may be so, but in fact we have very little evidence about Jesus' family life, and the traditional view is that Jesus Himself did not marry. Modern family life in Western society can bear little resemblance to first-century Middle-Eastern family life.

Modern life puts all sorts of strains on the family. Mobility separates people from their roots. The clear-cut authority of parents no longer exists now that schools, television, radio, newspapers, pop culture and youth culture make their own and often conflicting claims. Parents are not sure what to do. Very easily they find themselves feeling inadequate, taking refuge in either authoritarianism – laying down the law and running the risk of rebellion by their children – or permissiveness – allowing children to make their own choices and decisions, with the risk that they will make disastrous ones.

Reflecting on this, it is as well to remember that family life as we have it now is of recent origin, and we are still working out how to make it succeed. Fortunately human beings are resilient and children usually survive the well-intentioned mistakes of their parents – and parents those of their children.

E.3.c. Marriage Breakdown

Despite good intentions and real effort, marriages do break down. This happens to Christians as well as to others. The breakdown of a marriage causes great distress for all concerned – not just the partners. We often hear of divorce statistics and forget the deep pain which every statistic represents. Those who actually have to go through this pain need all the compassion and help Christians can give.

Many Christians have always recognised that some marriages break down and separation – living apart by agreement – has been seen as a way of dealing with the situation. So far the matter is simple, if painful. The real difficulty for Christians comes with the question of divorce and remarriage. This is one of the issues that divides Christians into Absolutists and Relativists (E.1.a). The Absolutist would say that if marriage for Christians is for life, then a second marriage is totally out of the question. If contracted it would involve adultery because, in the eyes of God, the first marriage cannot under any circumstances be unmade. This is what Jesus seems to mean when He said: 'Whoever divorces his wife and marries another commits adultery against her: so too, if she divorces her husband and marries another, she commits adultery' (Mark 10:11–12). But other Christians look at things in a different way. In Matthew 5:32 Jesus says, 'If a man divorces his wife for any cause *other than unchastity* he involves her in adultery'. This so-called Matthean exception seems to show that Jesus accepted that adultery was sufficient cause for divorce.

Marriage is for life – 'till death us do part'. So it has always been accepted by the Church that after the death of one partner, the other may remarry. The Eastern Church has traditionally extended this to allow for the idea of 'moral death', by which is meant behaviour such as adultery or bigamy. In recent years some Christians have spoken of the 'death' or breakdown of the marriage as grounds for cancelling the bond and allowing remarriage.

In some Christian traditions clergy have not usually been prepared to allow second marriages to take place in church. It seems nonsensical for someone to make the same permanent promises for a second time to a different person. And yet the same clergy have been unable to deny that many second marriages are good, successful and apparently blessed by God. If God blesses the marriage, should a clergyman refuse to do the same? Today more clergymen are prepared to officiate at second marriages, but of course they are criticised by Absolutists as pandering to modern ideas and being disloyal to the difficult teaching of Christ and His Church.

Absolutists and Relativists alike deplore the breakdown of marriages because of the pain caused. Two things are done to try and help. First, there are marriage counsellors, trained to deal with the problems that arise when two individuals live very closely together. If people seek help soon enough, they can often be guided through their problems and their marriage may be stronger because of difficulties shared and overcome together. Secondly, stress is being placed on more careful preparation for marriage. Clergy bring together groups of couples who are planning marriage and together they

187

explore the meaning of marriage and prepare for the opportunities and difficulties it will bring.

E.4. INFLUENCES ON AND USE OF TIME AND MONEY

E.4.a. Education

Christians believe that the purpose of education is to help the individual fulfil all his or her potential and grow to be a mature and useful member of society. Education is always more than acquiring information. St Paul's words about Christians growing to maturity, 'measured by nothing less than the full stature of Christ' (Eph. 4:13), express for many the ideal of education.

In Europe, for centuries the Church was the only educator; schools, colleges and universities were Christian foundations. It was only in the nineteenth century that the state began to take responsibility for education. In the UK, Church schools were not abolished, and there is now a dual system with a number of Church schools (usually Roman Catholic and Anglican) alongside the vast majority of state or local authority schools.

Most people would agree that the purpose of a Church school is not to indoctrinate children with Christianity. It is rather that the ethos, or atmosphere of a school should be Christian. Some think that Church schools are divisive in society. Their usual policy of admitting first (and sometimes only) the children of Church families means that in some areas they accidentally exercise a colour bar.

In the UK, most independent or private schools are Christian in origin. As far as race and religion are concerned they take in a broad cross-section. As they are fee-paying schools, they are again open to the charge of being divisive. In the USA public (state) schools do not teach religion, though Churches are involved in private educational institutions.

Christian education has never and can never be limited to schools. Home and the local worshipping community have a vital role in the educating of a child in the Christian faith.

Christians must be concerned about the quality of education. If it becomes merely a means of getting a good job (important though that is) or if it teaches, by example rather than by words, that success is all that matters in life, then it is not good education. The curriculum of all schools should include subjects which are concerned with meaning and values. Every good school, Christian or not, will have those two issues clearly before it.

E.4.b. Work

Christian attitudes to work grew largely out of Jewish attitudes (see D.4.6). Work is honourable as well as being a necessity. All Jewish boys were taught a trade. At the same time burdensome work was seen as a consequence of

Man's disobeying God, according to the early story in Genesis 3:17–19.

For Christians, work was consecrated by Jesus' work as a carpenter (Mark 6:3). Acts 18:3 records that St Paul earned his living by his trade as a tent-cloth maker. Paul also gives clear advice: 'Let it be your ambition to keep calm and look after your own business, and to work with your hands ... so that you may command the respect of those outside your own number, and at the same time may never be in want' (1 Thess. 4:11–12). He also sternly rules that Christians should not be spongers: 'We laid down the rule: the man who will not work shall not eat' (2 Thess. 3:10).

Jewish influence thus led to the Christian belief in the dignity of work. Greek thought also influenced Christianity and ancient Greeks had slaves to do heavy and dirty jobs. This seems to have affected Christianity in that academic, intellectual, professional and 'white-collar' jobs are often seen as superior. Further, when Christians speak of vocation they usually have in mind a job such as priest, nurse, doctor or teacher. It should be more fully understood that any job which is not morally wrong (as being a pimp or thief) may be a vocation in which a person can fulfil God's purpose.

What of unemployment? The traditional view of the dignity of work naturally makes unemployment undignified. Many people suffer depression and despair because they are unemployed and it is a serious problem in modern society. One of the obvious reasons for increasing unemployment is that advances in technology have meant machines doing work previously done by people. Since this is not likely to change, full employment may be a thing of the past. Further, people will probably not do one job for the whole of their working life so retraining will be necessary. It may even be that some people will never have a job. This makes understanding leisure a necessity.

E.4.c. Leisure and its Use

For a Christian it is as bad to be a workaholic as it is to be lazy. Leisure is a necessary and good part of life. In the first creation story in Genesis it says that God rested on the seventh, or Sabbath day (Gen. 2:2–3). Also the second version of the Ten Commandments gives people's need of rest as the reason for the institution of the Sabbath:

> But the seventh day is a Sabbath of the Lord your God; that day you shall not do any work, neither you, your son or your daughter, your slave or your slave-girl, or your ox or your ass, or any of your cattle, nor the alien within your gates, so that your slaves and slave-girls may rest as you do. (Deut. 5:14)

For Christians the rightness of rest and leisure is underlined by Jesus: 'He said to them, "Come with me by yourselves, to some lonely place where you

189

can rest quietly". For they had no leisure even to eat, so many were coming and going' (Mark 6:31).

All this means that leisure is good and to be enjoyed (see D.4.c). We use the word 'recreation' because pastimes are intended to make a person 'new' again. This renewal process is good in itself, so pastimes do not need to be serious or 'improving' to be good. Sometimes some Christians have given the impression that pastimes are all right as long as you do not enjoy them. This is a distortion of Christianity, which is about fullness of life and joy and good news.

At certain times in history there has been concern that people did not get enough leisure. Great Christians like Lord Shaftesbury fought to reduce the hours which people (particularly children) worked in factories and mines. Today, it seems, there is the opposite problem: many who have no work whose lives are wholly leisure. Others have what can seem to be a great deal too much of leisure time. Hence the growth of a 'leisure industry' producing things that help people use time. Much of this is 'passive leisure' – listening or watching, rather than doing. Churches can make a contribution here by encouraging people to organise worthwhile activities or to see time spent in prayer and quiet as worth while.

E.4.d. Wealth

Christianity has an ambivalent attitude to wealth. On the one hand there is great wealth in, for example, the Church of England and the Church of Rome. Further, there are individual Christians with private fortunes and there are millionaire television evangelists in the USA. On the other hand, there are Christians who choose to live in poverty because they believe that Jesus both led and commended that way of life.

Christians believe that the world is God's creation and that humankind should enjoy God's gifts. Comfort and the good things of life are not evils. Also it is clear that money in itself is neither good nor bad. A pound or a dollar (or a million of them) does not have any moral quality. What matters for a Christian are the circumstances in which a person lives and the use he or she makes of wealth in those circumstances.

Things have not changed much since the time of Jesus. He lived in a world in which some people were rich, even very rich, others were poor and often very poor. He had a lot to say both to and about the poor. He chose words from Isaiah 61:1–2 as the text of His first sermon: 'The spirit of the Lord is upon me because He has anointed me; He has sent me to announce good news to the poor' (Luke 4:18). Luke also records that Jesus met a tax collector named Zacchaeus who, under Jesus' influence, said 'Here and now, sir, I give half my possessions to charity; and if I have cheated anyone, I am ready to repay him four times over' (Luke 19:8).

Mark records that Jesus met a rich young man who was not satisfied with life. Jesus said 'go, sell everything you have and give to the poor, and you will have riches in heaven' (Mark 10:21). The young man could not take up the challenge. It is sometimes said that this was particular advice to this young man and that Jesus might have met someone even wealthier but for whom wealth was not a barrier either to the kingdom or to fullness of life. That may be true but Mark records that Jesus went on to say that wealth brings with it grave dangers: 'how hard it is to enter the kingdom of God. It is easier for a camel to pass through the eye of a needle than for a rich man to enter the king- dom of God' (Mark 10:24, 25).

Jesus' teaching has often been proved right. Recently, both in the UK and the USA, millionaires have been sent to prison for cheating the taxman. It is as if the more you have, the more you think you need. Greed can take over and a sense of proportion about life be lost. Money has the power to enslave so that instead of a person owning wealth, the wealth owns the person. Jesus said it neatly: 'you cannot serve God and Money' (Luke 16:13). Finally from the New Testament we should note that St Paul wrote, 'The love of money is the root of all evil things' (1 Tim. 6:10).

Where does that leave Christians? It leaves them in a world where there is great inequality of wealth: the affluent nations of the West and the Third World stand in stark contrast. In our society we can consider television sets and refrigerators to be necessities, while for many people in the world one meal a day would be a luxury. Everyone is urged by advertisers (see E.4.g) to buy things which are often not needed. From time to time the needs of the world's poor or our country's poor become headlines, and many people give generously. Obviously this is good but it can be a way of relieving our guilt while we do nothing about the deep-seated causes of poverty and need that continue when the fund-raising campaign is over.

All Christians have a duty to care for the poor. Some believe that the only way to do this properly is by identification. St Anthony, an Egyptian Christian of the fourth century, read the story of the rich young man in Mark 10:17–22 and felt that it applied to him personally. He gave up everything and went to the desert to live in poverty. St Francis also followed the way of poverty literally, giving away everything he possessed. The ascetic ideal of voluntary poverty amongst the monks, nuns and friars who followed the same path has made an important contribution to Christian living.

This is not the way required of all Christians. All have a duty to help according to their means, and many have done so secretly because of what Jesus said about the right hand not knowing what the left hand is doing in giving charity (Matt. 6:2–4). Christians in an affluent society have the two- fold responsibility of ensuring that they do not give in to the temptations wealth presents, while thinking and acting compassionately towards the poor

191

of the world. Christians cannot ignore the needy by saying they are feckless or lazy because Jesus said that the way we treat others is the way we treat Him (Matt. 25:31–46).

E.4.e. Drugs

Most Christians would say that the careful medicinal use of drugs is perfectly acceptable and good. Drugs in this case are seen as God's gifts in creation and properly used they benefit mankind. It must, however, be admitted that the medical use of drugs is not without danger. Some patients have become increasingly and permanently dependent on drugs prescribed to help them through a temporary crisis. A Christian would see such a condition as being less than the fully free person which God intended human beings to be.

In reality, of course, there are few people who are not drug-takers in the widest sense of the term. Tea and coffee (containing the drug caffeine) are widely consumed. Though drugs like cocaine, heroin and cannabis hit the headlines, the uncontrolled drugs, alcohol and nicotine, are for most people of far greater danger. This is why it is often said that if society were being planned anew from scratch, both nicotine and alcohol would be made illegal. Because they have been accepted for so long we have to live with them and people therefore need to be made fully aware of their dangers.

There are, nevertheless, certain drugs it is illegal to possess – controlled drugs – without the proper authority or prescription. This means that those who become dependent upon a certain drug will have to obtain it illegally unless they become registered as an addict and, under medical supervision, receive the drug – or more likely a less dangerous substitute – in the hope it will help them break the addiction. To obtain controlled drugs illegally will usually mean addicts having to steal the drug, which is difficult and usually impossible. More likely they will try to get money or saleable goods in order to pay dealers, even resorting to cheating and stealing from their own families at first and then later from anyone, anywhere. To finance their own addiction addicts may sell, or 'push', drugs to others. Inevitably, the drug-taker becomes involved in crime – often a seemingly unstoppable downward spiral of physical and moral deterioration.

The person whose life is dominated and ruined by drugs, whether it is alcohol, heroin or any other, is a person in desperate need. Jesus said quite clearly it was people in need He was chiefly concerned about. 'It is not the healthy that need a doctor, but the sick. I did not come to invite virtuous people, but sinners' (Mark 2:17). The whole of chapter 15 of St Luke's gospel is about Jesus' concern for the lost. Anyone trying to rewrite the Parable of the Prodigal Son (Luke 15:11–32) in modern terms might well make the younger son a drug addict.

With Christ's clear example before them Christians can only respond to the problem of drug addiction with love and compassion. But besides caring for those addicted, they will try to discover the causes, both in individuals and in society, that lead to the situation. They will then try to do something about it.

The care given to drug addicts by Christians is exactly the same as that given in hospitals, clinics, hospices and other medical institutions by people of other faiths or of no faith. Christians cannot and do not claim a monopoly of compassion in the world. Their motivation, however, is different. No matter how degraded someone may become, to the Christian they are a person for whom Christ died. Many Christians would say that in helping such a person they are in fact helping Christ. This is because Christ is present in all people, and also because Jesus said 'Anything you did for one of my brothers here, however humble, you did for me' (Matt. 25:40). This whole parable of the sheep and the goats (Matt. 25:31–46) illustrates how Christians see Christ in other people, and it helps them understand the motivation of people like Mother Teresa and Dame Cicely Saunders both outstanding examples of Christian compassion.

While Christians can be fairly certain that they are doing the work of Christ if they love and care for addicts, it is much more difficult to be certain about how they prevent people reaching the stage at which they need such help. A Christian response to the drug situation would reject the attitude that it is people's own concern whether they drink, smoke or take drugs, not the concern of anyone else. In the first place even passive smoking – having to breathe in the smoke of other people's cigarettes – is known to be harmful while people's addiction to alcohol or illegal drugs often leads to terrible unhappiness, the breakdown of family life and sometimes to crime.

But beyond the effects on others, Christians believe that all people are God's creatures. We did not create ourselves: we do not own ourselves: our bodies are not our own to use or misuse as we please. St Paul wrote, 'Do you not know that your body is a shrine of the indwelling Holy Spirit, and the Spirit is God's gift to you? You do not belong to yourselves; you were bought at a price. Then honour God in your body' (1 Cor. 6:19–20). In the latter part of the nineteenth and the earlier part of the twentieth century the dangers and evils of alcohol were well known. Many people drank to drown the sorrows of lives lived in appalling conditions. Still, many Christians in those days 'signed the pledge', that is, they promised never to drink alcohol. This is still a requirement, voluntarily undertaken, for members of the Salvation Army who promise that they will neither drink nor smoke.

Many Christians think that today's drug problem arises from a dissatisfaction with life which is similar to that which led people to drink heavily a hundred years ago. Today it is not usually, or not only poor housing conditions, poverty or appalling working conditions which people suffer.

But perhaps the root causes are much the same. It seems that many people experiment with drugs because their lives are empty and they are bored. They want more excitement and they think that drugs will give them wonderful new experiences.

Christians would say that the emptiness people feel in their lives is because they live (as do most people) on the purely materialistic level. They lack depth, and that depth can only be provided by faith in God. (It should be said that people of other faiths might well say the same thing.) It is sometimes said that modern people have a God-shaped hole in their lives. Christians would argue that if people were more open to the spiritual dimension of life, their lives would not be so empty. They would have the excitement of discovering experiences beyond ordinary everyday life. Taking drugs is a poor substitute for religious experience.

E.4.f. The Media

Radio, television and the press are immensely powerful and influential because they make an immediate and profound impact. They cannot be neutral: they inevitably represent the views of their editors, producers and owners. It is important, therefore, that there should be a variety of news-papers and radio stations and a choice of television channels – including the choice of switching them all off.

So effective are the media at shaping people's minds that there are Christians who feel the Churches should use the media more fully to proclaim their own faith and standards. The so-called 'God slot' on television and radio and the religious correspondents of the allegedly serious news-papers give Christians the opportunity to use these modern methods of teaching and preaching.

Some Christians even believe that the influence of the media is so great that the contents of programmes and papers should be closely monitored, and if necessary censored, lest people are corrupted by what they see, hear and read. Others think censorship restricts human freedom and would be a backward step. Yet others hold that what people see, hear or read does not influence their behaviour. If this is true, though, it raises the question why advertisers spend so much to put their products before the public.

E.4.g. Advertising

There is little or no advertising in Ethiopia for advertising is a by-product of an affluent society. To simplify, it seems there are two sorts of advertising. The first tries to persuade people to buy one particular brand of something that is genuinely needed, like, for example, soap. The other kind tries to make people buy things they certainly do not need. This sort of advertising encourages acquisitiveness while playing on people's weaknesses and

194

inadequacies to suggest that unless they have or use a certain product they will not be manly or feminine, trendy or popular. Christians cannot be happy with that sort of advertising as it diminishes one's view of a human person and presents a value-system which is at odds with Christianity.

E.5. THE QUALITY AND VALUE OF LIFE

E.5.a. The Elderly

Advances in medical science have made it possible for diseases and conditions which were at one time 'killers' to be conquered or controlled. The result is that many people live longer. Longer lives and the mobility of population (see E.3.b) mean that some old people become isolated and lonely when their grown-up children move away. The very length of their lives, small private houses and the patterns of life in society today mean that many old people cannot live with their married children.

Christians inherited from Judaism (see D.5.a) a respect for the elderly which seems to be in some danger from modern society's preoccupation with the young, the active and the successful. The elderly have much to give to the young. There is often a very special bond between grandparents and grand-children. But in general it is doubtful whether society as a whole makes the best of the accumulated wisdom and experience of the old. George Bernard Shaw, who himself lived to a great age, regretted the fact that people go through life gaining knowledge and experience and then, just as they are getting wise, they die and the world is deprived of their wisdom. Shaw thought 200 would be a good age to live to! Some of his plays, particularly *Back to Methuselah*, deal with this theme.

When those of a younger generation think about the elderly, they often think of them in terms of problems or needs. The elderly, of course, do have needs. They need security, which includes an adequate pension and confidence that bills can be paid. They need companionship, something which may be difficult if their children live a distance away. They may need special medical care; and there is a strong possibility they will have special housing needs, such as the need to live on the ground floor or where there is readily available help.

The young and active look at the elderly through their own eyes and perhaps misunderstand. Sometimes the very passiveness of the elderly is thought of as an inferior quality of life to the active life. This is not necessarily the case. The 20-year-old rarely longs for the return of life as it was at 10, or the 40-year-old for life as it was at 20. Perhaps the young cannot understand the satisfactions and joys of the life of an 80- or 90-year-old. We should not regard it as an inferior sort of life because we cannot understand it.

In a beautiful little book, *The Stature of Waiting*, Canon W. H. Vanstone considers the state of being passive, as the old and ill often have to be. He discusses it in relation to the passiveness of Jesus in the later part of the Gospels. He suggests that we cannot fully understand the nature of God until we understand something of being passive ourselves, when things are done to and for us, rather than by us. This insight should be part of any Christian consideration of the needs and contributions of the elderly.

E.5.b. Those in Need

When people use the term 'the needy', they often have in mind individuals or nations who lack the material things which, in the twentieth century, are considered to be the basic necessities of life – food, shelter, clothing and reasonable comfort. Thus Third World nations (see E.9.a) are needy, as are the homeless and poor of more affluent societies. We shall return to them shortly.

At this point it might be helpful to point out that Christians believe that everyone is in need in some way. All human beings are imperfect and need the love of God. Even the most materially advantaged can have profound needs; illness, unhappiness, anxiety, loneliness, the fear of death, bereavement affect them as much as anyone else.

The Christian response to the needy is based on the teaching and practice of Jesus, which in turn was formed by His own Jewish background (see D.5.b). In the Sermon on the Mount he spoke of the way His followers should practise the three great aspects of their religion – prayer, fasting and the giving of charity. He did not have to argue for the rightness of giving charity, or helping the needy; He could simply assume that it was an accepted part of their Jewish faith.

At many points in the Gospels Jesus is seen in contact with the needy. He often speaks of the needs of the poor, the disabled and those who are at a particular disadvantage such as widows and orphans. (See, for example, Luke 7:11–17; John 5:1–9.)

St Paul and other New Testament writers demonstrate how the care of the needy became an accepted part of Christianity (as it is of all faiths). Paul wrote, 'Let us never tire of doing good, for if we do not slacken our efforts we shall in due time reap our harvest. Therefore, as opportunity offers, let us work for the good of all, especially members of the household of faith' (Gal. 6: 9–10).

The Epistle of James warns against a so-called faith which does not place the care of the needy high on its list of priorities. 'Suppose a brother or sister is in rags with not enough food for the day, and one of you says, "Good luck to you, keep yourself warm, and have plenty to eat" but does nothing to supply their bodily needs, what is the good of that?' (James 2:16). James also writes: 'The kind of religion which is without stain or fault in the sight of

God our Father is this: to go to the help of orphans and widows in their distress and keep oneself untarnished by the world' (James 1:27).

The Christian response to the needy in the twentieth century is directed to individuals and to nations through agencies like Christian Aid. There is always a double aim. One is the response to the immediate problem, perhaps providing as an emergency measure food, warmth, clothing, medicine and healing. The second is perhaps even more important. It is the attempt to discover the causes of need and deprivation, so that they can be addressed. Long-term projects to prevent famine, to plan agricultural development, to provide homes, food, skills and work for individuals is a vital part of Christian care for those in need.

E.5.c. Abortion

Abortion sometimes happens naturally and then it is called 'miscarriage'. What is being considered here is the deliberate removal and destruction of a foetus which cannot survive outside the womb. This is an issue on which Christians are widely divided. There are rigorists who believe that all abortions are wrong. There are liberals who believe that the decision should be left to the individual woman. Every possible position between the two extremes has Christians among its advocates.

Christian teaching down the centuries has not been consistent. In the first two centuries of the Christian era, when abortion and infanticide were common, the Church was firmly against them. Later a distinction was made between the 'unformed' foetus which, it was believed, did not possess a soul, and the 'formed' foetus which did. This change was believed to take place sometime between forty and eighty days after conception. It has also been held that the time of change was at 'quickening', when the mother could feel the movement of the foetus within her.

People today may not discuss whether the foetus has a soul, but they do discuss at what point it becomes a separate, unique, person. Because of the knowledge of how the foetus changes and develops, different terms are used: 'embryo' for the organism between conception and the ninth week of pregnancy, and 'foetus' from the ninth week until birth. The law (the Abortion Act in Britain in 1967) states that it is illegal for foetuses to be aborted after twenty-eight weeks of pregnancy. This time was chosen because after then the foetus is normally viable, that is, it can live outside the womb. Most people agree that to kill a viable foetus would be murder.

Before the 1967 Act in Britain and the 1973 Act in the USA, abortions, which were then illegal, were often carried out by people unqualified to perform such operations, usually in unhygienic conditions. They put the woman in grave danger and were accompanied by deceit and sordidness.

The 1967 Act allowed abortions to take place up to twenty-eight weeks after conception but only if two registered doctors confirmed that the continuance of the pregnancy would involve risk to the life of the pregnant woman, or injury to either her physical or mental health or that of any existing children of her family, greater than if the pregnancy were terminated. Abortions could also be performed if it were testified that there was a substantial risk of the child being born with such physical or mental abnormalities as to be seriously handicapped.

A Bill was introduced to the UK Parliament in late 1987 which attempted to reduce the legal time for abortions to eighteen weeks. There were two main reasons for this. One was that advances in medical science mean that the foetus is viable at an earlier time. The other was a general desire to reduce the number of abortions that take place because, the promoters of the Bill argued, the Abortion Act 1967 is open to abuse and abortion is virtually available on demand. The sponsor of the Bill was a Roman Catholic but it had supporters in all parts of the Christian Church.

The Roman Catholic Church is the only part of the Church to lay down precise teaching in this century on abortion. The Roman Catholic view is that a unique life is formed at conception and therefore abortion is wrong at any time. The life of the embryo and foetus is, in theory, as important as that of the mother. If a Roman Catholic doctor has to save one life at the expense of the other, in practice it is usually the life of the mother which is saved as this is common medical practice.

Christians who are not Roman Catholics may support this view, as may some members of other religions and people with no religious allegiance at all. Many others want to look at each individual situation and ask what factors ought to be considered – the health of the mother and family (as the Act of 1967 lays down), the circumstances under which the woman became pregnant (was she raped?), the age of the woman (is she very young, or rather old to be having a child?). They might also ask (as in the case of killing in war, see E.8.b) whether a society which readily accepts abortion may be valuing life cheaply, giving cause for fears that the destruction of life might be extended to that of the old and the handicapped (see E.5.d).

E.5.d. Euthanasia

Euthanasia or 'dying well' has been discussed increasingly as people live longer. Usually it is taken to mean voluntary euthanasia. The question is: does a person for whom life has become a burden, or for whom it is intolerably painful, have the right to ask for that life to be ended? Many factors have to be considered.

First let us deal with 'artificially preserving life'. Machines can be used to keep the heart and lungs working when the brain is dead. Few people today would argue that a doctor who advises that the machines should be switched off in such a case is 'killing' the patient and breaking his or her Hippocratic oath.

Many Christians argue that people do not own their lives. Life is God's gift and no one has the right to terminate it. This is why suicide is still seen as wrong by most Christians. The person who reaches the state in which he or she attempts to commit suicide requires the most gentle and loving care. But that does not make the act right. In the same way euthanasia, however desirable it may sometimes seem, takes God's prerogative and gives it to humans.

For Christians who do not take the above view questions to be faced are: which is the more important, length or quality of life?; should drugs be used to prolong life if that life will be one of pain and distress?; if it is agreed that there comes a point when life should not be prolonged, who should make the decision?; should it be the patient? Sick people may make a decision during a period of pain or depression which later they would change. So should it be the relatives who decide? But, then, is it acceptable to lay on people under strain the extra burden of a life-and-death decision? And suppose there were disharmony between patient and relatives. Would that plant fear in the patient? Finally, what about doctors? Is it right to place the burden on them when they would have to make the decision repeatedly? More importantly, would it undermine the confidence a patient has in a doctor who is professionally committed to saving life?

Despite these problems, many people today, including some Christians, believe that euthanasia should be made lawful. In the UK the Voluntary Euthanasia Society is a reputable body and its literature gives examples of prolonged suffering and distress which support its view powerfully. This approach to the problem has the virtue of taking death seriously, and of insisting that people ought to be able to prepare for it with care and dignity. Some Christians are comfortable with arguments for euthanasia and do not consider that God wishes for unnecessary suffering nor is angry at a decision to bring death forward.

In recent years the hospice movement has gained strength and support. Hospices provide care for the dying rather than attempt healing. Patients are surrounded by love and understanding. They and their families are taken fully into the confidence of the medical staff, so that they can discuss and prepare for death and consider the future of the family and dependants. Hospices relieve the pain, physical and emotional, of the dying and help them meet death in dignity and peace. Many of the Christians who are involved in hospices think that the care provided undermines arguments for euthanasia.

Finally something must be said about compulsory euthanasia. Of course, all forms of euthanasia are at present unlawful. But some people fear that if voluntary euthanasia became lawful it could be 'the thin end of the wedge'. If decisions were made for patients who were paralysed or comatose, could we guarantee that they would not be extended to the senile, the mentally disturbed, the severely disabled and so on? It is perhaps only a remote possibility, but nevertheless it deserves serious consideration.

E.6. QUESTIONS OF RIGHT AND WRONG

E.6.a. The Purpose of Law

Christians believe that God created the world in such a way that there can be said to be laws which govern the world and humanity's place in it. These are generally called laws of nature or laws of God. Fire burns. If you put a kettle of water on a gas flame, it will boil. If you put your hand into the flame, the same law holds, you will feel pain. These are the physical laws which govern the way physical objects interact. Christians believe that there are moral laws as well as such physical laws and failure to observe them can also lead to pain. The Bible sometimes speaks of the 'wrath of God'. This does not mean that God rather maliciously watches people, noting their actions, ready to pounce and punish those who break His laws. Rather it means that if God has ordered the world in a certain way, actions which contravene His instructions are likely to carry their own result, even punishment.

The concept of Law is very important in Judaism (see D.6.a). The Torah (Law) contained in the first five books of the Jewish Bible (Old Testament) is regarded as God's revelation of the way people should live, and the oral Torah, exemplified in the debates of the rabbis, discusses its application. The earliest Christians were Jews and they naturally respected this teaching. Jesus said 'Do not suppose that I have come to abolish the Law and the Prophets; I did not come to abolish, but to complete. I tell you this: so long as heaven and earth endure, not a letter not a stroke, will disappear from the Law ...' (Matt. 5:17–18). St Paul wrote, '... the Law is in itself holy, and the commandment is holy and just and good' (Rom. 7:12). But Jesus also came into conflict with the religious authorities of His day, and challenged the authority of the Law. Sometimes He seems to have heightened the demands of the Law: 'You have learned that they were told, "Do not commit adultery". But what I tell you is this: If a man looks on a woman with a lustful eye, he has already committed adultery with her in his heart' (Matt. 5:27–8).

St Paul, brought up as a Pharisee, had desperately tried to keep the Law, hoping it would help him win God's approval: 'In the practice of our national religion I was outstripping many of my Jewish contemporaries in my boundless devotion to the traditions of my ancestors' (Gal. 1:14). His experience was one of disappointment: he never felt that he succeeded in keeping the law and felt no nearer to God's love. When he became a Christian he found that the problem was solved. He discovered that he did not need to keep the law to win God's approval: God's love was freely given despite Paul's failures.

He wrote 'But now, quite independently of law, God's justice has been brought to light … all alike have sinned … and all are justified by God's free grace alone' (Rom. 3:21, 23–4).

Paul made this the central point of his teaching. Man cannot, and does not need to seek God's favour by keeping the Law. It is the other way round. God loves people no matter how badly they keep the Law. Acceptance of this free gift – grace – of God's love enables people to be free to keep the Law. For Christians God's unconditional love comes first; living a good life and keeping the Law follow from it. Nevertheless, Christianity has often been practised as a religion of law and Christians normally obey the laws of the land (see E.1.e and E.6.c).

E.6.b. Sin and Sins

The most superficial consideration of human life would lead most people to say that all is not well with humanity. We cannot claim that the twentieth century, with two world wars, Hitler's Holocaust, Stalin's Purges, materialism, apartheid and so on, is better than any other period in mankind's history.

Christians speak of 'sin' as being the reason for the mess. Often the word 'sin' is used of particular wrong actions such as stealing, lying and adultery. But it is more accurate to understand sin as the condition of being alienated or separated from God. This, for Christians is the root of all human problems. Sin began, Christians believe, when humankind first began to disobey God (see Genesis). After that, human nature became flawed and no generation escapes its effects. This is what Christians mean by 'original sin'. Separation from God, Christians also believe, leads to separation from fellow human beings (with results such as hatred, conflict, war) and even separation from oneself (with results such as anxiety, insecurity and a feeling of worthlessness).

E.6.c. Punishments

Because Christians live in society they are subject to civil, national and international laws. The laws are made for the good of society as a whole, and failure to keep them will lead to punishment. There may sometimes be circumstances when Christians feel that the laws are not good as, for example, in the case of apartheid in South Africa and they have a duty to disobey them. Generally, however, Christians accept that punishment is right. It demonstrates that laws cannot be broken with impunity; it reassures society that it is protected by laws which carry some weight; it also satisfies the offender that his or her guilt can be expunged by taking the punishment.

Christians must always be concerned that punishments are fair and appropriate. They must not be degrading either to societies or to the offender. To take one example: some Christians oppose capital punishment on the grounds that it brings society down to the level of the offender and leaves no room for rectifying the mistakes which sometimes will be made by judges and juries.

E.6.d. The Wrongdoer and the Wronged

Punishment is not incompatible with love. Parents may punish a greatly loved child so that the child will learn what is acceptable and what is not. Similarly society has the responsibility both to punish and care for the wrongdoer. It should be aiming to reform as well as punish; this is not likely to happen if offenders are subjected to punishments which are overly severe. So, for example, a prison sentence is intended to deprive offenders of their freedom, to separate them from family and friends, to take away their rights as citizens as well as prevent them continuing their wrongdoing. It is not intended to brutalise them, or make them ill. So, even though prison is a punishment, reasonable conditions, food and exercise are necessary.

Sometimes the zeal to be fair and humane in the punishment and care of offenders seems to some people to have outstripped efforts made to relieve, care for and compensate the victims. Suggestions are often made that the work offenders do in prison should be used (and should be seen to be used) to help repay the victims. This is a very difficult topic. It is easy to be idealistic. Actual contact between offender and victim might simply fuel hatred and recall past hurt. Only in exceptional cases and with exceptional people is there likely to be benefit from direct contact – and who could decide which were the exceptional cases? Christians teach that human beings should forgive each other as this is how God is prepared to deal with them. This sometimes seems to be in tension with the decisions about and implementation of systems of law and punishments.

E.7. EQUALITY AND DIFFERENCE

E.7.a. Differences between People

Christians believe in one God, the creator and father of all humankind. They believe that the love of God for all people has been demonstrated in the life of Jesus: 'God loved the world so much that He gave his only Son, that everyone who has faith in Him may not die but have eternal life' (John 3:16). Differences of race, sex, colour, physique and capacity undoubtedly exist within the human race but they are all seen by Christians as part of the richness of humanity. For they are insignificant in comparison with the fact that everyone is related as a child of God. St Paul expressed the Christian attitude when he wrote, 'There is no such thing as Jew and Greek, slave and freeman, male and female; for you are all one person in Christ Jesus' (Gal. 3:28).

This view of the unity of humankind is held by almost all Christians. But there have been exceptions. Some members of the Dutch Reformed Church in South Africa have claimed that white races are superior to black or coloured races, and the political system of apartheid reflected this. Other Christians vigorously oppose this view as totally unchristian. Some of the greatest and most effective figures in the struggle for freedom and human rights for all people have been Christians: people like Martin Luther King, Trevor Huddleston and Desmond Tutu.

E.7.b. Attitudes to Other Religions

Christians today vary in their attitudes to other religious traditions. Three main positions have been identified by Alan Race in his book *Christians and Religious Pluralism*, but there are a whole range of approaches between the three he describes.

Exclusivism is the approach often associated with Christians by those of other faiths. It expresses the conviction that the only way to God is 'through Jesus'. Exclusivists often use the text in St John's Gospel in which Jesus is quoted as saying 'I am the way, the truth and the life and no one comes to the Father except through me' (John 14:6). Until recently exclusivism was the majority Christian view and was expressed in the phrase 'outside the Church there is no salvation'. This was applied to those different Christian groups seen to be misguided and outside what was thought of as the true Church, as well as to members of different religions.

Particularly after the Second Vatican Council of the Roman Catholic Church and the writing of Karl Rahner, another position was developed which is called inclusivism. Inclusivists often refer to the story in the Acts of the Apostles in the New Testament 17:22–34 where Paul is visiting Athens and recognises that in their search for an Unknown God to whom they have built an altar, the Greeks were on a genuine religious path. Inclusivists see members of other religions who lead a life in harmony with Christian moral standards and whom Christians can respect as 'anonymous Christians'; they include them in those who are saved.

The third position is called pluralism and is expressed in particular in the work of the Christian philosopher of religion John Hick. He argues that all religions focus on 'Reality' (a term he uses to include even those who do not talk about a personal God) and enable people to move from self-centredness to reality-centredness. If we look at the records of religions, he says, they have all produced good and bad moral fruits. Also they all indicate that Reality is beyond human expression and that the final verification of the truth of what people believe is eschatological, that is it lies at the end of time, when everyone is saved. To the pluralist Christianity is only one of the possible ways to liberation or salvation.

The shift in the attitudes of many Christians that has taken place in the twentieth century owes a great deal to the increased knowledge and understanding that these Christians now have of faiths other than their own and many Christians are involved in interfaith dialogue.

E.7.c. Attitudes to Other Races

Christianity is not and cannot be limited to any particular race or nation. It began in the Middle East and its earliest members were all Jews. Within fifty years of the death of Jesus there were Christian Syrians, Cypriots, Turks, Greeks, Italians, Ethiopians and Egyptians.

Between the first century and the present day, Christianity developed mainly as a religion of the white, Western world. In the nineteenth century in particular, the Churches of Europe and North America saw it as their duty to send missionaries to Africa, India, China and elsewhere, to try to convert people of other races, nations and religions to Christianity.

As the twentieth century has passed, there has been a great change in the distribution of Christians throughout the world. European and North American countries are sometimes said to be secular post-Christian, meaning that despite much outward observance and vestiges of Christianity in society, religion makes little impact on the lives of most people. It is now a fact that the majority of Christians in the world live south of the Equator, and that Christianity is spreading especially rapidly in Africa.

All this might be said to demonstrate that Christianity is not tied to any particular race or nation. The principles which have made such a history and development possible spring from the teaching of the New Testament, and especially from the teaching and work of St Paul. His words in Galatians 3:28 are the starting point: 'There is no such thing as Jew and Greek, slave and freeman, male and female; for you are all one person in Christ Jesus.' Thus, for Christians, people of other races and nations are brothers and sisters in Christ under the one fatherhood of God.

E.7.d. Women and Men

Some people might argue that if the wording of the title of this section were reversed, it would read more naturally. Others would say that it would then discriminate against women by placing them second.

Christians are sometimes accused of discriminating against women because of the roles traditionally assigned to them in Church life and in Western society, which has been much influenced and shaped by Christian attitudes and teaching. It is certainly true that in Church life women have often been required to perform lowly tasks and be subservient to men. For example in local churches women have been expected to arrange flowers, make tea, scrub floors, polish pews and perhaps sing in the choir or teach in Sunday School. In most denominations they have not been allowed to lead worship. Until recently most people, including women, accepted this situation.

Things have, however, changed and are continuing to change. In most Churches women now play, if not yet the leading part, at least a part, in public worship. The Methodist, Congregational and United Reformed Churches have had women ministers for some time now, and the Salvation Army has had women officers from its earliest days. In the Church of England in recent years women have been made Deacons and Priests for the first time. The Roman Catholic and Eastern Orthodox Churches, however, still do not think this would be right. Another symptom of the concern being shown over the place of women in the Church is seen in the way the wording of services is being changed to avoid phrases like 'fellow men' or 'all men' when what is meant is the human race; many people now find such phrases discriminating and offensive.

What is happening in the Church is, of course, a part of what is happening in society at large. Women are being accepted in, or are forcing their way into many professions and walks of life that would not have been open to them even twenty years ago.

So what are the reasons for the Church's traditional stance and its present changing attitude? Jesus chose twelve men to be His closest companions and to share His work of preaching and healing (Mark 3:14–19); women were there to 'wait on Him' (Mark 15:41). But it is also the case that in the accepted social customs of His time, Jesus was very liberal in His attitude to women. His conversation with the Samaritan women (John 4:8–26), His judgement on the woman accused of adultery (John 8:2–11), His friendship with Mary and Martha (John 11:1–44 and Luke 10:38–42) and His acceptance of Mary Magdalene are evidence of an open and relaxed attitude to women. It is noteworthy too that women were the earliest and most important witnesses of the resurrection of Jesus (Mark 16:1–8; Matthew 28:1–8; Luke 24:1–11; John 20:1–2). One might argue that it is surprising in the climate of opinion of the time that such a crucial role was given to women, and that the gospel writers faithfully recorded it.

It is St Paul upon whom the wrath of feminists chiefly falls. As we have already noted in E.3.a, St Paul, more conventionally than Jesus, reflected the ideas and practices of his own day. So we find him writing that 'the man is the head of the woman, as Christ is the head of the Church' (Eph. 5:21). He wrote too that a wife should 'obey' her husband, while a husband is told to 'love' his wife (Eph. 5:22, 23, 25) (see E.3.b). When considering arrangements for public worship Paul wrote 'I do not permit a woman to be a teacher, nor must woman domineer over man; she should be quiet' (1 Tim. 2:12). We might say that this statement, carrying the authority of St Paul, together with the fact that Jesus chose twelve men as His closest companions, has been the main reason for women having been kept out of positions of leadership in the Church. There is also a close association in Christian teaching, though not in Jewish, of women with Eve who is seen as the temptress in the story of the Fall in Genesis 2–3.

But there is another side of St Paul. It was he who wrote 'There is no such thing as Jew and Greek, slave and freeman, male and female; for you are all one person in Christ Jesus' (Gal. 3:28). In this sentence Paul instinctively stated the ideal relationship within the Christian community, no matter how far from it he and his fellow Christians have been in practice.

In practice the Church has often been better than the accepted standards of society, and women have been both recognised and influential in Church life. Some of the great figures of the Church have been women like Hilda of Whitby (614–80 CE), Teresa of Avila (1515–82 CE) and in our own day Catherine Bramwell Booth. These women were great leaders and organisers. The Church also recognises many women saints and it is significant that the most highly revered of all saints is Mary, the mother of Jesus.

Christians believe that God created the two sexes: the differences are important and we should not pretend they do not exist. Christians are now frequently challenged about the ambivalent attitudes towards women that arise from their interpretations of the story of the creation of Adam and Eve and the Fall in the first chapters of Genesis. Eve has been seen as inferior to Adam, the cause of the Fall and herself a temptress. Ambivalence towards women has been part of Christianity's ambivalence towards sex and marriage. It has often held up the ideal of celibacy and avoidance of women as necessary for high spiritual attainment (see E.3.a). But most Christians would now emphasise that the differences between men and women, like all other differences between human beings, count for little compared with our shared nature as children of God, created and loved by God.

E.7.e. Are All People Equal?

I cannot claim to be equal in intelligence to Einstein. I am not equal in musical genius with Bach. I am not as athletic as Carl Lewis nor as well known and good looking as Princess Diana. Yet according to the Christian faith I am equally loved by God and equally important to Him.

There might be said to be two sides to the Christian belief about equality. On the one side, even the cleverest, most talented person is still imperfect, still a sinner and in need of God's forgiveness. St Paul wrote in Romans 3:22–3 'there is no distinction; since all have sinned and fall short of the glory of God'. On the other side there is the belief that God deals totally impartially with all. There is a story in Acts 10 which records how St Peter found the truth about God's impartiality forced upon him. In the key verse 34 Peter says, 'Truly I perceive that God shows no partiality, but in every nation any one who fears Him and does what is right is acceptable to Him.' Most Christians accept that people differ in their abilities, appearance and character, but that all are of equal value in the sight of God (see E.7.a). Although Christians have not always lived up to this ideal many have worked against slavery, apartheid, prejudice and the oppression of women.

E.8. NATIONAL DIVISIONS, WAR AND PEACE

E.8.a. Why do Different Nations Exist?

Since people began to live in settled communities, they have felt a closer link with those geographically nearer than with those they seldom meet. Seas, mountains and rivers formed natural boundaries which separated groups from each other. These natural boundaries still form the borders of many modern nations. France is an excellent example, separated from the UK by the Channel, from Spain by the Pyrenees and from Italy and Switzerland by the Alps.

Separation by nature led to the development of different languages and these in turn have become invisible but real barriers between nations. The story of the Tower of Babel in Genesis 11:1–9 ponders why different people speak different languages (see D.8.a).

Nations can be comparatively small communities within a small geographical space, such as Luxemburg or many small Pacific Islands, or they can be vast geographical areas such as North America or Australia. In each case the majority of each nation will share a common history, descent, language or political system – sometimes some of these, sometimes all of them.

Nations seem to be a natural development in the history of mankind. For people to favour their own nation seems a simple and natural extension of the biological and social necessity to care for, and therefore favour, one's own family. For most people, therefore, patriotism is a virtue. But as communications make the world smaller, in the sense that people can talk of a global village, narrow patriotism of the 'my country right or wrong' sort is seen to be inadequate and unchristian. Not only are there fellow Christians in other nations (see E.7.c) but Christians believe that God created people of all nations and that Jesus exemplifies God's love for the whole world.

St Paul was very proud of his Jewishness, of his birth in Tarsus in Turkey and of being a citizen of the Roman Empire, and yet he knew that national divisions were secondary to mankind's essential unity as creatures of God: 'He created every race of men of one stock, to inhabit the whole earth's surface' (Acts 17:26).

E.8.b. Conflict between Nations

The 'fallen' nature of mankind (see E.6.b) makes it inevitable that conflicts will occur between individuals and between communities. The study of history shows that wars have been a constant element in the human story.

When Christians think about the issues of war and peace, they will use all three sources that were mentioned in E.1.a. They will look to the Bible, to tradition and to conscience.

The Old Testament is the history of God's dealing with Israel – a history in which there is plenty of war. Incidents can be found in which God is regarded as encouraging war of the bloodiest sort. The Book of Joshua, commenting on the resistance of the Canaanites to the Israelite invasion, says, 'It was the Lord's purpose that they should offer an obstinate resistance to the Israelites in battle, and that thus they should be annihilated without mercy and utterly destroyed, as the Lord commanded Moses' (Joshua 11:20).

At the same time, the Old Testament offers an inspiring vision of a peace which is not just the absence of war but a settled, contented security:

> They shall beat their swords into mattocks
> and their spears into pruning knives;
> nation shall not lift sword against nation
> nor ever again be trained for war,
> and each man shall dwell under his own vine
> under his own fig-tree, undisturbed. (Mic. 4:3–4).

Christians study with particular care the teaching and example of Jesus. On the one hand He vigorously opposed evil: He denounced people He believed were hypocrites (Matt. 23:13,15) and used a whip of cords to drive animals (and perhaps people) from the Temple when He believed they were defiling it (John 2:13–17). But He also told Peter to put away his sword (Matt. 26:52), and taught His disciples not to resist an evil person but to offer the other cheek (Matt. 5:39), and love their enemies (Matt. 5:44). It was, he said, the peacemakers who are blessed (Matt. 5:9).

The central theme of the teaching of Jesus was the coming of the Kingdom of God (Mark 1:15). His apparent refusal to be associated with the Zealots who were dedicated to driving out the occupying Romans suggests that He did not regard violence as a possible way to go about setting up the Kingdom. Some scholars think that when Jesus said 'love your enemies', he was deliberately offering an alternative to the Zealots.

For the first three centuries of the Church's existence, Christians seem to have believed that Jesus forbade His followers to engage in war or violence of any kind: it was a pacifist religion. Christian pacifists today look back to these early centuries as the time when Christians got it right. But it is not a simple matter. What was possible when Christians were a persecuted minority is not necessarily possible when the religion becomes a majority movement and its members involved in governing and directing the fate of nations.

Christians believe that God desires peace, but also desires that mankind should live in justice and freedom. What happens when peace and justice conflict? Does a moment occur when injustice becomes so intolerable that to fight against it is the lesser of two evils? Christians may decide to accept violence against them without resistance. But is a Christian justified in standing idly by when someone else, perhaps weak and defenceless, is attacked?

In response to these hard questions some Christians say that war is and always has been morally wrong, and that the conditions of life created by war are never better than the conditions of oppression or injustice which some people would go to war to remove. Other Christians say that in certain circumstances war may be the lesser evil. This sort of sincerely held belief led to the idea of the 'just war'. A just war, theologians said, is one in which the cause is just, one which will establish a better state of affairs than that existing before and one in which only proper means and weapons are used (see E.1.e). It might be possible, if very difficult, to engage in a just war today.

Though war has always been a feature of human history, the situation is radically different in this century. The dropping of the atomic bomb on Hiroshima in 1945 marked a turning point in world history. In the late twentieth century the capacity to destroy is many, many times greater. With nuclear, chemical or biological weapons one person, pressing a button, could end life on the planet. This makes the killing of 100,000 people in one night when Dresden was bombed look almost trivial. Such is the appalling power people now have at their command.

Where can Christians stand in the face of these terrible dilemmas about war and peace? First, Christians always regard war as evil. It may in certain circumstances not be the greatest evil, and some Christians therefore justify war as a last resort. The World Council of Churches meeting in Amsterdam in 1948 stated its position clearly: 'War as a method of settling disputes is incompatible with the teaching and examples of our Lord Jesus Christ'. Those Christians who fully embrace this are pacifists. They believe that war is unjustifiable under any circumstances and that better results come from opposing wrong by non-violent means. It should be noted that this is no coward's option. Jesus, Gandhi and Martin Luther King practised non-violent resistance and all were killed. Pacifism is one of the main tenets of the Quakers (the Society of Friends) but many Christians of other Churches are also pacifists.

In addition to condemning war in general as evil, Christians join with others in their horror and fear of the potential of modern weapons. In 1983 the World Council of Churches said that Christians should be against both the use and the possession of nuclear weapons. Many Christians agree with this statement because they believe that nuclear, chemical and biological weapons make the idea of a just war impossible. However, not all Christians oppose the actual possession of nuclear weapons. They point to the fact that for more than fifty years they have acted as a deterrent in the world.

Christians know, of course, that there is no such thing as complete safety in life. We are all subject to disease and accident and it is unrealistic to expect a world free of war and conflict. They agree upon the desirability of peace, upon the evil of war and the need to work to resolve international disputes by means other than war.

E.9. GLOBAL ISSUES

E.9.a. Responses to World Poverty

A third of the world's population is affluent, well fed and comfortable. The other two-thirds – commonly called the Third World – are poor, underfed and powerless. It has been said that while they starve for lack of food, the affluent worry about diets and slimming because of overeating.

The Christian feels a responsibility about world poverty for two reasons. First there is the clear example and teaching of Jesus, in which the poor are said to be specially blessed (Luke 6:20) and deserving of special concern (Mark 10:21). The conditions prevailing on our planet mean that some areas of the world are likely to suffer drought, famine, flooding and perhaps other natural disasters. This makes the cultivation of land and the founding of a successful economic state very difficult. Christians find, in the words of Jesus, reason to try and help.

Secondly, the countries of the Third World have often suffered not only from natural disasters, but also from exploitation. The UK, for example, has taken a great deal out of India and Africa and Christians believe it has a moral responsibility to put something back, and to try to right some of the wrongs its past actions have caused.

Christian responses to world poverty are rather like the responses a Christian might make to those needing or asking for help (see E.4.d). The Christian might give them some money and then, conscience satisfied, forget them. The money might provide a meal or a bed for the night. Or it might be used to buy alcohol or drugs. In either case the problem will still exist the following day: it might be worse; it will probably be no better. No permanent solution has been found. International aid can be like this. Of course, sometimes emergency aid is required and money or food is an urgent necessity if people are to be saved from starvation. But generally Christian charity has moved far beyond this: it is now well recognised that tomorrow's problem must be solved as well as today's. Long-term projects such as digging wells, building hospitals, training doctors, agriculturalists and teachers are all attempts to help Third World countries grapple with their problems to find permanent solutions.

This is nearly always difficult and complicated. For example, it may seem a good idea to give a village a tractor. But what happens when the tractor breaks down? You need to give the village mechanics as well, or even better, people who can train mechanics. You also need to give spare parts. Through facing problems such as these, Christian responses to world poverty have become practical and thoughtful.

Of course, Christians are not the only people who are involved in relief and aid work in the Third World, but Christian individuals and organisations have often been at the forefront of the work. Among the agencies which are not specifically Christian, but are widely supported by Christians are Oxfam, War on Want, and the efforts inspired by Bob Geldof such as Band Aid, Live Aid and School Aid. Examples of specifically Christian relief organisations (which of course are supported also by many non-Christians) are Christian Aid, Tear Fund and CAFOD (Catholic Fund for Overseas Development). Inspired by the teaching and example of Jesus, Christians try to respond to the words of St John, 'If a man has enough to live on, and yet when he sees his brother in need shuts up his heart against him, how can it be said that the divine love dwells in him?' (1 John 3:17).

E.9.b. Responses to Population Control

Population control means different things in different parts of the world. To a couple in the affluent West it might mean a decision not to have children, so that they can enjoy a high standard of living. It may mean a decision to limit the number of children in the family so that they can provide proper care, upbringing and education for those they have. It may mean the reluctant but necessary avoidance of having children for health or social reasons. To a government in the Third World, population control probably means trying to cope with the problems of food, living space, education, employment, housing and health requirements for a population that is growing faster than resources.

For Christians, both situations involve the moral question of whether it is right to frustrate the normal procreative function of sexual intercourse, and if it is, what methods are normally acceptable. Historically, population control has been fairly common. In the Graeco-Roman world, for example, people would get rid of unwanted children by abortion or 'exposure' – leaving children to die. The early Church rejected both these practices as being evil. St Augustine stated that the only purpose and justification of sexual intercourse was the procreation of children. St Thomas Aquinas gave a rather more positive place to sexual activity within marriage. The result of these two immensely influential views was that traditionally the Church taught that the only permitted method of contraception was abstinence from sex.

In general this has continued to be the official view of the Roman Catholic Church. In this century an encyclical in 1930 from Pope Pius XI reaffirmed the traditional teaching. In 1951 Pope Pius XII referred to 'periodic absti- nence' and so the use of the monthly infertile period became accepted as a way for married couples to enjoy sexual relationships without conceiving children. This is sometimes called 'the rhythm method' of contraception. The 'rhythm' is rather irregular for many women and it is by no means an infallible method. In the 1960s the Second Vatican Council stated that sexual intercourse was a means of strengthening and expressing the marital union, as well as a means of procreation.

In the West, circumstances of life are now far different from those of past ages. At one time large families were normal and necessary because children were additional 'hands' in the family's struggle for existence. It could also be expected that several children would die at birth, in infancy or childhood. Advances in medicine have drastically altered the death rate. Also children are no longer an economic help – on the contrary, parents are required to ensure they receive full-time education until the age of 16, and in today's social conditions children are an inevitable drain on a family's resources.

Christians have tried to take these new circumstances into account in their thinking about birth control. For example, the Anglican Church has tried to move from the traditional teaching to something which is equally Christian and more relevant to the lives of Christians in the modern world. The mar- riage service speaks of 'mutual society, help and comfort' between couples as well as the duty of having children (see E.3.a). Christians have placed an increasing stress on the non-procreative purposes of sexual intercourse within marriage. A report published in 1958 , *The Family in Contemporary Society*, and another in 1959, *The Mansfield Report*, admitted that it was difficult to see any moral difference between the use of the rhythm method and any other form of contraception.

A drastic method of contraception is the sterilisation of one of the part- ners. In effect this involves making one far-reaching moral decision instead of a series of decisions. Christians would usually say that sterilisation is only permissible on health grounds, such as it being dangerous or socially highly undesirable for a couple to have further children. Sterilisation for a woman is a more serious operation than is vasectomy for a man – and this brings us to the other part of the problem of population control.

In the end most Christian couples would say that their conscience, in- formed by the teaching of the Bible, the traditions of the Church and their own thought and prayer, must be the final judge about whether and what sort of contraception they should practise. Some Roman Catholic couples, believing that the current teaching of their Church does not reflect God's will for them, make their decision in a similar way.

This sort of thoughtful approach to the problem is often spoken of as responsible parenthood. *The Lambeth Report* of 1958 explained what was meant by this: 'responsible parenthood ... requires a wise stewardship of the resources and abilities of the family as well as a thoughtful consideration of the varying population needs and problems of society and the claims of future generations.'

E.9.c. Planet Earth and Ecology

Two things make people aware that they are inhabitants not just of a country, a town or a city, but of a planet. One is the wonderful advance in communications, so that it is possible to see and hear events happening in all parts of the planet as they take place. The other is the vast increase in industrialisation, so that using up the resources of the earth becomes a real possibility. In the past twenty-five years or so, people have become increasingly aware that just as we have to take care of our homes and belongings, and live within our finances and resources, so also the human race must be responsible about the way it lives on the planet and uses its resources. A short time ago few people knew the meaning of the word 'ecology'. Today many more know that it means the study of living things in relation to their environment. This is one of the areas of ethical discussion and action in which Christians may identify the same problems and suggest the same courses of action as other people but, their basic reasons will often be different (see E.1.a).

It is not possible here to look at specific ecological issues. Sufficient to say that most responsible people are concerned about what is being done to the planet, its air, land and water. Quite recently it has been reported that serious damage has been inflicted – and is continuing to be – to the ozone layer which protects the planet from the harmful rays of the sun. The removal of trees and hedges to provide larger areas for farming has resulted in the destruction of the habitat of wildlife, and the erosion and loss of soil. Removal of the rain forests of South America is causing other serious problems – even the reduction of the supply of oxygen. Pollution of the sea by dumping waste and by the gradual build-up of chemicals washed in from rivers destroys sea life. These are the types of problems which are rightly causing so much concern.

The Christian approach to all this is based on the belief that the universe is the creation of God and that humans, as God's creatures, should treat it as such. The poem of creation in the first chapter of Genesis speaks of the goodness of God's creation: 'And God saw all that He had made, and it was very good' (Gen. 1:31). The poem also speaks of humanity's special role in creation: 'God blessed them and said, "Be fruitful and increase, fill the earth and subdue it, rule over the fish of the sea, the birds of heaven and every living thing that moves upon the earth"' (Gen. 1:28). A re-evaluation of the relationships between human beings and animals is an important part of the contemporary Christian concern (see Linzey 1994).

Christians (and, of course, not only Christians because this is Jewish scripture also) believe, then, that the world is not an accident. To the contrary, it was made by God who also gave humankind a place of special responsibility for and within creation.

However, the current state of the planet indicates that people have not always exercised this responsibility and have often despoiled God's creation out of greed, carelessness or ignorance. Christians would say that this is because humanity is flawed (see E.6.b) and that just as everyone falls short of God's ideal in personal and social life, so they do in global or environmental life. This is probably where the essential difference in the Christian approach to ecology is seen.

Christians say that just as Jesus came to reconcile humanity to God and people to people, He also came to reconcile humanity to nature. Jesus began this great work of reconciliation, and Christians believe the final outcome is assured. But until then they must work to bring it about. St Paul wrote of the universe waiting to be restored to the perfection God intended: 'the universe itself is to be freed from the shackles of mortality and enter upon the liberty and splendour of the children of God. Up to the present, we know, the whole created universe groans in all its parts as if in the pangs of childbirth' (Rom. 8:21–2).

Christians believe that they are called to share the work of bringing about this freeing of nature. At this point they join with many others who have social, scientific, humanitarian and other reasons for caring for the planet. Many Christians join with Friends of the Earth, Greenpeace and other similar movements, to convert into action what their Christian faith teaches them about their relationship to planet earth.

GLOSSARY

Anglican	Churches in England and abroad which are in communion with the see of Canterbury. In England the Anglican Church is often called 'The Church of England'
Apartheid	(Literally 'apartness'.) The term used for the racial segregation which was practised in South Africa
Archbishop of Canterbury	The senior Bishop, and often the spokesman, of the Church of England and the Anglican Church
Bible	The sacred book of Christianity. The Bible contains

	the thirty-nine books of the Old Testament (which is also the Jewish Bible) and the twenty-seven books of the New Testament which contains specifically Christian writings.
Bishop	The highest order of Minister in the Christian Church. The word comes from 'episcopus' – one who has oversight
Charity	The word is used in two ways by Christians. It is the greatest virtue and is synonymous with 'love', which is God's greatest attribute and gift to men. It has also come to mean the act of caring for those in need
Church	A community of Christians. Sometimes the term is used to refer to all Christians in the world. Places of Christian worship can also be called 'churches'
Congregational Church	A Church which emphasised the independence and authority of local groups of Christians. In 1972 the Congregational Church joined with Presbyterians to form the United Reformed Church
Conscience	Traditional Christian teaching holds that people have an inborn capacity for deciding what is right and what is wrong. This is 'conscience', sometimes called the 'inner voice' or 'the voice of God'.
Deacon	The word means 'servant'. It is the first rank in the three-fold Christian ministry of Bishops, Priests and Deacons
Encyclical	A letter sent by a Bishop to all churches in his area. Commonly it is used of letters sent by the Pope to all parts of the Roman Catholic Church
Evangelist	One who transmits good news. The Four Evangelists are the writers of the Gospels – Matthew, Mark, Luke and John – which are in the New Testament. The term is also used for those particularly skilled in or concerned with spreading the Christian good news
Grace	The free gift of God's love
Holy Spirit	Christians believe that the One God has revealed Himself in many ways, but most clearly as 'Father', the source and creator of everything; as 'Son', in the person of Jesus; and as 'Holy Spirit' which is the continuing and present activity of God's divine energy
Hospice	The hospice movement was started early this century, but spread particularly after the opening of St Christopher's Hospice in 1967. Hospices care for the

	terminally ill. They seek to give patients the opportunity to live out their lives in dignity and with as much medical and social support as possible.
Kingdom of God	The 'Kingdom of God' or 'the reign of God' was the central theme of Jesus' teaching. He taught His followers to proclaim, work and pray for the establishment and recognition of God's Kingdom on earth
Lambeth	Lambeth Palace is the London residence of the Archbishop of Canterbury and a major centre for the administrative work of the Church of England. Every ten years the Bishops of the Anglican Communion meet in conference at Lambeth
Martyr	A person who dies for the faith
Minister	The word means 'servant' and is applied to leaders of Christian groups. They are to be servants of God and their fellow Christians
Missionary	Someone who is 'sent'. Missionaries try, by teaching and service, to convert people to Christianity
Monk	A male member of a religious community. He takes vows of poverty, chastity and obedience. His most important work is prayer
Nun	A female member of a religious community
Orthodox	The Eastern Churches in communion with Constantinople – the ancient name for Istanbul
Pope	The Bishop of Rome, who is head of the Roman Catholic Church throughout the world
Prayer	Communication with God. Prayer can be public or private, verbal or silent, meditative or contemplative
Priest	A minister of the Church ranking between Bishop and Deacon
Quaker	A term used for a member of the Society of Friends which was founded by George Fox in 1668. Quakers stress the guidance of God to individuals through the 'inner light'. They are pacifists
Reconciliation	The bringing together as friends those who were separated. Christians believe that Jesus reconciled humankind to God, human beings to each other and humankind to nature
Resurrection	The rising from the dead of Jesus on the Sunday after His death on a Friday. This was achieved by the power of God. Christians believe that God will also raise believers

Roman Catholic	That part of the Church which owes allegiance to the Pope
Sabbath	A term imported from Judaism. Because of the resurrection of Jesus on a Sunday, Christians keep that day as their special day of worship. Opinions vary about precisely how Sunday should be observed.
Sacrament	A sign, symbol or action representing a sacred and invisible grace or gift. Most Christians recognise seven sacraments – the two great sacraments of Baptism and the Eucharist, and the five lesser sacraments of Confirmation, Marriage, Ordination, Unction (annointing of the sick) and Penance
Saint	The word is commonly used of people whose holiness is or has been exceptional. Originally it referred to all Christians as they were 'set apart' from the rest of the world by their beliefs
Salvation Army	A branch of the Church devoted especially to social and evangelistic work. It was founded in 1865 by General William Booth
Sanctification	The process of growing in holiness, which can begin when a person has accepted the free gift of God's forgiveness
Scripture	The sacred books of Christianity – the Bible
Sin	Sin is often thought of as acts of disobedience against God and is linked by Christians to the account in Genesis 3 which they call The Fall. It is perhaps better regarded as the state of being separated from God, which leads to wrong acts. The idea that we inherit this state of separation has been called Original Sin by Christians
Soul	Christian teaching about the soul is not precise. Generally we might say that it is the 'self', or the identity of an individual, the 'I' which speaks of 'my hand', 'my body', 'my head', or 'my brain'
Synoptic Gospels	The first three Gospels of the New Testament – Matthew, Mark and Luke. Synoptic means they share a common viewpoint
Tradition	'That which is handed over' from generation to generation in Christianity – its beliefs, practices and attitudes
United Reformed Church	Founded in 1972 by the uniting of the Congregational Church and the Presbyterian Church in England

Vatican	The residence of the Pope in Rome and the administrative centre of the Roman Catholic Church
Virtues	The Theological Virtues are Faith, Hope and Charity. The Cardinal Virtues are Prudence, Temperance, Fortitude and Justice
Vocation	This means 'calling'. The word is used to express the belief that some occupations are more than mere jobs: the way a person responds to the 'call' of God

REFERENCES

Texts

Biblical quotations in the text are taken from the New English Bible edition, published by The Bible Societies in association with Oxford University Press and Cambridge University Press 1961 and 1970.

General

Barclay, W., *The Plain Man's Guide to Ethics*, Fount, 1986.
Beune, R., *Ordinary Saints*, Fortress, 1988.
Breuilly, E. and M. Palmer (eds), *Christianity and Ecology*, Cassell, 1992.
Brown, D., *Choices*, Basil Blackwell, 1983.
Childress, J. and J. Macquarrie (eds), *A New Dictionary of Christian Ethics*, SCM, 1987.
Chirbban, J. T. (ed.), *Ethical Dilemmas: Crises in Faith and Modern Medicine*, University Press of America, 1994.
Collins, R. F., *Christian Morality: Biblical Foundations*, Notre Dame, 1986.
Cook, D., *The Moral Maze*, SPCK, 1988.
Cupitt, D., *The New Christian Ethics*, SCM, 1988.
Curran, C. E., *Issues in Sexual and Medical Ethics*, Notre Dame, 1978.
Gill, R., *Christian Ethics in Secular Worlds*, T & T Clark, 1991.
Hart, R. E., *Ethics and Environment*, University Press of America, 1992.
Holmes, A. F., *War and Christian Ethics*, Baker, 1975.
Jones, R. G., *Groundwork of Christian Ethics*, Epworth, 1984.
King, R., *Ethics and Civil Rights*, OUP, 1992.
Lambeth Report, The, also called *The Family in Contemporary Society* (no editor), Lambeth Conference 1958, SPCK.
Linzey, A., *Animal Theology*, SCM, 1994.
Macnamarra, V., *The Truth in Love*, Gill and Macmillan, 1988.
Mansfield Report, The, also called *Responsible Parenthood and the Population Problem*, *Ecumenical Review* vol. 12, no. 1, Oct. 1959.
Patey, E., *Questions for Today*, Mowbray, 1986.
Preston, R. H., *The Future of Christian Ethics*, SCM, 1987.

Race, A., *Christians and Religious Pluralism*, 2nd edn, SCM, 1994.
Ramsay, P., *The Just War: Force and Political Responsibility*, Scribners, 1968.
Ramsay, P., *Ethics at the Edges of Life*, Yale University Press, 1978.
Saunders, J. T., *Ethics in The New Testament*, SCM, 1986.
Taylor, M. H., *Good for the Poor: Christian Ethics and World Development*, Mowbray, 1990.
Wogaman, J. P., *Economics and Ethics: A Christian Enquiry*, SCM, 1986.

USEFUL ADDRESSES

UK

Actions by Christians Against Torture, Quex Road Methodist Church, Kilburn, London NW6 4PR.

CAFOD, 2 Romero Close, Stockwell Road, London SW9 9TY.

Centre for Black and White Christian Partnership, Selly Oak Colleges, Birmingham B29 9LQ.

Christian Aid, PO Box 100, London SE1 7RT.

Churches Commission for Inter-Faith Relations, Church House, Great Smith Street, Westminster, London SW1P 3NZ.

Council of Churches for Britain and Ireland, Inter-Church House, 35 Lower Marsh, London SE1 7RL.

Ecumenical Forum for European Christian Women, 10a Osbourne Terrace, Edinburgh EH12 2HE.

Environmental Issues Network, National Agricultural Centre, Stoneleigh Park, Warwickshire CV8 2IZ.

Feed the Minds, Robertson House, Leas Road, Guildford GU1 4QW.

Justice, Peace and Integrity of Creation Group, 39 Eccleston Square, London SW1V 1PD.

North America

Alcoholism Treatment Associates, 24 E 12 Manhattan NY, USA.

American Friends' Services Committee, 1501 Cherry St, Philadelphia, Pennsylvania, USA.

Direct Relief International, 2801-B, De La Vina Street, PO Box 30820, Santa Barbara, CA 93130, USA.

Foundation for Field Research, PO Box 2010, Alpine, CA 91903, USA.

National Wildlife Federation, 1400 16th St, NW, Washington DC 20036, USA.

Peace Corps of the United States, 1990 K Streeet, NW, Washington, DC 20526, USA.

Student Conservation Association, PO Box 550, Charlestown, NH 03603, USA.

World Peace Foundation, 22 Batterymarch St, Boston, MA 02109, USA.

F. ISLAM

Mashuq ibn Ally

F.1. RELIGIOUS IDENTITY AND AUTHORITY

F.1.a. On Being a Muslim

Islam is described as a way of life (*dīn*), but what does this mean to a Muslim? What is the framework of life within which a Muslim lives? What determines obligations, good and bad, right and wrong, in Islam? Underpinning the Islamic way of life is an ethical system which shapes and determines the Muslim world view. This section attempts to outline the basic beliefs, concepts, values, morals, and standard of conduct of the Islamic ethical system.

At the core of the Muslim religious experience is God (*Allah*), the Creator (*khaliq*), Sustainer (*razzāq*), and Sovereign (*mālik*) of all creation. Commitment to God means being in witness (*shahāda*) to His will, both as His servant (*'abd*) and as His trustee (*khalīfa*).

This trusteeship (*khalīfah*) confers both responsibility and obligation (*taklīf*) for the whole universe; it is the basis of the Muslim's humanity. For God has invested Muslims with His divine trust which is the fulfilment of the ethical part of the divine will, by virtue of the powers delegated to them by God, Muslims are required to exercise this authority within the limits prescribed by God. For instance, suppose an estate which you own is given to someone to administer on your behalf. You will be very concerned that four conditions are upheld; first, that the real ownership remains with you and not with the administrator; second, that the estate is administered only in accordance with your instructions; third, that the administrator exercises his authority within the limits prescribed by you; and fourth, that in the administration of the trust the administrator executes your will and not his own. Failure to meet these conditions will result in the administrator being blamed for not meeting the responsibilities which were implied in the concept of trusteeship; on the other hand success in fulfilling the trust would result in his being rewarded.

In the course of being a Muslim – that is, one who is in a state of *Islam* or peace in commitment to One God, there is no aspect of life at the individual level, or at the communal (*ummah*) level which is not touched and transformed in keeping with the two basic concepts of the Lordship and Sovereignty of God (*rab*) and the human being's responsibility to Him.

For the fulfilment of responsibility and therefore of divine will, knowledge is required. The source from which a Muslim seeks knowledge (*'ilm*) of God and guidance (*hidāyah*) for human behaviour is the Qur'ān – the book (*al-kitāb*) believed by Muslims to contain the revealed word (*wahī*) of God to humanity; the direct and immediate disclosure of what God wants to be realised on earth.

The Qur'ān brings together all the eternal beliefs (*aqīda*): oneness of God (*tawhīd*), revelation (*wahī*), prophethood (*risāla*), belief in beings beyond our perception (*gayb*), and life after death (*'akhira*). It encapsulates the fundamental ethical institutions of religious life: worship (*'ibāda*), fasting (*saum*), charity (*zakat*), and pilgrimage (*hajj*) (see F.2.a). It projects universal religious norms and virtues: faith (*imān*), God-consciousness (*taqwa*), justice (*'adl*), sincerity (*ikhlās*), trust in God (*tawakkul*), wisdom (*hikma*), mercy and compassion (*rahma*), courage (*shajā'a*), repentance (*tawba*), gratitude (*shukr*), temperance (*'iffa*), love (*hubb*), hope (*rajā*), fear (*khawf*), and patience (*sabr*). It discerns the root vices: gluttony, excess in sexual relations, excessive speech (*sharah al-kalām*), cursing (*la'n*), hypocrisy (*nifāq*), slander (*namīma*), backbiting (*ghība*), strong anger (*shiddat al-ghadab*), rancour (*hiqd*), envy (*hasad*), love of the world (*hubb ad-dunyā*), love of wealth (*hubb al-māl*), love of influence (*hubb al-jāh*), ostentation (*riyā*), and pride (*kibr*).

The Qur'ān draws on allegory and history to encourage, exhort and inspire Muslims to an ethic of action. Vices, if left unchecked, lead to evil (*munkarāt*); virtues when allowed to flourish, lead to goodness (*mar'ūfāt*). The former will lead to destabilisation; giving way to chaos and injustice – disturbing the natural order of things. The latter give way to order, equilibrium (*wast*), and justice (*'adl*) – maintaining the natural order. The Qur'ān does not, however, limit itself to an inventory of good and evil; rather, it lays down an entire scheme of life whose aim is to make sure that good triumphs, and that evil does not destroy or harm human life.

It is this moral responsibility to strive for and uphold God's sovereignty, struggle for what is right, good and just, and maintain equilibrium and order, which is the fulfilment of the ethical part of the divine will. The responsibility or obligation (*taklīf*) laid upon the Muslim knows no bounds, as far as the possible scope and theatre of action are concerned; it comprehends the whole universe. All humanity is the object of moral action; all earth and sky are the Muslim's theatre, his and her material. For the Muslim's *taklīf* is universal, cosmic. It comes to an end only on the day of judgement.

This concept of the Muslim's place in the universe leads to the expectation of accountability to God. The degree to which the Muslim is able to fulfil the divine trust is to be accounted for on the day of judgement; one day he or she will die and will have to stand before the divine court of justice, where no special pleading will be of avail. It is this belief in accountability to God which is the real force behind the moral law of Islam.

Islam's first requirement then, is belief, and its second is action. Out of its concepts and beliefs emerges a certain attitude towards life, towards one's own self, towards other human beings, and towards the universe. This leads to the development of a certain kind of personality, a distinctive type of human interaction, along with a particular mode of worship, family life, manners and living habits.

The second source of ethical knowledge (*'ilm al-akhlāq*) for the Muslim is the life examples (*sunnah*) of prophets (see F.4.a). Each one of the prophets was a human being like any other, with the same human needs and feelings; Islam most emphatically denies any suggestion of the divinity or super-human nature of God's prophets. However, prophets were men of special qualities whom God singles out from the rest of humanity for the task of conveying His revelation (*wahī*) and guidance (*hidāyah*). Such individuals, the first of whom Muslims believe was Adam and the last of whom was Muhammad, are characterised by their total commitment to God; their pure and upright natures; the extraordinary righteousness of their conduct; their exemplification of the divine will. After the name of each prophet a Muslim will say or write the Arabic phrase which is translated into English as 'peace and blessings be upon him', or PBUH.

The life of a prophet is a beacon light for the rest of humanity. For example, Abraham (PBUH), out of obedience, love and trust in God, was prepared to sacrifice his most loved child on God's command. Moses (PBUH) struggled against the oppression of the children of Israel; Jesus (PBUH) was compassionate towards the sick and infirm; Muhammad (PBUH) stood up for all those who suffered from oppression and tyranny. These men stood for good in opposition to the men of evil some of whom were represented by Nimrod, Pharaoh, Caesar and the Quraysh.

Therefore, prophets were not mere messengers, but exemplars of the messages they brought and which they struggled to establish in the world. The ethical and moral principles of the prophets is one long continuum: beginning with Adam (PBUH), and completed by Muhammad (PBUH). Islam holds that there is no basic difference in ethics from one prophet to another.

The ethics of all prophets was one of moderation and balance (*wast*), therefore fanaticism, or fundamentalism as it is mistakenly called, has no place in Islam. Fanaticism is an attitude of faith which arises out of fear of the unknown, and may lead to extreme behaviour; fundamentalism is the literal interpretation of scripture. However, Muslims would understand it as a legitimate process of interpreting the Qur'ān and *sunnah* to meet the demands of a changing world; the ethical mission of prophets was to temper faith with reason, and to guide humans to apprehend the unknown through reflection, search and discovery.

The Salman Rushdie issue is a contemporary example of the conflict between moderation and extremism. On the one hand the majority of Muslims would like to see the *Satanic Verses* withdrawn from publication because they believe it contains offensive material – in very crude language – against the Prophet Muhammad and his family. On the other hand there is a minority which calls for the death of the author. Although, Muslims have no objections to the life of Muhammad coming under scrutiny and criticism, they do object to this being undertaken insensitively and without regard for the ethical standards which should be applied when speaking of the dead; Islam prohibits speaking ill of the dead, whether saint or criminal.

Apart from prophets Muslims are not encouraged to emulate the lives of any other member of the faith because no other Muslims can claim to be totally exemplary of the Islamic ethical system. However, that does not stop them being encouraged and inspired by the goodness reflected in some aspects of the lives of others. That is why, in some parts of the world, some Muslims may gather around an individual who, because of his or her morality, they feel can give spiritual guidance and inspiration.

F.1.b. Authority

Islam is not a faith of isolation or a faith which encourages monasticism. Its moral order demands an ethical system which requires the Muslim to meet and fulfil the responsibility and obligation (*taklīf*) of the divine trust at the individual level; it also demands that this task be fulfilled with the assistance and co-operation of other human beings. This involvement with other humans is what is meant by *ummatism* (community).

This notion requires the Muslim to involve others in doing good, in struggling (*jihād*) for justice (*'adl*). But since the desired end is moral, it can only be achieved in a condition of moral freedom: it should be willed, for the sake of God, if it is to be moral at all. Islam therefore prescribes that people be invited, and educated to join a community (*ummah*) which serves God by fulfilling His divine will. 'Let there arise a *ummah* which establishes good, Which enjoins good works and prohibits evil. Those are truly felicitous' (Qur'ān 3: 104).

The term *ummah* is not synonymous with 'people' or 'nation', or 'state'.

These are always determined by race, geography, language or history. The *ummah* is trans-local and trans-racial: its territory is not only the whole earth, but all of creation. The *ummah* is the universal social order of Islam, and though the individual has freedom and authority to exercise responsibility and obligation (*taklīf*), he or she does so within the framework and structure of community (*ummah*), which constrains excesses. It is the *ummah* which has the authority for formulating law within the framework of the Qur'ān; deciding on issues of war and peace, electing leadership and determining policy.

F.1.c. Authority Figures in the Faith

Though there is no priesthood or Church in Islam, four terms denote power and authority in the *ummah*. These are *khalīfa, amīr al-mu'minūn, 'imām, qadī*.

Khalīfa, in the general Qur'ānic sense, is an expression of the concept which gives Muslims the ability to manage and control their world as a trust (*amānah*), through which they achieve what they are worth and thus decide their eternal destiny in the hereafter. To realise this goal at a collective level individuals must organise themselves into a community (*ummah*) from among whom they elect a *khalīfa* who carries the mantle of leader. In the contemporary world this title has also become synonymous with 'President' and 'King'. The *khalīfa* is bound by the *sharī'ah* (Qur'ān and *sunnah*) and has no authority to modify doctrine. His pronouncements only attempt to buttress the power and authority of his office under the *sharī'ah* against any single member of the *ummah*'s authority. In addition the *khalīfa* is also called the *amīr al-mu'minūn*, the Commander of the Faithful. If the occasion arises where the *ummah* has to go to war in its struggle to maintain justice (*'adl*), the *khalīfa* becomes leader of the Muslim army.

'Imām signifies leadership with more emphasis on the spiritual affairs of the *ummah*. The word itself means leader, and such a position can be held by anyone who is nominated and elected by the community (see F.1.d). *Qadī* are individuals in the community trained in the law of Islam and are therefore responsible for formulating judgements on any issue which they deem relevant to the welfare of the community in its pursuit of justice.

F.1.d. Duties of Leaders

The duties of the *khalīfa*, whether a king or president, is to uphold the *sharī'ah* and maintain the unity of the community. This is achieved by co-ordinating all the services and utilities of the community which would result in equilibrium (*wast*) and justice (*'adl*).

The *'imām*, by contrast, operates at a very local level, and particularly from the mosque. His responsibilities include leadership of all congregational prayers (*salāh*) and rites of passage, as well as the organisation of social welfare activities such as education, youth, visiting both the sick and infirm, and those in penal institutions. The *'imām* may delegate or share these responsibilities with other members of the community. Like the *khalīfa*, maintaining equilibrium (*wast*) and justice (*'adl*) among community members is paramount in the *'imām*'s function. However, his status should not be confused with that of an ordained priest, since an *'imām* can be removed by the community should it lose confidence in him.

The *qadī*'s role is to serve the *ummah* in difficult judgements of law. Because of the special training they receive in the Qur'ān and *sunnah*, the *qadīs* guide and advise the *ummah* or even act as arbiters in disputes of social or spiritual concern.

F.1.e. Duties of Subjects

Islam is emphatic that final obedience should be to God alone and to the teaching of the Prophet. The earthly ruler rules under God and the law (see F.1.c) and to be afraid of him or her can be seen as a form of *shirk*, associating with God what is not God (see F.6.b). However, all members of the *ummah* have a duty to support and serve those whom they have elected to lead. Should differences of opinion occur between the leaders and the led, the Qur'ān and *sunnah* become the final arbiter.

> O you who believe!
> Obey God, and obey the Apostle,
> And those charged with authority among you.
> If you differ in anything
> Among yourselves, refer it
> to God and His Apostle,
> If you do believe in God
> And the Last Day:
> That is best, and most suitable for final
> determination. (Qur'ān 4: 59)

The ideal for Muslims is to live in an Islamic State where the Islamic ideals of rule and *sharī'ah* prevail. However, if Muslims are citizens of any country they are obliged to obey the laws of the country which gives them protection. In the case of the rulings of other countries which have Muslim governments, for instance *fatwas* (legal advice) need not be obeyed by Muslims living outside the country in which that *fatwa* is issued. In addition, there are some questions amongst Muslim scholars about the applicability of legal decisions across Muslim theological schools – for example, between Shiites and Sunnīs – which affect the obligation that Muslims may feel to listen to the rulings of another school than their own.

F.2. PERSONAL AND PRIVATE?

F.2.a. Personal Qualities

Islam makes a distinction between a person who submits to God's guidance by believing in His laws (a *muslim*) – one who possesses *imān*; and one who has the deep inner certainty of faith (a *mu'min*) – one who possesses this faith and acts on it.

Faith or conviction (*imān*) to the *mu'min* is a great deal more than merely believing that God exists. Rather it is the realisation and personal experience that God is in absolute control of the universe, including human beings, and that together with the rest of God's creation, each one of us is wholly dependent upon God and will return to Him for account (see F.1.a). With this conviction the Muslim is fired into action through the process of prayer (*salāh*), fasting (*saum*), charity (*zakāt*), and pilgrimage (*hajj*). Each of these acts of worship (*'ibāda*) bring the Muslim nearer to God, so that consciousness of God (*taqwa*) is developed. *Taqwa* is a quality which is absolutely essential in the personality of the Muslim. It is a vital attitude which develops little by little, for instance in the heart of a Muslim child as he or she is taught about God – His existence and omnipresence, beneficence and kindness, and everyone's personal responsibility and accountability to Him.

As Muslims embrace this consciousness of God (*taqwa*), they begin to reflect it in the everyday etiquettes of life. For instance, they will begin every act by seeking God's blessings and help – *bismi'lāhi'r-rahmāni'r-rahīm* (I begin in the name of God who is the Most-merciful, the Most-compassionate). When they meet relatives and friends, they will offer *salāms*, greetings of peace – *as-salāmu alaykum wa rahmatū'llāhi* (peace be on you and the mercy of God). And to cement the deep feeling generated by the *salām*, Muslims customarily shake hands, embrace and kiss each other. Lastly, they show gratitude for success for the fulfilment of any act, whether their own or anyone else's – *al-hamdū li 'illāhī rabbi'l-'ālamīn* (praise be to God, Lord of the Worlds). It is not customary for Muslims to cheer or show gratitude to someone by clapping hands.

By becoming conscious of God the Muslim becomes aware of the qualities which will bring about moral goodness – qualities such as love, mercy, compassion, humility, forgiveness, honesty, sincerity, integrity and justice (see F.1.a). Such an individual, a Muslim would claim, never loses sight of the ultimate goal – to merit God's mercy and pleasure. As part of the means of attaining it, the Muslim must be active in the world, taking responsibilities seriously and trying to fulfil them to the best of his or her abilities, and being always conscious of the duty owed to society.

However, it should be pointed out that faith (*imān*) and God-consciousness (*taqwa*) are not constant, they don't remain at the same level, and no two

Muslims have them in the same way. This is particularly true when we consider that Muslims like any other religious people may have to cope with non-religious beliefs and values which impinge upon their lives. Therefore it will not be surprising to find a variation in personal qualities between one Muslim and another and between Muslims in different parts of the world.

F.2.b. Friendship

It is a natural consequence of life to be able to share with others those things which we love most, be they our ideas, our possessions, or our pleasure in the company of those we like. A quality which is vital to any friendship is sincerity. Through sincerity towards God (*ikhlās*) the Muslims are prompted to be absolutely honest with themselves regarding their motives and intentions, and to strive continuously to weed out from their character whatever traces of hypocrisy, greed, selfishness and envy are present. Sincerity towards a friend, and for that matter towards any fellow human being, should lead to openness and straightforwardness. A friend should never be manipulated.

> The example of a good or a bad friend is like that of a dealer of musk-perfume. If nothing, at least the benefit of sweet smell can be derived from this friend. The bad friend is like a furnace; if your clothes are not set ablaze, your dress will certainly be blackened by its fumes. (*Hadīth: Bukhari* 3: 314)

Friendships may be established in any number of situations: at school; whilst travelling; through work or in a neighbourhood. The reasons for friendship can be just as varied. Friendships can be made between two people because of their attractiveness, their interests or their worldly status. But Islam wants friendships to build on the love of someone in order to gain God's love (*hubb bil-Allāh wa fī Allāh*). This in turn will lead to fulfilling the divine trust. 'God will ordain on the Day of Judgement: Where are those people who used to love their fellows for my sake only. I shall place them under My shadow' (*Hadīth: Muslim* 6225). The Prophet, giving an inspiring description of the meeting of two friends, observed:

> A man set out to call on his friends who lived in another habitation. God appointed an angel to await him on the way. The angel enquired of him: 'Where are you going?' The man made the answer: 'I am proceeding to that village to see my brother.' The angel further enquired: 'Does he owe you a debt of favour which you are now going to receive from him?' The man replied: 'No, I am going to meet him only because I love him for the sake of God.' The angel thereupon told him: 'Listen then! God has sent me to convey to you the glad tiding that God loves you as much as you love your friend for God's sake. (*Hadīth: Muslim* 6226)

Love (*hubb*), however, has many shades. There is love between husband and wife, between brother and sister, and between two unrelated individuals. In each case the intensity of the love is dependent upon the closeness of the relationship and the level of commitment between one other. However, Islam does not condone homosexual and lesbian relationships (see F.2.d). 'By Him [God] in Whose hand is my soul, a man does not believe until he loves for his brother [friend] what he loves for himself' (*Hadīth: Nawawī* 13).

Ten duties can be identified from the Qur'ān and *sunnah* as essential for a good relationship: (1) to help a friend with one's wealth, even to the extent that a friend has a right to that wealth; (2) to assist a friend before he or she asks for assistance, and to do so with a cheerful countenance; (3) to speak good of a friend and to conceal his or her faults; (4) to express to the friend love for him; (5) to offer guidance to the friend whether it be of a spiritual or material nature; (6) to forgive the friend's faults and shortcomings; (7) while praying to God for oneself, to pray for the friend during his lifetime and also after his or her death; (8) to take care of his or her family, and to be kind to all those who are an object of his or her love; (9) to be natural in the relationship; (10) lastly, to consider oneself neither superior nor equal to, but humbler than one's friend.

Being truthful and just to a friend leads to mutual respect and understanding, and contributes to integrity. That is why the Qur'ān is very concerned that Muslims, through being conscious of God are truthful and meet their commitments. 'O you who believe, be conscious of God and be with the truthful' (Qur'ān 9: 119). And '[The virtuous are] those who honour their trusts and promises and those who stand firm in their testimonies' (ibid. 70: 32–3).

The main concern for Islam is that the Muslim live in co-operation, not competition, with fellow human beings, whether they are of the same or a different faith, race, culture or status (see section F.7). Through this spirit of co-operation and in fulfilment of his or her trusteeship, the Muslim is concerned with the welfare – spiritual, psychological and material – of his or her friend. The friend's honour, dignity and nobility must be maintained. That is why friends are described as a mirror because they reflect back to us, through their reactions, the virtues which they see within us. 'Each one of you serves as a mirror to his brother, If you see any fault in your brother, eliminate it (*Hadīth: Mishkat* 4985).

F.2.c. Sex before Marriage

Sexual intercourse is an act of worship (*'ibāda*) for Islam. It fulfils the emotional and procreational needs of human beings. Emotionally it is the culmination of the love which two people have for one another. Just as pilgrimage is a means of union with God, so sexual intercourse is the ultimate physical union between two human beings to express their love and commitment to each other (see F.3.a). The result of sexual intercourse, procreation, is the contribution which human beings make towards the continuation of God's creation. For the Muslim therefore both the emotional satisfaction of sexual intercourse and the procreational contribution to human existence are noble acts, which are to be cherished as gifts (*ni'ma*) from God. They are, therefore, part of the Muslim's trusteeship: the divine trust.

To maintain the importance, seriousness and value of sexual intercourse, to ensure that it can be handled responsibly, Islam prohibits sex outside marriage (see F.3.a). Marriage is the crucible within which both the emotional and creative power of sexual intercourse can be controlled. When there is excess or deficiency in the desire for sexual intercourse an imbalance can occur in the personality. Deficiency, for whatever reasons, may result in a person unnecessarily feeling shame, guilt, frustration or lack of dignity. Excess overpowers reason and leads to adultery, fornication and other mortal sins, which, besides an imbalance in the personality, affects the spiritual development of the individual. The creative consequence of sexual intercourse – the birth of a child – requires the warmth of love which parents involved in the creative process can offer. However, without any contractual commitment, mother or father, or both, can refuse to meet their moral obligations and responsibilities to the child (see F.3.b).

Marriage provides a moderating force on emotional extremes, as well as the legal and moral framework for bringing up children (see F.3.a). True happiness (*sa'adah*) in sexual relations can only be achieved when there is a balance (*wast*) between the two emotional extremes and when there are clear moral obligations for the consequences of such relations.

F.2.d. Homosexuality

Though love is the basis of all relationships, Islam forbids homosexual and lesbian relations. Islam views such relations as unnatural and a deviation from the norm. Specific mention is made of its practice in the Qur'ān (26: 165–6): 'What! Of all creatures, do you approach males and leave the spouses whom your Lord has created for you? Indeed, you are people transgressing [all limits]'. This verse reminds Muslims that the Prophet Lot was sent by God to warn his people against the practice of homosexuality and lesbianism. In addition sodomy is considered to be an act against the natural disposition of human beings (see F.6.c).

F.3. MARRIAGE AND THE FAMILY

F.3.a. The Meaning of Marriage

As the example of the prophet shows, marriage is seen as the norm for

Muslims. In Islam, marriage is a social contract (*nikāh*), which has divine sanction, 'And it is He Who created man from water, then He has made for him blood-relationship and marriage-relationship' (Qur'ān 25: 54). It is not a sacrament but rather a legal, binding contract between a man and a woman. This contract establishes the permanence and responsibility of their relationship and an acceptance of one another as spouses with a mutual commitment to live together according to the teachings of Islam. 'And of His signs is this, that He created mates for you from yourselves that you may find tranquillity, and He put between you love and compassion' (Qur'ān 30: 21). In the Qur'ān, marriage has been specifically referred to as a strong covenant (*mīthāqan ghalīzah*, Qur'ān 4: 21). It is a noble contract which leads to a number of relationships and engenders a set of mutual rights and obligations. The consent of both spouses is an explicit condition for a valid marriage and its public declaration is essential: secret marriages are not allowed. 'The father or any other guardian cannot give in marriage a virgin or one who has been married before without her consent' (*Hadīth: Bukhari* 7: 67). Many Muslim marriages are assisted or arranged. How this is done depends on the culture in which a Muslim lives, but there should always be consent to the future partner according to Islam.

Marriage should be from among those possible partners who share a common outlook on life and morality, and who participate in this joint venture to fulfil their destiny as God's trustees (*khalīfa*). Therefore a Muslim is generally not permitted to marry a non-Muslim. The only exception is that a Muslim male can marry a Jewish or Christian woman, on the principle that Muslims, Christians and Jews believe in revealed books and as such share, to a certain extent, a common outlook on life. The Muslim woman is not permitted to marry a Christian or Jew, except when he embraces Islam. Here the concern is that the woman may not receive the same rights and privileges which Islam confers on her. To ensure that these considerations are realised, those contemplating marriage are encouraged to appoint guardians who can give sound advice. Guardians can be parents, relatives or close friends. Their degree of involvement will vary according to cultural traditions from which the family, or prospective partners come.

Islamic law (*sharī'ah*) does not insist on any particular form of contract or on any specific religious ceremony. This allows for different traditional forms according to the customs of the country in which the ceremony is taking place. However, the Prophet encourages simplicity. 'The best wedding is that upon which the least trouble and expense is bestowed' (*Hadīth: Mishkat* 3097). Ostentation is frowned on. 'The worst of feasts are those marriage feasts to which the rich are invited and the poor left out. And he who refuses to accept an invitation to a marriage feast verily disobeys God and His Prophet' (*Hadīth: Muwatta* 28.21.50).

According to the *sharī'ah* there must be at least two witnesses to the marriage contract. The groom must give a gift (*mahr*) to the bride as good-will for completing the contract. This gift is for her sole and exclusive use and benefit. 'And give women their dowries as a free gift' (Qur'ān 4: 4). Being a social contract, both spouses retain their personal rights; the wife is seen as a person in her own right, not merely as an adjunct to her husband. Therefore, for example, she has the full right of ownership and disposal of her own property and earnings even after marriage, and when she marries she retains her own family name instead of taking that of her husband.

The relationship in a Muslim marriage should be a permanent and enduring one and both partners are expected to make a serious and sustained effort to live together in harmony and with mutual respect. It is a relationship of mutual understanding, kindness, love, companionship and harmonious interaction. Husband and wife are friends and partners sharing each other's lives and concerns, cherishing and protecting each other, and helping to bear responsibilities which would be difficult or impossible for either to handle alone. 'They [wives] are your garments and you [husbands] are their garments' (Qur'ān 2: 187).

The marriage relationship also involves another fundamental responsibility: the responsibility of both husband and wife to meet one another's sexual needs. They should enjoy this aspect of life in such a way that pleasure and responsibility go hand in hand. Sexual intercourse in marriage provides the control mechanism for the sexual urge; it acts as a safety-valve for sexual morality. Through marriage, fulfilment and sublimation are achieved in a balanced way and equilibrium is attained. The Qur'ān calls marriage a 'castle' (*hisn*) against a life of debauchery. 'So marry them with their guardian's permission and give them their marriage portions as wives, they being chaste, not commiting fornication or having illicit friendships' (Qur'ān 4: 25).

Islam regards both spouses as completely equal in terms of accountability to God and in possessing unique personalities of their own (see F.7.d). It prescribes for both the same religious obligations, apart from the concessions made for women's reproductive cycle. They are both, in fulfilment of their trusteeship, to strive for good, develop their spirituality, and acquire the knowledge to achieve this. 'And whoever does good, whether male or female, and he [or she] is a Believer, these will enter Paradise and they will not be wronged by so much as the groove of a date-stone' (Qur'ān 4: 124).

Though Islam recognises the marriage of one man to one woman as the norm, under exceptional circumstances it allows a man more than one wife. 'And if you fear that you cannot do justice to orphans, marry such women as seem good to you, two or three or four; but if you fear that you will not do justice [between them], then [marry] only one' (ibid. 4: 3). This is the only

231

passage in the Qur'ān that mentions polygamy, and it should be noticed that it does not enjoin polygamy but permits it and that only conditionally. This characteristic of Islam is related to pressing human problems particularly when women outnumber men, for example after wars or due to imbalances in the birth rate. In such situations, it is thought to be in the interests of society and of women themselves to be co-wives of men instead of spending their entire lives without marriage, deprived of the peace, affection, and protection of marital life and the joy of motherhood.

The condition which Islam lays down for permitting a man to have more than one wife is confidence on his part that he will be able to deal equitably with his two or more wives. Unless a person can give assurances that he will be able to fulfil his obligations with justice and equity, he is prohibited from marrying more than one woman. For these reasons polygamy is not practised widely by Muslims. Muslims are also obliged to live within the law of the country in which they reside, which will affect Muslim practice.

F.3.b. Family Relationships

The family plays a very important part in Muslim society. It is a basic institution of the community (*ummah*) and is organised in such a way that it operates as a society in miniature. The network of rights and obligations that provides the basis of family life aims to produce those virtues that Islam wants to foster in the individual and in the community (*ummah*) (see F.1.a and F.2.a).

Through companionship, it is possible to achieve psychological, spiritual and emotional stability. However, relationships between all the members of a family, and most important of all between the husband and wife, are important not merely because they are useful. They are spiritual relationships which sustain and generate love, kindness, mercy, compassion, mutual confidence, self-sacrifice, solace and succour. Muslims claim that it is only in the context of the family that the ethical and moral potential in human beings becomes real; Islam encourages the flowering of goodness and virtue both within the family and in the world beyond it. The virtues of fellowship, of love and compassion, of sacrifice for others, of tolerance and kindness are implanted in children's characters as they grow up within the family (see F.2.a). It is the family that provides the most congenial climate for the development of those characteristics necessary to fulfil the divine trust.

On one occasion Aqra' ibn Habis came to the Prophet who was, at the time, engaged in playing with his grandson Hassan, Aqra' was surprised and asked, 'O Prophet do you play with children. I have ten children and have never shown fondness to even one of them'. The Prophet raised his eyes and taking a look at Aqra' observed: 'If God has deprived your heart of kindness and affection, what can I do!' (*Hadīth*: *Bukhari* 8: 26)

Socialisation and establishment of values are other important functions of the family. Child-bearing remains incomplete without child-rearing and upbringing, that is to say, overseeing children's education, character building, gradual initiation into Islam and recognition of the obligations and responsibilities of fulfilling the trusteeship. 'Of all that a father can give to his children the best is their good education and training' (*Hadīth*: *Mishkat* 4977). It is because of this that care of members of the family is a full-time job and an act of worship (*'ibāda*). 'Our Lord! grant us in our spouses and our offspring the comfort of our eyes and make us a model for the heedful' (Qur'ān 44: 6). The rewards for diligence in raising children are great. 'And whosoever has cared for his three daughters or three sisters and given them a good education and training, treating them with kindness till God makes them stand on their own feet, by God's grace he has earned for himself a place in Paradise' (*Hadīth*: *Abū Dawūd* 5128).

The family does not only function as a moral and social entity, it extends to the economic sphere as well. The Prophet Muhammad said 'When God endows you with prosperity, spend first on yourself and your family' (*Hadīth*: *Mishkat* 360). The financial maintenance of the family in Islam is a legal duty of the husband, even if his wife is wealthy. Financial support strengthens and extends cohesion and mutual respect – providing for a system of material security.

Through marriage, the family becomes a means of widening the area of one's contacts and developing relationships between different groups. 'Matrimonial alliances (between two families) increase friendship more than anything else' (*Hadīth*: *Mishkat* 3093). Marriage acts as a bridge between different families and communities and is instrumental in the absorption of diverse people into wider relationships. In practice, marriage has played an important role in the expansion of Islam.

Importantly, the family is seen as encouraging and increasing its members' sense of responsibility while inducing them to make greater efforts towards fulfilling their potential, talents and aspirations, in relation to the divine will. The harmony of the family is dependent upon the roles and responsibilities carried out by its members. In the Muslim family the key role is played by women. In an Islamic community (*ummah*), they should be free from the rigours of trying to make a living and attending to the demands of employment, so that they can play their role in developing the family. The mother in a Muslim home is responsible for the affairs of the household and for the proper management of her husband's possessions and property. However, that does not mean she may not pursue a career or profession, she is free to do so, but the demand of fulfilling the divine will in the home has first priority.

Although the leadership of the family is vested in both spouses, and decisions are arrived at through mutual consultation (*shūra*), the husband remains head and is the final authority in the family. He is also responsible for the financial maintenance of the family. Even if his wife pursues a career or profession, any income she receives is for her exclusive use, and her husband has no rights over it. The husband is responsible for assisting his wife with the household work following the example of the Prophet Muhammad, who used to mend his own clothes and help in carrying out chores in the home. While the mother is generally the primary means of training the children, Islam neither expects nor wants her to carry out this extremely important task alone. It is the joint responsibility of husband and wife to bring up the children. Together husband and wife must provide an Islamic atmosphere in their home and a consistent approach to training in which they reinforce and support one another.

Children are very much loved and wanted by Muslims – they are a precious gift (*ni'ma*) and trust (*amānah*). Although contraception is not prohibited (see F.9.b), Muslim families are large by choice. Parenthood is regarded as desirable and rewarding; parents and their children are encouraged to be very close emotionally and physically. The birth of a child is an event of great joy and thanksgiving which is shared by relatives and friends. Within seven days of a baby's birth the call to prayer (*adhān*) is whispered into the child's ear by the father, a name is given, the first crop of hair is shaved, and an animal is slaughtered (*'aqīqa*) as a token of thankfulness to God for the new family member. The meat of the slaughtered animal is shared with friends, relatives and the poor. If it is a boy, the child should be circumcised.

Training and guidance begin very early. The goal is to develop the personality of the child to meet the obligations and responsibilities of the ethical and moral systems in response to the divine will. Therefore emphasis will be on strong Islamic principles, sound Islamic knowledge, good character and morals. Such training does not consist merely of setting objectives but, far more important, of providing a living example of unfailing submission to God. An essential part of this training, beginning very early in life, is obedience, respect and consideration for the parents themselves, as the embodiment of the well-known Muslim proverb 'The pleasure of God is the pleasure of the parents'. 'Say: Come I will recite to you what your Lord has made a sacred obligation for you: that you associate nothing with Him [as partner in his divinity] and that you do good to parents ...' (Qur'ān 6: 151).

Although training and the upbringing of children is shared by both mother and father, it is the Muslim woman's role as mother which is regarded as being

of the highest importance, the most serious, and most challenging responsibility. The maternal role is not only rewarding enough to stimulate and give
her great satisfaction, but it also provides her with status and position in the
community (*ummah*). Muslim women as a rule possess a deep certainty that
this role has been entrusted to them because of their innate fitness and
capacity for the most important of all tasks: the shaping of the future generation of humanity. Islam acknowledges the immense importance of this role.
The Prophet Muhammad says:

> A man came to the Prophet and said: 'Messenger of God, I desire to go
> on a military expedition and I have come to consult you'. The Prophet
> asked him if he had a mother and when he replied that he had, the
> Prophet said, 'Stay with her, for Paradise is at her foot'. (*Hadīth*:
> *Mishkat* 4939)

A mother must, also, the Prophet insists, be given due consideration.

> Someone asked God's Messenger to whom he should show kindness
> and he replied, 'Your mother'. He asked who came next and the Prophet
> replied, 'Your mother'. He asked who came next and he replied, 'Your
> father, then your relatives in order of relationship'. (*Hadīth*: *Abū Dawūd*
> 5120)

The love, respect and honour of parents developed in Muslim children should
endure throughout their lives. While there is a natural branching-off when
young people leave home, either for marriage, education or work, parents are
not replaced in their affection by newly formed relationships. Although they
may live in separate homes or locations, or even at the opposite ends of
the earth, parents and children remain part of a single family unit whose
members are bound together by the strongest ties of duty and affection.

When parents get older and their vitality diminishes, they are looked after
by the family. In traditional Muslim societies, the aged are cared for by their
children as a matter of course or by other relatives if there are no children. A
Muslim does not regard this as a burden, no matter how demanding their
care may be, but as part of the divine trust (see F.5.a). As Muslims live in
different cultural contexts they will try to determine what care for family
members, whether children or elderly parents, is the best that is available.

> Your Lord has commanded that you worship none but Him and that
> you be kind to parents. If either or both of them reach old age with you,
> do not say to them 'Uff'! nor chide them but address them in terms of
> honour, and out of kindness lower to them your wing of humility and
> say 'My Lord; have mercy on them as they cherished me in childhood'.
> (Qur'ān 17: 23–4)

Thus, the mutual love, compassion and sympathy between parents and children lasts throughout life; when death comes to parents, their children will continue to mention them in their prayers and make supplication (*dua'*) for God's mercy on them.

Family relationships are not restricted to parent and child, they extend to the wider family. One who strengthens relationships with relatives (*silat ar-rahīm*) is loved by God, and one who severs them is hated by Him. Visiting relatives regularly and caring for them contribute towards maintaining such ties. A non-Muslim relative should be treated in the same way as a Muslim relative, because relationships based on blood remain the same all the time.

Muslim grandparents are very much like one's mother and father and are to be treated as such; aunts and uncles are regarded similarly. Sisters and brothers are usually very close, and their children are like one's own. Family ties are so close that it is not unusual for Muslims to assume responsibility for their younger brothers or sisters or for nieces and nephews or grandchildren and cousins if the need arises. If any of these relatives – including an elderly aunt or uncle, a widowed, divorced or unmarried sister, or an orphan – are destitute, infirm or alone, they are to be provided for by some member of the family (see F.5.b). The real core of family life is the sharing of each other's joys, sorrows, hopes and fears.

F.3.c. Marriage Breakdown

There are occasions when the best of partnerships break down: marriage is no exception. People's hearts and minds change in different ways for different reasons. The change may be so unavoidable and profound as to defeat the purpose of marriage. So that while Islam takes for granted the continuity and permanence of marriage, it does not exclude the possibility of its dissolution. 'Divorce is the most detestable in the sight of God of all permitted things' (*Hadīth: Abū Dawūd* 2173).

The grounds upon which a divorce can take place are indicated in general terms in the Qur'ān. Divorce results in the failure of one or both partners to the marriage of being able to discharge their marital duties and to live with each other in kindness, peace and compassion. Although this is a question which rests ultimately within the individual's sense of relationship to God and the divine trust, Muslim jurists have developed indices of that failure and specified the major situations which may be accepted as grounds for divorce or annulment.

From the wife's point of view the following situations justify divorce: long absence without knowing the whereabouts of the husband; his long imprisonment or capture by war enemies; a refusal to provide for the wife; severe poverty; impotence. There are another set of circumstances which may involve either party: desertion, chronic disease, insanity, misrepresentation at the conclusion of the marriage contract, incongruity, mistreatment, debauchery or moral laxity. There are also circumstances which may actually necessitate the dissolution of marriage: the wife's acceptance of Islam when her husband remains a non-Muslim; apostasy and the established illegality of the initial marriage contract.

It is interesting to note, first, that the wife has more grounds for seeking a divorce and is given greater justification than the husband. Secondly, when one or both parties are entitled to take the course of divorce, it does not necessarily mean that they must or will definitely use it. Divorce is the very last resort, and if it must take place, the parties are encouraged to be charitable, kind and just to each other as if the marriage bond were still intact.

If all efforts at reconciliation and restoration of good relationships between the two partners fail, and husband and wife consider it impossible to live together, then they cannot be forced or pressured to continue the marriage. They may seek divorce in peace, and each of them may seek fulfilment of the divine trust with somebody else in a new marriage relationship. There are three forms of divorce: by the husband (*talāq*), by the wife (*khul*), and by a court as arbiter. The divorce may take three to nine months depending on circumstances. Thus, there are a number of variations to procedure but the one most widely practised requires first, that divorce takes place before two witnesses; it can either be given in writing or orally. Secondly, a woman cannot be divorced during her monthly period: the husband will make the first pronouncement of divorce after this, the second after the next monthly cycle, and after the third monthly cycle the final pronouncement. Thirdly, if the wife is discovered to be pregnant, the divorce cannot be concluded until after the birth of the child.

The three monthly cycles are called 'waiting periods'. During these periods the divorce can be revoked and the marriage reconciled. That is why, if the wife is pregnant, the divorce cannot be concluded – the birth of the child may contribute to a change of heart by the parents. In addition, the child's legitimacy and identity will be established. All during the waiting periods the wife is to be treated with kindness and provided with all the usual necessary comforts, and she cannot be evicted from her home.

Young children remain in the custody of their divorced mother, unless she is proved to be unfit. It is the father's responsibility to bear the full cost of the children's care, and equitably compensate the mother. In addition, he alone is responsible for their housing, clothing and food even though they are in their mother's custody or home. The wife keeps the gift given to her by the husband at the time of marriage.

One consequence of divorce is the freedom to remarry. Being divorced does

237

not stigmatise those involved, nor must they spend their lives in loneliness. Divorced people are offered every possible opportunity to remarry if they intend peace and desire harmony. Many Muslims live in countries where the Islamic law described above is not the law of the land. They will then live, as Muslims, within that secular law and decide its effect upon their Islamic life and values.

F.4. INFLUENCES ON AND USE OF TIME AND MONEY

F.4.a. Education

Muslims are required to fulfil the divine trust from a position of knowledge. Three sources of knowledge are available: The Qur'ān, *sunnah* and knowledge derived from experience.

The Qur'ān is believed by Muslims to be divine revelation (*wahī*). It was revealed by God to the Prophet Muhammad over a period of twenty-three years. It consists of 114 chapters of varying lengths, the longest chapters coming first and the shorter ones later. It is the revealed Word of God in the form of a book (*al-kitāb*) written in Arabic. Arabic was the language of the Prophet Muhammad, it is therefore obvious that the Qur'ān should be revealed in this language. Every word is believed to be the word of truth and the Qur'ān's role must be understood to be much wider than that of a sacred text because for the Muslim it is the first source of all knowledge and underpins every aspect of human existence.

The concern for its preservation has resulted in its still being read in Arabic and many Muslims have committed it to memory. A Muslim child is taught to recite it from a very early age, either by attending a Qur'ān school or at home through the efforts of parents. Understanding of the texts is through translations if the first language is not Arabic.

The Qur'ān provides the Muslim with all the moral and ethical principles of life, in addition to the framework within which that life is to be lived. It is the source of spiritual development, because by absorbing its teaching it purifies (*tazkīya*) the heart and mind of the individual so that goodness and virtue flourish. By so doing the spiritual personality develops to meet the responsibilities and obligations of the material world.

Meeting the realities of the material world requires a guide. This guidance is provided by prophets, in the case of Muslims, the Prophet Muhammad (see F.1.a). His way (*sunnah*) is the exemplification of divine revelation, through his interaction with it. He becomes the first human interpreter of the Qur'ān and he expounds an understanding of it – his sayings and teachings in relation to the Qur'ān are embodied in the *hadīth*. The *hadīth* is understood by Muslims to be distinct and separate from the Qur'ān, although it has the sanction of the Qur'ān. This distinction is important for Muslims because the Word of God – the Qur'ān – must not be confused or mixed up with the Prophet's interpretation of the word – *hadīth*.

The *sunnah*, the way of the Prophet, provides the second source of knowledge for the Muslim. The life of the Prophet is the living proof and example of the divine will; a body of knowledge of how to live in this world. The *hadīth* is a collection of the Prophet's teachings on what is good and bad; practical examples of how to enhance goodness and contain evil. It identifies the primary and secondary institutions and processes by which inner spiritual development can be externalised to meet the aspirations of the individual and the expectations of the wider society.

The Qur'ān and *sunnah* are complemented by the third source, knowledge gained from the sum of human experience. This knowledge which is subsidiary to the first two sources includes all the arts and sciences and provides the skills, tools and knowledge of the world necessary for fulfilling the divine trust within the wider society. This knowledge may be obtained from any source. However, all scientific or practical knowledge and skills must be subjected to Islamic criteria and standards. Whatever is appropriate and beneficial for the building of a society governed by God's laws in all aspects of life is then applied, and whatever is not appropriate or useful is put aside.

Knowledge is to be sought both for its own sake, for the love of learning, and for its application. It is the duty of those who have knowledge to impart it to others. According to a *hadīth*, a Muslim who has gone out in search of knowledge is 'in the way of God until he returns': seeking knowledge is an act of worship (*'ibāda*) (*Hadīth: Mishkat* 220). It is also a binding duty. 'Seeking knowledge is a duty on every Muslim man and woman' (ibid.: 218).

F.4.b. Work

The knowledge a Muslim acquires should not only be used to know God, to know oneself, to know the rest of creation, and to know one's responsibilities and obligations, but also to fulfil the divine trust by administering the affairs of the earth (*khalīfa*) in the best possible manner. This means, managing resources, developing science, industry and technology, while developing human potential and abilities so as to help the effective and smooth running of society. This working or striving (*'amal*) is a religious obligation, an act of worship (*'ibāda*). The Qur'ān is explicit in stating that God's help comes only to those who work and strive with commitment: 'And those who strive hard for Us. We will most certainly guide them in Our paths, for Verily God is with those who do right' (Qur'ān 29: 69).

Working means being in service to God, not to a human being. Therefore work has a wide meaning in Islam and it does not necessarily imply a financial return. Islam respects honest effort and work of any kind, and does not consider any necessary or useful endeavour degrading. If a need for some

239

service or skill is felt by the Muslim community, whether it be nursing or rubbish collecting, it becomes the obligation of some members of the community to master the necessary knowledge or skills. In addition whatever work is done it should be done well, in keeping with the Prophet Muhammad's saying, 'God loves that when any of you does anything, he should do it in the best way' (*Hadīth*: *Abū Dawūd* 6370).

While Islam does not prohibit women from working outside the home, it should not be at the expense of the welfare of the home. The attitude and skills developed in managing a home may be much wider and more comprehensive than those required by a job outside. Women may take up any career which is dignified and which draws upon their unique qualities, but women should not be stereotyped into a particular job, such as sewing, typing or cleaning. Should a woman receive financial income in return for her work or service, that income is for her sole use and expenditure, she is not obliged to contribute it to the family income, though she may, out of love for the family, do so.

In the Islamic system of life, every member of the community must contribute whatever he or she is capable of, for the good of the community (*ummah*). This is true of a child or youth who is studying, a woman in her role as the manager of her household, or a man with whatever physical or intellectual abilities he may possess. Islam is not a system which permits praying or meditating all day long or living the life of an ascetic while making no effort either for oneself or for others. Once the Prophet Muhammad was told about a man who spent all his time in the mosque praying. He asked, 'Then who feeds him?' 'His brother', was the reply. 'Then his brother is better than he', said the Prophet, underscoring the point that the religion of Islam does not consist merely of piety and devotional activities but also of hard work and reliance upon one's own efforts.

Islam therefore discourages people from remaining unemployed for too long. If owing to economic reasons a particular skill or service is not required, then the individual should retrain, remembering work is linked to service to God. Thus, while Islam has made it the responsibility of Muslims to take care of people who for any reason are unable to meet their own needs (see F.4.d and F.5.b) it certainly does not encourage deliberate dependence from any source. This underlines the respectability of any type of useful work and the undesirability of living by the labour of others or by charity. Islam frowns upon idleness, prohibits asceticism and discourages begging, for it makes it clear that a human being's dignity and sense of self-worth, as well as the well-being of society, are intimately tied up with sincere and honest effort, not merely of some but of all its members.

F.4.c. Leisure and its Use

In Islam there is no particular day, or time of the day reserved for leisure. Time and life are gifts (*ni'ma*) and trusts (*amānah*) from God. Time should be used wisely and life spent responsibly. For the Muslim, the whole of life is perceived to be a time of happiness and pleasure when lived in service of God.

However, apart from working and generally being of service to humanity, Muslims are encouraged to spend some time on their own or with dear ones, enjoying those activities which are of personal interest, whether it be swimming, horse-riding, archery or reading. Being physically healthy is just as much an act of *'ibāda* as nurturing one's spiritual health. The spiritual, psychological and physical equilibrium (*wast*) of each Muslim effectively contributes to the equilibrium of the *ummah* as a whole. Muslims are encouraged to take up any pursuit which contributes to this goal. The Prophet took care to preserve his physical energy and strived to enhance it, he liked to swim, shoot arrows and ride horses. 'Learn archery and horse-riding. I like the archers more than the horse-riders. He who learns the art of shooting arrows and then gives it up has paid scant regard to a Divine Blessing' (*Hadīth: Abū Dawūd* 2507).

Gambling, taking intoxicants such as drugs (see F.4.e) or alcohol, or indulging in magic are not leisure activities in Islam. These are activities which contribute to the loss of sense and reason, and lead to disobedience to God.

> O you who believe!
> Intoxicants and gambling,
> Dedication of Stones,
> Divination by arrows,
> are an abomination that you will not prosper.
> (Qur'ān 5: 93)

Leisure is perceived to be part of the ethical and moral system of the *ummah* in that the well-being of the individual contributes to a healthy society.

F.4.d. Wealth

Love of wealth and possessions (*hubb al-māl*) – money, houses, land, valuables – is part of human nature, but a Muslim is expected to keep their relative importance in perspective so that their acquisition does not become the object of all endeavour. 'Alluring to men is the love of things they covet – women, sons, hoarded treasures of gold and silver, highly bred horses, cattle and land. This is the provision of this world's life. Yet with God is a better Abode' (Qur'ān 3: 14).

Wealth is created by God, and is His property. This underpins the Muslim's attitude to its acquisition. The right of property which accrues to a human being is delegated to him by God because all a person can do is to invest his labour in the process of production; God alone can cause this endeavour to be fruitful. It is God who has bestowed wealth upon the Muslim, and it is God who has the right to demand how it should be used. Thus all wealth and possessions are a gift (*ni'ma*) and trust (*amānah*) from God, not by right or simply due to one's own efforts, but from God's beneficence. As such, wealth is to be spent not only on oneself and one's family but also to help others who are in want or distress as well (*miskīn*). 'And in their property is the right of the beggar and those devoid of riches [poor]' (Qur'ān 51: 19). 'You give to your relative his right and to the poor and a way-farer' (ibid. 30: 38).

There are a number of mechanisms adopted in Islam to distribute wealth but two – *zakat* and *sadaqah* – have been the most frequently mentioned in the Qur'ān, and of these two *zakat* is one of the pillars of the faith. Every Muslim is required to pay *zakat*, which is two and a half per cent of their cash wealth to the poor (*miskīn*). This should not be considered an act of charity, but an obligation, in service to God, to the welfare of the disadvantaged: an act of worship (*'ibāda*). On the other hand *sadaqah* is a voluntary contribution, out of altruism (*īthār*), given by individuals over and above the payment of the compulsory *zakat* to relieve the problems and sufferings of fellow human beings. *Sadaqah* must be given in such a way that 'even the left hand of the donor does not know what the right hand gives'. No distinction is made between the poor among Muslims and non-Muslims. 'A man who helps and spends his time and money in looking after widows and the poor, holds the same position in the eyes of God as one who fights in the war, or fasts every day and prays the whole night over a number of years' (*Hadīth: Bukhari* 8: 35–6).

Through these teachings, Islam tries to inculcate in Muslims the basic virtue of generosity (*sakhā*) which gives contentment (*qanā'a*) to both the giver and recipient of wealth; contribution to balance and equilibrium (*wast*). At the same time, Islam discourages wastefulness in unreasonable luxuries, and most of all ostentation (*riyā*). Neither does it wish that wealth should be earned through dubious or evil means, such as selfishness, dishonesty or bribery. 'O you traders, beware of telling lies [in your business] transactions' (*Hadīth: Mishkat* 2799).

Islam also prohibits giving and taking interest on anything borrowed or lent because it exploits those in need and eliminates the sense of responsibility of both lender and borrower; both should share justly in any profit or loss. 'God will deprive usery of all blessings, but will give increase for deeds of charity for He loves not creatures ungrateful and wicked' (Qur'ān 2: 276).

And miserliness (*bukhl*) is condemned because it is hoarding wealth at the expense of society. 'And render to the kindred their due rights, as [also] to those in want, and to the wayfarer, but squander not [your wealth] in the manner of a spendthrift' (ibid. 17: 26).

Simplicity, contentment (*qanā'a*) and gratitude (*shukr*) for whatever God has seen fit to bestow on one are important qualities, while pride in one's wealth, a sense of being above others who have less, greed or miserliness are very great evils. Money is of value only for what it can do, not for itself. It is therefore not to be hoarded or allowed to sit idle in the form of savings but is either to be spent for legitimate needs, to help others, or to be kept in circulation by appropriate and beneficial investment.

F.4.e. Drugs

The use of drugs which affect mood and psychological development has been a feature of human life in numerous social contexts throughout history and there have inevitably been people whose pattern of use was at odds with contemporary norms and customs. In Islam drugs such as marijuana, cocaine, opium and the like are definitely prohibited because their use produces illusions and hallucinations, which impairs the faculty of reasoning and decision-making. Such drugs are taken as a means of escape from the inner reality of one's feelings and the outer realities of life and religion into the realm of fantasy and imagination. In addition, there are serious moral consequences – moral insensitivity, weakening of will power, and neglect of responsibilities. Eventually, addition to drugs renders a person a diseased member of society, which may result in the destruction of the family or even in a life of crime. The following extract from a well-known thirteenth-century CE Muslim scholar, Shaikh al-Islam ibn Taymiyyah, sums up the general Muslim attitude on drugs.

> This solid grass [hashish] is prohibited, whether or not it produces intoxication. Sinful people smoke it because they find it produces rapture and delight, an effect similar to drunkenness. While wine makes the one who drinks it active and quarrelsome, hashish produces dullness and lethargy; furthermore, smoking it disturbs the mind and temperament, excites sexual desire, and leads to shameless promiscuity, and these are greater evils than those caused by drinking. (Ibn Taymiyyay, Fatawa vol. 4, p. 262)

F.4.f. The Media

In an age of high technology and mass communication it becomes even more important that the virtues (see F.1.a) which Islam wishes to inculcate are reflected in the media. The media do not form an impartial looking-glass;

they select what they wish to mirror. They cannot help doing that. They must decide how much space or time they will give and what they will show. This serious business of selection and portrayal is important because the media justifiably claim that society needs information to function efficiently, happily and justly. There is therefore a moral base to the media. Muslims are understandably concerned when the media highlight in an unsympathetic and biased way what it calls Islamic fundamentalism or fanaticism. The work of Edward Said (1981) has highlighted some important issues here, and Muslims feel the need for fair and representative media coverage in the different countries in which they live.

In the Muslim community (*ummah*) the media are perceived as tools for communicating to its members information about the community, and about other communities. The media play an educative role: they provide knowledge of development in the community and beyond it, knowledge of the kind which should improve the individual and collective quality of the *ummah*. Therefore the media should become an embodiment of the virtues and ideals of the community of which it is part. However, it should also be recognised that most Muslims live in countries which are multi-faith and in some cases secular societies. The media there may well reflect a variety of viewpoints which may conflict with established Muslim values and norms. In these cases Muslims may see the role of the media as a help in highlighting their views, allowing for discussion and debate which will contribute towards enrichment and resolution.

F.4.g. Advertising

Advertisers can play a central role in shaping the views of those exposed to adverts and also in determining the values of the system through which they are conveyed, for instance newspapers, television and radio. The main source of income for the media system apart from the BBC is advertising revenue, therefore advertisers can have powerful influences on the ethical stance of the media as well as on viewers. For instance cigarette advertisements will not only encourage people to buy the product, they will reinforce views that smoking is justifiable. There are also advertisements which exploit women, some by conveying that their principal function is to look pretty and to gaze admiringly at ruggedly handsome men. However, advertisements can also contribute towards developing new tastes in society and expanding the options open to its citizens following new inventions, or new imports from other countries. In most cases, therefore, advertisements can be determinants on what is good or bad.

Muslims recognise the power of advertising and remember a caution of Prophet Muhammad to be truthful and balanced when promoting their products. 'Be careful of excesses in promoting sale, because it may find you a market but then reduces blessing' (*Hadīth*: *Mishkat* 903).

F.5. THE QUALITY AND VALUE OF LIFE

F.5.a. The Elderly

Just as youth is the future wealth of the *ummah*, Muslims view the elderly as its present wealth, because of the effort and sacrifices they have made in this world, as well as the vast amount of knowledge and experience which they hold. Therefore, the decorum and respect which is accorded to parents should also be shown to the elderly.

> Your Lord hath decreed that you worship none but Him, and that you be kind to parents. Whether one or both of them attain old age in their life, say not to them a word of contempt, nor repel them. But address them in terms of honour, and, out of kindness, lower to them the wing of humility, and say: 'My Lord! bestow on them your Mercy even as they cherished me in childhood'. (Qur'ān 17: 23–4)

It is the responsibility of the Muslim to take care of the elderly, whether they are related or not. Islam does not encourage the elderly to live on their own. They are to be part of a household where their material wants and need for love, care and companionship can be met in a human manner (see F.3.b). This idea of the extended family is one that Muslims try to maintain, even in cultures where it is not the norm.

F.5.b. Those in Need

The Qur'ān identifies those in need as orphans (*yatīm*), the needy (*miskīn*), and the wayfarers (*ibn as sabīl*). Each of these are to be understood both in their literal as well as symbolic sense. 'What God has bestowed on His Messengers [and taken away] from the people of the township, belongs to God and Apostle and to kindred and orphans, the needy, and the wayfarer' (Qur'ān 59: 7).

Orphans (*yatīm*) are frequently mentioned in the Qur'ān; their central need is the feeling of love and the warmth and support of a family. Thus orphans are as a rule brought up by relatives or by families within the community, not put into institutions. Islamic law is very strict in the maintenance of the rights of orphans, particularly with regard to their identity and inheritance. Identity is crucial to a person's status, therefore an orphan has a right to his or her geneological history. In addition an orphan has rights to any inheritance from deceased parents, and the guardian has the obligation of seeing those rights realised. 'To orphans restore their property [when they reach their age], nor substitute [your] worthless things for their good ones;

and devour not their substance by mixing it up with your own. For this is transgression' (Qur'ān 4: 2).

The needy (*miskīn*) extends to the poor, the disadvantaged, handicapped and diseased, etc. 'It is no fault in the blind, nor in one born lame, nor in one afflicted with illness' (ibid. 24: 61). It is the concern of the *ummah* to cushion the difficulties experienced by the handicapped and those families responsible for looking after them. The Muslim is reminded that normality and abnormality in human beings is the result of the divine will, therefore the welfare of those disadvantaged is part of the divine responsibility. A Muslim is not allowed to despair or perceive handicap with superstition.

The wayfarer (*ibn as sabīl*) may be a beggar, a traveller or a person who has lost hope. A Muslim is responsible for the care and welfare of all such individuals (see F.4.d). Islam wants all human beings to be encouraged and inspired, and this can only be achieved through stability and security, hope and optimism (see F.5.d): 'and never give up hope of Soothing Mercy; Truly no one despairs of God's Soothing Mercy except those who have no faith' (Qur'ān 12: 87).

F.5.c. Abortion

Islam values human life and is concerned with its preservation, therefore it does not allow abortion unless the continuation of the pregnancy will result in the death of the mother. The basis of the Muslim position is highlighted in the following quotation from 'Imām al-Ghazali (CE 1058–1111), in his *Ihya Ulūm-id-Dīn*.

> Contraception is not like abortion. Abortion is a crime against an existing being. Now, existence has stages. The first stages of existence are the settling of the semen in the womb and its mixing with the secretions of the woman. It is then ready to receive life. Disturbing it is a crime. When it develops further and becomes a lump, aborting it is a greater crime. When it acquires a soul and its creation is completed, the crime becomes more grievous. The crime reaches a maximum seriousness when it is committed after it [foetus] is separated [from the mother] alive. (Al-Ghazali 1982: 74)

Muslim jurists agree unanimously that after the foetus is completely formed and has been given a soul, aborting it is prohibited provided the mother is in no danger. Social and economic factors are not valid reasons for an abortion in Islam. 'And do not kill your children out of fear of poverty; we shall provide for them and for you. Truly, the killing of them is a great sin' (Qur'ān 17: 31). Most Muslims understand this verse to apply to unborn children as well.

246

F.5.d. Euthanasia

Euthanasia and suicide are perceived by Muslims to be morally equivalent. The hardships and sufferings of this life are a test of a person's *imān* (faith) and *taqwa* (God-consciousness), therefore a Muslim is required to approach life optimistically, and not to give up or run away from the difficulties of life. That is why the Qur'ān implores people 'not to kill yourselves; indeed, God is merciful to you' (Qur'ān 4: 29).

> The Prophet Muhammad (PBUH) said: 'In the time before you, a man was wounded. His wounds troubled him so much that he took a knife and cut his wrist and bled to death. Thereupon God said: 'My servant hurried in the matter of his life.' Therefore he is deprived of the Garden. (*Hadīth: Bukhari* 8: 603)

From this quotation Muslims are prohibited from taking their own lives. If, out of despair, some people do resort to suicide, on the one hand the individual has destroyed what does not belong to him, and on the other hand the community (*ummah*) has failed in its responsibility to meet the needs of one experiencing a psychological and spiritual void. Islam views it as a duty to maintain an optimistic attitude to life. Hence, Muslims may not give permission to others to take their lives, nor may they assist them. Euthanasia has no place in Islam, not even for the very old whose lives are just as sacred as those of the young. Death is a time allotted by God. 'Nor can a person die except by God's leave, The term being fixed as by waiting' (Qur'ān 3: 145).

A Muslim, then, is not the absolute owner of his or her life. God is its owner, since in Islam, God gave it. A person has the responsibility to preserve and prolong that life, not the right to destroy it. Suffering, resulting from old age, is never to be endured for its own sake, so far as it is possible to be eased, but it is the occasion of spiritual growth. Even the manner in which it is endured can have moral effects upon those who are privileged to be in attendance.

F.6. QUESTIONS OF RIGHT AND WRONG

F.6.a. The Purpose of Law

In F.2.a, the relationship between *imān* (faith) and *taqwa* (God-consciousness) was mentioned. It was pointed out that neither remains static; both are dependent upon the spiritual capacity by which a Muslim can absorb them so as to shape his or her personality. In this process of absorption, the influences of the wider society, Muslim or non-Muslim, must be taken into account. The resolution of this perennial question of tension between the individual and society is determined by the *sharī'ah*, Islamic law: its objective is justice (*'adl*). Justice is a comprehensive term, and may include all the virtues of good behaviour. But the religion of Islam asks for something warmer and more human; the doing of good deeds even where perhaps they are not strictly demanded by justice, such as returning good for ill.

Sharī'ah literally means the 'way to water' – the source of all life – and signifies the way to God, as given by God. It is the way which encompasses the totality of a Muslim life. For the Muslim the *sharī'ah* is for all times to come, and is equally valid under all circumstances. The human condition must change in relation to the *sharī'ah* not vice versa. That does not mean human reason has no role to play in the *sharī'ah*. On the contrary, human reason is required to understand and interpret divine guidance in new or changed situations and to apply it to actual situations in human life. Reason is also vital to help frame rules, regulations and byelaws for implementing basic principles and injunctions and to legislate in those vast areas where nothing has been laid down in the Qur'ān and *sunnah*. This exercise of understanding, interpretation and application is achieved through forming opinion (*'ijtihād*), consultation (*shūra*), and consensus (*'ijma*) by those trained in the formation and understanding of law (*qadī*).

The two principle sources from which Islamic law is drawn are the Qur'ān and *sunnah*. They divide human acts of heart and body into five categories: (1) those which are expressly prohibited (*haram*) and (2) those expressly enjoined (*wajib* or *fard*); (3) those which are disliked but not prohibited (*makrūh*) and hence are permissible under certain circumstances; (4) those recommended but not enjoined (*mandūb*), hence with no obligation to comply; and (5) those without any injunction or opinion, and hence permitted through silence (*mubah*).

It is a principle of Islamic law that no human being has the authority to prohibit what God and the Prophet Muhammad have not forbidden. A Muslim has the right, whenever it is claimed that something is obligatory or prohibited, to demand the basis for this assertion in the Qur'ān or the *sunnah*. At the same time while the Qur'ān simply lays down the principle that all affairs of Muslims must be settled by consultation (*shūra*), how that consultation and the ensuing consensus are to be achieved has been left to be decided by Muslims in each age according to their own circumstances. An example of this would be the related challenges Muslims face living in a secular society like Britain where no facilities are provided at work for their uniquely religious observances, such as the five daily prayers and the Friday prayers.

F.6.b. Sin and Sins

No matter how purified and reformed an individual is, he or she will still be open to temptations. Sin is essentially an act of injustice to one's own self, against God, and also perhaps against society. In Islam there is no equivalent to the idea of original sin. However, it can be understood to be an aberration against one's basic natural disposition (*'asl-al-fitrā*). Since the human being is born pure it errs towards goodness, therefore inclination towards evil is against its original nature.

A first order sin would be associating someone or something – inevitably inferior – with God in His divine essence, attributes, powers or rights; this is known as *shirk*, and a person practising it is a *mushrik*. Second order sins are things like murder, theft, suicide, illegal sexual relations and defamation. These are known as *zalim*, violation of the rights of oneself and of others through disobeying the rules of Islam. Third order sins would be, for example, lying, cursing, backbiting, envy. All of these sins, if allowed to spread or go uncontained, will result in corruption on earth (*fasād fil'ard*). They are manifestations of human selfishness, avarice, revenge, caprice and egoism. The acts of worship (*'ibāda*) are meant to control such characteristics in the human being so that the virtues of goodness can flower.

F.6.c. Punishments (*'uqūbāh*)

When aberrations from the natural disposition of the human being do occur, God and society must apply some form of containment. This is achieved through punishment.

Punishment in Islam has nothing to do with notions of atonement, expiation or wiping away of sin. Only God can forgive, and because God is compassionate (*rahmān*) and merciful (*rahīm*), He does this when a person turns to Him, truly repentant (*tawbah*) and seeking forgiveness (*'istighfar*). So between the human being and God, there is total emphasis on repentance and forgiveness. But a crime is also an act against the social order, and in this sphere mere repentance cannot be a substitute for punishment, which is a means of protecting and strengthening society.

Punishment has always been considered an integral part of the concept of justice, but it is important to recognise that in the Islamic scheme there is no concept of the punishment being exactly and justly proportional to the crime. Absolute and truly proportional justice would require the exact evaluation of such complex factors as intentions and motives, the surrounding circumstances, the causes and repercussions all of which only God knows. Human judges must consider but cannot fully evaluate them. Therefore Islamic punishments are not to be judged on the scale of proportional and full retribution.

At the same time punishments in Islam cannot be understood, nor successfully or justifiably implemented in isolation. Law is not the main vehicle in the total framework for the reinforcement of morality. It is faith (*imān*) and God-consciousness (*taqwa*) – those inherent and innate qualities which make a person want to refrain from what displeases God and do what pleases Him. In addition, justice is a positive ideal which permeates and dominates the entire community life; it is not merely an institutionalised means of inflicting punishment. Consequently, a whole environment is needed where to do right is encouraged, facilitated and found easy and to do wrong is discouraged, inhibited and found difficult.

Penalties in Islam have a more functional nature, to regulate and deter people from overstepping the boundaries of what is good and just. It is significant, therefore, that penalties are called *hudūd* (boundaries) not punishments: they are liabilities incurred as a result of violating the limits set by God and, crucially, designed to keep alive the sense of justice in the community by public repudiation of such violations.

It is evident, therefore, that *hudūd* is limited to punishments for crimes mentioned in the Qur'ān and *sunnah*, for example homicide (*qatl*): 'if any one kills a person – unless it be for murder or for spreading mischief in the land – it would be as if he killed the whole people and if anyone saved life, it would be as if he saved the life of the whole people' (Qur'ān 5: 32). It is, however, vital to distinguish between homicide and the destruction of life carried out in pursuit of justice. 'Do not kill a soul which God has made sacred except through the due process of law' (Qur'ān 6: 15).

The punishment for adultery (*zinā*) is spelt out in detail. 'The woman and the man guilty of adultery or fornication, flog each one of them with a hundred stripes; let no compassion move you in their case, in a matter prescribed by God, if you believe in God and the Last Day and let a party of believers witness their punishment' (Qur'ān 24: 2).

Zinā means sexual intercourse between a man and a woman who are not married to each other. It is immaterial whether one or both parties have their own spouses or are unmarried. The word also applies to fornication. Sodomy (*liwāt*) is another form of fornication which is totally condemned.

> We also sent Lut: he said to his people: 'Do you commit adultery as no people in creation [ever] committed before you? For you practise your lusts on men in preference to women: You are indeed a people transgressing beyond limits'. (Qur'ān 7: 84)

Sodomy (see F.2.d) is considered to be an act against one's natural disposition (*'asl-al-fitrā*) because it is considered to be sex merely to satisfy one's passion and performed with part of the body for which sexual intercourse was not created. It also includes anal sex with one's wife. All Muslim jurists agree that sodomy is a sexual offence but they differ as to its appropriate punishment. They also differ on the punishment for bestiality. Some agree with the literal understanding of this *hadīth* – 'Kill the animal and the person who committed sexual intercourse with it' (*Hadīth*: *Abū Dawūd* 4449) – some do not. Still others maintain that only an individual can be punished but not an animal since it has no guilty mind.

Defamation (*qadhf*) is deserving of serious punishment. 'And those who launch charge against chaste women, and produce not four witnesses [to support their allegations], flog them with eighty stripes. And reject their evidence even after. For they are transgressors' (Qur'ān 24: 4). The honour, dignity and nobility of human beings is sacred because it is part of their divine nature, therefore defamation is considered a grave crime, since it undermines that divine nature. It is also a crime to take from someone what is rightly theirs (*sariqa*). 'As to the thief male or female, cut off his hands or her hands: a punishment by way of example, from God, for their crime: and God is exalted in Power and Wise' (Qur'ān 5: 41). The punishment of cutting off hands is carried out only if the person is sane, adult and was neither compelled to commit theft nor hungry while doing so.

Apart from penalties, the Qur'ān also provides for retribution (*qisās*). When a person causes physical injury or harm to a fellow human being, Islam gives the injured party the right of equal requital. In this case this right belongs to the individual or family who has suffered an injury, and not to society or the state.

> O you who believe! The law of equality is prescribed to you in cases of murder: the free for the free, the slave for the slave, the woman for the woman. But any remission is made by the brother of the slain, then grant any reasonable demand and compensate him with handsome gratitude. This is a concession and a mercy from your Lord. After this, whoever exceeds the limits shall be in grave penalty. (Qur'ān 2: 178)

The injured person or family may forgo the right to retribution by forgiving, or may agree to accept token recompense instead. The Qur'ān highly recommends the act of forgiving. Thus, under *qisās*, punishment is available without burdening the executive or judiciary with the dilemma of whether to exercise mercy. Very few realise that the principle of *qisās* even allows capital punishment to be avoided.

Why does Islam want to punish and not reform? Because every institution in the community (*ummah*) is value oriented and is responsible for the moral development of every person, the emphasis is on prevention of crime. The Islamic scheme attempts to ensure that inducement to commit crime is minimal. Once the crime is committed, the best place for reform is in the family and in society, where a criminal is to live after punishment, not in a prison where every inmate is a criminal. This is unless of course a society considers itself to be more corrupt and less competent to effect reform than a jail. Muslims are aware that the codes of law in many of the countries where they are resident are based on completely different principles from these and that any statement of the *sharī'ah* position as it affects, for example, perceptions of homosexuals is highly controversial.

F.6.d. The Wrongdoer and the Wronged

There are three commonly used terms in the Qur'ān for those who indulge in wrongdoing: *zalim* (usurper of rights), *fāsiq* (transgressor), *mushrik* (idolator). The term criminal has no meaning in the vocabulary of Islam. So long as an individual transgresses he or she is in one of these categories. As soon as people accept punishment, repent (*tawbah*) and seek forgiveness ('*istighfar*), both from God and from those they injured, they immediately return to their natural (*fitra*) self. They do not have to bear any further guilt or be stigmatised. Repentance and forgiveness are here and now, the wronged must not feel any revulsion towards the wrongdoer, life must go on.

F.7. EQUALITY AND DIFFERENCE

F.7.a. Differences between People

The unity of God (*tawhīd*), acknowledging God as Creator of all creation, extends also to the oneness of humanity. All are equally His creatures. 'O Mankind, We have generated you all from one pair, a male and a female. We have constituted you into peoples and tribes that you may know one another. Noblest among you is the most righteous. God is omniscient, all-knowing' (Qur'ān 49: 13). Thus, to the Muslim, the colours, races and languages of human beings – the obvious external differences within the family of humanity – are signs of God's wondrous creativity, the God-ordained diversity of humanity within its overall unity.

The differences should not impede co-operation, but, on the contrary, enrich one another. What is evident from the above verse is that external differences can never constitute a reason for looking up to or despising another individual; the only criteria for distinction among human beings are spiritual and moral qualities, the excellence of a person's character. Material considerations such as wealth, status, power, family and education do not count at all in the sight of God, unless an individual uses them to follow His guidance and seek His pleasure.

It is human nature which places all humans as equal before God, they are all created in the divine image and this constitutes their essential humanity. It is the human being's most noble and precious possession, and where it is missing there is no human being. The universalism of the divine will leaves no human being outside its relevance. The whole world is its object, and the whole of humanity is both its object and subject of moral striving. It is the degree to which the consciousness of God (*taqwa*) has been realised which distinguishes human beings from one another, and only God can be the judge of that. As a consequence the *ummah* can never restrict itself to the members of any tribe, nation, race or group; it must expand to include all humanity.

F.7.b. Attitudes to Other Religions

The all-inclusiveness mentioned in F.7.a means that the *ummah*'s boundaries are always open. Islamic law, therefore, has provided principles about the treatment of those who do not consider themselves Muslims. Non-Muslims, whether they belong to a faith community or not, who live among Muslims in an Islamic state, hold the status of *dhimmī*, which means pledged (*'ahd*), guarantee (*damān*), and safety (*amān*). *Dhimmis* are so called because they are under the pledge of God, the pledge of the Prophet and the pledge of the Muslim community so that they can live under the protection of Islam. In other words, they are under the protection of Muslims and their guarantee. 'Whoever persecuted a *dhimmī* or usurps or took work from him beyond his capacity, or took something from him with evil intentions, I shall be a complainant against him on the Day of Resurrection' (*Hadīth*: *Abū Dawūd* 3046).

Muslims are required to deal with non-Muslims kindly and justly. Jews and Christians and all those who believe in one God have been given a special position in the Qur'ān, since their religions were originally based on revelation.

> And dispute you not with the People of the Book [Jews and Christians], except with means better [than mere disputation], unless it be with those of them who inflict wrong but say: 'We believe in the Revelations which have come down to us and in that which came down to you; Our God and your God is One and it is to Him we bow. (Qur'ān 29: 46)

There is also a clear indication of the status of other faiths with regard to their rewards: 'Verily those who believe in God and His Guidance and those who are Jews, and Christians, and Sabians – whoever believe in God and the Last Day and do good deeds shall have their reward with their Lord, on them shall be no fear, nor shall they grieve' (Qur'ān 2: 62).

The fundamental rights of non-Muslims are of two kinds: the right to protection from all external threats and the right to protection from all internal tyranny and persecution. In addition non-Muslims have the freedom of religious practice and personal status and since they are not subject to *zakat*, they pay a tax known as *jizyah* which will be utilised in the defence and administration of the state.

F.7.c. Attitudes to Other Races

Islam regards religious communities (*millah*) as the ones which give people their basic identity: for example, Muslim, Christian, Jewish, Zoroastrian,

Sabean, Hindu, Buddhist and Sikh religious communities. This is opposed to tribalism and nationalism, for it regards ethnocentrism, whether based on racial, geographical, linguistic or cultural particularism, as unbecoming to humans whom God created. Every human being, Muslims believe, would rather be identified by his or her thoughts and ideals, voluntary deeds and accomplishments than by circumstances of birth and biological or social formation, which are never of the person's own choosing. Religion ideally does involve personal commitment.

The universalism implied by *tawhīd* (see F.7.a) demands a new formation which would make an effort to fulfil the divine will. Islam would hope that those communities organised on racial and national frameworks would outgrow their ties and reorganise themselves on the basis of ideals or of religion. Islam does not hold that religion is a backward perspective, nor stagnant, prejudicial or exclusivist; it is the most important aspect of human life on earth.

With the development of the nation state, the world, in the Muslim perception, is divided into Muslim and non-Muslim states. Because this situation is a recent development, Muslims have yet to formulate their ideas on international relations (*siyar*).

F.7.d. Women and Men

Islam does not compare women to men, just as it does not accept that two men or two women are equal but that each is unique. However, men and women are equal in relation to their religious, ethical and civil rights, their duties and responsibilities. 'Whether male or female, whoever in faith does a good work for the sake of God will be granted a good life and rewarded with greater reward' (Qur'ān 16: 97). With respect to primary functions in the *ummah*, Muslims regard men and women as created for differing but complementary functions. The functions of motherhood are regarded as home care and children's upbringing. Those of fatherhood are taken to be home protection, earning a livelihood and overall responsibility (F.4.b). Both call for different physical, psychic and emotional constitutions in men and women. Islam sees this differentiation as necessary for the self-fulfilment of both sexes. Both roles are equally subject to the ethical-moral norms; and both require all the intelligence, talent, energy, and self-exertion that those involved can master (see F.3).

It should be pointed out that where natural aptitudes make it desirable, or where necessity makes it expedient, men and women may cross into each other's realm of activities without prejudice to the main differentiation of role established by God in nature. Otherwise, the Qur'ān would not have granted to women the full civil rights which it did.

F.7.e. Are All People Equal?

Material already given in this section makes the Muslim view on this issue clear, as do points made elsewhere about the place of, for example, the elderly in society (see F.5.a). It is part of a whole world view and needs no further comment. When Muslims go to Mecca on the *hajj* (pilgrimage), they wear simple white garments which show their equality before God. These simple garments are also those placed on the bodies of the dead before burial for the same reason.

F.8. NATIONAL DIVISIONS, WAR AND PEACE

F.8.a. Why do Different Nations Exist?

Islam holds that the existence of nations is the result of humanity's disobedience to God's law and of humankind's forgetfulness of the divine trust. 'Mankind was but one nation, but differed later. Had it not been for a Word [revelation] that went forth before from your Lord, their differences would have been settled between them' (Qur'ān 10: 19). Humanity drifted away from God's central message of commitment and worship to Him only, resulting in new sovereignties developing: the sovereignties of land, resources, languages and race (see Section 7). These sovereignties replaced the sovereignty of God, and humanity began to worship them and created artificial boundaries and barriers to protect itself from intruders. History shows us people struggling to protect their interest. As a result a wedge was driven into the life of humanity. People began to witness in themselves the conflict between their loyalty to spiritual values, on the one hand, and the claims which were being made on them by worldly values on the other. Humankind disintegrated into small partisan groups and out of these nations gradually emerged.

To some degree these were the factors which resulted in the creation of Pakistan in the twentieth century although some Muslims perceived Pakistan not as a disintegration, but as the coming into being of a truly Islamic state. At the time Muslims of India were fearful that they would receive harsh treatment by a predominantly Hindu society when India became independent after the Second World War. Equally, Pakistan itself may still be very far away from fulfilling the dream of an ideal Islamic state but there are Muslims who continue to work to see it realised.

F.8.b. Conflict between Nations

The conflicts which nationalism has created have resulted in a desire, by Muslims, for an international order which would establish a just and permanent peace without tyranny; one which recognises the differences and distinctions – religious, cultural, social and economic – of the peoples of the world as legitimate. This desire has become even greater as we have seen the world threatened by nuclear holocaust.

The struggle (*jihād*) for a world government – whatever its form – has now become an absolute and inevitable necessity. Weapons of mass destruction have increased, along with greed for the world's wealth. Humanity seems to be seething with hatred and discontent, and growing ever more radical and restive. The fact remains that in the field of international ethics, as well as law and jurisprudence, the world needs a new order.

Many Muslims regard themselves as commited to the task of bringing about that new world order. They regard this commitment as the only viable response to the present predicament. This is because, first, it is the only way they can render obedience to God, who has commanded all humans to enter the realm of peace and order their lives in justice and responsible brotherhood. Secondly, because this is the only way to save humanity from endless competition and meaningless suffering in the present and from destruction in the future.

A Muslim commitment to a world order of peace and justice is both religious and utilitarian. Islam holds that desiring this world order, working for it, and sacrificing to bring it about are constituents of virtue and God-consciousness (*taqwa*). To lay down one's life in the process of bringing it about is *shahādah* – martyrdom – earning a place in eternal paradise. No nobler or stronger motivation is possible. Muslims themselves are critical of strife between nations who call themselves Muslim, and the wider concept of *jihād* as struggle against injustice and oppression which is outlined above can be carried out by the pen and diplomacy as well as within a person. Only if all else fails and the faith is threatened should Muslims resort to *jihād* as holy war. It is never a true *jihād* if carried out against another Muslim nation or involves destruction of crops, places of worship and homes.

F.9. GLOBAL ISSUES

F.9.a. Responses to World Poverty

The concern for world poverty is of considerable relevance to Muslims, because, though there may be some Muslim communities which are wealthy, owing to the discovery of oil, there are many parts of the world where huge numbers of Muslims are desperate for the necessities of life. Muslims hold that this situation has mostly been artificially created. The reasons are both historical and contemporary, largely to do with the transfer of wealth from one part of the world to another – rich North and poor South.

For justice (*'adl*) and equilibrium (*wast*) to be realised there must be a strong correlation between the spiritual and material well-being of the individual, and this is a right of all human beings (see F.5.b). From this major premiss, Islam holds two main principles. First, that no individual or group may exploit another; and second, that no group may insulate and separate itself from the rest of humanity with a view to restricting its economic condition to themselves be it one of misery or of affluence.

Human nature makes it unlikely that the needy would isolate themselves from sharing the well-being of the affluent. History has shown that it is the affluent who have been more keen to restrict their affluence to themselves. In our age of colonialism, neo-colonialism and imperialism, this phenomenon has had appalling manifestations. The 'North' permitted itself a high rise in the standard of living at the cost of cheap labour and natural resources in Africa and Asia. The technological revolution of today would have been impossible without countless millions of Asians and Africans labouring on plantations and in mines, without infinite numbers of ships carrying the wealth of Asia and Africa – whether in produce, raw materials, mineral or semi-finished products – to Europe and America.

This is all utterly opposed to Islam where the first ethical principle is that every person is entitled to the fruits of his or her labour (see F.4.b). 'To every person whatever gain he/she has earned; against every person whatever loss he/she has earned' (Qur'ān 2: 286). Until a new economic order can be established Muslim communities all over the world, rich or poor, have established philanthropic agencies which are committed to transferring wealth to those parts of the world which need capital for establishing projects to feed the local people. Muslim volunteers are also to be found in poor countries assisting villagers to run basic amenities. This is an expression of *zakat* for Muslims.

F.9.b. Responses to Population Control

It is claimed that one of the causes of world poverty is the size of the world's population. Most Muslims would agree that there is a need at the individual level to take account of family circumstances before adding to the number of children. However, global control of population would result in the loss of the right of procreation: a right given by God. In addition, it would contradict a fundamental principle of Islam, that not only is God creator but also sustainer of all that is in the world. 'How many are the creatures that carry not their own sustenance? It is God who feeds [both] them and you: For He hears and knows [All things]' (Qur'ān 29: 60).

Generally Muslims would claim that the world is not overcrowded but that there are parts of the world where there is a high concentration of people in relation to land, and that movement to the less populated areas of the world is impeded by the creation of artificial national boundaries. Also most Muslims would agree that the causes of world poverty have more to do with the factors mentioned above in F.9.a than with over-population.

F.9.c. Planet Earth and Ecology

The responsibility and obligation of the divine trust requires the Muslim to live in harmony with the rest of creation. Though the world has been created by God for humanity's use, the utilisation of nature must be done with responsibility (see F.1.a). Islam leaves it to the *ummah*, acting through its duly constituted organs, to regulate the use of nature in fulfilment of the divine trust. Responsibility (*taklīf*) countenances neither waste nor extravagance. Islam encourages the Muslim to use nature in the amounts and ways required for production which in turn must be justifiable in terms of human need. The ethical responsibility demands that no damage occurs to nature in the process of humanity's use of it. Nature is a resource granted by God to us. The owner is and always remains God.

The 'rape of nature' and her pollution which recurrently plague societies are the result of humanity's irresponsible use of God's gift. Such abuse of nature runs counter to the ethic of *tawhīd* (unity of creation, see F.7.a). As Muslims see it, production must take into account the ecology of the environment. Neither animal, plant nor human may be hurt by it. Where damage occurs, it must be compensated for. The *ummah* has the right to bring the offending entrepreneur to justice, as trustee (*khalīfa*) of nature.

GLOSSARY

'Abd	Slave; servant
Adhān	Call to prayer
'Adl	Justice
'Ahd	Pledged, covenant
'Akhira	Life after death
Allah	God
'Amal	Work; action
Amān	Safety
Amānah	Trust
Amīr al-mu'minūn	Commander of the Faithful
'Aqīqa	Slaughtering of a sheep in thanksgiving to God for the birth of a new-born child
'Asl-al-fitrā	Natural disposition
Bukhl	Miserliness
Damān	Guarantee
Dhimmī	Non-Muslims living in an Islamic state
Dīn	Way – in many respects a better word than religion for Islam
Dua'	Supplication
Fasād fil'ard	Corruption on earth

Fāsiq	Transgressor of God's limit
Fitra	Nature; natural
Gayb	Things, beings, beyond human perception
Ghība	Backbiting
Hadīth	Sayings and practices of the Prophet Muhammad (see *sunnah*)
Hajj	Pilgrimage to Mecca (Makka) to commemorate Abraham's intended sacrifice of his son. One of the five pillars of Islam
Haram	Unlawful; prohibited
Hasad	Envy
Hidāyah	Guidance from God
Hikma	Wisdom
Hiqd	Rancour
Hisn	Castle
Hubb	Love
Hubb ad–dunyā	Love of the world
Hubb al–jāh	Love of influence
Hubb al–māl	Love of wealth
Hubb bi–allah wa fi–allah	Love for the sake of God
Hudūd	Boundary limits set by God in relation to what is lawful
'Ibāda	Worship
Ibn as–sabīl	Wayfarer
'Iffa	Temperance
'Ijma	Consensus, which contributes to the making of *Shari'ah* in Islam
'Ijtihād	Opinion formation, which contributes to the making of *Shari'ah* in Islam
Ikhlās	Sincerity towards God
'Ilm	Knowledge
'Ilm al–akhlāq	Knowledge of ethics
'Imām	Leader. This is sometimes used for the leader of prayer in a mosque and sometimes for the leader of the community
Imān	Faith
Islām	Peace, through submission to the will of God
'Istighfar	Seeking forgiveness from God
Īthār	Altruism
Jihād	Striving, struggle – a broader concept than the frequently used translation of 'holy war'

259

Jizyah	Tax paid by non-Muslims living in an Islamic state
Khalīfa	Trustee of God, used for the leader of the community and of the place of the human being in the world
Khaliq	Creator, one of the ninety-nine beautiful names of God
Khawf	Fear
Khul	Divorce by a woman
Kibr	Pride
Al-kitāb	The book
La'n	Cursing
Liwāt	Sodomy
Mahr	Gift from groom to bride at the time of marriage contract
Makrūh	Disliked but not prohibited
Mālik	King; sovereign
Mandūb	Recommended but not enforced
Ma'rūfāt	Goodness
Millah	Religious communities
Miskīn	Poor; disadvantaged
Mīthāqan ghalīzah	Strong covenant
Mubah	Permissable
Mu'min	One who has inner certainty of faith
Munkarāt	Evils
Mushrik	One who practises idol-worship
Muslim	One who submits to God, or whose will is in harmony with the will of God
Namīma	Slander
Nifāq	Hypocrisy
Nikāh	Marriage contract
Ni'ma	Gift of God
Niya	Intention
PBUH	'Peace be upon him', a phrase used after the names of all the prophets from Adam to Muhammad
Qadhf	Defamation
Qadī	Judge
Qanā'a	Contentment
Qatl	Homicide
Qisās	Retribution
Qur'ān	Noble reading or recitation. The name of the Holy Book of Islam
Rab	Lord; Master
Rahīm	Merciful, one of the ninety-nine beautiful names of God

Rahmān	Compassionate, one of the ninety-nine beautiful names of God
Rajā	Hope
Razzāq	Sustainer
Risala	Prophethood
Riyā	Ostentation
Sa'ādah	Happiness
Sabr	Patience
Sadaqah	Charity
Sakhā	Generosity
Salāh	Five daily prayers. Prayer is one of the five pillars of Islam
Sariqa	Theft
Saum	Fasting, one of the five pillars of Islam
Shāhādah	Witness, particularly that 'There is no God but God and Muhammad is the Messenger of God'. One of the five pillars of Islam or martyrdom, earning a place in paradise
Shajā' a	Courage
Sharah al-kalam	Excessive discussion
Sharī'ah	Islamic system of law. Literally, 'the way to water', which is the source of life
Shiddat al-ghadab	Strong anger
Shirk	The practice of idol-worship or more widely associating with God what is not God
Shukr	Gratitude
Shūra	Consultation which contributes to the making of *Sharī'ah* in Islam
Silat ar-rahīm	Strengthening of relationships with relatives
Siyar	International relations
Sunnah	The way of the Prophet – after the Qur'ān, the second source of authority for Muslims
Taklīf	Responsibility; obligation
Talāq	Divorce by a man
Taqwa	God-consciousness
Tawakkul	Trust in God
Tawbah	Repentance
Tawhīd	Unity of God, which leads to a sense of the unity of all life under God for the Muslim
Tazkīya	Spiritual purification
Ummah	Community. This is a central concept in Islam which dates its beginnings from 622 CE when the first community was established in Medina

261

'Uqūbāh	Criminal law
Waḥī	God's revelation
Wajib	Obligatory
Wast	Equilibrium
Yatīm	Orphan
Zakāt	Obligatory contribution to the poor. Almsgiving is one of the five pillars of Islam
Zalim	Transgression by usurping others' rights
Al-zawāj	Marriage
Zinā	Adultery

REFERENCES

Texts

Qur'ān

'Ali, 'A. Y. (trans.), *The Holy Qur'ān*, Islamic Foundation, 1995. (The Arabic text with English translation.)

Pickthall, M. (trans.), *The Meaning of the Glorious Qur'ān*, Daset Press, n.d.

Hadīth

Hasan, A., *Abu Dāwūd*, 3 vols, Ashraf Publications, 1984.

Ibrahim, E. and Johnson-Davies, D. (trans.), *Nawawi – Forty Hadith*, The Holy Koran Publications, 1980.

Khan, M. (trans.), *Bukhari*, 9 vols, Islamic University, 1994.

Malik, *Al-Muwata*, Diwan Press, 1982.

Robson, J. (trans.), *Mishkat al Masabih*, 2 vols, Edinburgh University Press, 1967.

Siddiqui, A. H. (trans.), *Muslim*, Ashraf Publications, 1976.

General

Ahmad, K., *Islam: Its Meaning and Message*, Islamic Foundation, 1976.

Ahsan, M., *Islam: Faith and Practice*, Islamic Foundation, 1976.

al-'Ati, H. 'A., *The Family Structure in Islam*, American Trust Publications, 1977.

Azami, M., *Studies in Early Hadīth Literature*, American Trust Publications, 1978.

Cragg, K., *The House of Islam*, Wadsworth, 1975.

Fakhry, M., *Ethical Theories in Islam*, Leiden, 1991.

al-Ghazali, A., *Ihya Ulum-id-Din*, vol. 2, Kitab Bhavan, 1982.

Haddad, Y. Y. and A. T. Lummis, *Islamic Values in the United States*, Oxford University Press, 1987.

Hamid, 'A. W., *Islam: the Natural Way*, Muslim Education and Literary Services, 1989.

Haneef, S., *What Everyone Should Know about Islam and Muslims*, Kazi Publications, 1979.

Ibn Taymiyya, *Fatawa*, vol. 4, n.p. and n.d.

Irving, T. B., K. Ahmad and M. Ahsan, *The Qur'ān: Basic Teachings*, Islamic Foundation, 1979.

al-Kaysi, M. I., *Morals and Manners in Islam*, Islamic Foundation, 1984.

Khalid, F. M. and J. O'Brian, *Islam and Ecology*, Cassells, 1992.

Memissi, F., *Women and Islam*, Oxford, 1987.

Mir, M., *Coherence in the Qur'ān*, American Trust Publications, 1986.

Rahman, F., *Health and Medicine in the Islamic Tradition*, The Crossroad Publishing Co., 1987.

Said, E., *Covering Islam*, Routledge & Kegan Paul, 1981.

Sardar, Z., *Muhammad: Aspects of His Biography*, Islamic Foundation, 1978.

USEFUL ADDRESSES

UK

Centre for Islamic Studies, University of Wales, Lampeter, Dyfed SA48 7ED.

Centre for the Study of Islam and Christian Muslim Relations, Selly Oak Colleges, Bristol Road, Birmingham B29 6LQ.

Council of Mosques, 46 Goodge Street, London W1P 1FJ.

Islamic Academy, 23 Metcalfe Road, Cambridge CB4 2DB.

Islamic Book Centre, 120 Drummond Street, London NW1 2LY.

Islamic College London, 84–92 Whitechapel Road, London E1 1JQ.

Islamic Foundation, Markfield Conference Centre, Ratby Lane, Markfield, Leicester LE6 0RN.

Islamic Information Service, 233 Seven Sisters Road, London N4 2DA.

Islamia Schools Trust, 2 Digswell Street, London N7 8JX.

Muslim Educational Trust, 130 Stroud Green Road, London N4 3RZ.

Muslim Institute, 6 Endsleigh Street, London WC1H 0DS.

North America

American Trust Publications, 10900 West Washington St, Indianapolis, Indiana, 46231, USA.

The Institute of Islamic Information and Education, 4390 North Elston Avenue, Chicago, ILL 60641, USA.

International Institute of Islamic Thought, PO Box 669, 555 Grove Street, Herndon, VA 22070, USA.

Islamic Circle of North America, 166–26, 89th Avenue, Jamaica, New York 11432, USA.

Islamic Information Foundation, 8 Laurel Lane, Halifax, N.S. Canada, B3M 2P6.

Islamic Society of North America, PO Box 38, Plainfields, Indiana 46168, USA.

The Islamic Society of Orange County, Garden Grove, PO Box 1330B, California 92642, USA.

GENERAL
BIBLIOGRAPHY

Armstrong, K., *Holy War*, Macmillan, 1988.
Berthrong, J. (ed.), *Interfaith Dialogue: An Annotated Bibliography*, Multifaith Resources, 1993.
Bowker, J., *Worlds of Faith*, BBC/Ariel, 1983.
Carman, J. and M. Juergensmeyer (eds), *A Bibliographical Guide to the Comparative Study of Ethics*, Cambridge University Press, 1991.
Chichester, D., *Patterns of Action: Religion and Ethics in a Comparative Perspective*, Wadsworth, 1987.
Cohn-Sherbok, D., *World Religions and Human Liberation*, Orbis, 1991.
Cole, W. O., *Moral Issues in Six Religions*, Heinemann, 1993.
Crawford, S. C., *World Religions and Global Ethics*, Paragon House, 1989.
Dickenson, D. and M. Johnson, *Death, Dying and Bereavement*, Sage, 1993.
Eliade, M., *Encyclopedia of Religion*, Macmillan, 1988.
Ferguson, J., *War and Peace in World Religions*, Sheldon Press, 1977.
Goodacre, D., *World Religions and Medicine*, Institute of Religion and Medicine, 1983.
Green, R. M., *Religion and Moral Reason*, Oxford University Press, 1988.
Hastings, J. (ed.), *Encyclopaedia of Religion and Ethics*, T & T Clark, 1926.
Holm, J., *Keyguide Information Sources on World Religions*, Mansell, 1991.
Holm, J. with J. Bowker, *Making Moral Decisions*, Pinter, 1994.
Jenkins, J., *Contemporary Moral Issues*, Heinemann, 1993.
Küng, H. and K. J. Kuschel, *A Global Ethic*, SCM Press, 1993.
Merkl, P. H. and N. Smart, *Religion and Politics in the Modern World*, SUNY, 1983.
Parrinder, G., *Sex in the World Religions*, Sheldon Press, 1980.
Prickett, J. (ed.), *Marriage and the Family*, Lutterworth, 1985.
Richardson, E. A., *Strangers in this Land*, Pilgrim Press, 1988.
Rouner, L. S., *Human Rights in the World Religions*, Notre Dame, 1988.
Sharma, A. (ed.), *Women in World Religions*, SUNY, 1987.
Weller, P. (ed.), *Religions in the UK: A Directory*, University of Derby, 1993.

World Religions in Education, the annual journal of The Shap Working Party on World Religions in Education, is often devoted to ethical issues: e.g. Women (1988); Humankind and the Environment (1989); Death and Dying (1994). The address of the Working Party is in the list of general addresses.

GENERAL ADDRESSES

UK

Age Concern, Sunley House, 60 Pitcairn Road, Mitcham, Surrey CR4 3LL.
Alcoholics Anonymous, PO Box 1, Stonebow House, Stonebow, York YO1 2NJ.
Amnesty International, 5 Roberts Place, London EC1R 0EJ.
Help the Aged, Freepost, London EC1B 1BD.
Howard League for Penal Reform, 322 Kennington Park Road, London SE11 4PP.
Inter-Faith Network, 5–7 Tavistock Place, London WC1H 9SS.
International Interfaith Centre, Westminster College, Oxford OX2 9AT.
LIFE (Save the Unborn Child), 118–20 Warwick Street, Leamington Spa, Warwickshire
    CV32 4QY.
OXFAM, 274 Banbury Road, Oxford OX2 7DZ.
Shap Working Party on World Religions in Education, c/o 36 Causton Street, London
    SW1P 4AU.
World Congress of Faiths, 2 Market Street, Oxford OX1 3EF.
World Wildlife Trust, Panda House, Weyside Park, Godalming GU7 1XR.

NORTH AMERICA

Canadian Coalition for Ecology, Ethics and Religions, 22 Carriage Bay, Winnipeg, Canada
    MMB R2Y 0MS.
Council of Societies for the Study of Religions, Directory of Departments and Programmes
    of Religious Studies in America, Valparaiso University, Valparaiso, IN 46 383–64 93 USA.
Department of Religious Studies (Professor Seshaqiri Rao), Cocke Hall, University of
    Virginia, Charlottesville, Virginia, VA 22903, USA.
Freedom, Justice and Peace Society Inc., 150 Werimus Lane, Hillside, New Jersey 07642,
    USA.
Institute for Dialogue Among Religious Traditions, Boston University School of Theology,
    Suite 110, 745 Commonwealth Avenue, Boston MA 02215, USA.
Multifaith Resources, PO Box 128, Wofford Heights, California, CA 93285 0128, USA.
Religious Pluralism Project, Center for Study of World Religions, Harvard 42, Francis
    Avenue, Cambridge MA, USA.
World Inter-Faith Education Association, PO Box 7384, Station 'D', Victoria British
    Columbia, Canada V9B 5B7.

NOTES ON
CONTRIBUTORS

DR MASHUQ IBN ALLY is Director of the Centre for Islamic Studies associated with the Department of Theology and Religious Studies, and Sub-Dean for post-graduate affairs at the Federal University of Wales, Lampeter. He has written widely on Islam and is involved with the Muslim community internationally as well as with the UK Islamic Mission. He is a trustee of the Birmingham Central Mosque.

CLIVE LAWTON was at one time education officer for the Board of Deputies of British Jews and is now Director of Jewish Continuity. He has also been headmaster of King David's High School in Liverpool, and Deputy Director of Education for the Liverpool Education Authority. He is a past chair of the Shap Working Party on World Religions in Education, and has published widely on Judaism, especially for teachers and schools.

DR WERNER MENSKI is senior lecturer in Hindu and Modern South Asian Laws at the School of Oriental and African Studies, University of London. He is also trained as a social scientist, knows the North American scene, and has worked in Germany as well as Britain. He has contributed to many journals and books on Hindu law, Indian marriage and divorce laws, and immigration law. He is particularly interested in ethnic minorities in the UK and Europe and in customary law. His home is in Leicester where he is immersed in Hindu community life.

PEGGY MORGAN is senior lecturer in Theology and Religious Studies at Westminster College, Oxford, a lecturer at Mansfield College, and a member of the University of Oxford Faculty of Theology, for which she teaches the study of religions papers. She is a member of the Shap Working Party on World Religions in Education and has published widely on Buddhism. She has considerable experience of Buddhist life, of working with Buddhists and of interfaith dialogue.

ELEANOR NESBITT is a lecturer and research fellow in the Department of Arts Education at the University of Warwick, and is engaged in ethnographic research with religious communities, particularly in the Coventry area. She has taught in Northern India and subsequently conducted socio-anthropological research for a thesis entitled 'Aspects of the Sikh Tradition in Nottingham'. She has published widely on classical Sikhism as well as many ethnographic papers, and has a broad experience of Sikh communities worldwide.

REVD CANON TREVOR SHANNON is an ordained priest in the Church of England. He serves at present as area dean of Redbridge in Essex and rector of Great Ilford. He has previously taught religious education in schools and been a secondary-school headmaster. He was for many years a member of the Shap Working Party on World Religions in Education and is the author of books on Christian themes for the Chichester Project.

INDEX

INDEX

Buddhism 55–61
Christianity 175–80
Hinduism 1–10
Islam 220–5
Judaism 135–9
Sikhism 99–104

Baal Shem Tov 138
Baba, Kerichowale 103
Baba, Sai 11, 24, 25
Babel, Tower of 159, 164, 207
Bahadur, Banda 102
Bahadur, Guru Tegh 104, 105, 124
Band Aid 211
Bangladesh 44
Baroda, Gaekwads of 32
begging 26, 48, 240
bestiality 250–1
Bet Din 138
Bhago, Mai 122
Bhago, Malak 113
Bhai Gurdas 104
Bhatia 46, 47
Bhindranwale, Sant Jarnail Singh 103
Bible
Christianity 177, 208
Judaism *see* Tenakh
bigamy 21, 187, 231–2
birth control *see* contraception
bonded labourers 23
Bonhoeffer, Dietrich 180
Booth, Catherine Bramwell 206
boundaries, Islam 250
Brahma 6
brahma-viharas 61
brahman 6
Brahmins 23, 37, 38–9
Buddhism
addresses 97–8
equality and difference 82–7
global issues 90–3
glossary 93–6
life, quality and value of 74–8
marriage and the family 64–7
national divisions, war and peace 87–90
personal and private 61–4
references 96–7
religious authority 55–61
right and wrong, questions of 78–82
time and money, influences on and use of 67–73
Buddhist, on being a 55–8
Buddhist Peace Fellowship 89
Buddhist Society 64
Buddhist Women's Movement 86

caffeine 192
CAFOD 211

capital punishment
Buddhism 81
Christianity 201–2
Hinduism 37
Islam 251
Sikhism 118
cardinal values 181
Caro, Rabbi Joseph 142
caste system
Hinduism 23, 29, 40, 41, 43
Sikhism 112, 119
Casuists 177
Catholicism *see* Roman Catholicism
celibacy xvii
Buddhism 91
Christianity 184, 206
Judaism 168
censorship 194
Chand, Duni 113
charitable giving
Buddhism 71
Christianity 197, 210–11
Hinduism 26, 27
Islam 242
Judaism 140, 147–8, 151, 156–7, 168
Sikhism 113, 115, 125
chastity
Buddhism 63
Hinduism 12, 13, 14, 42, 43
chief rabbis 138
child marriages 13
Christian, on being a 175–8
Christian Aid 197, 211
Christianity
addresses 219
equality and difference 202–7
global issues 210–14
glossary 214–18
life, quality and value of 195–200
marriage and the family 184–8
national divisions, war and peace 207–10
personal and private 180–4
references 218–19
religious identity and authority 175–80
right and wrong, questions of 200–2
time and money, influences on and use of 188–95
Church of England (Anglican Church) 205, 212
circumcision, Islam 234
citta 68
colonialism 257
community, Islam 223–4
compassion, Buddhism 76
compensation, Hinduism 39
concentration, right 58
confession, Judaism 157
conflict between nations xxv

268

INDEX

INDEX

INDEX

nuclear war xxv
  Buddhism 89–90
  Christianity 209, 210
  Judaism 166–7
  Sikhism 101, 125
nuns
  Buddhism 56
    authority 58, 59; founding of order of 85;
    meditation 69; needy people 75; precepts
    57; wealth 71
  Christianity 184

obedience 9, 185
Oral Torah 135
order, Hinduism 3, 6, 34–5
organ transplants 77
  Judaism 153–4
original sin 201
orphans, Islam 245–6
Orthodox Christians 182
Orthodox Jews 136, 142–3, 145, 162, 163
outmarriage 108, 121, 142–3
ownership, Hinduism 26
Oxfam 211

pacifism 89, 209
Pakistan 44, 255
Pali Canon 65, 66, 72
patience, Buddhism 81
patriotism 88, 207
Paul, Saint
  authority 178
  drugs 193
  education 188
  equality of people 206
  family relationships 186
  homosexuality 183
  law, purpose of 200–1
  national divisions 207
  needy people 196
  people, differences between 202
  personal qualities 180–1
  planet earth 214
  races, attitudes to other 204
  religions, attitudes to other 203
  religious identity 175, 176
  sex before marriage 182
  wealth 191
  women and men 185, 205–6
  work 189
peace and war xxiv–xxv
  Buddhism 87–90
  Christianity 207–10
  Hinduism 44–7
  Islam 255–6
  Judaism 164–7
  Sikhism 123–5
penances, Hinduism 35–6, 38

pensions, old-age 30
people, differences between xxiii
  Buddhism 82–3.
  Christianity 202–3
  Hinduism 39–40
  Islam 252–3
  Judaism 158–9
  Sikhism 119
perfections, Buddhism 61
personal and private xv–xvii
  Buddhism 61–4
  Christianity 180–4
  Hinduism 10–14
  Islam 226–9
  Judaism 139–42
  Sikhism 104–7
Peter, Saint 179, 206–7
physical health, Islam 241
Piara Singh Sambhi 101
pigs, Judaism 154
pilgrimage, Muslims 255
pill, contraceptive 169
Pingalwara 115
Pius XI, Pope 212
Pius XII, Pope 212
planet earth see ecology
pluralism, Christianity 203
polygamy
  Buddhism 65
  Hinduism 17–18
  Islam 231–2
  Judaism 145
  Sikhism 108
Pope 179
population control, responses to xxvi
  Buddhism 91–2
  Christianity 211–13
  Hinduism 48–9
  Islam 257
  Judaism 168–9
  Sikhism 126
possessions, Buddhism 57
poverty, responses to xxvi
  Buddhism 70–1, 90–1
  Christianity 210–11
  Hinduism 47–8
  Islam 256–7
  Judaism 151, 167–8
  Sikhism 125
prayer 156, 177, 240
precepts, Buddhism 56–7, 63, 65
Prem Sumarg 101
Prithivī 50
private and personal see personal and private
Progressive Jews 136, 139, 143, 145, 162
prophets, Islam 222–3
protests, Sikhs 104, 117
Pu-Tai 87

INDEX

Saraswati, Dayanand 13
sati 34
Saunders, Dame Cicely 193
savings, Islam 243
School Aid 211
Schumacher, Ernst F. 69, 91, 92
scriptures *see* texts and scriptures
secret Jews 160
secular societies xiv
segregation of sexes, Hinduism 19
self-control 12, 43, 63, 126
self-defence, Judaism 165–6
self-denial, Buddhism 71
sensual pleasure 12
separation, marital 187
Seven Noahide Laws 158, 161
Seven Virtues 181
sexes, differences between *see* women and
  men
sexual intercourse xvi–xvii, 185, 231
  before marriage *see* marriage, sex before
Shabbat 136, 137, 146, 147
  current affairs 149
  women and men 162
Shaftesbury, Lord 190
Shan, Sharan-Jeet 121
Shaw, George Bernard 195
Shiites 225
Shiromani Gurdwara Parbandhak Committee
  101, 126
Shūdras 4
Shulkan Arukh 137, 147–8, 149
sick people 31–2, 151
Sigalovada Sutta 72
Sikh, on being a 99–101
Sikhism
  addresses 134
  equality and difference 119–23
  global issues 125–7
  glossary 127–32
  life, quality and value of 114–16
  marriage and the family 107–10
  national divisions, war and peace 123–5
  personal and private 104–7
  references 132–4
  religious identity and authority 99–104
  right and wrong, questions of 117–19
  time and money, influences on and use of
    110–14
sin and sins xxiii
  Buddhism 79–80
  Christianity 201
  Hinduism 35–6
  Islam 248–9
  Judaism 155–6
  Sikhism 117–18
sincerity, Islam 227
Singh, Avtar 104

Singh, Baba Dip 124–5
Singh, Balwant 126
Singh, Bhai Randhir 122
Singh, Bhai Taru 125
Singh, Bhai Vir 114
Singh, Guru Gobind 101, 102, 103
  conflict between nations 124
  differences between people 119
  duties of leaders 103–4
  education 111
  halāl meat 127
  personal qualities 104
  religions, attitudes to other 120
  sin and sins 118
  wives 108
Singh, Indarjit 121
Singh, Maharaja Ranjit 102, 104, 119, 123
Singh, Sant Puran 103
Singh, Shahid Bhagat 118
Singh Sabha 111
Sita 50
Situationists 177
slander, Judaism 149
smoking
  Christianity 192
  Hinduism 27
  Judaism 148
  Sikhism 112, 114
social action, Buddhism 55
socialism and Judaism 167
Society of Friends 181, 209
sodomy 229, 250
solemnisation, marriage 15
Solomon 139
song, Hinduism 24
speech, right 57
spiritual friendship, Buddhism 62
Spiro, Melford 80
sterilisation 49, 126, 212
strangers, Judaism 151–2
students, Hinduism 4, 22, 25
subjects, duties xv
  Buddhism 60–1
  Christianity 180
  Hinduism 9–10
  Islam 225
  Judaism 138–9
  Sikhism 104
suffering, Buddhism 79, 80
suicide
  Buddhism 77, 78
  Christianity 199
  Hinduism 33, 34
  Islam 247, 249
Sunnīs 225
supercession, Hinduism 20
suttee 34

276